The Crusades
A Short History

By the same author
*The First Crusade
and the Idea of Crusading*
(Athlone, 1986)

.

The Crusades

A Short History

JONATHAN RILEY-SMITH

YALE UNIVERSITY PRESS
New Haven and London

First published in Great Britain in 1987 by The Athlone Press Limited
First published in the United States in 1987 by Yale University Press

Printed in the United States of America by
BookCrafters, Inc., Chelsea, Michigan.

Library of Congress catalog card number: 87–50214

International standard book number: 0–300–03905–0 (cloth)
0–300–04700–2 (pbk.)

The paper in this book meets the guidelines for
permanence and durability of the Committee on
Production Guidelines for Book Longevity of the
Council on Library Resources.

10

For
Dominie, Hamish, Prosper, Tristram,
Sebastian and Torquil

Ecce quam bonum et quam iucundum
habitare fratres in unum!
(Psalms 132 (133): 1)

Contents

Maps

Drawn by András Bereznay

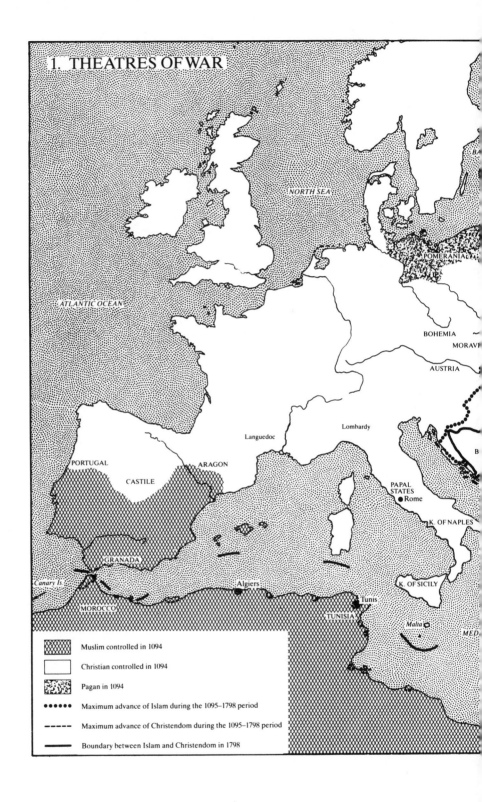

1. THEATRES OF WAR

NORTH SEA

ATLANTIC OCEAN

POMERANIA

BOHEMIA

MORAVI

AUSTRIA

Lombardy

Languedoc

PAPAL
STATES
● Rome

K. OF NAPLES

PORTUGAL   ARAGON

CASTILE

K. OF SICILY

GRANADA

Canary Is

Algiers

Tunis

MOROCCO

TUNISIA

Malta

MED

▨	Muslim controlled in 1094
☐	Christian controlled in 1094
▨	Pagan in 1094
●●●●●●	Maximum advance of Islam during the 1095–1798 period
-----	Maximum advance of Christendom during the 1095–1798 period
——	Boundary between Islam and Christendom in 1798

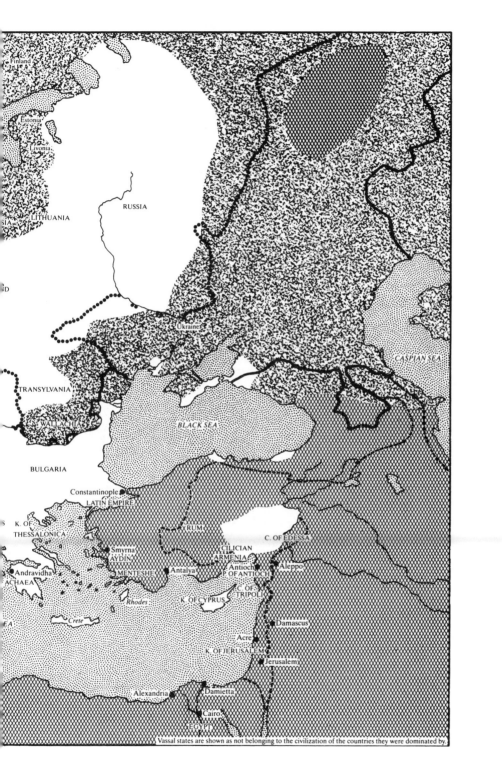

Finland

Estonia

Livonia

LITHUANIA

RUSSIA

Ukraine

CASPIAN SEA

TRANSYLVANIA

WALLACHIA

BLACK SEA

BULGARIA

Constantinople
LATIN EMPIRE

K. OF
THESSALONICA

RUM

C. OF EDESSA

Smyrna
AYDIN

CILICIAN
ARMENIA

Andravidha

MENTESHE

Antalya

Antioch
P. OF ANTIOCH

Aleppo

ACHAEA

Rhodes

K. OF CYPRUS

C. OF
TRIPOLI

Crete

Damascus

Acre

K. OF JERUSALEM

Jerusalem

Alexandria

Damietta

Cairo

EGYPT

Vassal states are shown as not belonging to the civilization of the countries they were dominated by.

London
Dartmouth
Ypres
Lille ● Tournai
Antwerp
Compiègne
Gisors
Cambrai
Bouillon
Frankfurt
Gelnhausen
Paris
Soissons
Trier
Mainz
Würzburg
Tachov
Chartres
Reims
Verdun
Metz
Worms
Speyer
Nuremberg
Le Mans
Étampes
Troyes
Haguenau
Angers
Blois
Cairvaux
Tours
Sancerre
Vézelay
Poitiers
Bourges
Cîteaux
Constance
Razès
Cluny
Limoges ● St Léonard-de-Noblat
Clermont
Lyon
Le Puy
Vienne
Valence
Milan ●
Toulouse ●
Nîmes
Avignon
Genoa
Aigues ● St Gilles
Mortes ● Marseille
Pisa
Perpignan ●
Hyères
Barcelona
Rome
Naples
Bari
Brindisi
Amalfi
Taranto
Cagliari
Trapani
Palermo
Messina
Algiers
Tunis
Mahdia
Malta ● Valletta
MEDIT
Jerba
Tripoli

Bremen
Verden
Minden
Osnabrück
Hildesheim
Münster
Magdeburg
Paderborn
Cologne
Liège
Aachen
Legnica
Wesseli
Prague
Regensburg
Vienna
Nitra
Wieselburg
Pannonhalma ●
B
Danube
M
Zer
Venice
Bologna
Zadar
Split
Dubr
Otrar

- - - - - - Boundary between Islam and Christianity in 1054
————— Boundary between Islam and Christianity in 1094
–·–·–·– Boundary between Islam and Christianity in 1144
▨▨▨ Controlled by Islam in 1270
–··–··– Boundary between Islam and Christianity in 1380
━━━━━ Boundary between Islam and Christianity in 1500
–·–·–·– Boundary between Islam and Christianity in 1550

Vassal states are shown as not belonging to t

2. EUROPE AND THE NEAR EAST

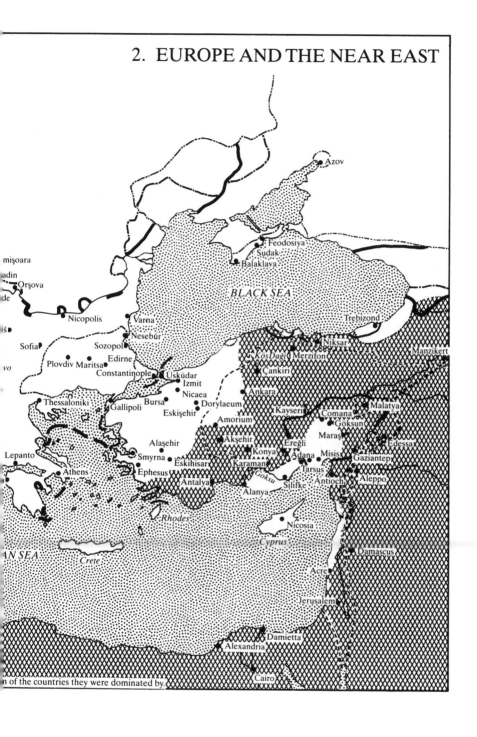

Azov

mişoara
adin
Orşova
de

Feodosiya
Sudak
Balaklava

BLACK SEA

Trebizond

š

Nicopolis
Varna
Nesebŭr
Sofia
Sozopol
Niksar
Manzikert
Kös Dağı Merzifon
Edirne
Çankırı
vo
Plovdiv Maritsa
Constantinople
Üsküdar
Izmit
İzmit
Ankara
Thessaloniki
Nicaea
Bursa
Dorylaeum
Kayseri
Malatya
Gallipoli
Eskişehir
Amorium
Comana
Göksun
Maraş
Alaşehir
Akşehir
Edessa
Lepanto
Smyrna
Konya
Ereğli
Misis
Athens
Eskihisar
Karaman
Adana
Gaziantep
Ephesus
Tarsus
Aleppo
Antalya
Göksu Silifke
Antioch
Alanya
Damascus
Rhodes

Nicosia
Cyprus

AN SEA
Crete
Acre

Jerusalem

Damietta
Alexandria

n of the countries they were dominated by.
Cairo

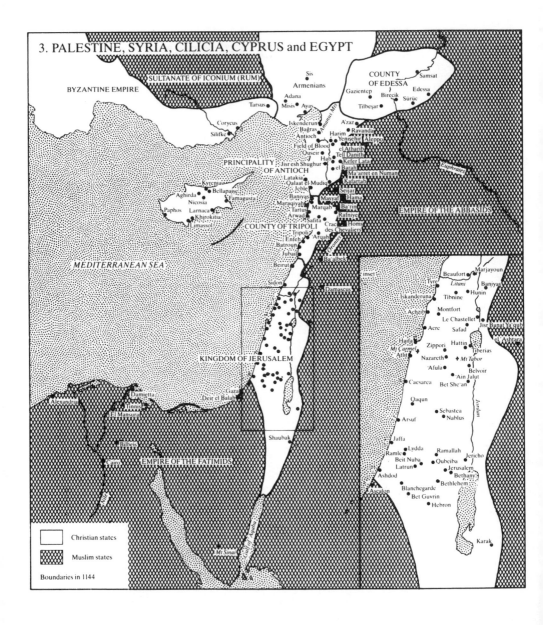

3. PALESTINE, SYRIA, CILICIA, CYPRUS and EGYPT

BYZANTINE EMPIRE

SULTANATE OF ICONIUM (RUM)

Sis
Armenians
Adana
Misis Ayas
Tarsus

Corycus
Silifke

COUNTY
OF EDESSA
Samsat
Gazientep
Birecik Edessa
Tilbeşar Sürüc

Iskenderun
Bağras
Antioch
Field of Blood
Quseir
Jisr esh Shughur
Latakia
Qalaat el-Mudiq
Jeble
Baniyas
Maraqiyah
Tartus
Arwad
Safita

PRINCIPALITY
OF ANTIOCH

Kyrenia
Aghirda
Nicosia
Paphos
Larnaca
Khirokitia
Limassol

Bellapaise
Famagusta

A'zaz
Harim
Ravanda
Yenisehir Aleppo
el-Atharib
Tell Danith
Hab
Kefer Lata
el Barah
Ma'arret en Numan
Kafartab
Seijar
Masyat Hama
Marqab
Rafniye
Homs
Crac
des Chevaliers

EMPIRE OF THE ABBASIDS

COUNTY OF TRIPOLI

Tripoli
Enfeh
Batroun
Juball
Beirut

Arquah

Ba'albek

MEDITERRANEAN SEA

Sidon

Damascus

Beaufort
Marjayoun
Tyre
Litani Baniya
Iskanderuna
Hunin
Achziб
Tibnine
Montfort
Le Chastellet
Acre Safad
Haifa Zippori Hattin
Mt Carmel
Atlit Nazareth
'Afula
Caesarea
Bet She'an
Belvoir

Jisr Banat Ya'qub
el-Ashtara

Tiberias
Mt Tabor

Ain Jalut

KINGDOM OF JERUSALEM

Gaza
Deir el Balah

Shaubak

Qaqun
Arsuf

Schastea
Nablus

Jaffa
Ramle
Beit Nuba
Latrun
Ashdod
Ascalon

Lydda
Ramallah
Qubeiba
Jericho
Jerusalem
Bethany
Bethlehem
Blanchegarde
Bet Guvrin
Hebron

Alexandria
Damietta
Tinnis
El Mansura

Bilbeis
Cairo

EMPIRE OF THE FATIMIDS

Karak

Mt Sinai

Christian states

Muslim states

Boundaries in 1144

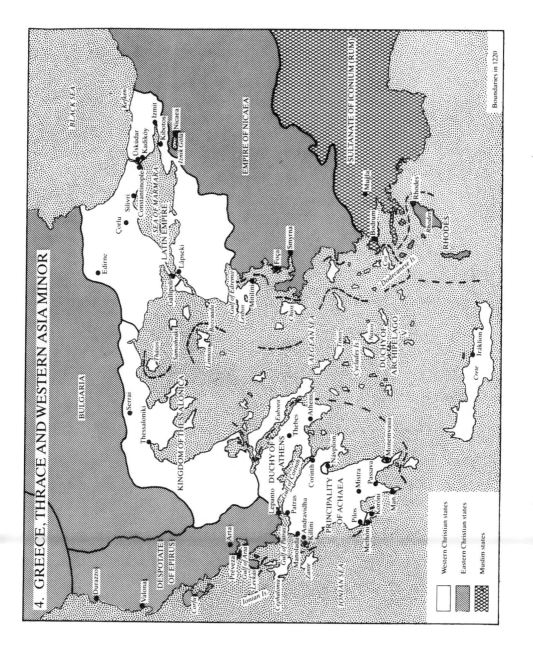

4. GREECE, THRACE AND WESTERN ASIA MINOR

BLACK SEA

BULGARIA

Edirne

Çorlu

Silivri

Serrai

Thessaloníki

KINGDOM OF THESSALONICA

SEA OF MARMARA

LATIN EMPIRE

Üsküdar
Kadiköy
Constantinople
Kibotos
Izmit
Izmit Gulf
Nicaea

EMPIRE OF NICAEA

SULTANATE OF ICONIUM (RUM)

Keşan

Gallipoli
Lápseki

Gulf of Edremit
Edremit

Lesbos

Smyrna

Foça

Chios

AEGEAN SEA

Tínos

DUCHY OF
ARCHIPELAGO

Cyclades Is

Muğla

Bodrum

Rhodes

Rhodes

RHODES

Dodecanese Is

DESPOTATE
OF EPIRUS

Durazzo

Valona

Arta

Prevesa

Lévkas

Corfu

Ithaca

Cephalonia

Ionian Is

IONIAN SEA

Lepanto

Gulf of Patras

Patras

Andravidha

Manolada

Killini

DUCHY OF
ATHENS

Euboea

Thebes

Athens

Gulf of Corinth

Corinth

PRINCIPALITY
OF ACHAEA

Návplion

Mistra

Passavá

Monemvasia

Pílos

Koróni

Methóni

Maïna

Crete

Iráklion

Western Christian states

Eastern Christian states

Muslim states

Boundaries in 1220

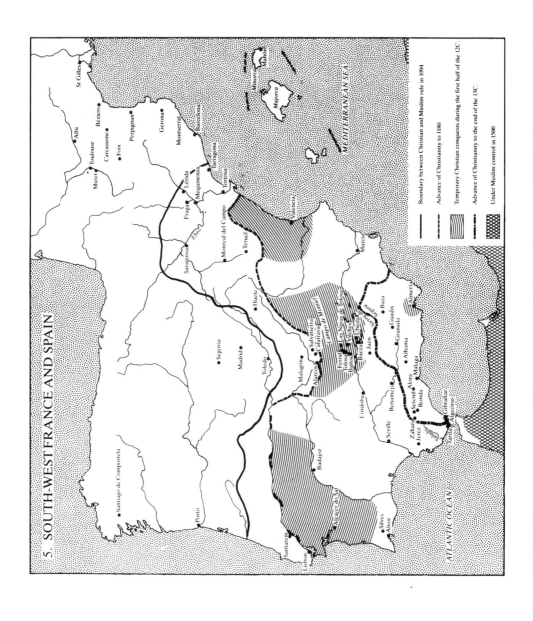

5. SOUTH-WEST FRANCE AND SPAIN

MEDITERRANEAN SEA

ATLANTIC OCEAN

St Gilles
Albi
Toulouse
Béziers
Carcassonne
Muret
Foix
Perpignan
Gerona
Montserrat
Barcelona
Tarragona
Lérida
Mequinenza
Tortosa
Fraga
Saragossa
Ebro
Montreal del Campo
Teruel
Valencia
Huete
Segovia
Madrid
Toledo
Murcia
Baza
Huescar
Las Navas de Tolosa
Campo de Montiel
Salvatierra
Calatrava
Vilches
Guadix
Granada
Alhama
Almeria
Malagón
Alarcos
Ferral
Tolosa
Baños
Baeza
Úbeda
Jaén
Benamejì
Alora
Málaga
Setenil
Ronda
Córdoba
Badajoz
Seville
Zahara
Jerez
Gibraltar
Algeciras
Tarifa
Santarém
Alcácer do Sal
Lisbon
Silves
Albor
Porto
Santiago de Compostela
Minorca
Mahon
Majorca

Boundary between Christian and Muslim rule in 1094
Advance of Christianity to 1180
Temporary Christian conquests during the first half of the 12C.
Advance of Christianity to the end of the 13C.
Under Muslim control in 1500

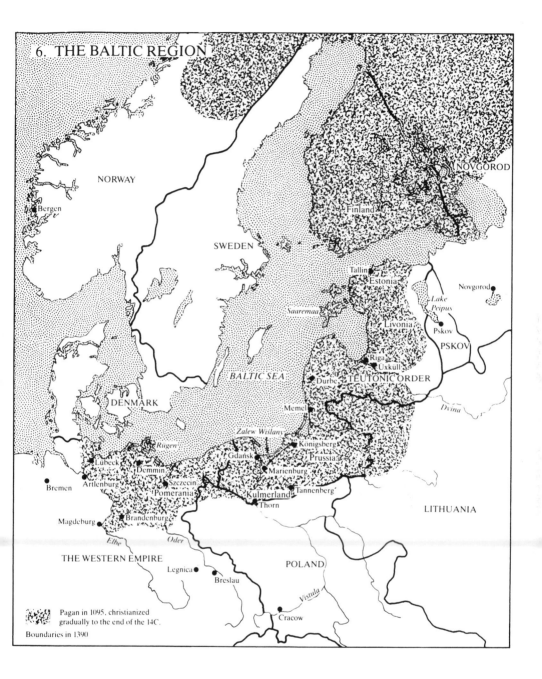

6. THE BALTIC REGION

NORWAY

Bergen

SWEDEN

NOVGOROD

Finland

Tallin
Estonia

Saaremaa

Novgorod

*Lake
Peipus*

Livonia

Pskov

PSKOV

Riga

BALTIC SEA

Uxküll

TEUTONIC ORDER

Durbe

DENMARK

Memel

Dvina

Rüggen

Zalew Wislany

Königsberg

Lübeck

Gdańsk

Prussia

Demmin

Marienburg

Bremen

Artlenburg

Szczecin

Pomerania

Kulmerland

Tannenberg

LITHUANIA

Magdeburg

Brandenburg

Thorn

Elbe

Oder

THE WESTERN EMPIRE

POLAND

Legnica

Breslau

Vistula

Pagan in 1095, christianized
gradually to the end of the 14C.

Boundaries in 1390

Cracow

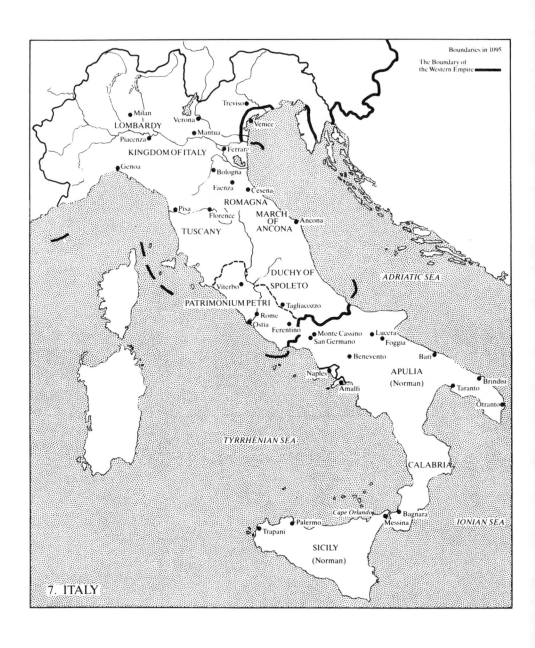

Boundaries in 1095

The Boundary of
the Western Empire ━━━

Milan

Verona

Treviso

LOMBARDY

Mantua

Venice

Piacenza

KINGDOM OF ITALY

Ferrara

Genoa

Bologna

Faenza

Cesena

ROMAGNA

Pisa

Florence

MARCH
OF
ANCONA

Ancona

TUSCANY

ADRIATIC SEA

DUCHY OF
SPOLETO

Viterbo

PATRIMONIUM PETRI

Tagliacozzo

Rome

Ostia

Ferentino

Monte Cassino

Lucera

San Germano

Foggia

Bari

Benevento

Naples

APULIA

Amalfi

(Norman)

Taranto

Brindisi

Otranto

TYRRHENIAN SEA

CALABRIA

Cape Orlando

Bagnara

Palermo

Messina

IONIAN SEA

Trapani

SICILY

(Norman)

7. ITALY

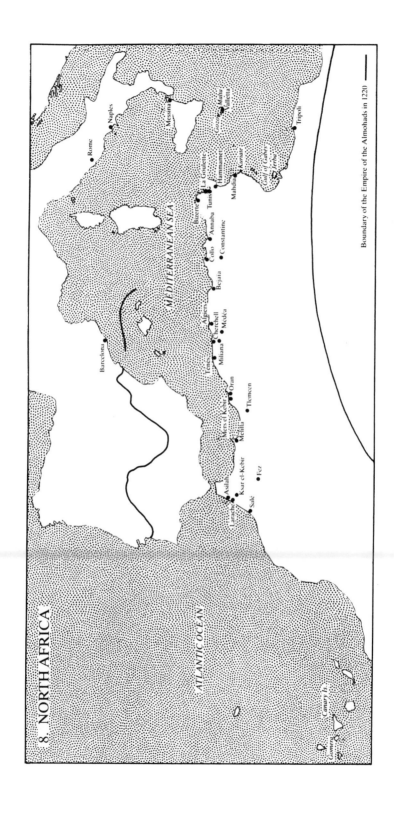

8. NORTH AFRICA

ATLANTIC OCEAN

MEDITERRANEAN SEA

Rome
Naples
Messina
Malta
Valletta
Gozo

Barcelona

Bizerte
La Goulette
Tunis
Hammamet
Mahdia
Kuriate
Annaba
Collo
Constantine
Bejaïa
Qal'i ibn Gabès
Djerba
Tripoli

Algiers
Tenès
Cherchell
Miliana
Medéa

Oran
Mers el-Kebir
Tlemcen
Melilla

Asilah
Ksar el-Kebir
Larache
Salé
Fez

Canary Is.
Gomera Is.

Boundary of the Empire of the Almohads in 1220 ⎯⎯

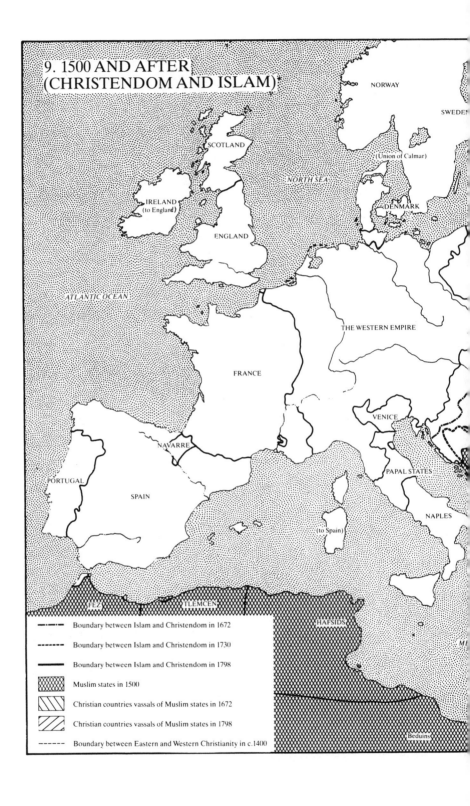

9. 1500 AND AFTER (CHRISTENDOM AND ISLAM)

NORWAY

SWEDEN

(Union of Calmar)

SCOTLAND

NORTH SEA

DENMARK

IRELAND
(to England)

ENGLAND

ATLANTIC OCEAN

THE WESTERN EMPIRE

FRANCE

VENICE

NAVARRE

PAPAL STATES

PORTUGAL

SPAIN

NAPLES

(to Spain)

FEZ

TLEMCEN

HAFSIDS

M

Beduins

---·—·— Boundary between Islam and Christendom in 1672

------- Boundary between Islam and Christendom in 1730

———— Boundary between Islam and Christendom in 1798

Muslim states in 1500

Christian countries vassals of Muslim states in 1672

Christian countries vassals of Muslim states in 1798

------ Boundary between Eastern and Western Christianity in c.1400

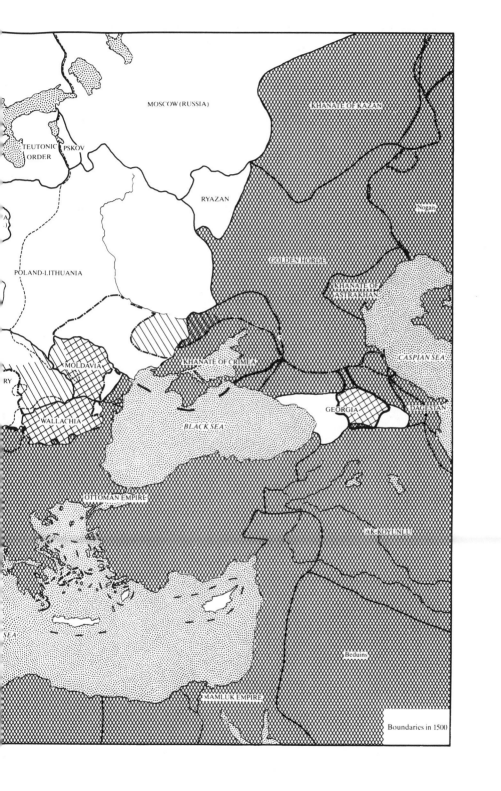

MOSCOW (RUSSIA)

KHANATE OF KAZAN

TEUTONIC PSKOV
ORDER

Nogais

RYAZAN

GOLDEN HORDE

POLAND-LITHUANIA

KHANATE OF
ASTRAKHAN

CASPIAN SEA

MOLDAVIA

KHANATE OF CRIMEA

RY

GEORGIA

DAGESTAN

WALLACHIA

BLACK SEA

OTTOMAN EMPIRE

AK-KOYUNLU

SEA

Beduins

MAMLUK EMPIRE

Boundaries in 1500

Abbreviations

MGHS	*Monumenta Germaniae Historica Scriptores in Folio et Quarto*, ed. G. H. Pertz et al., (1826 ff.)
MGHS rer. Germ.	*MGHS rerum germanicarum in usum scholarum separatim editi* (1840–1937)
PL	*Patrologiae cursus completus. Series Latina*, comp. J. P. Migne (1844–64)
RHC	*Recueil des Historiens des Croisades*, ed. Académie des Inscriptions et Belles-Lettres (1841–1906)
RHC Lois	*RHC Lois. Les Assises de Jérusalem* (1841–3)
RHC Oc.	*RHC Historiens occidentaux* (1844–95)

Preface

Crusades were waged in many theatres of war and it is no coincidence that some of the regions involved have changed hands many times over the centuries. So many places have more than one name. On the assumption that some of my readers may want to visit the more important sites, I have followed *The Times Atlas of the World* (6th comprehensive edition, 1984) for place-names whenever possible, but I have modified its practice for places too well-known to readers of English to change (Gdańsk rather than Danzig, but Fez not Fès, and Marienburg rather than Malbork). In every case I have included any alternative name in parentheses after the first mention and also in the index.

The Times Atlas has adopted a system of transliteration which is used widely in Britain and the United States, but it is not one employed by historians and I decided that it would be confusing if I tried to recast Arabic personal names to agree with it. Arabists will not like the way I use one system of transliteration for places and another for persons, but my chief aim has been to make things as easy as I can for the general reader.

Every university historian knows that his greatest debts of gratitude are owed to his undergraduate and post-graduate students. To two of mine, Dr Peter Edbury and Dr Norman Housley, are owed special thanks because they read this book in typescript and saved me from blunders and in-felicities. I did not always follow their advice, however, and so take full responsibility for the interpretations and opinions, which are my own. I would also like to thank Janet Daines, who typed the final version.

The translations of documents quoted in the text on pp. 6, 8–9, 89, 95, 97–8, 104, 107, 109, 120, 132–3, 140, 142–4, 158–9, 257 are taken from L. and J. Riley-Smith, *The Crusades: Idea and Reality, 1095–1274* (Edward Arnold, *Documents of Medieval History*, 4), London, 1981.

J. S. C. R-S.

Introduction

In the early thirteenth century the great preacher James of Vitry addressed the Knights Templar. His sermon was certainly preached in the East, probably in Acre, where he was bishop and where the Templars had their headquarters in a massive convent-fortress by the sea. He began by drawing attention to the fact that while the Templars and their fellow Christian soldiers battled on a lesser plane than the first 'soldiers of God', the apostles and martyrs, and the last, those souls who would remain firm during the final trial before Doomsday, they had the important duty of countering a real and present threat to Christians from the devil and his agents, idolators, pagans, heretics and pacifists, the last of whom sought to undermine the rôle of the Templars. He justified Christian violence with theological arguments, drawn almost entirely from the pages of Gratian's *Decretum*, the standard textbook of canon law. This would have been over the heads of his audience, for most of the Templars were uneducated and would have perceived only dimly, if at all, the intellectual case for force. They must have been relieved when, as was his custom, James told some good stories, one about a Templar 'in the days when the Templars were poor and most fervently religious' – a typical dig at his listeners – before ending his sermon with an exhortation to eschew their own glory and place their trust only in God.

Reading the sermon now, it does not come across as a great success. There is an artificial break between the scriptural allusions and quotations from the Fathers in the first three-quarters of it and the anecdotes and simple message with which it ends. It manages only to illustrate the deep gulf that has always separated the intellectual abstractions of theologians from the forces that move ordinary men and women. Popes and preachers, who had to present the theology of violence to ordinary Christians in terms they could understand, never succeeded in building satisfactory bridges across the divide. This is one reason why they could never fully control the passions they aroused. But it is important to stress at the start that the crusading movement flourished against a background of ideas on violence which were upheld by most educated men. Without them the Church would never have embarked on the dangerous course of encouraging laymen, let alone religious like the Templars, to resort to arms: it had had

enough trouble trying to cope with the anarchic turbulence in contemporary society.

The standard Christian criteria for justifiable war had been developed in
the fourth century: a right intention on the part of the participants, which
should always be expressed through love of God and neighbour; a just
cause; and legitimate proclamation by a qualified authority. But holy wars
such as the crusades required two additional premises. The first was that
violence – defined crudely as an act of physical force which threatens,
deliberately or as a side-effect, homicide or injury to the human body – was
not intrinsically evil. It was morally neutral until qualified by the intention
of the perpetrator. If his intention was altruistic, like that of a surgeon
who, even against the wishes of his patient, amputated a limb – a measure
which at the time certainly endangered the patient's life – then the violence
could be regarded as being positively good.

The second premise was that of a political Christ. Sacred violence always
stemmed from the conviction that Christ's wishes for mankind were
associated with a political system or course of political events in this world.
For the crusaders his intentions were embodied in a political conception,
the Christian Republic, which was thought to be a single, universal, trans-
cendental state ruled by him, whose agents on earth were popes, bishops,
emperors and kings. A personal commitment to its defence was believed
by many to be a moral imperative for those qualified to fight. Propagandists gave this theory expression in terms the faithful could understand: the Holy Land was Christ's royal domain or patrimony; Livonia
(approx. Latvia) on the Baltic was the Blessed Virgin Mary's private
estate, a kind of queen mother's dower.

God, whether in the rôle of Father or Son, would, of course, approve of
acts of force in defence of his wishes and it was also believed that he could
personally and directly authorize them. He was reported to have done so
on many occasions in the Old Testament and on a few in the New
Testament, among them Christ's apparent approval of the possession of
two swords by the Apostles at the Last Supper (Luke 22: 38), which,
coupled with his injunction a few hours later to St Peter not to throw what
was obviously one of these swords away, but to put it back into its scabbard
(Matthew 26: 52–3; John 18: 11; also Luke 22: 49–51), suggested that his
precepts of mercy and forgiveness had not entirely reversed the
belligerence in divine revelation under the old dispensation. Christ was
believed to authorize crusades himself – this was one of their characteristic
features – and he did so through his chief representative on earth, the
pope.

A crusade was a holy war fought against those perceived to be the
external or internal foes of Christendom for the recovery of Christian
property or in defence of the Church or Christian people. As far as the

crusaders were concerned, the Muslims in the East and in Spain had occupied Christian territory, including land sanctified and made his very own by the presence of Christ himself, and they had imposed infidel tyranny on the Christians who lived there. The pagans in the Baltic region threatened new Christian settlements. The heretics in Languedoc or Bohemia were rebels against their mother the Church and were denying the responsibility for teaching entrusted to her by Christ; they and the Church's political opponents in Italy disturbed rightful order. These people all menaced Christians and the Church, and their actions provided crusaders with the opportunity of expressing love for their oppressed or threatened brothers in a just cause, which was always related to that of Christendom as a whole. A crusading army was therefore considered to be international, even when it was actually composed of men from only one region. I have already drawn attention to the fact that the war it fought was believed to be directly authorized by Christ himself, the incarnate God, through his mouthpiece the pope. Being Christ's own enterprise it was regarded as positively holy. Being proclaimed by the pope assured a measure of control by the Church. At least some of the participants had taken a vow which originated in that of pilgrims, and pilgrimage terminology was often used of crusaders and their campaigns; while the privileges they enjoyed, particularly the protection of themselves, their families and properties, were based on those given to pilgrims. They were also granted indulgences and when they were not fighting in the East the popes often, but not always, related indulgences specifically to those given to crusaders to the Holy Land.

The thirteenth-century popes would have recognized this definition. But the crusade became a clearly defined institution only gradually and not all Christians saw crusading in the same light as did the papacy. While there is general agreement that crusades to the East always had greater prestige and provided the standard against which all others were judged, one controversy among historians today is whether the majority of the faithful regarded crusades in Europe as being qualitatively their equals. The argument is rather a pointless one, because even if most Latin Christians had disagreed with the papacy – and the evidence suggests that on this issue they did not – so many of them took part in crusades within Europe that the western theatres of war cannot be ignored if one is to give a balanced account of the movement. The popes made judgements on the respective importance at a given time of a range of options. So did the faithful; but the fact that they sometimes disagreed with the papal curia is not proof that they always disagreed. Developments within one theatre could influence events in another and sometimes two theatres would be directly linked, as when Spaniards argued that the best way to reach and protect Jerusalem was to extend the *Reconquista* into a liberation of North Africa, or when the Teutonic Knights made use of Prussia as a training-ground for Palestine. The controversy anyway becomes irrelevant when we reach the later fourteenth century, for by then the wars with Islam were coming to involve the defence of Europe itself. Was the Crusade of Nicopolis of 1396 any less of a 'crusade' because it was a 'voiage d'Onguerie', with the aim of driving the Turks from the Hungarian frontier rather than liberating Jerusalem?

The definition I have given here would hold good for crusades to the East, some of the campaigns fought during the Reconquest of Spain, the perpetual crusade in Prussia and Livonia and some expeditions on the Finnish-Russian border, the crusades against the Albigensians, Hussites and Mongols, and those against opponents of the papacy and its allies in Italy. But it would not cover many other engagements which have to be considered in this book. The brothers of the Military Orders were never crusaders, since they did not take crusade vows – of their nature temporary commitments – but were professed religious permanently committed to the defence of Christendom. The secular lords and knights of Latin Palestine and Syria were not crusaders either and the campaigns they fought in defence of their homes and properties were not usually crusades. The leagues formed to combat the Turks from the fourteenth to the late seventeenth centuries were not crusades because, although provided with papal authorization and with participants who had taken vows and were granted indulgences, they were technically alliances of separate Christian powers, even when support for them was preached outside the borders of the states involved, and so they lacked the supra-national ethos which was a characteristic of all crusades. And yet all these were so closely associated with crusading that it would be absurd to treat them separately. It is best, I believe, to consider crusades as expressions of a crusading movement which underlay them and found other outlets as well. It was this movement which outlasted the crusades and only ended with the surrender of Malta to Napoleon Bonaparte by the Hospitallers of St John in 1798. Its vestiges, in other words, were, like those of other decayed institutions of the *ancien régime*, swept away by the French Revolutionary wars. It is sobering to think that only seven generations separate its last adherents from ourselves.

CHAPTER 1

The Birth of the Crusading Movement: The Preaching of the First Crusade

Background

In the first week of March 1095 Pope Urban II presided over a church council at Piacenza in northern Italy. There was present an embassy sent by the Byzantine emperor Alexius to ask for help against the Turks, whose advance across Asia Minor had brought them within striking distance of Constantinople (Istanbul). This appeal set off the chain of events that led to the First Crusade and provided it with a *casus belli*.

By the early eighth century the Christians had lost North Africa, Palestine and Syria and most of Spain to the Muslims. But then the frontier between Christendom and Islam had stabilized until the Byzantine emperors, ruling from Constantinople what remained of the eastern Roman empire, went on to the offensive in the second half of the tenth century. The comparatively subdued reaction of the Muslims to the First Crusade can be partly explained by the fact that their confidence had already been shaken 130 years before, when the ancient cities of Tarsus and Antioch (Antakya) had been retaken and the Byzantine frontier had advanced into northern Syria. A violent shock had been felt throughout the Islamic world at that time: 600 volunteers had arrived in Mosul from Khorasan, 1,200 miles away, in 963; they were followed three years later by a further 20,000 men. The Christian victories had coincided with internal developments that had transformed the western Islamic scene. The authority of the 'Abbasid caliphs in Baghdad had atrophied and they themselves had fallen under the control of Shi'ite princes, whom they regarded as heretics. In 969 Egypt had been occupied almost without opposition by another Shi'ite dynasty, the Fatimids, and a rival caliphate had been established. Thereafter the Fatimids struggled to wrest Palestine and Syria from the 'Abbasids until in the 1060s and 1070s they had to give way to the Turks who, taking advantage of seventeen years of internal disorder in Egypt, drove them out of most of their Syrian possessions and left them with only a shaky hold on parts of Palestine. It was these Turks who at the same time revived Muslim fortunes on the Christian frontier.

Far to the East, among the nomadic Turkomans on the borders of the Turkish steppe east of the Aral Sea who had converted to Islam in the tenth century, there had been a large group under a chief called Selchük.

Brought into the settled Islamic area as hired warriors, his people were in control of Khoorasan by 1037 and their victory at the Battle of Dandanqan in 1040 opened Iran to them. In 1049 the motley following of Tughrul, Selchük's grandson, comprising barely controllable nomadic Turkomans and more regular forces, penetrated Armenia. In 1055 Tughrul entered Baghdad and by 1059 he was master of Iraq as far as the Byzantine and Syrian marches. He established a sultanate which ruled Iran, Iraq and part of Syria in the name of the 'Abbasid caliph. At their conversion to Islam the Selchük Turks had absorbed the aggressive and strict religion of the frontiers and they justified their progress westwards as a campaign against the corruption in Islam which, they believed, manifested itself in the scandal of an orthodox Sunnite caliphate being for over a century under the dominance of Shi'ite princes. Their concern thereafter was to proceed against the heretical caliph in Egypt and their early moves against Christendom were haphazard and spasmodic. From the later 1050s, however, parties of nomads were making deep raids into Byzantine Armenia and by the late 1060s they were to be found in Cilicia and in Anatolia proper, at Amorium and Konya, being, in fact, sometimes engaged as mercenaries by Greek generals. As they moved across the borders they passed beyond the control of Tughrul's nephew and successor Alp Arslan, who was forced to intervene in the region. This in turn provoked a Byzantine military reaction. In 1071 Alp Arslan conducted a campaign which, although it involved capturing several Christian places in order to consolidate his frontier, was concerned primarily with bringing Aleppo to heel. The city fell to him, but he then heard that the Byzantine emperor Romanus IV Diogenes was preparing an offensive. Rounding on the Greeks, he annihilated them and captured the emperor at the Battle of Manzikert.

Byzantine military power had been in decline and Manzikert opened the empire to the Turkoman nomads, a process hastened by the short-sighted actions of Greek generals competing for the throne, who enrolled Turks in their service and established them in the interior. Asia Minor rapidly passed out of Byzantine control and it was this that lay behind the appeal to the West in 1095.

Pope Urban II

The papacy had for some time been worried by the disintegration of Christendom's eastern frontier. News of the Turkish advances had led Pope Gregory VII in 1074 to make an extraordinary proposal to lead personally a force of as many as 50,000 volunteers to 'liberate' their Christian brothers in the East; he stated that with this army he might even push on to the Holy Sepulchre in Jerusalem. Pope Urban II, who had been in touch with the Byzantine emperor from the beginning of his pontificate, with the aim of improving relations between the Latin and Greek churches, may have considered calling for French volunteers to lend military aid to the Greeks as early as 1089. It is, therefore, highly improbable that his behaviour after the Council of Piacenza was a spontaneous response to the appeal just made by the Greeks. It is far more likely to have been one that he had long premeditated.

With hindsight one can see how Urban II's upbringing and career had prepared him for the step he now took. He had been born c. 1035 into a North French noble family: his father was probably a vassal of the Count of Champagne. Educated at the prestigious school attached to the cathedral at Reims, he became canon and archdeacon there, before leaving soon after 1067 to enter the great Burgundian abbey of Cluny, perhaps under the influence of that desire for a stricter religious life which was to lead his teacher St Bruno to found the Carthusians. By 1074 the abilities which had made him archdeacon at a very young age had brought him to the office of grand prior of Cluny, the second-in-command to the abbot. Cluny was at the centre of ecclesiastical affairs and its monks were called upon to serve at the Roman curia under Pope Gregory VII. Urban was appointed to the cardinal-bishopric of Ostia, the senior office in the college of cardinals, succeeding another past grand prior of Cluny. He went to Rome in 1080 and was caught up in the Investiture Contest, especially during the winter of 1084–5 when he was trying to shore up the crumbling support for Pope Gregory in Germany. He was one of three persons nominated by Gregory as his possible successors, and after the short pontificate of Victor III Urban was elected pope on 12 March 1088. His time as canon of Reims and monk and prior at Cluny had brought him into contact with some of the best elements in the reform movement, about which more below, and had exposed him to views associated with Cluny on the functions of secular knights in the service of the Church. His career in Italy and as papal legate in Germany had introduced him to the latest reform ideas and to their application in ecclesiastical politics. But above all by birth he was particularly qualified to know the minds of the knights of France.

After staying in Piacenza for about a month he began a leisurely journey through northern Italy before moving on to France. On 15 August 1095 he was at Le Puy, the bishop of which, Adhémar of Monteil, was to play an important part in the crusade. From there Urban summoned the French bishops to a council to be held at Clermont in the following November. He then travelled south to St Gilles, in the dominions of Raymond of St Gilles, the count of Toulouse and a future leader of the crusade, before travelling up the Rhône valley to Cluny, which he reached on c. 18 October. One of the reasons for Urban's visit to France had been to dedicate the altar of the great new church that had been built at Cluny. He reached Clermont on 15 or 16 November and opened the council on the 18th. On the 27th he proclaimed the crusade to a large but predominantly clerical gathering, after which he journeyed through central, western and southern France, skirting the area directly controlled by the king, whose excommunication for adultery had been confirmed at Clermont. Urban must have preached the crusade a good deal himself, although we have evidence only of sermons at Limoges at Christmas 1095, at Angers and Le Mans in February 1096 and at Nîmes in July. He also presided over ceremonies at which knights took the cross: possibly at Le Mans, certainly at Tours in March 1096. He re-crossed the Alps into Italy in August. By then the crusade was under way.

There were many descriptions of the message Urban was trying to get across at Clermont and on his tour of France, but most are not to be trusted because they were written after the crusade had liberated Jerusalem, when no writer was immune from a general euphoria that bathed the immediate past in an artificial glow. But there is enough contemporary material, particularly in his own letters, for us to discern at least the outlines of Urban's appeal. He called for a war of liberation, thus echoing the message of progressive churchmen for the past fifty years, a half-century that was one of the most remarkable in Christian history. The Church had entered one of its periodical bouts of reform. The reformers wanted to free it from corrupt practices which they imputed above all to an excessive influence of the laity in ecclesiastical appointments. They wanted a purer institution, more akin to the Early Church they perceived in reading the Acts of the Apostles. And since most of the reformers were monks, engaged in a reform of monasticiscm which pre-dated and ran parallel to the more general reform of the Church, they viewed the Early Church through monkish eyes. It is no exaggeration to say that they wanted to monasticize the Christian world. They dreamed of a clergy, celibate and untainted by worldly values, ministering to lay men and women who as far as they were able lived lives and adopted devotional practices that corresponded to monastic ones. The energy expended on the cause was remarkable. So too were the vigour with which the reformers encouraged the physical transformation of the Church's presence all over Europe through the building of parish churches, each in its way a large conventual chapel for a lay community, and the intelligence that led them to foster scholarship, particularly the study of grammar, history and canon law, to justify the campaign. Most extraordinary of all is the way the papacy was captured: it is no coincidence that so many of the popes of this period were monks themselves. For most of its 2000-year history the papacy has not been in the forefront of reform. It has supported reformers and it has taken over and controlled reform once it has begun, but only once, in the late eleventh century, can it be said that the popes found themselves in the invigorating but dangerously exposed position of being the leaders of a radical party in the Church.

So when Urban called for liberation, he was using a concept coloured by its employment in the last half-century by reformers who, it must be admitted, had an exaggerated notion of liberty, bred in great exempt abbeys like Cluny, communities which had been accustomed to enjoy 'liberties' granted them by the popes, which freed them from the power of bishops and kings. This pressure for liberation in the West had already led to violence. For over forty years popes had occasionally supported the use of force against those who resisted the new ideas, most notably when around 1080 a party of German magnates had dragged Pope Gregory VII into war in Germany with the king and emperor-designate Henry IV. This war had spread to Italy and Gregory had been driven from Rome and an anti-pope established there in his place. Urban II had begun his pontificate in exile, opposed by powerful forces in Europe. His success in rebuilding support had culminated in his entry into Rome in 1094 and in the Council of Piacenza itself, which was attended by a large body of bishops and by a significant number of representatives of lay powers. During this period of conflict the popes, moreover, had taken the extraordinarily brave step of renouncing imperial protection on principle, thus exposing themselves to the greedy ambitions of the local Roman nobles, who had shown in the past that unless checked they were capable of treating their bishopric as a pawn. Faced with conflict within Christendom and fearing the nobility at home, the popes, therefore, had every reason for trying to build up all over Europe a party of 'knights of St Peter' at their disposal and they had turned for help to allies in Italy, particularly the Normans in the south. It was natural that this should have been accompanied by hyperbolic de-nunciations of the wickedness of their opponents, by demonstrations of the justice of their cause and by assurances of absolution, even the crown of martyrdom, for their soldiers. They had also turned to scholars for justification of Christian violence and Gregory VII had found in Anselm of Lucca a partisan who, through a careful reading of the Fathers, above all St Augustine of Hippo, would build a convincing case for Christian violence as something which could be commanded by God, was at the disposal of the Church and would, when properly used, be an expression of Christian love.

Since the summons to liberation in the eleventh-century western Church had already led to the use of liberating force it was only a matter of time before it would be extended to areas in which Christians suffered from far more serious disabilities than any of their western brothers. Urban also used the term 'liberation' of the Norman Count Roger's reconquest of Sicily and of the Reconquest of Spain, where the Christians had begun to reoccupy the territories lost to the Muslims in the eighth century: the fall of Toledo to the Christians in 1085 had been a sensation. And it was certain – Gregory VII's proposal of 1074 had shown this – that when reformers, accustomed as monks to constant references to Jerusalem and Zion in the psalmody of the divine office, thought of the East their minds turned naturally to Jerusalem. In this respect the First Crusade hardly required a *casus belli*: the inner momentum of the reform movement would probably have led to it sooner or later.

When he preached the crusade, however, Urban proclaimed a war with two distinct liberating goals. The first was the freeing of the eastern Churches, and especially the Church of Jerusalem, from the savagery and tyranny of the Muslims. This was the liberation of people, the baptized members of the Churches, and Urban apparently painted a lurid picture of life under Muslim rule and exaggerated the threat the Turks now posed to Constantinople – their advance had petered out in 1092 – although it must have seemed real enough to the Greeks. It is clear that he coupled this liberation with that of the whole Church. In this he was like his predecessors, who had always linked the liberation of specific groups of the faithful to the needs and renewal of the Church at large; but there was also another factor which made it impossible for him to treat the crusade in isolation. Since almost the start of his pontificate Urban had enthusiastically supported – indeed the evidence suggests that he himself had inaugurated – a drive to reoccupy Tarragona, a ghost town in no man's land fifty miles down the Spanish coast from Barcelona. The Count of Barcelona, who was being encouraged to take it, made it over to the pope as a 'land of St Peter'. Urban appointed an archbishop, fostered colonization, enjoined, in the language of indulgences, about which more below, the notables of the region to rebuild the town 'in penitence and for the remission of sins', and suggested that those planning to make penitential pilgrimages, even to Jerusalem, should instead work for and make financial contributions to the restoration of Tarragona which, he assured them, would gain the same spiritual benefits. It is not at all suprising that when, after he had preached the crusade, he learnt that Catalans were planning to take the cross for Jerusalem he ordered them to stay at home where, he promised them, they could fulfil their crusade vows

> because it is no virtue to rescue Christians from Muslims in one place, only to expose them to the tyranny and oppression of the Muslims in another (P. F. Kehr, *Papsturkunden in Spanien. 1. Katalonien* (1926) p. 288).

For the rest of his pontificate he specifically equated the war in the East with the reconquest of Spain.

> 'In our days (God) has fought through Christian men in Asia against the Turks and in Europe against the Moors' (Urban II, 'Epistolae et Privilegia', *PL* vol. 151, col. 504).

In respect of the liberation and defence of people, therefore, he made little distinction between the East and Spain. This must be stressed because only with it in mind does the future of crusading become understandable. Some historians have suggested that crusades aimed elsewhere than to the East were deviations from an original ideal, but in fact the first deviation occurred during the First Crusade, was proposed by the originator of crusading, and stemmed from a concern of his to preserve an initiative that pre-dated it.

The other goal of the crusade was the liberation of Jerusalem, a specific place. Many historians have found it hard to believe that Urban was really serious about Jerusalem and the idea of a western Christian army battling its way through Asia Minor and Syria to Palestine does look at first sight to have been quixotic. The theory has evolved that in fact the goal of Jerusalem was secondary, perhaps long-term, and that Urban's first concern was to help the Greeks against the Turks, thus improving relations with the patriarchate of Constantinople. There is, however, overwhelming evidence, above all in the charters of departing crusaders, for Jerusalem being a prime goal from the start, which is understandable in the context of contemporary attitudes. The concern of eleventh-century Catholics with Jerusalem – the centre of the world, the focus of God's interventions in history and a relic, since its streets had been walked by Christ and its ground had soaked up Christ's blood – was becoming obsessive, fostered by pilgrimages which, in spite of the fact that Urban apparently made play of the sufferings of pilgrims at the hands of the Muslims, were increasing in frequency and numbers.

It was the goal of Jerusalem, of course, that made the crusade a pilgrimage. There is no doubt that Urban preached it as a pilgrimage and that he extended to crusaders the privileges and practices of pilgrims: the protection of the church for crusaders and their property, and the public vow, similar to the pilgrimage vow, made by a crusader and signified by his wearing of a cross, which enabled some sort of control to be exercised over him, since a pilgrim was treated in law as a temporary ecclesiastic, subject to Church courts. It is clear from their charters that the crusaders regarded themselves as pilgrims and while on crusade they engaged in the devotional and liturgical exercises characteristic of pilgrims. They were, of course, warrior pilgrims, but although this was novel – there had never been pilgrims who set out with the intention of conquest – there had often been pilgrimages armed for self-preservation. There was, moreover, a tradition of violence associated with some of the great pilgrim centres in the West, in which the saints whose relics were the objects of the cults used miracles of force to protect the guardians of, or visitors to, the shrines.

But in another way the crusade was a very odd sort of pilgrimage. Since it was also a war, Urban tried to limit participation to arms-bearing knights, in other words to youngish, healthy men. He absolutely forbade monks to go:

> We were (he wrote) stimulating the minds of knights to go on this expedition. . . . We do not want those who have abandoned the world and have vowed themselves to spiritual warfare either to bear arms or to go on this journey; we go so far as to forbid them to do so (W. Wiederhold, 'Papsturkunden in Florenz', *Nachrichten von der Gesellschaft der Wissenschaften zu Gottingen. Phil.-hist.* K1. (1901), p. 313).

He wanted to limit the number of priests to as few as was necessary. He stated that the old, the infirm and women were not suitable, although women apparently could accompany their husbands or brothers with permission from Church authorities. His statements on the unfit laity could not, however, be prohibitions, merely recommendations. Pilgrimages were traditionally devotional exercises for all penitents, whatever their condition – indeed those to healing shrines were for the sick – and it was clearly impossible to limit a pilgrimage to healthy men, which is one reason why so many of the 'unsuitable' did eventually take part in the crusade.

He authorized the war in his capacity as pope, but it is clear that he also stated that he was acting on Christ's behalf. He wrote of the crusaders being inspired agents of God who were engaged in God's service out of love for him. He told them they were followers of Christ and he may well have referred to them as 'knights of Christ'; throughout France the crusade was known as 'the way of God'. He was, of course, using the expostulatory language already employed by reformers when they referred to the engagements of their military supporters: Gregory VII had written of his *fideles* as 'knights of Christ' and Urban used this kind of language himself when writing of military operations against the Muslims in Spain, North Africa and Sicily. But it is noticeable that his approach was somewhat more restrained than that of his predecessors. Had it not been for the crusade's success we would now be thinking of his summons at Clermont merely as a variant of the pronouncements of Gregory VII. We shall see that it was the crusaders themselves, engaged in triumph in Asia, who came to consider that they really were involved in a divine enterprise.

Urban appealed particularly to French knights, although as enthusiasm spread he was prepared to extend his summons to other nationalities, except of course Spaniards, and from the summer of 1096 he was anxious to make use of the maritime power of the Italian ports. In this he must have betrayed his origins and he was playing on the emotions of a class he knew intimately. It is significant that he addressed his appeal not just to the great magnates but also to their followers, the castellans and knights, from whose ranks he himself had sprung. They were also members of classes which had reduced France to chaos, which is why he stressed the difference between the old robber warrior – the successful castellan – and the new knight whose altruistic participation in this war would be an act of Christian charity, expressing love of God and of his neighbour. In this regard he cited three passages of scripture: *If any man will come after me, let him deny himself and take up his cross and follow me* (Matt. 16: 24 or Luke 14: 27); *Every one that hath left house or brethren or sisters or father or mother or wife or children or lands, for my name's sake, shall receive an hundredfold and shall possess life everlasting* (Matt. 19: 29); and *Greater love than this no man hath, that a man lay down his life for his friends* (John 15: 13).

By appealing to French knights Urban was reviving an alliance between France and the Holy See which had not been operative for two centuries. By preaching the crusade as a meritorious act of love which laymen were particularly qualified to undertake he was presenting crusading in a way that marked the culmination of a period in which the Church had progressively turned to the laity for support. But he went further in proposing the crusade as a 'way of the cross' for laymen. Hitherto that way had been a withdrawal from the world, a renunciation of earthly things in a retreat into the cloister. Now laymen were given something to do that was almost equivalent to monasticism:

> God has instituted in our time holy wars [wrote one contemporary], so that the order of knights and the crowd running in their wake, who following the example of the ancient pagans have been engaged in slaughtering one another, might find a new way of gaining salvation. And so they are not forced to abandon secular affairs completely by choosing the monastic life or any religious profession, as used to be the custom, but can attain in some measure God's grace while pursuing their own careers, with the liberty and in the dress to which they are accustomed (Guibert of Nogent, 'Gesta Dei per Francos', *RHC Oc*. vol. 4, p. 124).

Urban had taken a step along the road that would lead the Church to recognize the lay condition as a vocation in itself.

He sealed his remarks on the merit of crusading by the grant at the Council of Clermont of the indulgence. To understand what he did we must remember that the popes of the time appear still to have maintained that penances, self-imposed punishments for sin, could be 'satisfactory', by which they meant that the pain and suffering thus voluntarily accepted could outweigh the punishments God would impose in this world or in the after-life for sin. Urban's indulgences were authoritative declarations that the crusade would be so arduous and unpleasant that it would make good all penance owed to God by individual sinners, although he appears to have made a distinction between the less demanding exercise of fighting in Spain – the indulgence was granted only to those who died in the Spanish war – and the rigours of the campaign to the East, for the survivors of which the indulgence was granted absolutely.

It should be stressed that apart from the appeal to the French and the idea of a war-pilgrimage confined to healthy males, there was little that was novel in Urban's message. For almost every element precedents can be found in the practice of earlier popes or in the discussions taking place in reforming circles in Italy. It is true that the summons appeared to be radical and exciting to many in France, but that is only evidence for the backwardness of the provinces and the difficulty reformers had had in getting their views across. Urban, of course, combined these elements into a synthesis which had never been quite achieved before and therefore he really was the originator of the crusades. But just as important to the development of the idea of crusading were the response to his call and the experiences of the first crusaders in Asia. Out of the enthusiasms and traumas of the participants the elements found embryonically in Urban's message formed themselves into an ideology.

The response

Urban not only preached the crusade personally during his journey through France after Clermont; he also sent letters or embassies to Flanders, Genoa, Bologna, Pisa and Milan; and the crusade was discussed at councils he held at Bari in October 1098 and Rome in April 1099. At Clermont and probably at the Council of Nîmes in the following summer he encouraged all the bishops present to preach the cross themselves. Several followed his instructions, among whom the most prominent was Hugh of Die, the Archbishop of Lyon and an ardent reformer, but there is evidence that many did not. Very few surviving manuscripts of the decisions of the Council of Clermont included the decree on the crusade indulgence; they tended to contain only the selection of interest to the bishops who had them copied. And one which did include the decree, a list made for Bishop Lambert of Arras, may not even have reflected Lambert's concern, since he has left us his own account of the Council, in which no mention is made of the crusade at all; for him the most important result was the pope's confirmation of the standing of his own bishopric. Monks seem to have been more enthusiastic and many were active recruiting-officers. There were also free-lancers like Peter the Hermit. But the news of the pope's appeal spread fast – so fast, according to one contemporary, that there was no need of preaching – and it soon became clear that there was going to be a significant response in France, Italy and South and West

Germany. This response was large enough to cause comment at the time, but just how large is now difficult to judge. Leaving aside the great numbers on the third wave of the crusade – the so-called Crusade of 1101 – which were affected by the news of the liberation of Jerusalem in 1099, the following figures can be suggested very tentatively. A fair, perhaps too conservative, estimate of the numbers on the second wave that gathered before Nicaea (Iznik) in June 1097 would be 43,000. Crusaders continued to overtake and join the army right up to the fall of Jerusalem and beyond, even though the total in the army during the siege of Jerusalem had fallen to 15,000. We might add 3,000 for late departures. The armies of the first wave were at least as large, possibly larger, than those of the second. So a guess for them would be 45,000 persons. This gives us a total of 91,000, of whom perhaps 7,000 would have been knights. We then have to take into account the substantial number who took the cross but did not leave; perhaps 45,000 or 50 per cent of the total number departing would be reasonable. So we end with a figure of 136,000, of which less than 10 per cent would have been knights.

These are guesses of course, but even much lower estimates produce a figure in excess of 100,000, which is very substantial for the time and begs the question why so many did respond. The population of Europe, which had been steadily growing, had reached the point at which the systems of inheritance and marriage practices were being put under severe pressure. It is not surprising that the age was one of colonization on the frontiers and even in forests and on marginal lands within old Europe. It was, therefore, natural for a few commentators at the time and for many historians since to assume that the crusade was a colonial venture, that the prospect of new territory for settlement in a land referred to in scripture as 'flowing with milk and honey' situated in a region of legendary wealth, moved peasants, landless unmarried sons and members of families collectively sharing smaller sub-divisions of holdings to opt for a new life. On the other hand, the majority of commentators then and a minority of historians now have maintained that the chief motivation was a genuine idealism.

It is important to get out of the way certain matters on which all can agree. First, any conclusion must be a generalization: there were naturally both adventurers and idealists on the crusade. Secondly, it is certain that conquest was intended from the first. It was discussed at Clermont, since the pope had to make a ruling that churches in any conquered territory would appertain to the 'prince' who took it, although he must have assumed at the time full Byzantine collaboration and so would have expected that the 'prince' would be the Byzantine emperor. It is true that the great majority of the first crusaders returned home after Jerusalem had been liberated – the settlers were on the whole men and women who travelled out to the Levantine territories after they had been conquered –

but the exodus of crusaders from Palestine in late 1099 is not evidence that few of them had intended to settle there when they had left western Europe three years before; their experiences on the march had been so terrible that many could have changed their minds. Thirdly, it is worth remembering that, however, popular the First Crusade was, it did not appeal to everyone by any means. Most western Europeans did not respond at all to the pope's summons. Even in the classes of nobles and knights, about whom we have most information, the figure of, say, 13,000 respondents (of whom about half did not actually depart) represents a fraction of the total numbers: in England alone there were c. 5,000 knights; in France and the French-speaking imperial territories at least 50,000. So we are concerned with the reactions not of an entire class but of a fraction of it, which makes the argument for a general idealistic motivation more credible. Fourthly, we should not expect this idealism to be similar to ours, or even, as many recent studies have shown, to have corresponded to that of senior churchmen and theologians. Lay knights had their own ethos, the features of which are gradually becoming clearer to us. Christian morality certainly played a large part in it, but just as important were other codes: of honour, of social generosity and of family and feudal solidarity which found expression in vendettas.

With these points in mind the situation and expectations of those who took the cross in 1096 can be discerned fairly clearly. Information about the distance to Palestine must have been freely available to them: many western Europeans had been on pilgrimage and a significant number of knights had served in the Byzantine forces as mercenaries. The distance and consequent expenses may not have deterred the very poor, who expected nothing and could, perhaps, have believed that their situation could only improve. But for knights it was a different matter. They were expected to bring with them the equipment, horses, pack-animals and servants required to fulfil their function efficiently. Half a century later a German knight called upon to serve the emperor in Italy needed to put by for such a campaign twice his annual income. The factor by which a French knight would have had to multiply his income to estimate his expenses for a campaign in the East in the late eleventh century can only be guessed at, but a factor of four or five would not be unreasonable. Substantial sums, therefore, were required by a knight before he could contemplate going on crusade, which makes the traditional picture of landless knights departing without a care in the world ridiculous. Landless knights did go, but at the expense of richer men. It can also be seen that so many western European knights planning to fight their way to the East involved the raising of substantial sums of money. There were various options open to them. They could tax their tenants, but I have found only one example of this, perhaps because the shortages at the time were so acute that little could be gained.

They could, if they had been involved in disputes over rights and property, renounce claims that in the past they had sometimes enforced by violent means in return for cash payments. This seems to have been fairly common, although a feature of the agreements of renunciation was the abject and humiliating way in which many of the claims were given up: either, like all pilgrims, the individuals concerned were truly anxious not to depart from Europe leaving any residual ill-feeling behind them; or the other parties to the agreements had now so much of the upper hand that they were able to dictate terms that included expressions of regret for past offences. But in an agricultural economy the sums involved could only be raised by a final option, the negotiating of mortgages or sales of property, including fiefs and allods, those freeholds which were so valuable to families but were more easily disposed of than fiefs. That is why the pope and bishops at the Council of Clermont legislated to protect the sales and mortgages negotiated by crusaders and why so many charters of these types are still to be found in the cartularies of churches and monasteries.

The crusade, however, was preached at a time of agricultural depression caused by a succession of bad harvests due to drought. The run was broken by a magnificent harvest in 1096 after a wet spring that seemed to be a physical expression of God's approval of the enterprise, but this obviously came too late for many of the crusaders, who had already been engaged in selling or mortgaging their lands. And the seriousness of their situation was compounded by the facts that sales and mortgages were so numerous and the number of individuals or institutions capable of providing ready cash on so large a scale so few that the value of goods in France was said to have fallen.

Reading the charters that have survived one thing becomes clear. What was being mortgaged or sold was often patrimony, family land, and any transaction had to involve not only the crusader but also the other members of his family, who would be covered by its terms and would signal their agreement to it. While one occasionally finds special payments being made to relatives to secure their assent and the odd case in which members of a family were later involved in litigation over the measures taken, the general picture is one of relatives making substantial sacrifices, actual and potential, in agreeing to the disposal of property to provide cash for departing crusaders. There is very little evidence to support the proposition that the crusade was an opportunity for spare sons to make themselves scarce in order to relieve their families of burdens, or for landless knights to seek an easy way to make a future for themselves overseas. The evidence points overwhelmingly to families taking on burdens to help individual members fulfil their vows, quite apart from the fact that among the magnates, castellans and knights it was common for several members of a family to go – Baldwin of Guines took his four sons, of whom one,

Fulk, was to remain in Palestine – and frequently it was the senior rather than the junior members who went.

This makes it difficult for me to believe that most crusaders, or at least most crusading knights, were motivated by crude materialism. The disposal of assets to invest in the fairly remote possibility of settlement after a 2,000-mile march to the East would have been a stupid gamble. The odds, moreover, could have been lessened simply by waiting until after the agricultural depression had passed and the flood of properties on the market had subsided. It makes much more sense to suppose that they, and especially their families, were moved by idealism. This was an age of ostentatious and extravagant generosity and monasteries and religious communities benefited greatly from it. If the phenomenal growth of monasticism of the period was due as much, if not more, to those who did not enter the communities but endowed them from outside as to those who did, then the same is true of the crusading movement. Behind many crusaders stood a large body of men and women who were prepared to sacrifice interest to help them set out.

To understand why lay men and women were in the frame of mind to respond in this way to the pope's appeal we must go back a hundred years to late tenth-century France. By that time the central power of the Carolingian state had already fragmented. Real authority was no longer exercised by the king but by the great magnates, each in his own province. Then, in a process that is still mysterious but may have had something to do with the fact that a society constructed for war no longer had any function other than to turn its aggression inward upon itself, many of the provinces themselves fragmented into smaller units, based on castles from which castellans and their bodies of knights so terrorized their neighbourhoods that they came to represent the only authorities, violent, arbitrary and demanding, that men knew. This breakdown even of provincial government was accompanied by uncontrollable violence which reached a peak in the 1020s. The Church reacted in two ways. First, it preached a near pacifism and took the lead in a movement for the 'Peace of God', which expressed popular concern in great assemblies of free men, meeting round piles of relics collected from all the local churches and decreeing the immunity of the clergy and poor from violence and exploitation; the peace movement was eventually to ban all violence at certain times of the year and days of the week. Attempts were made to force the castellans and knights to accept peace provisions, but these warriors could only be compelled by force and so the peace movement itself engendered military actions against peace-breakers, conducted in the name of churchmen who, if they were bishops and abbots, anyway had their own retinues of knights.

The reform movement was getting under way at the same time and the reformers, particularly those inspired by ideas associated with Pope Urban's own community of Cluny, began to try to construct a bridge to the secular world across which they could carry the ideas and values with which they wished to infuse it. They spearheaded the intense evangelization of the faithful, out of which came the conviction that the very aggressiveness that had broken up society could be put to good, God-given purposes if only the laity could be disposed to canalize their energies into the service of the Church. The historians employed by the reformers were able to find many texts to justify the use of such force, as we have seen, and the popes were not alone in turning to laymen for military support. All over Europe churchmen were doing the same, while chaplains, concerned to put across the Christian message in terms their employers and their households would understand, drew on the Old Testament stories and Christian hagiography for heroic and martial tales which would appeal to their listeners and perhaps inspire them to do better.

Their efforts were rewarded in the sense that, although society in the late eleventh century was still violent, it was less violent than it had been. There is, moreover, clear evidence for growing piety and outward shows of devotion among many lords and knights. In a society which was so public that private devotions were impractical for laymen, these generally took the form of participation in pilgrimages, themselves semi-monastic in tone and liturgy and closely linked to the monasteries because many of the shrines were in monastic hands, and in the endowment of new religious communities. Those magnates and knights who had been touched by the reform movement and were known for their piety were to be prominent among the crusaders. If it cannot be said that before 1095 the Church had been outstandingly successful in its appeals for armed assistance, in the response to Urban's call it is as though the hand it had been holding out to the laity for fifty years was suddenly grasped and that at last its perception and the laity's aspirations met. It is surely no coincidence that the pope who engineered this meeting of minds was himself a product of that class the Church had been most concerned to energize.

The appeal to crusade also succeeded because it could be interpreted by the lay knights in accordance with their own thinking. In their minds it would take on a colouring that churchmen did not like much but which they could do little to control. For instance, this was an age of vendettas. Western European society consisted of many tight, interlocking circles, made up of families, at this time more widely encompassing than in the later Middle Ages, each bound by the knowledge that its members were kin and therefore 'friends', obliged to guard each other's interests, and of feudal groupings, of vassals round lords, which made the same demands on their members. Both familial and feudal relationships imposed on a man the obligation of the blood-feud in which he was bound to draw his sword in the interests of his relatives, lord or fellow vassals. It is significant that the first appeal for crusaders was expressed in intimate, even domestic, terms. Men were called upon to go to the aid of their oppressed 'brothers', the eastern Christians, whom they were obliged to love, and to the aid of their 'father' and 'lord', Jesus Christ, who was humiliated and disregarded and had lost his 'inheritance' or patrimony. That was a summons to a vendetta.

> I address fathers and sons and brothers and nephews. If an outsider were to strike any of your kin down would you not avenge your blood-relative? How much more ought you to avenge your God, your father, your brother, whom you see reproached, banished from his estates, crucified; whom you hear calling, desolate and begging for aid (Baldric of Bourgueil, 'Historia Jerosolimitana', *RHC Oc.* vol. 4, p. 101).

That is an extract from a crusade sermon constructed about ten years later by a commentator, but it certainly corresponded to reality. In September 1098 the leaders of the crusade in Syria informed Urban that

> The Turks, who inflicted much dishonour on Our Lord Jesus Christ, have been taken and killed and we Jerusalemites have avenged the injury to the supreme God Jesus Christ (H. Hagenmeyer, *Die Kreuzzugsbriefe aus den Jahren 1088–1100* (1901), p. 161).

The potency of the idea of the vendetta was clearly demonstrated in the opening act of the crusade, the 'first holocaust' of European Jews. The first outbreaks of violent anti-semitism seem to have occurred in France shortly after the Council of Clermont. They then spread to Germany and eastern Europe, where they were associated with the first wave of crusaders leaving for the East in the spring of 1096. On 3 May the storm broke over the Jewish community at Speyer, where a South German army under Emich of Leiningen, the most merciless of the persecutors, had gathered. Emich proceeded to Worms, where the massacres began on 18 May, and then to Mainz, where he was joined by more Germans and by a large army of French, English, Flemish and Lorrainer crusaders. Between 25 and 29 May the Jewish community at Mainz, one of the largest in Europe, was decimated. Some crusaders then marched north to Cologne, from where the Jews had already been dispersed into neighbouring settlements. For the next month they were hunted out and destroyed. Another band seems to have gone south-west to Trier and Metz, where the massacres continued. Meanwhile another crusading army, probably Peter the Hermit's, forced almost the whole community at Regensburg to undergo baptism and the communities at Wesseli and Prague in Bohemia suffered probably from the attentions of yet another crusading army, led by a priest called Folkmar.

These pogroms were attributed by some contemporaries to avarice, and the crusaders certainly made financial demands of the Jewish communities and despoiled them; indeed, given the demands of the journey they were about to make they were obviously obsessed with cash. But the Hebrew accounts ascribed greed more to the local bishops, their officials and townspeople than to the crusaders, who seem to have been more interested in forcing conversions. Everywhere Jews were offered the choice of conversion or death, and synagogues, Torah scrolls and cemeteries were desecrated. The Jews feared that the crusaders intended to wipe Judaism out of the regions through which they passed. There is overwhelming evidence that uppermost in the crusaders' minds was a desire for vengeance. They found it impossible to distinguish between Muslims and Jews and if they were being called upon, as they saw it, to avenge the injury to Christ's 'honour' of the loss of his patrimony to the Muslims, why, they asked, should they not also avenge the injury to his person of the Crucifixion – a far deeper disparagement of his 'honour' – particularly in the light of a popular legend circulating at the time in which Christ on the cross had called on the faithful to avenge him? In fact the forcible conversion of non-Christians was prohibited in canon law and the German bishops, with varying degrees of success, tried to stop it. To educated churchmen the Crucifixion in 33 and the Muslim occupation of Jerusalem in 638 were not the issues. It was a present injury, the fact that the Muslims were still in occupation of the Holy City, which justified the crusade, not some woolly concept of past disparagement of honour. But once the crusade had been preached as an expression of love for God and brothers it was impossible for churchmen to control the emotions their appeal had aroused and throughout the twelfth century every major call to crusade gave rise to pogroms against Jews.

CHAPTER 2

The Course of the First Crusade

Since for reasons which will be given later it is not helpful to describe the various groups of crusaders as 'armies', it is best to think of them in terms of three waves of men and women leaving Europe between 1096 and 1101. Even that analogy is not a particularly good one, because there was a continuous stream travelling East, so that the forces of the second wave were being overtaken all the time by new recruits, and crusaders were still entering Palestine as those who had won Jerusalem were leaving for home. There was, moreover, a counterflow of deserters back along the path and from as early as the winter of 1096 the disillusioned, the sick and the fearful were drifting back to western Europe.

The first wave

The first wave of crusaders left very early, in fact far too early, in the spring of 1096. The most famous of its leaders, a popular preacher called Peter the Hermit, had begun to preach the crusade in central France as soon as the Council of Clermont had met, perhaps even before. He collected a substantial following before moving on to the Rhineland in April. In advance of him, and probably on his instructions, a large body of foot, led by only eight knights under the command of Walter Sansavoir (not 'the penniless', as is popularly supposed: Sansavoir was the cognomen of the lords of Poissy) entered Hungary on 21 May and marched in a fairly orderly way to Constantinople. There was one serious outbreak of violence at Belgrade, predictably over foraging, and the absence of more trouble is remarkable considering the fact that Walter's early arrival took the Byzantine authorities by surprise.

At Constantinople Walter was joined by parties of Italian pilgrims and on 1 August by Peter the Hermit, who had left Cologne on 20 April and had had a much more difficult crossing of the Balkans, for which the indiscipline of his followers was largely to blame. His army marched peacefully through Hungary, but at Zemun, the last town in the kingdom, a riot broke out, the citadel was stormed and a large number of Hungarians were killed. The crusaders were naturally anxious to escape retribution by crossing the river Sava into Byzantine territory as soon as possible, and the attempts by a Byzantine force to restrict their movement were violently resisted. They were in an ugly mood by the time they reached a deserted Belgrade which they probably sacked. Nevertheless the Byzantine governor at Niš, unprepared though he was, tried to be cooperative and allowed them to buy supplies in exchange for the surrender of hostages. As they were leaving, some Germans set fire to mills outside the town and the governor sent troops to attack the rearguard. Many of Peter's followers, ignoring his orders, turned on their attackers, but they were routed and scattered. The crusaders lost many men and women and all their cash. Luckily, by the time they reached Sofia the Greeks were ready to receive them. They were now kept supplied and on the move and reached Constantinople without further incident.

Walter and Peter were received well by the Byzantine emperor Alexius and were advised to wait until the other bands of crusaders, which were known to be assembling in Europe, arrived. But Peter's impatient followers took to raiding the surrounding countryside and it is not surprising that the Greeks decided that the sooner the crusaders were moved on the better. On 6 August they were ferried across the Bosporus; they then marched to Kibotos, a suitable assembly-point where they could wait for the rest of the crusade. Differences arose between the Germans and Italians on one side, who elected their own leader, an Italian noble called Rainaldo, and the French on the other. From Kibotos the French raided as far as Turkish Nicaea and Rainaldo's party sought to emulate them. The Germans and Italians broke away and established a base beyond Nicaea, but on 29 September they were surrounded by the Turks and surrendered eight days later. Those who agreed to apostasize were sent to the East, but all who refused were killed. When the news of this disaster reached the main body, Peter the Hermit was away in Constantinople and the French crusaders, ignoring Walter Sansavoir's pleas for caution, advanced into the interior on 21 October. They were ambushed by the Turks and were annihilated.

Walter and Peter at least reached Asia Minor. Three other armies, which marched at about the same time, got no further than Hungary. A force of Saxons and Bohemians under the priest Folkmar was destroyed at Nitra. Another unruly band under a Rhineland priest called Gottschalk was forced to surrender to the Hungarians at Pannonhalma. And the large army of Rhinelander, Swabian, French, English and Lorrainer crusaders under Emich of Leiningen, which had been persecuting the Jews in the Rhineland, was halted before Wieselburg on the Hungarian frontier where, after taking six weeks to build a bridge over the river in front of the town, its first assault dissolved into panic and flight.

It is wrongly assumed that these forces, 'The People's Crusade', consisted almost entirely of peasants, in contrast to those that left Europe later in 1096. This was certainly an explanation given by contemporaries for their massacres of Jews, their indiscipline in the Balkans and their failure in Asia Minor. But, although there may have been more non-combatants than in the later armies, there was a strong knightly element as well. Walter Sansavoir was an experienced knight; so appear to have been Peter the Hermit's captains, one of whom, Fulcher of Chartres, was to end his days as a great lord in the county of Edessa, the earliest Latin settlement. Attached to Peter's following, moreover, was a body of Swabian nobles under the Count Palatine Hugh of Tübingen and Duke Walker of Tegk. Emich of Leiningen was an important South German noble. So was Count Hartmann of Dillingen-Kybourg, who joined him at Mainz. They were probably accompanied by at least four other German counts. The army of French, English, Flemish and Lorrainer crusaders, which also met Emich at Mainz and was apparently large and well-equipped, was under the leadership of an outstanding group of French knights: Clarembald of Vendeuil, Thomas of Marle lord of Coucy, William the Carpenter viscount of Melun, and Drogo of Nesle. They may have made up a French advance-guard, since after the destruction of Emich's forces they joined Hugh of Vermandois, the king of France's brother, and continued their journey to the East with him. We cannot allow ourselves to be lulled by the comforting belief that the persecution of Jews was perpetrated by mere gangs of peasants, too unprofessional to cope in the Balkans and Asia Minor.

I have already tried to explain the pogroms. One of the reasons for the catastrophes that befell this first wave of crusaders was that they left Europe before the date set by the pope, which was 15 August 1096. Leaving while western Europe was still in the grip of near famine conditions, before the marvellous harvest of that summer, they were short of food from the start. In the Balkans they had to pillage when the markets were not available to them; and even with access to markets they were anxious about supplies. It is clear that over and over again it was disputes about provisions that led to disorder. The Byzantine government, moreover, was unprepared. It had not set up the organization to guide the crusaders; nor did it have the supplies to give them. And the failure of the armies of Folkmar, Gottschalk and especially Emich of Leiningen to get through at all meant that Peter the Hermit and Walter Sansavoir did not have adequate forces in Asia Minor.

The second wave

The second wave of crusaders began to leave western Europe in the middle of August, on or after the date fixed by the pope. At this stage they travelled in separate corps, each mustered from a region and many under the leadership of great magnates. Hugh of Vermandois left France in the middle of August and travelled by way of Rome to Bari, from where he set sail for Durazzo (Durrës). But a storm scattered his fleet and Hugh, who was forced to land some way from Durazzo, was briefly detained before being escorted to Constantinople. At about the same time Godfrey of Bouillon, the Duke of Lower Lorraine, left with his brother Baldwin of Boulogne and a party of Lorrainer nobles. Godfrey is the most famous of the first crusaders, but the one we can understand the least. He had been born c. 1060, the second son of Count Eustace II of Boulogne and Ida of Lorraine. His elder brother, Eustace III, inherited Boulogne and the family's great estates in England a little after 1070. Six years later Godfrey's maternal uncle left him the duchy of Lower Lorraine, the marquisate of Antwerp, the county of Verdun and the territories of Bouillon and Stenay. But King Henry IV of Germany postponed confirmation of the grant of Lower Lorraine and Godfrey only acquired the duchy in 1087, while he had to fight what amounted to a ten-year war against his aunt, the formidable Mathilda of Tuscany, who had no intention of renouncing her claims to her husband's lands, and the Bishop of Verdun and the Count of Namur, who backed her, before he was firmly in control of the other properties. Until he took the cross he had not shown any marked piety and it is clear from the terms of the mortgage agreements he drew up that in 1096 he had no definite intention of settling in the East. In ecclesiastical politics, moreover, he had been firmly on the side of the German king and against the reforming papacy. His maternal grandfather and uncle had been imperialists, and those who had stood in the way of his inheritance, Mathilda of Tuscany and the Bishop of Verdun, were partisans of Pope Gregory VII. He himself had fought for Henry IV and had probably taken part in the seizure of Rome from Gregory in 1084.

The personality of Godfrey's younger brother Baldwin is clearer to us. Born between 1061 and 1070, he had been destined for the Church and had been presented with prebends at Reims, Cambrai and Liège. But in the new climate of reformist opinion such pluralism was intolerable and it may be that he was forced to surrender some of his benefices. At any rate he had left the Church by 1086, too late to enjoy a share in the family inheritance which had already been divided between his brothers. This helps to explain the animosity Baldwin was to show later to reformers and reform ideas. He was poor and his need for money may have led to his marriage in c. 1090 to Godehilde of Tosny, the child of a powerful Anglo-Norman family, who was to die during the crusade. He was an intelligent, calculating and ruthless man. He was not pleasant, but his strength of personality and quickness of mind were to be of great value to the crusaders and the early settlers in the East.

Passing through southern Germany, the two brothers and their following reached the Hungarian border in September. Here they delayed to get clearance from the king, who had already smashed three crusading armies. Baldwin was persuaded to be a hostage for the crusaders' behaviour and

Godrey issued strict instructions against plundering. Late in November he reached Byzantine territory. Hearing a rumour that Hugh of Vermandois was being held prisoner by the emperor, he allowed his followers to pillage the region around Silivri until he was assured that Hugh was free. He reached Constantinople on 23 December and camped outside the city near the head of the Golden Horn.

Bohemond of Taranto had crossed the Adriatic with quite a small force of South Italian Normans a fortnight after Hugh of Vermandois. About forty years old, he was Robert Guiscard's eldest son and had played a leading part in his father's invasion of Byzantine Albania in 1081. Robert had left him his conquests on the eastern shore of the Adriatic, which the Normans were already losing, and in consequence Bohemond had found himself effectively disinherited, since his younger brother Roger had been left Apulia. Although in the late 1080s he had carved out for himself a large lordship in southern Italy, he was still relatively poor. There is no doubt that he was ambitious and wanted a principality, possibly to be won at the expense of the Greeks who had retaken the lands he should have been enjoying in Albania. The Greeks, who believed that he had also inherited from his father designs on the Byzantine empire itself, recognized that he was very able; in fact he was to prove himself to be one of the finest generals the crusading movement produced. He was also intelligent and pious, and he was perhaps the only leader who really understood the motives of the reforming papacy. Byzantine officials were prepared for his arrival, but the local inhabitants, who had after all experienced a Norman invasion quite recently, refused to sell him provisions. So his followers had to forage until they were assured of supplies by the Byzantine government once they had passed Thessaloniki. They also destroyed a small town which they thought was occupied by heretics and they had a brush with imperial troops who tried to hurry them along. Bohemond, in fact, had to spend time and energy trying to restrain his followers from looting even in Thrace and when he went on ahead to Constantinople, which he reached on 10 April 1097, his second-in-command, his nephew Tancred who was to prove himself to be one of the ablest of the early rulers of the settlements in the East, allowed the Normans to forage in the countryside not far from the Byzantine capital.

Bohemond was closely followed by the Count of Toulouse, Raymond of St Gilles, who was now in his mid-fifties and was by the standards of the time an elderly man. He had spent thirty years patiently reassembling his ancestral lands, which had been scattered into other hands, and was now master of thirteen counties in southern France. He was connected by marriage to the Spanish royal houses and it is possible, though not certain, that he had fought in the Spanish Reconquest. For at least twenty years he had supported the cause of church reform, although it is by no means clear

that he really understood what it entailed. At any rate Pope Urban regarded Raymond as an ally and before the crusade was proclaimed at
Clermont had already picked him to be the leader. The pope had visited St
Gilles before the council and may have discussed the expedition with
Raymond there since, in what must have been a pre-arranged *coup de
théatre*, the day after Urban's sermon the Count's ambassadors arrived at
Clermont to commit their master to the enterprise. There were rumours
that Raymond had vowed never to return home. Whether they were true
or not this elderly man had made the remarkable decision to desert the
lands he had taken so long to consolidate, leaving his eldest son in charge
of them, and to go with his wife on a hazardous journey to the East. There
is evidence that he had prepared for this more efficiently than any of the
other leaders; certainly his followers fared better in the ordeals ahead than
did the other crusaders. But he seems to have been chronically ill, which is
not surprising when one considers his age. He shared leadership of perhaps
the largest force with Bishop Adhémar of Le Puy, who had vigorously
upheld the cause of reform in southern France from the 1080s, had been
appointed papal legate on the crusade by Urban, and was to dominate the
councils of the leaders until his early death. Raymond and Adhémar had
marched through northern Italy, round the end of the Adriatic and through
Dalmatia, where the locals had been hostile. Escorted by imperial troops,
who were prepared to treat roughly any who diverged from the route, they
had reached Thessaloniki at the beginning of April. Raymond himself
reached Constantinople on the 21st, but before they arrived six days later
his troops were severely bruised in a clash with their Greek escorts, who
were doubtless trying to prevent them from foraging.

Duke Robert of Normandy, Count Robert of Flanders and Count
Stephen of Blois left France in the autumn of 1096. They journeyed by way
of Rome and Monte Cassino to Bari. Robert of Flanders crossed the
Adriatic almost at once and reached Constantinople at about the same
time as Bohemond. Robert of Normandy and Stephen of Blois wintered in
southern Italy and joined the others in Constantinople c. 14 May.

The crusaders' experiences at Constantinople crucially affected the rest of
the campaign. No one was certain what part would be played by the
Greeks, but it seems that most of the leaders were expecting their full
participation in the campaign and possibly even that the emperior Alexius
would himself take overall command. In the spring of 1097 Alexius discussed with the leaders already in Constantinople, Godfrey of Bouillon,
Robert of Flanders, Bohemond and perhaps also Hugh of Vermandois, the
possibility of taking the cross himself and assuming command. Any response on his part may simply have been politic; certainly when Raymond
of St Gilles arrived and made the emperor's leadership a pre-condition of

his acknowledgement of his subordination to him, Alexius excused himself on the grounds that his presence was needed in Constantinople. And although there was close cooperation between Greeks and Latins during the siege of Nicaea and then a token, but welcome, Greek presence as far as Antioch – welcome because the Byzantine's government's representative, a Hellenized Turk and experienced military commander called Tatikios, provided guides – there remained, after Tatikios's withdrawal in February 1098, only a few Greek officers and clergy, while, in the crusade's wake, an imperial army concentrated on re-establishing Byzantine control over the coast of Asia Minor as far as Antalya. By June 1098 Alexius himself had moved with an army of Greeks and lately-arrived crusaders only as far as Akşehir, under half-way from Constantinople to Antioch. Erroneous reports of the situation in Antioch and rumours of the mustering of a large Turkish army in Anatolia led him to withdraw even from there, abandoning the crusade to its fate. By the summer of 1098 Greek participation had shown itself to be half-hearted at best.

As far as Alexius himself was concerned, another issue was paramount. Help of a very different sort to that he had envisaged had arrived and the crusaders had already caused him major problems as they had advanced through the Balkans and approached Constantinople. He was thoroughly suspicious of them, particularly of Bohemond of Taranto, and he must have felt that he had to find some means of controlling them. He may have worked out a method of doing so in the late autumn of 1096 when Hugh of Vermandois was his prisoner-cum-guest. Alexius tried to isolate the leaders in order to deal with each of them separately – his daughter Anna in her encomium of him wrote that he feared for an attack on Constantinople if they mustered together – and he demanded two oaths, in return for which he presented them with large sums of money, gifts not as lavish as they might seem, since he obliged the crusaders to pay for goods bought in his markets. They were, of course, desperate for supplies and therefore at a disadvantage, which was compounded by the fact that the only real alternative to refusal of the emperor's demands was to return home.

The first of the oaths was a promise to hand back to the empire all the lands to be liberated which had once belonged to it. This provided Alexius with legitimate grounds for claiming sovereignty over the territories likely to be won, since it is clear that the crusaders had no intention of trying to conquer land that had not once been Christian. The second was an oath of homage and fealty, similar to the contracts entered into by *vassalli non casati* in the West which were not accompanied by the reciprocal grant of a fief. It gave Alexius a measure, admittedly limited, of control. The leaders' reactions to the demands for these oaths were not consistent. Hugh of Vermandois (as far as we know), Robert of Normandy, Robert of Flanders and Stephen of Blois raised little objection. Godfrey of Bouillon and Raymond of St Gilles made difficulties, and although Bohemond of Taranto did not, his second-in-command Tancred did, perhaps revealing Bohemond's real attitude. It has been suggested that it was no coincidence that the objectors were the men who eventually settled in the East and that the divisions among the leaders that surfaced in Constantinople continued for the rest of the crusade. But in fact it was not at all clear at this stage who would settle in the Levant and it is more reasonable to look at the leaders' predicaments in turn.

Hugh of Vermandois was a near prisoner when the oath was demanded of him. He was also virtually alone. As for Godfrey, it has already been pointed out that he had set out in 1096 with every intention of returning to Europe, at least if the East was to offer him nothing better. It is, therefore, unlikely that the oaths were unattractive because they might limit his freedom of action in the future. He was obviously distrustful, concerned that Hugh of Vermandois's agreement had been extorted from him, and unwilling to take any step before consulting the leaders whose arrival was expected. Alexius put pressure on him by cutting off his supplies. Godfrey responded to this threat to his force's existence by authorizing his brother Baldwin to raid the suburbs of Constantinople. Supplies were restored and there followed three months of relative peace until Alexius, hearing of the approach of more crusading armies, cut off supplies once more. Again the crusaders' response was to use force, the only weapon at their disposal. This culminated in an attack on the city on Maundy Thursday, which was beaten off by the Greeks. Godfrey must have realized that force would not get provisions restored, and so, in a desperate situation, he and his leading followers took the oaths and his troops were immediately transported out of the way, across the Bosporus.

By the time Bohemond of Taranto arrived, therefore, Alexius had successfully wrung oaths from Hugh of Vermandois and Godfrey of Bouillon. So Bohemond was in no position to refuse outright, although Tancred managed to slip through Constantinople without submitting. There is little doubt that Bohemond wanted to carve out a principality for himself in the East, but he was not particularly well off and his force was a small one. If the report that he requested the office of Grand Domestic – commander-in-chief of the Byzantine army – is true, it was quite a sensible move on his part, because he could then have ensured adequate Greek military support for the crusade.

Since Raymond of St Gilles may have made a vow never to return to his native land he may have hoped for an eastern principality, but it was the performance of homage and oath of fealty rather than the promise to return territory to the empire that raised difficulties for him. He appears to have believed that the making of homage conflicted with his crusade vow to serve God, and in spite of the efforts and irritation of the other crusade leaders he would not change his mind. He compromised by taking a more limited oath to respect and maintain the emperor's life and honour, for which there were parallels in the region of France from which he came. We know nothing of Robert of Flanders's reaction, but by the time Robert of Normandy and Stephen of Blois arrived the precedents had been set and, whether they liked them or not, there was little option but to follow them. The various parties were shipped separately across the Bosporus from April 1097 onwards and in early June they all assembled in one army before Nicaea, the first important city in Asia Minor which was in Turkish hands.

The events in Constantinople left the crusade leaders frustrated and disillusioned. After long marches they had arrived short of supplies and uncertain about the future rôle of the Greeks. They found the emperor reluctant to take on the burden of leadership, apparently only interested in the recovery of imperial territories – which, to be fair, was what he had wanted in the first place – and prepared to use every measure at his disposal, from the distribution of largesse to the denial of supplies, to force each prince in turn to take the oaths before his confrères arrived. Although Alexius gave them rich gifts of cash, moreover, these only provided the means to buy provisions in his own markets. No wonder that from this time onwards most of the crusaders distrusted and disliked the imperial government.

Although its inhabitants were still mostly Christian, Nicaea was the chief residence of the Selchük sultan of Rum, Kilij Arslan, the most powerful Turkish prince in Anatolia. The capture of the city was essential before the crusade could advance down the old military road to the East. It had been well-fortified by the Greeks and was held by a strong Turkish garrison. But Kilij Arslan himself was away with the bulk of his forces, disputing Malatya with his chief rival, an emir called Danishmend, and was out of touch. By the time the first of his troops had been rushed back the city was invested and the main body of his army failed to break through the cordon on 21 May, although it inflicted heavy losses on the crusaders. Kilij Arslan withdrew, leaving the city and his wife, family and much of his treasury to their fate, but it was not until Greek ships had been launched on Iznik Gölü (Lake Ascanius), on the shore of which it stood, that Nicaea was entirely isolated. The garrison opened negotiations with the Byzantines and on 19 June, the day appointed for a general assault, the crusaders saw imperial banners flying over the town. Alexius had saved himself any embarrassment by having Nicaea surrender directly to himself, but he now took the opportunity of demanding and receiving oaths from those leaders, including Tancred, who had not yet made them.

Between 26 and 28 June the crusaders set out across Asia Minor, marching in two divisions, one a day ahead of the other. The first, under Bohemond's command, consisted of the Normans from Italy and France together with the followers of Robert of Flanders and Stephen of Blois, and the Greeks; the second, under the command of Raymond of St Gilles, was made up of the southern French and the Lorrainers and the force of Hugh of Vermandois. Close to Dorylaeum at dawn on 1 July Kilij Arslan's Turks, supplemented by troops provided by Danishmend and the ruler of Cappadocia, who had surrounded Bohemond's corps during the night, launched an attack, forcing the Christian knights back on to the mass of armed and unarmed pilgrims with them. This confused crush of men, although unable to strike at the enemy, could defend itself quite effectively and the battle remained deadlocked for two or three hours until the arrival of the second corps, hurrying in separate columns, each of which was answering Bohemond's call for help as best it could, surprised and routed the Turks.

The crusaders rested for two days after this great victory and then resumed their march by way of Akşehir and Konya through a country already laid waste in the aftermath of the Turkish invasions and further devastated by a scorched-earth policy adopted by their enemies. At Ereğli, c. 10 September, they put an army blocking their way to flight. Tancred and Baldwin of Boulogne now broke away to raid Cilicia, taking advantage of the existence in that region of a string of petty Armenian principalities, established precariously out of the chaos of the last few decades. The crusaders did not cooperate with one another, but their quarrelsome progress was welcomed by the Armenian population which had recently settled in the area and they took Tarsus, Adana, Misis and Iskenderun before rejoining the main army. Baldwin left again almost at once with a small force and with an Armenian adviser who had attached himself to him, to follow the seam of Armenian principalities eastward. He took two fortresses, Ravanda and Tilbeşar, with the assistance of local Armenians and was then invited by Toros, the prince of Edessa (Urfa), whose position was newly established and very insecure, to become his adopted son and partner. On 6 February 1098 he reached Edessa, but a month later the Armenians in the city rioted, perhaps with his connivance; on 9 March Toros was killed by the mob while trying to escape, and on the following day Baldwin took over the government entirely. He had established the first Latin settlement in the East, comprising Edessa, the fortresses of Ravanda and Tilbeşar and, within a few months, Birecik, Sürüc and Samsat. The region was prosperous and from the autumn of 1098 money and horses poured out of Edessa to the crusaders in Antioch. Godfrey of Bouillon himself was given the castle and estates of Tilbeşar and his comparative wealth was very apparent in the later stages of the crusade; by means of it he was able to augment his following, significantly at the expense of Raymond of St Gilles, and this may have contributed to his election as ruler of Jerusalem. We shall see that Baldwin at Edessa was able in another way to contribute to the crusade's salvation at a vital moment. But, in the light of the bitterness later felt by the Greeks at the refusal of the crusaders to abide by their oaths and restore Antioch to the empire, it is of interest to note that although Tarsus, Adana, Misis, Iskenderun, Ravanda, Tilbeşar and Edessa had all been Byzantine, no move was made to restore them to Greek rule or even to recognize Greek suzerainty. The Greeks were far away, of course. The only detachment was still marching with the main crusading army, which was why a French knight called Peter of Aups was appointed to hold Comana 'in fealty to God and the Holy Sepulchre and the princes (of the crusade) and the (Byzantine) emperor' when it was reached. The apparent refusal of Tancred and Baldwin even to consider the issue of Byzantine sovereignty was a pointer to the future.

The main force of crusaders, meanwhile, must have been advised that passage through the Cilician Gates in the Taurus mountains and particularly through the Syrian Gates, the Belen pass which cuts the Amanus range north of Antioch, was hardly possible if these were adequately defended. The leaders decided to add many miles to their journey by swinging north to Kayseri and then south-east by way of Comana and Göksun to Maraş (Kahramanmaraş), by-passing the main bulk of the Amanus. This brought the crusaders on to the open plain north of Antioch, which they reached on 21 October. They were in a moderately good state as far as provisions went, and a Genoese fleet, which docked at Mağaracik, the port of Antioch, in November, brought more supplies. But already, during the march across the wastelands of Asia Minor in the summer heat, the horses and beasts of burden had been dying like flies. This was disastrous, particularly to the knights who needed chargers to fulfil their functions and maintain their status and pack animals to carry their baggage. By the time the crusaders reached Antioch there were not more than 1,000 horses left – so already four out of every five knights were horseless – and by the following summer the numbers had shrunk to between 100 and 200. Most knights, among them powerful men at home, were now fighting on foot or riding donkeys and mules; even Godfrey of Bouillon and Robert of Flanders had to beg for horses for themselves before the Battle of Antioch in June 1098. Moreover the loss of pack animals meant that the knights had to carry their own heavy sacks of arms and armour and this had led to embarrassing scenes of panic as they struggled up steep paths during the crossing of the Anti-Taurus range of mountains.

An army of at least 40,000 men and women now found itself engaged in a siege that was to last until 3 June 1098. Situated between Mount Silpius and the river Orontes, with its citadel on the mountain-top 1,000 feet above it, Antioch could never be completely surrounded. During the siege the crusaders built camps and forts across the river and before the northern and southern gates, but these must usually have been lightly garrisoned. Most of the force was occupied with hunting for rations. Having marched into Asia without any proper system of provisioning – indeed it would have been impossible to devise one – the crusaders had to rely on foraging and it is not surprising that within a short time the countryside around the city was stripped bare. They were obliged to search further and further afield, travelling in foraging parties fifty miles and establishing foraging centres at great distances from Antioch: northwards towards Cilicia, north-eastwards towards Edessa, to the east to Yenişehir and Harim, to the south to the Ruj and Latakia. The abiding impression one has of the siege is not one of warfare but of a constant search for food. Predictably there was famine and death from starvation, illness and disease. Other crusaders besides Raymond of St Gilles seem to have been chronically sick. There was also impoverishment and even knights and lords found themselves compelled to enter service with the greatest princes for wages. All the princes were reduced to paying their followers these wages, which imposed great pressures on them, and already by January 1098 Bohemond was threatening to leave the siege because he did not have the resources for it; by the following summer both Godfrey of Bouillon and Robert of Flanders were in penury. In these stressful circumstances it is not surprising that there were manifestations of homesickness and fear, leading to panic and desertion.

The siege of Antioch lasted for seven and a half months, through a winter during which the crusaders suffered dreadfully. Early in February 1098 a Muslim relief force, which launched an attack in conjunction with a sortie from the garrison, was beaten off; but a large Muslim army, including detachments from Iraq and Iran, left Mosul under the command of its governor Kerbogha in May. It spent three fruitless weeks trying to reduce Edessa – the other example of the importance to the crusade's survival of Baldwin's initiative – and, collecting additional troops from Aleppo on the way, arrived in the vicinity of Antioch on 5 June. But by that time the crusaders' situation had been transformed. Bohemond, whose ambition to possess Antioch himself was already apparent, had entered into negotiations with one of the garrison captains, probably a renegade Armenian, who agreed to deliver the city to him. He persuaded all his colleagues, except Raymond of St Gilles, to promise him the city if his troops were the first to enter it and if the emperor never came to claim it in person. He then revealed the conspiracy and received their support. Before sunset on 2 June the crusaders engaged in an elaborate diversionary manoeuvre before returning to their positions after dark. Just before dawn on the 3rd sixty knights from Bohemond's force swarmed over the walls under the traitor's command, an area of the fortifications half-way up the slopes of Mount Silpius around a tower called the Two Sisters. They then dashed down the hill to open the Gate of St George and their confrères poured into the city, which was in their hands by evening, although the citadel still held out. The governor, who had fled, fell from his horse and was beheaded by some Armenian peasants.

The crusaders were now in occupation of a city that had suffered a long siege and they were almost immediatley besieged themselves, as Kerbogha's army came up and camped across the river. Kerbogha was in touch with the citadel, from which an assault was launched on 9 June. A crusader sortie failed on the 10th, and that night the Christians' morale sank to its lowest. There were so many desertions or attempted desertions that the leaders, fearing a mass break-out, were forced to seal the gates. Those who had fled joined Stephen of Blois, who had only recently been elected commander-in-chief but had retired to Iskenderun just before Antioch fell, probably because of ill-health. He was now panicked into flight. Reaching the imperial headquarters at Akşehir, he and his companions persuaded Alexius of the hopelessness of the crusade's situation, whereupon the emperor, anyway fearing a Turkish counter-attack in Anatolia, led his army northwards again, back to the safety of Constantinople.

Within Antioch, however, morale had begun to rise for an extraordinary but characteristic reason. Two visionaries revealed to the leaders that they had had supernatural experiences. One of them had seen Christ on the night of 10 June and had received the assurance that the crusaders would prevail, provided they repented of their sins. The other reported a series of visits from St Andrew, who had shown him the hiding-place of the Holy Lance, the tip of the spear with which Christ's side had been lanced during the Crucifixion. This relic was 'discovered' on 14 June at the bottom of a trench dug in the floor of the newly re-consecrated cathedral and, in spite of the fact that many of the leaders, including the papal legate, were sceptical, the ordinary crusaders were elated. It was decided to resolve the crisis in which they found themselves by seeking battle. One last embassy was sent to Kerbogha to seek terms and on 28 June the crusaders sortied out of the city under Bohemond's command. His generalship was exemplary, although Kerbogha's decision to allow the whole Christian army to emerge from a single gate before engaging it certainly assisted him. The crusaders were marshalled in four divisions, each made up of two squadrons of horse and foot: given the few horses left, the number of mounted knights must have been very small. Each division engaged in turn in a complicated manoeuvre, switching from column to line, so that in the end three of them were advancing side by side, with the infantry in front masking the few mounted knights, and with their flanks covered, on the right by the river Orontes and on the left by high ground. The fourth division, under Bohemond himself, marched in reserve. The crusaders then attacked in echelon, presumably at walking pace, and the Muslims fled, whereupon the citadel surrendered to Bohemond. The crusaders rationalized this remarkable victory by ascribing it to the appearance of a heavenly army of angels, saints and the ghosts of dead crusaders which intervened on their side.

It was, in fact, the turning-point of the crusade, but that cannot then have been apparent. The leaders quite sensibly decided to wait until 1 November, when the summer heat would be over, before continuing their march; but an epidemic, probably of typhoid, broke out, claiming the life of Adhémar of Le Puy and scattering the other leaders to their foraging centres. When they returned in September there were clear signs of division over two issues and in November these surfaced.

The first was the possession of Antioch, which Bohemond claimed for himself. Raymond of St Gilles, who still held some parts of the city, including the governor's palace and a fortified bridge over the Orontes linking the city to the road to its port, spoke up for the oaths sworn to the Byzantine emperor. He may have wanted Antioch for himself and envisaged the only way of achieving this was by an imperial grant. But no one could deny that oaths had been sworn and homage had been paid to the emperor. Before the city fell it had been agreed that it would be surrendered to him if he came in person to claim it. After the Battle of Antioch a high-powered embassy, led by Hugh of Vermandois and Baldwin of Hainault, was sent to invite the emperor Alexius to present himself and take the leadership of the crusade. His reply, however, did not reach the crusaders until the following April. He promised to join them in June and asked them to delay their advance until his arrival; he demanded the return of Antioch and his ambassadors complained bitterly about Bohemond's usurpation of the city in breach of his oath. On the other hand it was argued that the Byzantine emperor was indifferent, even hostile, to the crusaders and had failed as the leaders' feudal lord, which he was; that the oath had been extorted from them by force; that the departure of Tatikios and the withdrawal of Alexius and his army from Akşehir when the crusade was most in need had shown that the Greeks had not kept their side of the bargain; and that the long delay before Alexius's reply to the embassy of July 1098 revealed the military unpreparedness of the empire. Of course this was special pleading, but the crusaders had been let down by the Greeks and their need was pressing. It has already been pointed out that there was a steady stream of new recruits joining the crusade. By 1098, moreover, the crusaders were conscious of, even obsessed by, the large numbers of men whom they believed had taken the cross but had never left Europe. The existence of this reservoir of manpower was often in their thoughts and the bishops with the crusade excommunicated those who had not fulfilled their vows and expressed the hope that their colleagues in the West would do the same. The majority of late arrivals were coming overland and the crusaders expected that many others would follow the same route, as indeed they did in the crusade of 1101. Antioch, dominating the passes from Asia Minor into Syria and holding the northern coastal road open against the Muslim powers in Syria and Iraq, had obviously to be held by someone reliable. Alexius had not proved himself to be that; on the contrary he appeared to the crusaders to have cynically manipulated them to serve his own ends. It is important to remember that, although Bohemond stayed behind in Antioch and did not fulfil his own vow at the Holy Sepulchre until five months after its liberation, he was not at all blamed in the West for what he had done; in fact his visit to France in 1106 was a triumph.

The second issue was the date at which the march to Jerusalem should be renewed. As a step in this direction the ordinary crusaders forced the princes to agree to the investment of the town of Ma'arret en Nu'man, sixty miles south of Antioch. This fell on 11–12 December 1098, but the princes still could not bring themselves to make a firm decision and a conference in the Ruj early in January 1099, at which Raymond of St Gilles, under pressure from his followers to continue the journey, offered to take the other leaders into his service for large sums of money, came to nothing.

One of the chief reasons for this paralysis of will was the fact that the crusade had no proper leadership. On four separate occasions attempts were made to provide the army with a commander-in-chief. Alexius turned down the proposal in the spring of 1097; it was put to him again by the embassy that left Antioch in July 1098. In the spring of 1098 Stephen of Blois was elected over-all commander, but soon afterwards he deserted. In January 1099 Raymond of St Gilles, as we have seen, offered to take the other leaders into his service, but in vain. The fact is that not one of the leaders was strong enough to dominate the others. It is generally supposed that these men – Bohemond of Taranto, Godfrey of Bouillon, Hugh of Vermandois, Raymond of St Gilles, Robert of Flanders, Robert of Normandy and Stephen of Blois – led 'armies', but that is far from the truth. Each was accompanied by an entourage of relatives and dependents and each came to employ a wider body of men for wages as the shortages began to bite; but the bulk of effective soldiery, the petty lords, many of them commanding their own little forces, and the knights, were independent and their allegiances constantly shifted from one leader to another as circumstances changed and the ability of the princes to reward them came and went. So no leader's following was coherent or permanent enough to provide him with a platform from which he could dominate the rest. The crusade was, in fact, run by committees and assemblies. Each prince took counsel with his leading followers. There were general assemblies of the whole army. But most important was a council of princes. This was quite effective while Adhémar of Le Puy was alive, for he had the personality and authority to dominate it. His death on 1 August 1098 removed the one forceful and objective leader and the committees became deadlocked.

This paralysis was reflected in the breakdown of discipline in June 1098, when Adhémar fell ill. Indiscipline and lawlessness bore particularly hard on the poor, who suffered in the anarchy and feared starvation if the crusade remained becalmed much longer. In the middle of November, with the princes dithering, they became fiercely critical and threatened to elect their own commander. As we have seen, they forced Raymond of St Gilles and Robert of Flanders to lead them to Ma'arret. When c. 5 January Raymond of St Gilles's followers at Ma'arret heard that the conference in the Ruj was going badly they pulled down the town's walls, so depriving Raymond of his base. Raymond had no option but to recommence the march to Jerusalem on the 13th. The ordinary crusaders still in Antioch also began to raise their voices and Godfrey of Bouillon, Robert of Flanders and Bohemond had to bow to public pressure. They convened a general assembly on 2 February which decided on a muster at Latakia on 1 March as a prelude to an advance from there.

Syria was in as disorganized and unready a state to meet the crusade as Asia Minor had been and the crusaders faced very little opposition to their advance. The Turkish rulers of Aleppo and Damascus were at odds with one another. The Arab dynasties in control of Seijar (Shaizar) and Tripoli were even more hostile to the Turks than to the Christians. The Egyptians, who had been in touch with the crusaders and the Byzantines, had been driven out of Syria by the Turks. They had only just regained control of Jerusalem and reacted extraordinarily slowly to the developing threat to Palestine. Raymond of St Gilles marched by way of Kafartab, where he was joined by Robert of Normandy and Tancred, and Rafniye to 'Arqah, fifteen miles from Tripoli, which he reached on 14 February 1099. He settled down to besiege it and before the end of March was joined by the other crusade leaders, except Bohemond who remained behind to guard Antioch. The investment of 'Arqah did not go well and, demoralized by the failure of the ordeal and death of Peter Bartholomew, the visionary to whom had been revealed the whereabouts of the Holy Lance – his visions had become so eccentric that he had antagonized a large section of the army – the crusaders raised the siege and took the road south again on 13 May. They crossed the Dog river north of Beirut six days later and marched quickly by way of Tyre, turning inland north of Jaffa and reaching Ramle on 3 June. They arrived before Jerusalem on the 7th; on the previous day Bethlehem had fallen to Tancred, who had deserted Raymond of St Gilles, whom he had agreed to serve, and had transferred his allegiance and the service of the South Italian Norman contingent with him to Godfrey of Bouillon.

Jerusalem was, like Antioch, far too large to be surrounded. The crusaders at first concentrated most of their strength against the western wall, but then divided their forces between the western section of the northern wall, where Robert of Normandy, Robert of Flanders, Godfrey of Bouillon and Tancred took up positions, and Mount Zion to the south, where Raymond of St Gilles, bitterly at odds with Godfrey over the desertion of Tancred and probably of others of his following, took his post. For a time the siege went badly, despite the arrival of Genoese and English ships at Jaffa, and an expedition to the north into Samaria, which provided wood and other materials for the construction of two siege-towers, a battering-ram and some catapults. Meanwhile news arrived of the march of an Egyptian relief force that everyone, not least the garrison of Jerusalem, had been expecting. On 8 July, following the instructions transmitted by a visionary, a great penitential procession of crusaders wound its way from holy place to holy place outside the city walls and gathered to hear sermons on the Mount of Olives. The 14th was spent filling in the ditch to the south and by evening Raymond of St Gilles's tower was closing on the wall, but on the 15th Godfrey of Bouillon's men, who had switched their point of attack eastwards to level ground slightly to the east of the present-day Herod's Gate, succeeded in bridging the gap between their tower and the wall. Two knights from Tournai were the first across, followed by the Lorrainers. The trickle became a torrent as crusaders poured over the wall and through a breach already made by the ram, some making for the Temple area and some beyond, down to the south-west corner where the Muslims defending against Raymond of St Gilles withdrew. Jerusalem was given over to sack.

On 22 July Godfrey of Bouillon was elected ruler of the new settlement. His first task was to organize its defence against the Egyptian counter-invasion. He had some difficulty in persuading the other crusade leaders to commit themselves and their forces entirely, but by the evening of 11 August the whole Christian army was at Ashdod, where the herds the Egyptians had brought to feed their troops were captured. At dawn the following morning the Christians surprised the Egyptian host, still encamped just north of Ascalon (Ashqelon), and the charge of the European knights, who seem by now to have been able to replace their horses, routed the enemy.

The third wave

It was after this victory that most of the crusaders decided to return home. From the winter of 1099–1100 the triumphant warriors began to reappear in Europe, bringing with them not riches but relics, which they gave to local churches. The news of the liberation of Jerusalem swept the West, inspiring songs in its honour and investing the liberators with a fame that some of them retained for the rest of their lives. In the general euphoria new armies were raised and a third wave of crusaders left for the East. Already in the spring of 1099 Pope Urban had commissioned the archbishop of Milan to preach the crusade in Lombardy; there was a fervent response, and the movement gathered pace with the glorious news, which Urban never received: he died on 29 July 1099. His successor, Paschal II, threatened, as Urban had done, to excommunicate those who had not yet fulfilled their vows to crusade and this was taken up by the bishops. Paschal also threatened to excommunicate deserters. Hugh of Vermandois and Stephen of Blois were among many in this humiliating condition who decided to retrace their steps to the East, but thousands of men and women in France, Italy and Germany who had not taken the cross before now flocked to the banners. Papal legates were sent to France. They held a council at Valence in September 1100 and went on to Limoges, where Duke William of Aquitaine and many of his vassals took the cross; and then to Poitiers where, at a council assembled on 18 November, the fifth anniversary of the opening of the Council of Clermont, the papal legates preached the crusade.

The armies of the third wave were at least as large as those which had left in 1096. The ecclesiastical contingent under the chief papal legate, Hugh of Die, Archbishop of Lyon, was stronger. The lay princes were of equal or greater rank than their predecessors: William of Aquitaine, Stephen of Blois and Hugh of Vermandois, William of Nevers, Odo of Burgundy, Stephen of Burgundy and Welf of Bavaria. Under the surface glitter of light-hearted knight-errantry that may be a reflection of William of Aquitaine's ebullient personality, there are indications of a serious religious purpose and of attempts to learn from the mistakes of their predecessors: the very wealth, carried in cash and jewelry, that gave these crusaders such a bad name was one of them.

The first crusaders of the third wave to depart were the Lombards, who left Milan on 13 September 1100. Their wintering in Bulgaria and encampment outside Constantinople for two months in the spring of 1101 as they waited for other crusaders from Germany and France were marked by disorders. Alexius, as before, tried to force them to cross the Bosporus by refusing them licences to buy supplies. As their predecessors had done, the crusaders reacted violently and launched an attack on his palace of Blachernae, but this so embarrassed their leaders that they agreed to be ferried across to Asia. At Izmit (Nicomedia) they were joined by the first and smaller of the German armies, by men from Burgundy and northern France under Stephen of Blois and by Raymond of St Gilles, who had reached Constantinople in the summer of 1100 with his household and had reluctantly allowed himself to be attached to them as an adviser. He was not very successful. Against his advice and that of the Greeks and Stephen of Blois, the new crusaders decided not to wait for the rest of their confrères but to march for Niksar, where Bohemond, who had been captured in the previous summer by Danishmend, was incarcerated. It is even possible that, fired by wild talk in Europe as news of the successes had come in, the Lombards, who alone among the new crusaders had been inspired to further conquest rather than to lend aid to the Holy Land, were planning to enter Iraq from the north and lay siege to Baghdad itself. At any rate in June they marched from Izmit to Ankara and then north-east to Çankiri (Gangra) before swinging east again. In the early part of August, somewhere near Merzifon, they were met by an army raised by a coalition of Turkish princes, who had at last buried their differences. There followed several days of fighting before the crusaders panicked and fled.

An army under William of Nevers reached Constantinople in June 1101 and, overtaking the force of William of Aquitaine which was already there, crossed the Bosporus and on the 24th set off to catch up with the Lombards. At Ankara it gave up the chase and turned south towards Konya, which was reached in the middle of August, after a three-day running battle. William failed to take the town and moved on to Ereğli, which was deserted, its wells blocked. After several thirsty days the crusaders were routed. Meanwhile the third army, under William of Aquitaine, which had left France in the middle of March and had joined the Bavarians under Welf before marching in an unruly fashion through the Balkans, had reached Constantinople at the beginning of June. It remained near the city for five weeks, purchasing supplies and taking advice from the Greeks, although a number of Germans wisely chose to go directly to Palestine by sea. In the middle of July William and Welf set off eastward, along the route followed by the second wave of crusaders. But the way had been devastated by the Turks and the constant passage of crusaders and in spite of careful planning they soon ran out of food. Near Ereğli their army was ambushed and annihilated.

William of Aquitaine and Welf of Bavaria escaped, as had William of Nevers, Stephen of Burgundy, Stephen of Blois and Raymond of St Gilles from the earlier disasters. Hugh of Vermandois died of his wounds at Tarsus. Some of the survivors joined Raymond of St Gilles in Syria and took the town of Tartus, which was to be his base for the creation of another settlement. Then most gathered in Jerusalem where they fulfilled their vows. Some, delayed from departure by adverse winds, joined the settlers' forces to meet another Egyptian invasion. Unlucky to the last, they were heavily defeated on 17 May 1102 and poor Stephen of Blois was killed.

The development of the idea of crusading

It is easy to find in the First Crusade traces of most of the elements which were to make up later crusading. Pope Urban's message contained many and they were developed in the response to it and in the experiences of the crusaders themselves. The crusade, a pilgrimage on which knights could fulfil their normal function as warriors, with its elaborate liturgies, penitential processions and fasts – it is remarkable that solemn fasting was imposed upon the starving soldiers of the second wave before every important engagement – struck articulate contemporaries, who were mostly monks, as having the features of a quasi-monastery on the move. The laymen had made vows, temporary it is true but with similarities to monastic profession, while the exigencies of the campaign had imposed poverty and ought also to have imposed celibacy. Like monks they were 'exiles' from the normal world, who had taken up their crosses to follow Christ and had abandoned wives, children and lands for the love of God, putting their bodies at risk out of love for their brothers. Like monks they engaged in regular public devotions and just as monks made an 'interior' journey to Jerusalem, they made a corporeal one. Since an aim of the reform movement had been to monasticize the whole Church, it seemed that here at last the laity was falling into line. There was, in fact, an extraordinarily rapid transfer to crusading of phrases and images traditionally associated with monasticism: the knighthood of Christ, the way of the cross, the way to a heavenly Jerusalem, spiritual warfare. The monastic interpretation of crusading was not going to last, but it provided the Church with a starting-point in its approach to the problem of control.

This problem was an important one and the crusade had highlighted it. Parish priests had been given the job of regulating recruitment – no one was to take the cross without going to his parish priest for advice – but the parochial system was not yet adequate to cope with mass recruitment. Bishops were supposed to enforce the fulfilment of vows if need be; it is impossible to decide whether those who fulfilled their vows on the third wave did so because of threats of excommunication or because they were inspired or shamed by the news of the liberation of Jerusalem. The papal legates and clergy on the crusade were supposed to exercise some control, but the clergy on the second wave were mostly of poor quality, and as the house-priests of magnates, they were not the men to challenge or discipline their employers. Churchmen failed to prevent the massacres of Jews in the spring and summer of 1096 or the establishment of a secular state in Palestine in 1099.

There were also signs of independent ideas among the laity: I have already touched on the prevalence of the idea of vendetta. One can also discern the beginnings of those family traditions which were to play so important a part in the future. A century later Lambert of Ardres, writing of Arnold of Ardres who, in his family's view, had had a very distinguished crusade, had to explain the absence of his name from the lists of crusaders in the great vernacular epic, the *Chanson d'Antioche*, by the fact that he had indignantly refused to bribe the author in return for its insertion. Some individuals may have taken the cross in 1100 because close relatives had died on the second wave and so perhaps had not fulfilled their vows; there was certainly anxiety on this point. It cannot, moreover, have been coincidence that Miles of Bray and Guy of Rochefort, the two senior members of the family of Guy Trousseau, who had fled from Antioch in the summer of 1098, took part in the 1101 crusade.

Most important of all, the traumatic experiences of the crusaders on the second wave were crucial to the development of the belief that the crusade really was a divine enterprise. The conviction that nothing they did was outside the benevolent, if stern, control of God seems to have grown among them once Asia Minor had been crossed. It was reinforced by the discovery of relics, the veneration of sites familiar to every Christian mind – even quite minor ones like the supposed location of Emmaus would have been major cult centres in western Europe – and by fortuitous disturbances in the night skies, auroras, comets, shooting-stars, most of which were preludes to an intense period of solar activity, the medieval maximum, which began around 1120. The crusaders were not fools. They probably exaggerated their own numbers, but they knew how much at a disadvantage they were. They lacked provisions and had constantly to forage. They lost their horses and had to fight for much of the time on foot. They had no firm leadership and at times their army disintegrated into anarchy. And yet they still won through. There could be no satisfactory explanation of this other than that they had experienced God's interventionary might. It is not surprising that it was with the crossing of Asia Minor that visionaries began to see apparitions – Christ himself, angels, saints and the ghosts of dead crusaders – and that their dead began to be treated as martyrs. The failures of the third wave in 1101 actually reinforced this impression, for they suggested that the opposition crushed in 1097–9 had been more powerful than it was, and the disasters that overtook William of Aquitaine and his confrères could be attributed to their own luxury, pride and sinfulness and therefore to the judgement of God.

The idea of the crusade as a divinely inspired and directed war comes across vividly in the letters and eyewitness accounts of the crusaders, but it was crude and occasionally untheological, until it was taken up by a second generation of commentators, particularly by three French Benedictine monks, Robert the Monk, Guibert of Nogent and Baldric of Bourgueil, writing ten years later. They put the crusade into the context of providential history. To Robert it was the clearest sign of divine intervention in this dimension after the Creation and the redemption of mankind on the

Cross; and to Guibert the crusaders outclassed the Israelites of the Old Testament. They also put all the elements firmly into a theological context, relating martyrdom, for instance, to Christian love. In their writings the idea of the crusade as a war for Christ, which was muffled and fairly conventional in Urban's message and had been elaborated maladroitly by the crusaders themselves, was given proper theological expression.

And yet there was much that was still amorphous and unformed. Crusading took a long time, almost a century, to reach maturity, and many questions still had to be answered. What distinguished a crusade from any holy war, or armed pilgrimage for that matter? Under what circumstances and in what theatres of war could crusades be preached? Could crusades be proclaimed only by popes? What powers of control over crusaders did the Church have? How did indulgences work and to whom could they be granted? How were crusades, which were very expensive, to be financed? The twelfth century was to be taken up with providing answers to these questions.

CHAPTER 3

The Holy Places and the Catholic
Patriarchates of Jerusalem and Antioch

The founding of the Latin settlements

Early in the twelfth century four settlements of West Europeans in Syria
and Palestine were coming into existence. Their future was still uncertain.
Even the titles of the rulers were imprecise. There is no good evidence that
the title of Advocate of the Holy Sepulchre, supposedly assumed by
Godfrey of Bouillon, was ever adopted by him; he appears to have called
himself 'prince' or 'duke'. His successor, King Baldwin I, who sometimes
called himself 'king of the Latin people of Jerusalem', was once entitled,
with wild hyperbole, 'king of Babylon and Asia'. The future Counts of
Tripoli called themselves 'commanders of the Christian army in Asia'.

The first settlement to be established, as we have seen, was the county of
Edessa, which straddled the Euphrates, stretching from the fortresses of
Gaziantep and Ravanda in the west to an indeterminate frontier to the
east. Edessa was 160 miles north-east of Antioch and 45 miles east of the
Euphrates, a Latin salient in an area that had for centuries been border
country between Muslims and Greeks. It was very exposed and the
European settlement was sparse and confined to isolated fortresses. On the
other hand the population was mostly Christian, Jacobite and Armenian,
and the countryside was fertile. The counts tended to get on quite well with
their subjects and were comparatively rich.

Between Edessa and the sea lay the principality of Antioch. Its control
over Cilicia was spasmodic, but it came to hold the Syrian coastline as far
south as Baniyas and it extended inland to Maraş and A'zaz in the north-
east and, with its frontier skirting Aleppo which always remained in
Muslim hands, to el Atharib and Ma'arret en Nu'man in the south-east.
The bulk of this territory had been gained against the interests as much of
the Greeks as the Muslims. During the crusade the southern ports of
Latakia and Baniyas were handed over to Byzantine officials by Robert of
Normandy and Raymond of St Gilles. In 1099 and 1100, the emperor
Alexius, smarting under Bohemond's refusal to recognize his claims to
Antioch, reoccupied Cilicia by force and also took Maraş. In August 1099
Bohemond himself laid siege to Latakia. He was assisted by a Pisan fleet,
which had brought with it the new papal legate, Archbishop Daimbert of
Pisa, had raided Greek islands on its way to the East, and had fought an

engagement with a Byzantine fleet sent to intercept it. The Pisans helped to blockade Latakia and Byzantine occupation was only preserved for the time being by the intervention of Raymond of St Gilles, Robert of Normandy and Robert of Flanders, who arrived on their way from Jerusalem. Raymond travelled to Constantinople in the following summer, leaving Latakia in Byzantine hands. Within a few months Bohemond had been taken prisoner by Danishmend. After a dangerous interregnum of seven months his nephew Tancred assumed the regency of Antioch and at once embarked on a policy of expansion, recovering Cilicia from the Greeks and re-investing Latakia, which fell to him in 1103 after a long siege.

The climax in the early conflicts with the Greeks came in 1108. Bohemond had been released by the Muslims in 1103, but he had to deal with renewed Byzantine invasions that autumn and in the summer of 1104, when the Greeks reoccupied Tarsus, Adana, Misis and Latakia. At the same time the Muslims were advancing from the east. Bohemond returned to Europe where, as we shall see, he himself organized a new crusade openly aimed against the Byzantine empire. In October 1107 his crusaders landed at Valona (Vlorë) and marched on Durazzo, but after a year of near inactivity, surrounded by Greek forces, he was compelled to surrender and agree to the Treaty of Devol, in which he recognized that he held Antioch, the territories of which were defined, as the emperor's vassal.

Long before then, any advance to the south had been blocked by the activities of Raymond of St Gilles, who was in the course of founding the county of Tripoli. Ever since he first entered Syria Raymond had probably been looking for territory. Foiled at Antioch and again at Jerusalem, it is possible that he had tried to establish a principality in southern Palestine around Ascalon or Arsuf. On his way south in 1102 with the ragged remnants of the third wave of crusaders he had laid siege to Tartus. In doing so he was, strictly speaking, in breach of an oath he had been forced to make to Tancred, who had briefly imprisoned him after the disasters in Asia Minor and had made him promise not to take any territory between Antioch and Acre ('Akko); he doubtless considered this oath to be invalid since it had been made under pressure. Tartus soon fell and, although moves against Husn el Akrad (later to be known as Crac des Chevaliers) and Homs failed, Raymond set up a siege camp on high ground about three miles inland from the important port of Tripoli, which he gradually enlarged into the castle of Montpélerin. Tripoli was not to fall until 1109, long after his death, but in 1104 he collaborated with the Genoese in taking Jubail to the south.

This brings us to the kingdom of Jerusalem. The election of Godfrey of Bouillon on 22 July 1099 to the rulership is a shadowy affair. The formal decision seems to have been made by the leaders of the crusade after a debate in the presence of the whole army, but informal approaches had been made beforehand to at least three of the leadersd Raymond probably as a matter of form, since Godfrey then accepted it. Raymond was not pleased by this and was only persuaded with difficulty to hand over the Tower of David, the citadel of Jerusalem, to the Catholic bishop of el Barah, one of his own followers, who surrendered it immediately. Why Godfrey was chosen is unclear, but Raymond was old and chronically unwell, whereas Godfrey was now comparatively rich, thanks to the efforts of his brother Baldwin: we have seen that on the final stages of the march he had been able to draw into his following men who had been in Raymond's company. Up to that time Raymond had been the richest of the crusaders and this suggests that Godfrey was now better equipped to reward them.

When most of the crusaders left Palestine in August 1099 Godfrey was in control of Jerusalem and a belt of land stretching through Ramle to Jaffa on the coast. By the following year three other areas seem to have been entrusted to leading figures who had remained in the East with him. Galdemar Carpenel, a rich nobleman from near Lyon, who had decided to dedicate the rest of his life to the defence of Jerusalem, held the south-eastern frontier, including the towns of Hebron and Jericho. North of Jerusalem the territory round Nablus may have been given to Garnier, Count of Grez in Brabant, who was related to Godfrey by birth and probably also by marriage and was a prominent member of his entourage. Further north still Tancred held Bet She'an and Tiberias; the latter had been occupied by Godfrey probably early in September 1099 and was granted to Tancred first as a castellany and then as a fief. But that was the limit of Godfrey's conquests when he died on 18 July 1100, although he had forced the ports of Ascalon, Arsuf, Caesarea and Acre to become tributaries and was planning a campaign against Haifa and Acre in concert with a Venetian fleet that had just arrived.

The succession of his brother Baldwin was not straightforward. He and Bohemond were the two obvious candidates. Both had played important and positive parts in the crusade and had already consolidated their hold over substantial territories in the East. Of the other possible competitors Raymond of St Gilles was away in Constantinople and Godfrey's elder brother Eustace, who had taken part in the crusade, had returned to Europe. Within the little settlement in Palestine there was a division of opinion. Tancred naturally supported his uncle Bohemond. So did Daimbert of Pisa, the patriarch of Jerusalem. There can be little doubt that from the point of view of Church reformers, of whom Daimbert was one, Bohemond was preferable to a representative of a family which had provided partisans of the imperial cause in the Investiture Contest and, as events were to show, was unenthusiastic about reform. On the other side were members of Godfrey's household who held positions of trust in Palestine. Appeals were sent to both candidates by their adherents and the Lorrainers took the precaution of seizing control of Jerusalem in Daimbert's absence, for the patriarch and Tancred were with the army besieging Haifa, which fell to the Christians c. 20 August. Daimbert's appeal to Bohemond was intercepted by members of Raymond of St Gilles' household who were still at Latakia and anyway Bohemond was withdrawn from the scene in August when he fell into the hands of the Turks. It was Baldwin himself who saved the principality of Antioch by coming swiftly to its aid and reinforcing the Armenian garrison of Malatya, which blocked any Danishmendid advance. Before starting his journey south on 2 October he arranged for his cousin Baldwin of Le Bourcq to be invested with the county of Edessa. Baldwin entered Jerusalem on 9 November, assumed the title of king on the 13th and was crowned in the church of the Nativity in Bethlehem on Christmas Day.

The establishment of the Latin Church

The First Crusade had been fought to recover Jerusalem and the holy places. The possibility of western European rule over them, which certainly had been raised at the Council of Clermont, since Pope Urban had ruled that liberated churches would belong to the principalities of the princes who conquered them – in other words that the conqueror would determine the rite – must have been considered to be remote, given the part the Byzantine Greeks must have been expected to play. The events that followed showed how unprepared the Catholic settlers, few and isolated, were for the task that faced them. The *raison d'être* of their settlement was the maintenance and protection of these holy places. There was, it is true, already a Catholic Benedictine community in the abbey of St Mary of the Latins just to the south of the Holy Sepulchre compound, but extreme shortages of cash and clerical manpower meant that at first Catholic communities could be established only at three sites in Jerusalem; the Holy Sepulchre, the Temple, and the Marian shrine of St Mary of the Valley of Jehoshaphat. Mount Zion, St Anne's, the Mount of Olives, even Bethlehem for a while, seem to have been served only by individual Catholic priests. A prime objective was to encase the great shrines in proper buildings. Most were in ruins and one of the striking features of the first eighty years of Latin occupation was an extraordinarily ambitious and expensive building programme. Although Greek and indigenous craftsmen were employed, the design of the churches and monastic quarters was recognizably western. First-rate sculptors were recruited in Europe to work on particular commissions, such as the south façade of the church of the Holy Sepulchre, where their work appears to have been incorporated into a framework of local and perhaps even re-used Roman sculpture, and the capitals and doorway of the great church at Nazareth, or to create semi-permanent workshops in the East, in which their work inter-reacted with that of other western immigrants, as in the 'Temple workshop' in Jerusalem, active from c. 1170 to 1187 and assembled round a core of Provencal craftsmen.

As one might expect, the most remarkable of these Catholic buildings was the church of the Holy Sepulchre, which was dedicated, if not yet entirely completed, on 15 July 1149, the fiftieth anniversary of the liberation of Jerusalem. When the crusaders had arrived there had been three major shrines and several smaller ones within a compound. There was the Sepulchre itself, demolished almost to ground level at the orders of the Fatimid caliph Hakim in 1009, over which had been constructed an aedicule, or little chapel. Around and over the aedicule was a domed rotunda, open to the sky, with an eastern apse in which was the choir, high altar and patriarchal throne. North and south of the rotunda were rows of chapels, some of them fairly large. East of it, across a yard, were the unoccupied ruins of the *martyrium*, the church of the Emperor Constantine the Great, beneath which was the spot where the Empress Helena supposed herself to have discovered the relic of the True Cross. A little to the south of the Sepulchre rotunda and the *martyrium* was Calvary. The hill had been reduced by Constantine's engineers to a pillar of rock, now encased in dressed stone; at its top was a chapel. The whole compound was surrounded by a wall. With the inspired brilliance so characteristic of contemporary western architecture, the Latins decided to enclose these elements in one great Romanesque church, with a choir to the east of the Holy Sepulchre and north of Golgotha, relating the monuments of Christ's death and resurrection to one another under the same roof. The present state of the building makes it difficult, but not impossible, to recognize this as one of the most profound expressions of Catholic Christian art, a theological commentary and emotional statement in stone which ranks among the greatest achievements of the twelfth century. As in all these churches, the interior was decorated with mosaics and paintings, which in Palestine had a strong Byzantine influence; it has been written that 'one must imagine the church of the Holy Sepulchre glowing with all the subdued richness with which we are familiar in St Mark's at Venice'.

The splendour of the churches was reflected in their furnishings. A magnificent series of liturgical books survives, one a superb product for a royal patron, others witnessing to the presence of skilful masters in the scriptorium of the Holy Sepulchre itself. And a workshop producing illuminated manuscripts of the highest quality was to be found in late thirteenth-century Acre. These reveal a school of miniature painting which was not provincial or colonial but had a distinctive style of its own, combining eastern and western elements, although the western, particularly the French, influence was assertive.

Surveying the wealth of building in Palestine and Syria and considering how early much of it was and the fact that there was at the same time a programme of fortification on a massive scale, one is forced to conclude that it was far too costly for the settlements to have financed on their own. There must have been a large-scale transfer of funds from western Europe to beautify the holy places. And the urgency with which the programme was carried out demonstrates the importance the Latins attached to them. Their preservation, of course, also involved adequate staffing and endowment; and, given the sentiments of the crusaders, that meant the importation of Catholic churchmen and monks and the establishment of a Catholic hierarchy.

The Latin Church in Palestine and Syria was formed in the two decades after the conquest and retained until the end of the thirteenth century features it had by then developed. The crusaders had entered a Babel with a bewildering diversity of creeds. In the north the majority of the indigenous population may well have been Christian, probably mostly monophysite Armenians and Jacobites, although there were also strong Orthodox communities, particularly around Antioch. In the south the majority were Muslims, Sunnite and Shi'ite, but there were large numbers of Orthodox Christians, a few Armenians and Syrian Jacobites, a sprinkling of Egyptian Copts (in communion with the Jacobites) and Nestorians and a substantial Maronite population in the Lebanon; there were also groups of Druzes and some Jewish communities, especially in Galilee.

In time the Latins had to get on with the members of all these religious groups who were subject to them, but their earliest reactions seem to have been conditioned by three factors. First, the Crusaders were was determined to expel all infidels, whether Muslims or Jews, from centres of religious or military significance. Where there was an indigenous Christian population, of whatever denomination, that could remain; where there was not there was to be settlement by western Europeans. Secondly, they began by being careful not to displace the existing Orthodox bishops, whose legitimacy and authority they recognized. But thirdly, Pope Urban's ruling at Clermont that liberated churches would 'belong' to the principalities of the princes who conquered them was used to justify the appointment of Catholic bishops where no Orthodox see existed or where there were vacancies, particularly in the light of the abandonment of their cause by the Byzantine emperor. The policy can be seen in operation in the winter of 1097–8. At Tilbeşar, Ravanda and Artah the Muslims were slaughtered or driven out but the Christians were allowed to remain. The crusaders adopted exactly the same approach in the following June when they took Antioch, although it was said that in the darkness before dawn they found it hard to distinguish between the Christian and Muslim inhabitants of the city, and again in July 1099 when they took Jerusalem. The Muslims and Jews who had not been massacred were expelled from Jerusalem and theoretically were not permitted to live there thenceforward, although they could visit it as pilgrims; in fact a few were in residence later in the twelfth century. The indigenous Christians were allowed to stay; indeed the relatively small number of inhabitants led later to extraordinary measures to increase the size of the population. The Orthodox patriarch of Antioch, John IV, who had been inside the city and had suffered during the siege, was restored to his cathedral by the crusaders, once it had been reconsecrated, and was accorded the full honours of the patriarchate. And although a Catholic patriarch of Jerusalem was elected a fortnight after the city's liberation, he was appointed in the knowledge that there was a vacancy, for the Orthodox patriarch Symeon, who had accompanied the crusade for part of its journey, had just died in Cyprus. Meanwhile at those places which they felt obliged to occupy for strategic reasons and where they found no Christian inhabitants, the crusaders adopted a policy of depopulation followed by settlement by westerners. In many of the earliest examples – el Barah in Syria, taken by Raymond of St Gilles in the autumn of 1098, Ramle in Palestine, reached by the crusade in June 1099, and Caesarea, which fell to the settlers in May 1101 – settlement was accompanied by the foundation of a Catholic bishopric, the incumbent of which was expected to manage it and exercise military command along the lines of some frontier sees in western Europe.

These measures, born of desperation and isolation, could not be maintained indefinitely once it became clear that western immigration was not to be on a large enough scale to create a state solely for Christians. The taking of Sidon (Saïda) in 1110 marked a change of policy. Much earlier, the toleration of existing Orthodox bishops had begun to break down. At Christmas 1099 the new Catholic patriarch of Jerusalem, Daimbert, consecrated Catholic archbishops of Tarsus, Misis and Edessa and a Catholic bishop of Artah. These towns had substantial native Christian populations and it is hard to believe that in all of them the Orthodox bishoprics were vacant. All, moreover, were in the patriarchate of Antioch and it may be that the Orthodox patriarch John had refused to consecrate them, which is why Daimbert did so, presumably by virtue of his legation from the pope. It is noteworthy that the new Catholic bishops had accompanied their temporal masters, Bohemond of Antioch and Baldwin of Edessa, and Daimbert himself, south from Syria to Jerusalem; their consecration was obviously an act of full deliberation. It was followed six months later by the forcing of the Orthodox patriarch out of Antioch and his replacement by a

Catholic. John's position became, or was made, intolerable and he retired to the monastery of Oxeia. This was treated by the Latins as abdication. The change in policy towards resident Orthodox bishops has been put down to Daimbert's supposed Hellenophobia, but the background to it was the Byzantine invasions of Cilicia and the empire's manifest desire to gain control of Antioch. Tarsus and Misis commanded the roads in and out of Cilicia. Artah watched the road east of Antioch. Edessa had already proved its strategic worth in the summer of 1098. Antioch was the capital of Syria and back in Normandy it was said that the settlers feared that Patriarch John would betray it to the Byzantine emperor after Bohemond had fallen into the hands of the Turks. It is clear that the setting up of lines of Catholic bishops in place of existing Orthodox ones was a response to military and political pressure from the Byzantine government and it is surely no coincidence that in the early twelfth century Catholic dioceses were established much more rapidly in Syria than in Palestine, where as late as 1120 there were only four Catholic bishops besides the patriarch.

Most of the early appointments were of poor quality. The candidates available had come with the crusade and being on the whole the chaplains of the magnates were a compliant and mediocre body of men, unlikely to resist their patrons. Although the first bishops of el Barah, Ramle and Artah were reasonably able – the bishop of Artah was to become the first Catholic patriarch of Antioch – the first Catholic patriarch of Jerusalem, Arnulf of Chocques, was a learned and worldly chaplain of Robert of Normandy, and Baldwin, the first abbot of St Mary of the Valley of Jehoshaphat and first Catholic archbishop of Caesarea, who had been Godfrey of Bouillon's chaplain, had created a scandal by having had a cross branded on his forehead, which he had passed off as a sign miraculously imprinted by an angel, and had financed his crusade by accepting oblations made to it by the faithful. Standards in the settler Church were not helped by the political consequences of the conquest. The crusade had been preached by a reforming papacy, but the pope's chief representative, Adhémar of Le Puy, had died in 1098 and the first rulers of Jerusalem had in the past supported the imperialists in the Investiture Contest. That would not necessarily have precluded sympathy for reform ideas, for many of the imperialists were themselves reformers, differing from the papalists only on the means by which reform should be achieved; and anyway most laymen, even those like Raymond of St Gilles who supported the reform papacy, seem to have had only the vaguest notions of what reform meant. But neither Godfrey of Bouillon nor Baldwin I showed any sympathy for reform ideas; indeed Baldwin, who had been trained for the priesthood and so must have been conscious of some of the issues, was clearly antipathetic, perhaps, as has been suggested, because his prospects as a young man had been harmed by the movement.

It is against this background that Baldwin's conflict with Daimbert of Pisa should be viewed. There is now little doubt that Pope Urban had appointed Daimbert as his chief legate to replace Adhémar of Le Puy and that it was in this capacity that on his arrival in Jerusalem before Christmas 1099 Daimbert chaired a council which refused to confirm the election of Arnulf of Chocques. Daimbert was then elected patriarch himself and presided at a ceremony at which he invested Godfrey and Bohemond with their principalities. It is possible that in their minds and his was the idea either of vassal-states of the papacy, of which Daimbert was the representative, or of vassal-states of the Holy Sepulchre, along the lines of the lands of St Peter in Europe; after all, the first crusader lordship in Asia Minor had been established '*in fealty to God and the Holy Sepulchre* and the princes (of the crusade) and the emperor'. It may be that Daimbert was merely confirming the princes' rule as papal legate, the representative of a power qualified to grant this recognition. We cannot now tell what was in the minds of the participants in this ceremony, although future rulers of Jerusalem and Antioch were never to be regarded as vassals of the popes or the patriarchs.

Daimbert seems to have decided on a radical solution to the problem of the endowment of his church, the creation of a patriarchal patrimony, centred on Jerusalem, not unlike the papal patrimony in Italy. Twenty Catholic canons had already been installed in the Holy Sepulchre and to provide for them it seems that the Orthodox clergy there were deprived of their benefices. But Godfrey, who was very short of cash, was probably reluctant to give way to demands to restore to the Church of Jerusalem all the properties and rights it claimed to have enjoyed in the past. He was persuaded by Daimbert to confirm it in its ancient possessions at the same time as the new patriarch was consecrated – although his inventory may have been less extensive than Daimbert's – and six weeks later he granted it a fourth part of Jaffa. In ecclesiastical circles in Jerusalem there developed a tradition that Daimbert, whose claims were reinforced by the presence in the East of a powerful Pisan fleet, went further. At Easter 1100 he was believed to have forced Godfrey to cede to him the whole of the city of Jerusalem, including its citadel, and the remaining three-quarters of Jaffa, although Godfrey's need for resources was recognized to the extent that he was allowed to retain usufruct until the settlement was enlarged. Godfrey was also believed to have promised that should he die without an heir Jerusalem and Jaffa would pass immediately to the patriarch and to have confirmed this on his deathbed; it was said that only the quick action of his household frustrated Daimbert and assured their possession by Baldwin. The Church of Jerusalem briefly revived its claims to Jerusalem and Jaffa thirty years later. Tradition is not fact. But it is clear that Daimbert was ambitious, even if the only consequence seems to have been the development of a patriarchal lordship around the church of the Holy Sepulchre in the north-western part of the city of Jerusalem.

Whether Daimbert had been trying to found a theocracy or a patriarchal patrimony or if all he was concerned with was a properly reformed Church and the right balance, as he saw it, between secular and spiritual power, Godfrey's death and his failure to engineer the succession of Bohemond greatly weakened his position. Pope Paschal II, moreover, had now appointed a new legate, Maurice of Porto, who arrived at Latakia in September 1100 and met Baldwin on the latter's journey south to claim the kingdom. Baldwin was crowned king of Jerusalem, by Daimbert himself, on Christmas Day 1100 and he clearly had no intention of surrendering what he regarded as his rights. When the new legate arrived in Palestine in the following spring Baldwin went on to the offensive. He accused Daimbert of various crimes, including plotting his assassination after Godfrey's death, and he engineered his suspension from the patriarchal office; then, after allowing him to buy himself back into his grace, he demanded money to pay the stipends of knights; it should be remembered that at this time the settlement was very precarious and a large Egyptian army was mustering on the southern frontier. Daimbert made a contribution which was considered to be too small. When the king made an angry scene and demanded more, he retorted by raising the issue of the Church's liberty, asking Baldwin whether he dared make her a tribute payer and bondswoman when Christ had freed her. He threatened Baldwin with excommunication by the pope. But Baldwin insisted and a compromise worked out by Maurice of Porto failed becase Daimbert only half-heartedly fulfilled his side of the bargain. Baldwin then struck ruthlessly, accusing Daimbert of embezzling money sent to the East by Roger of Sicily and forcing him into exile in Antioch. Although in 1102 Daimbert was briefly restored to power, in fulfilment of a condition Tancred had made in return for military aid from Antioch, he was almost immediately tried again by a council presided over by another papal legate, Robert of Paris, and deposed. He appealed to the pope and accompanied Bohemond to the West in 1104. His successor in the patriarchate, Evremar, was summoned to the papal curia to defend his election, but neither he nor Baldwin sent representatives to Rome and the case went by default to Daimbert, who died at Messina on his way back to the East. Evremar now travelled to Italy to plead his case, but he was followed by Arnulf of Chocques bringing letters from those very people who had written the references with which Evremar had been armed, calling for his deposition. The pope, scandalized, chose a new legate, Gibelin of Arles, to decide the matter. In 1108 Gibelin declared Evremar's election to be invalid because Daimbert had been deposed under royal pressure. Gibelin in his turn was elected patriarch.

Daimbert, who had had a distinguished career as a reforming politician in Italy, clearly met his match in Baldwin. He has had a bad press from historians, who have relied on sources hostile to him, but on his arrival in the East he must have been horrified to find a newly established Church that was inadequately endowed and staffed by clergy of poor quality, often the chaplains of the crusading magnates, with some dioceses doubling as military frontier-posts, reminiscent of the bad old days in western Europe. And he must have been struck by the fact that power in Jerusalem was held not by a supporter of the reforming popes, like Bohemond, but by a man who had been closer to the papacy's arch-enemy, Henry IV of Germany. It is worth noting that Pope Paschal's decision was in his favour. His remedies had been nullified by Baldwin and – this must have caused him bitterness – the two papal legates had not given him wholehearted support. The problem was, of course, that neither they nor the pope could afford to assent to anything that might damage the settlement, the situation of which was perilous enough. Paschal took the step of confirming Baldwin's assumption of the crown and he later went further. The archbishopric of Tyre with its suffragan sees, including Acre, Sidon and Beirut, was part of the patriarchate of Antioch. Baldwin was naturally anxious that the Church in the northern part of his kingdom should not be subject to a patriarch outside his control and he and Patriarch Gibelin appealed to Rome. In 1111 Paschal ruled that the boundary between the patriarchates should be the political frontier between Jerusalem and the northern settlements, thus detaching a large part of the southernmost province of one ancient patriarchate and incorporating it into another. In the process Tyre lost its three northern sees, Tripoli, Jubail and Tartus, which became directly subject to Antioch. The patriarch of Antioch protested and Paschal gave signs of changing his mind, but the rights of Jerusalem were confirmed by Pope Honorious II in 1128, although the issue remained controversial until at least the middle of the century. This extraordinary and messy decision, which was always unsatisfactory, shows how far Paschal was prepared to go to meet the king's desires. It is not the only example in his pontificate of compliance with the wishes of secular rulers, but it also demonstrates how the need for strong government in the new settlements tended to take precedence over other considerations.

Characteristics of the Latin Church

A feature of the Latin Church in Palestine and Syria was the relatively small number of Catholics. By the summer of 1100, after the departure for home of most of the crusaders, it was reported that in the area under Godfrey's immediate control there were no more than 300 knights and the same number of foot. Allowing for the settlers in Galilee, Hebron and Nablus and in the north around Antioch and Edessa, there must have been only 2–4,000 western Europeans in the whole of the Near East at the time and, although the numbers increased substantially so that at their height there may have been as many as 140,000 of them in Palestine, the settlement was always small. There were some converts to Catholicism, perhaps a significant number, from among the indigenous peoples – the mere fact of native names appearing in the witness lists to charters testifies to this, since in law only the testimony of Catholics carried full weight in court – but it is impossible to estimate the size of the convert community because there was a natural tendency for convert families to adopt the names of Latin saints and so merge into anonymity. For instance, the Arrabi family first made its appearance in 1122, when Muisse Arrabi was a knight of Jaffa. Muisse had a son called George, whose four children were named Henry, Peter, John and Maria: had they not chosen to use their distinctive cognomen their origins would have been lost to us. A burgess of Acre called Saliba made a will in 1264 which reveals him to have been a Catholic, or perhaps a Maronite, since he made endowments to several Latin churches. His sister was called Nayme. His brother Stephen, who was no longer living, had been married to a woman called Settedar. He had two daughters, Katherine and Haternie (Hodierna), four nieces, Vista, Caolfe, Bonaventura and Isabellona, and six nephews, Leonard, Thomasinus, George, Dominic, Nicholas and Leonardinus.

The legal inferiority of non-Catholics, about which more below, obviously encouraged conversions and in the thirteenth century there was active proselytizing, and diplomatic pressure, from missionaries and legations from the West: the Franciscans and Dominicans were active in the Holy Land and the Dominican *studium* in Acre was a training-school for missionaries. Much the most important submission was that of the Maronite Church, a monothelete community under its own patriarch and bishops which held the allegiance of most indigenous Christians in the county of Tripoli. In c. 1181 it entered into full religious union with Rome and thirty years later its status was regularized. It became the first Uniate Church with its own rites, canon law and hierarchy, which was directly subject to the popes without the intermediation of the local Catholic bishops. In spite of a party within the community hostile to union, the Maronites remained sentimentally attached to the Holy See even after the Latins had been driven from the Lebanon. The other cases, however, were less impressive. In 1198 an important segment of the Armenian Church, that in Cilicia, formally entered into union with Rome. This was engineered by the Armenian ruler who in consequence was made a king by representatives of the western emperor, but the agreement had been reached without the consent of the majority of the Armenian bishops, who resided outside Cilicia, was misunderstood by most of the Armenian people, caused anxiety to those who did understand it and had few results, as the reforms requested by the papacy were never implemented. The Armenians remained in a state of semi-independence. Professions of Catholic faith made to the Dominicans in 1237 by the Jacobite patriarch and archbishop of Jerusalem and by a Nestorian archbishop were of even less consequence, being personal. In fact the work of the Dominican and Franciscan missionaries brought to light the fact that the Jacobite and Nestorian communities, although technically heretical, consisted of ill-educated, devout, good people who had very little understanding of, or concern about, the theological disputes that had led to separation. But this discovery of the realities of the situation came too late for anything to be done about it.

Even allowing for convert or uniate families we are still left with very few Catholics, a fact that is confirmed by the small number of Latin parish churches – usually one to each settlement – and by the practice of making the cathedral double as the sole parish church in the larger towns: even in Jerusalem the only Latin church with the *jus parochiale* was the Holy Sepulchre. Jaffa had two parishes after 1168; Acre and Antioch had multiple parishes in the thirteenth century. But these were very much exceptions. A full Catholic hierarchy was eventually established, but it stood on a very small base and its responsibilities were further reduced by the system of exemptions, which freed the greater monasteries and religious Orders – the Latin Church in the East was markedly monastic as a result of the granting of the custody of so many of the holy places to monastic communities – and in the thirteenth century some of the churches in the Italian merchant quarters from episcopal jurisdiction.

It is true, of course, that the Catholic bishops retained formal authority over members of other Christian denominations, although there was a distinction made between the Orthodox, who were regarded as Catholic at least until late in the twelfth century, and the others, who were technically heretical. The Orthodox had their own churches and monastic communities. There is no good evidence that they were ever expelled from the greatest cult centres, like the Holy Sepulchre, although their priests there were deprived of their benefices and presumably had to subsist on offerings from the faithful: they were actually present and witnessed the failure in 1101 of the annual miracle in Jerusalem, the auto-lighting of the Easter fire in the aedicule of the Holy Sepulchre, which has wrongly been attributed to their absence. In fact throughout the period of Catholic occupation the Orthodox liturgy seems to have been celebrated daily before the Holy Sepulchre at a large altar in a prominent place in the church and at an altar in the church of Our Lady of the Valley of Jehoshaphat, the chief Marian shrine at Jerusalem. It is noteworthy that when the church of the Nativity at Bethlehem was redecorated by Greek mosaicists at the expense of the Byzantine emperor Manuel the *filioque* clause, a contentious issue between

Orthodox and Catholics, was omitted according to Orthodox practice from the formula of the Procession of the Holy Spirit inscribed on the walls. The Orthodox hierarchies continued to work alongside the Catholic. Titular Orthodox patriarchs of Antioch and Jerusalem lived in exile, although for a brief period, from 1165 to 1170, the Orthodox Patriarch Athanasius was restored to Antioch. But many Orthodox bishops remained in residence; and some sees must have had new appointments after hundreds of years of vacancy. In the patriarchate of Antioch it seems that their presence was not recognized: the Catholic bishops, regarding themselves in every sense the successors of their predecessors, appointed vicars to watch over their Orthodox flocks. In the patriarchate of Jerusalem Orthodox prelates seem to have been treated by the Catholics as coadjutors: we know of individual bishops at Gaza and probably also at Sidon and Lydda (Lod). The only Orthodox prelate recognized by the Latins as a full diocesan bishop was the archbishop of Sinai far to the south and outside their direct control.

Of the other Christians the most numerous were the Jacobites and the Armenians. In practice they were left alone. In the north, where most of them lived and where the Jacobite patriarch and the Armenian catholicos resided, they were not interfered with by most of the Catholic bishops, although the vicar appointed to supervise the Orthodox in at least one diocese also oversaw them. In the south they were regarded as being under the authority of the Catholic patriarch and their archbishops of Jerusalem were treated as his suffragans, although this seems to have been no more than a legal technicality. Both communities had cathedrals in Jerusalem. The Jacobites were not admitted to the Holy Sepulchre but were allowed to have a chapel at the entrance, with a separate door in the outer wall, while the Armenians had a chapel in the courtyard.

The Latin Church, therefore, like the army of a banana republic, had far too many generals for the troops available. The Christians directly subject to the bishops were so few that the bishops themselves had very little to do. In the winter of 1216–17 James of Vitry, who as bishop of Acre was responsible for the largest Catholic community in the East, described his daily round (*Lettres*, ed. R. B. C. Huygens (1960), p. 90): Mass first thing in the morning; then the hearing of confessions until mid-day; then, after a meal – he claimed to have lost his appetite since he had come to Palestine – visiting the sick until the hours of None or Vespers; then a sitting of his court, which took up much of the rest of the day. He wrote that he had no time for reading other than from the lectionaries at Mass or Matins and that he had to reserve the night-time for prayer and meditation, but his responsibilities in a city crowded with ecclesiastical refugees from the interior, with all the disputes over rights that followed, were exceptional. By the time he was writing the situation had become absurd. As the Christians began to lose territory to the Muslims, exiled Catholic bishops and their chapters crowded into the cities on the coast, particularly Acre, and there most of them remained, either because their sees, like those of Hebron and Sebastea, were not recovered, or because, like those of Nazareth, Lydda, Tiberias and Jerusalem itself, they were too exposed to be safely reoccupied. Some lines of bishops lapsed, two were joined to other dioceses, but several continued, largely because their churches had been endowed with properties along the coast and in western Europe. The cathedral churches of the Holy Sepulchre, Sebastea, Nazareth and Bethlehem, along with the abbeys of St Mary of the Latins and St Mary of the Valley of Jehoshaphat, the priory of Mount Zion and the Military Orders, had been endowed with estates throughout Christendom, from which revenues continued to flow in. Their administration provided a living for some of the canons and religious. In new statutes drawn up in 1251 for the chapter of Nazareth it was laid down that if the archbishop's own lordship in northern Galilee did not provide a living for him and prebends for the chapter

> only the prior should remain living with the archbishop in Syria. The other canons shall be provided for as is honestly seen to be expedient or they will be sent overseas to govern the priories and churches belonging to the cathedral of Nazareth (Innocent IV, *Registre*, ed. E. Berger (1883–1921), no. 5538).

Even without cathedral churches and pastoral duties these chapters, like Oxford and Cambridge colleges, were, therefore, independently endowed and would have remained in existence for that reason alone. A curious result was that the walls of thirteenth-century Acre contained, besides its own clergy and the brothers of the Military Orders and the friars, the Augustinian chapter of the Holy Sepulchre, religious communities like Mount Zion and St Mary of the Valley of Jehoshaphat exiled from Jerusalem and titular bishops *in partibus infidelium* with their chapters.

The plethora of idle bishops was only one of several odd features of the Church. Representing a minority in a potentially hostile population it was forced, after the brutal depopulations of the first decade, to be tolerant not only of other Christians but also of those of other faiths. Of course there were limits to this. Only Catholics had full rights in law, because only their witness was fully valid in court: the weight given to the testimony of the members of other communities was graded according to their creeds. While all Christians, moreover, originally had the intrinsic right to freedom, non-Christians did not. This, in fact, so hindered conversions, because lords, even when they were churchmen, were reluctant to allow their slaves to be baptized and therefore freed, that Pope Gregory IX ruled that baptism would not affect their servile status, a measure also applied in

Spain and along the Baltic shores. And non-Christians suffered under further disabilities which seem to have stemmed from a modification of the Muslim *dhimmi* laws which the crusaders had found on their arrival: in these Christians and Jews were allowed to retain their beliefs and a measure of self-government in community affairs but were subject to special taxation and to discriminatory regulations, such as distinctions in dress. In Latin East *dhimmi* status seems to have been retained for Jews, lifted from all Christians and imposed on Muslims. But in accordance with these laws Muslims and Jews were allowed to practise their faiths. They had their own places of worship – we know of a a new mosque built near Ramallah in 1176–7 – their own religious tribunals, their own schools (the rabbinical academies in Tyre and Acre were famous), and their own places of pilgrimage; they were admitted under special terms to shrines venerated by all three faiths such as the tomb of the patriarchs at Hebron. Certain buildings were even shared: part of the Templar house in Jerusalem, which incorporated what had been the el Aqsa mosque, was set aside for Muslim worship; so was part of the cathedral of the Holy Cross in Acre, which had been the Great Mosque of the Muslim town. Most striking of all was the policy on tithes, which belonged to the Catholic bishops and were levied only on Catholics, not even on other Christians, which in practice meant that only the lord's share of a village crop was tithed. The studied tolerance was not particularly exceptional in the twelfth century, but it is significant that it was maintained in the thirteenth, in spite of a drive for Christian uniformity on papal terms, which began during the pontificate of Pope Innocent III, first in southern Italy and then in Greece after 1204. Pressure for change was resisted by the Catholic hierarchies in Palestine and Syria, probably because the bishops did not want to antagonize the indigenous population. So although conversions were made and Uniate churches formed, the picture, all in all, is one of an extraordinarily passive body.

In the twelfth century the Church was also one of the most unreformed in Latin Christendom. No doubt this was due to the poor quality of the first generation of churchmen and to the fact that the early secular rulers were unsympathetic to reform. The picture we have, above all from the pioneering work of Professor Mayer, is not unlike that which confronts us in the more backward parts of Europe. There were proprietary churches in the hands of laymen as late as the middle of the twelfth century. It was not until the Council of Nablus in 1120 that the king and lords could be induced to give up their control of tithes. Until the end of the twelfth century the kings kept a tight control of episcopal elections, partly through the enjoyment of honorary canonries, like their European counterparts, which gave them a share in elections, partly through influence and partly by means of the disreputable practice of dual postulation by which the electoral body first secretly submitted two names to the king, although on the surface there followed a free canonical election. After 1191 this was gradually driven out after it had drawn from the papacy a condemnatory decretal, while the translations of bishops from Europe to the eastern sees – something only the pope could do – reduced state interference in the thirteenth century, when anyway there was an absentee and often powerless monarchy. But one is left with the paradox of an old-fashioned, unreformed Church created by one of the greatest initiatives of the reformed papacy.

So the Church was of low quality and provincial, in spite of occupying magnificent buildings and being so well-endowed with lands thousands of miles away. It is true that by 1103 the church of the Holy Sepulchre had established a master of schools and that there was another in Antioch by the late twelfth century; theology was taught in Acre by 1218 and canon and probably civil law in Tripoli in the middle of the thirteen century. By the 1120s Nazareth was a cultural centre of some importance, referred to as a 'famous religious community' in a papal document of 1145 and providing livings to two figures of minor literary significance, Rorgo Fretellus and Gerard of Nazareth; its library, the catalogue of which survives, bears comparison with those of western schools. But bright young men like William of Tyre, who spent nearly twenty years studying at the best schools and under the best masters in France and Italy, had to go to Europe for their education; and this was still the case in the thirteenth century. The settlers looked to western Europe for their learning and culture: to judge from the literature that attracted them the interests of the lay nobility were practically indistinguishable from those of their confrères in the West; even the *Chanson des Chetifs*, commissioned by Prince Raymond of Antioch and composed by a priest who was rewarded with a canonry there, belongs in its legendary story of crusaders captured by the Muslims to a western genre. It is no coincidence that their society did not provide a good channel for the transmission of Arabic learning to the West. Although it should be remembered that the Near East, which had suffered so much instability in the eleventh century, was not itself a great centre of cultural activity at the time, Professor Prawer is surely right in suggesting that it was the low educational level in the Latin settlements that accounts for this remarkable fact.

The contribution of the Latin Church

But it would be wrong to deny this small, isolated and backward institution, in the pockets of the twelfth-century kings, any contribution to the Church at large. Apart from the confraternal orders of the Holy Sepulchre and Bethlehem, the Latin kingdom also provided Christendom with the Carmelites and with two important new forms of the religious life, the hospitaller and the military, which then fused.

From the First Crusade onwards Palestine naturally attracted large numbers of fervent westerners who wished to live out their days as hermits in caves near Jerusalem, or in Galilee, or on the Amanus mountain chain north of Antioch, where some of them formed themselves into particularly strict communities, or on Mount Carmel, a tongue of rock ending on the sea-shore by Haifa, where they settled in imitation of the prophet Elijah. The last group may have been given a rudimentary rule of life by Patriarch Aimery of Antioch (1140–93), who certainly also interested himself in the solitaries on the Amanus; according to tradition he had a nephew among the Carmelite hermits. So matters rested until early in the thirteenth century, when Patriarch Albert of Jerusalem drew up a rule for a group of Carmelite hermits under a leader called Brocard. This work, later confirmed by Pope Honorious III, became the primitive rule of the Carmelite Order, which was soon to transform itself into a brotherhood of mendicants and in future centuries was to produce some of the greatest saints in Christian history.

The hospitaller way of life is particularly associated with the Order of the Hospital of St John of Jerusalem. This body came into existence soon after the First Crusade, when the administrators of a pilgrim-hospice in Jerusalem, run by the abbey of St Mary of the Latins, broke away from their parent and, benefiting from the general enthusiasm for pilgrimages to the Holy Land, were endowed with property in the East and in western Europe and were recognized by the papacy in 1113 as belonging to an independent institute. The ethos of the early Hospitallers stemmed directly from the concerns of the eleventh-century reformers, who had encouraged foundations committed to charitable and pastoral work among the faithful. They venerated the 'holy poor'. They were the 'serfs of the poor of Christ'. Their clothing had to be humble

> because our lords the poor, whose serfs we acknowledge ourselves to be, go about naked and meanly dressed. And it would be wrong and improper for the serf to be proud and his lord humble (J. Delaville le Roulx, *Cartulaire général de l'ordre des Hospitaliers de St -Jean de Jérusalem (1100–1310)* (1894–1906), no. 70).

This veneration of poverty as something evangelical reached, of course, its fullest expression in the ideals of St Francis in the following century, but in their abject humility and loving respect for the poor the early Hospitallers foreshadowed the Franciscans.

They made their ideal a reality by ministering to the poor when they were sick and in the process treating them as though they were the grandest lords. The uninterrupted history of hospitals as we know them in western Europe only began in the eleventh century; and the first great Catholic hospital was that managed in Jerusalem by the brothers of St John. This establishment, the organization of which was influenced by Greek methods, was run on a staggering scale, with almost unimaginable luxury for the time. It could accommodate 2,000 sick of both sexes. It was divided into wards, one of which was devoted to obstetrics. There were separate beds throughout and in the obstetrical ward there were also little cots for the children born to women pilgrims. The diet of the inmates was lavish by contemporary standards. They were given white bread and on three days a week fresh meat: pork or mutton or, if they could not stomach these, chicken. Four physicians and four surgeons were on the staff, assisted by nine sergeants-at-service in each ward. The spiritual needs of the patients were carefully met. On reception each inmate made confession and received communion; thereafter he or she seems to have been encouraged to receive the Sacrament every Sunday.

The expenses of this hospital, catering for and serving up to 2,000 patients who were probably sleeping in separate beds for the first time in their lives and certainly would never have eaten white bread and meat regularly or have had such close spiritual supervision, must have been enormous. It is all the more remarkable that within fifty years of their foundation the Hospitallers had taken on another function as well and were on the way to transforming their institute into a Military Order. In this they were following a path already taken by the Knights Templar. These had their origins in 1118–19, when a knight from Champagne called Hugh of Payns formed eight companions into a regular community of lay brothers, committed to defend the pilgrim roads through Palestine to Jerusalem, which were still very insecure. The Templars gained the support of the king, Baldwin II, who gave them part of the royal palace in the Temple enclosure, and of St Bernard, the influential Cistercian abbot of Clairvaux, who persuaded the papal legate, two archbishops and ten bishops attending the Council of Troyes in 1128 to recognize them and draw up a rule for them. This was an extraordinary event. The duty, indeed the moral obligation, of qualified laymen to bear arms in support of the Church had been, and continued to be, a necessary pre-condition for the preaching of the crusades. But it was quite another matter, as contemporaries pointed out, for professed religious to engage themselves in warfare. The Church's recognition of a religious community dedicated to fighting as well as prayer was a revolutionary step, formally confirmed by the papacy in 1139. There can be no doubt that on the whole it was very popular: Hugh of Payns himself had come to Europe in 1128 to raise a crusade almost single-handed; his Order was granted its first important frontier march, in the Amanus mountains north of Antioch, as early as the 1130s; and the scale of the endowments amassed by the Templars throughout Christendom far exceeded the Hospitallers'. But it was also a development that could have undermined the entire crusading movement. The Templars were not technically crusaders, of course: they had not made temporary pilgrim vows but were permanently committed to the holy war. But they were associated with crusading and the fact that they were religious called into question the special function of the laity as warriors on behalf of churchmen whose vocation prevented them from using force themselves.

The new hospitaller and military forms of the religious life were highly influential. The regulations for many hospitals in western Europe echoed the practices of the brothers of St John, although those brothers, themselves evidencing the attraction of a military profession, diverted most of their energies away from the care of the sick when they adopted the features of a Military Order. In 1136 King Fulk of Jerusalem, who was trying to confine Ascalon, the last Muslim stronghold on the Palestinian coast, with a ring of fortresses, gave the Hospitallers one of these castles at Bet Guvrin. Under pressure from the highest authorities in the kingdom to accept the burden of its defence, they probably garrisoned it with mercenaries. Its acquisition, however, was followed by others, especially Crac des Chevaliers (1144), Belvoir (1168) and Marqab (1186). In 1148 there came the first reference to a brother knight; by that time the Order was taking part in the Second Crusade. Between 1163 and 1170 there was a rapid expansion of military activities, an expansion which was temporarily halted with the Order in debt and its master suffering from a nervous breakdown. But the military wing then resumed its growth, in spite of worries expressed by Pope Alexander III, and the statutes issued by a General Chapter which probably met in 1206 show that by that time the Hospital of St John was a fully-fledged Military Order and that military duties were already overshadowing hospitaller ones. Although the care of the sick was never abandoned, it took second place thereafter. The association by these brothers of hospitaller and military functions was imitated by the Teutonic Knights, who came into existence in 1198. The Order of St Lazarus, with its care of lepers and wing of leper knights, took the same road, although probably independently. Other Military Orders came to be founded, especially in Spain and Germany as we shall see; and we should not forget the English Order of St Thomas of Acre.

The Hospitallers and Templars were members of great international institutions, the first truly centralized Orders of the Church. They were freed from the authority of diocesan bishops by papal privilege, becoming answerable only to Rome. In the East they increasingly took on their shoulders an important share of the burden of defending the Latin settlements. They have been described as over-powerful 'states within a state', contributing to that fragmentation of authority which in the end so weakened the kingdom of Jerusalem. But this picture of them is a caricature. Constitutionally their position was no different from that of other great ecclesiastical institutions in Latin Christendom, most of which held property under terms that exempted them from feudal military service and the jurisdiction of secular courts. The difference, of course, was that they were relatively stronger. They were also competitive, sometimes selfish, occasionally quarrelsome, and their leaders, while often good administrators, were not usually subtle or reflective men. They appreciated, however, that the survival of the Christian Holy Land was the reason for their existence. In the twelfth century the contribution they made to the defence of the Latin East was comparatively modest. At the height of their power in the thirteenth century they controlled at times around 40 per cent of the frontiers, but even then their strength lay especially in the north; most fortresses in the kingdom of Jerusalem were not in their hands, or even in those of the crown, but were held by feudal nobles. In all the East in the thirteenth century there were never more than c. 300 brothers of the Hospital and rather more brothers of the Temple; these operated as the commanders of mercenary troops who made up the bulk of their garrisons and field reigments. But their commitment involved them in great expenses. Safad (Zefat), one of the largest Templar castles in Palestine, was rebuilt in the 1240s. An estimate made within the Order put the bill, over and above the income from the villages nearby, at 1,100,000 Saracen besants. Thereafter the annual cost of maintaining it ran to 40,000 Saracen besants. Expenses of this sort, which can be understood if one remembers that in the thirteenth century knights' fees in Palestine ranged in worth from 400 to 1,000 Saracen besants *per annum*, were crippling. In spite of their great estates in the West and the elaborate machinery evolved for exploiting them, the Military Orders in the East were often over-burdened by their commitments and in financial difficulties.

CHAPTER 4

Settlement, Government and Defence of the Latin East, 1097–1187

Countryside and town

The region settled by the crusaders, nearly 600 miles from north to south, has a geographical unity. Mountains, in some places two parallel mountain ranges, bounded or broken by a depression carrying the watercourses of the Orontes, Litani and Jordan, run parallel to and at some distance from the coast, towards which, every now and then, rocky fingers of hillside extend. Since the wind is a prevailing westerly, winter rainwater is deposited on the high ground which retains it (more then than now because there were greater numbers of trees) and gradually releases it back to the coast throughout the dry season. The plains between the mountains and the coast are, therefore, relatively fertile and were well-populated. Some areas beyond the mountains, the land east of the Sea of Galilee for instance, are quite fertile too, before they merge into the desert which borders the region to the east and south.

The native villagers were technically serfs, being tied to the land, unable in ordinary circumstances to leave or alienate their shares in the arable fields. Each village seems to have been run by a council of elders presided over by a headman whom the Europeans called a *ra'is*, a common Arabic title for one with authority over a community, who acted as intermediary between government and governed. His office carried with it more land and a larger house than the other villagers had, and he presided over the agricultural decision made by the community as a whole, levied the returns owed by villagers to the lord and was almost certainly the community judge. A village of this type consisted generally of an inhabited nucleus, a knot of houses huddled together, with a cistern, perhaps a mill, an oven and threshing-floors, around which were vineyards, gardens and olive-groves held in personal possession by the villagers. Beyond were the arable lands, which were communally farmed and often stretched so far that abandoned settlements some distance away were occupied for a few weeks each year to work the fields around them. In certain regions, at least, a two-year crop rotation was practised, the fields being divided into those sown in mid-November with wheat or barley and those which were partly left fallow until sown in the following spring with a summer crop like sesame and partly given over to vegetable cultivation. The harvest was threshed on the village threshing-floors before it was divided into piles of grain, of which each family had a share, expressed in terms of a fraction of the village lands. Before the division took place, of course, the lord's share was subtracted, to be sub-divided itself if the village had several lords. This was the ancient Muslim tax of *kharaj* which usually amounted to one-third or one-quarter of the arable crop and one-half or one-quarter of the produce of vineyards, olive-groves and orchards; to it was added a poll tax on Muslims and Jews, a 'personal gift', again very ancient, called *mu'na*, a charge on those who owned goats, sheep and bees, and various minor impositions. It was quite common for these duties to be combined and commuted for a cash payment, but it was also common for them to be paid in kind, which is why one can still occasionally see in the countryside the ruins of great barns in which the returns from several villages could be stored.

There were also villages of western European peasants, whose settlements were strikingly different in appearance and were very similar to western *villeneuves*: instead of a formless huddle of houses one would come across a planned development along a street, with a tower, courthouse and Latin church. At Qubeiba there are still the foundations of very superior stone houses of two storeys, each with an elaborate cistern. The settlers came from all over Europe: at Bet Guvrin in the mid-twelfth century, for instance, one can identify among them men from France, the empire, Italy and Catalonia, attracted by generous terms. Each colonist received a reasonably large parcel of land to cultivate, which he was free to alienate if he wished. The returns he paid were not burdensome – 10 per cent together with certain other dues at one settlement – and were treated as rent. His community had its own system of justice. As in the West, it was presided over by an official called a *dispensator* or *locator*, who combined the responsibilities of president of the court and agent of the lord in the advertising and disposal of shares in the settlement. All the *villeneuves* which have been identified were established in the twelfth century and the movement must have run out of steam in the thirteenth as the territories under Christian control diminished. But some of the old communities survived and one *dispensator* was still active around 1200.

Whether indigenous or immigrant, one feature of the village economy was significantly different from that in western Europe. There was very little demesne land, the home farm which in the West involved a lord in the agriculture of his village and on which the peasants performed labour services for him. In the East demesne land was generally only to be found in the gardens and sugar-cane plantations that lined the coast; and very few villages were coastal. One consequence was that the villagers owed little in the way of labour services – usually not more than one day a week – and in many areas this seems to have consisted of transporting the lord's share of the harvest to collection centres, together with some work on roads and aqueducts. Another was that there was very little reason for a lord to involve himself directly in the agriculture of his villages since his chief concern would only be to get his due share of the crop. On the whole, therefore, landlords do not seem to have resided in the countryside – only a very few buildings have been identified as 'manor houses' and these may well have had other purposes – and the feudatories tended to congregate in the towns, where so many of them anyway enjoyed money fiefs.

The region, in fact, was one in which there was still a flourishing urban life. Its hinterland contained great cities, Damascus and Aleppo, for which the coastal ports in Christian hands were necessary outlets. Its own products, especially sugar, were in demand throughout the Mediterranean region and beyond. It straddled a major trade route to the Far East. It was to the towns that most of the Europeans came: of c. 140,000 Latins resident in Palestine, c. 120,000 lived in the towns, the majority being burgess freemen. These burgesses, members of a class which included the Europeans in the colonial villages as well as those in the towns, paid rent rather than servile dues for their properties, called *borgesies*, which they had the right to buy and sell; cases concerning them were subject to their own courts, the *Cours des Bourgeois*. They were not vassals and therefore were not tied by feudal obligations. They were subject to public law, the *assises des Bourgeois*, which varied a good deal from place to place: in fact each settlement had its own. Only two collections of these laws has survived, one from Antioch, which is incomplete and one from Acre, where there was the largest burgess community. The latter has been dated to the early 1240s by Professor Prawer, who has shown that it was strongly influenced by a Provençal treatise on Roman law which had a wide diffusion in Europe.

In spite of the early attempts to drive away Muslims and Jews there were also substantial indigenous communities in many towns, not only of proletariat but also of shopkeepers, merchants and artisans. In the twelfth century, the dyeworks at six towns were in Jewish hands, although the most famous, those at Tyre, were owned by Syrians. Jews played a part in the great glass industry at Tyre and engaged in trade as money-lenders and ship-masters: at Tyre they had sea-going vessels. There were also Muslim sea-captains: a safe-conduct from a king of Jerusalem for one trading between Egypt and Tyre has survived. In the thirteenth century there was an important Syrian trading community in Tyre. The most impressive evidence for indigenous participation in trade concerns a company which successfully appealed to Genoa in 1268 for compensation for a ship taken by the commune's fleet off the Cilician coast five years earlier. The city government of Genoa agreed to pay damages of 14,900 Genoese pounds. Partners in the enterprise, which seems to have been organized from

Mosul, deep in Islamic territory, were twenty-three men, all indigenous, of which six resided in Ayas (Yumurtalik) in Cilician Armenia, five in Antioch, two in Tyre and six in Acre. One of them was the burgess convert or Maronite Saliba, referred to in the last chapter. He was obviously quite prosperous: his will revealed that he had 1,275 Saracen besants invested in property and 1,156 Saracen besants and 10 royal pounds of Acre in cash. But he must have had more since he left the residue of his estate, for obvious reasons not itemized, to the Hospitallers, and one of his daughters, to whom he had left nothing, sued them for it.

Administration

Throughout history conquerors have adapted rather than destroyed the institutions in the territories they have conquered. The crusaders took over a region accustomed to fairly advanced government. Since most of the native population stayed to live under their rule it is not surprising that outlines of the previous administration remained in place, if occasionally altered to suit the westerners' preconceptions and requirements. Syria and Palestine had been Roman and Byzantine before falling to the Muslims. Much of northern Syria had, in fact, been Byzantine until recently and the survival of the Byzantine system there is evidenced by the appearance under the Latins of dukes, praetors and judges, the administrators of the late eleventh-century themes or provinces, although the rôle of the Antiochene dukes was very similar to that of the viscounts in the kingdom of Jerusalem who presided over burgess justice. Elsewhere the changes over the centuries had been less drastic than one might suppose. The basic Roman unit of administration had been the *civitas* – a city with the territory run from it – and several *civitates* had been combined to form the Roman province, of which there had been seven in the region. Roman provinces had become, with some changes, Muslim *junds*, and in a description of them as late as 985 some of the outlines of the old Roman provincial system can still be discerned. The stability of administrative boundaries can be illustrated with examples from Latin Palestine. The lordship of Caesarea exactly corresponded to the *civitas* of Caesarea on the eve of the Muslim invasions and must have survived as an entity. The same is probably true of the lordships of Ascalon and Arsuf, while the Palestinian boundaries of the principality of Galilee more or less corresponded to the borders of the Roman province of Palaestina Secunda.

Mediating between the new Latin lords and the villagers there were two officials whose offices, in one case certainly, in the other probably, predated the conquest and suggest that organs of Muslim local government had survived. One of these officials was called a scribe (*scriba*), an accurate translation of the Arabic *katib*, the officer in Muslim treasury departments. He was responsible for the collection of revenues, which were mostly

traditional ones, and the overseeing of property boundaries. A high proportion of those whose names are known to us – 14, perhaps 16, out of 25 –
were indigenous, but among them were a group called *scribani* who appear
to have held their offices in fief; perhaps here too there are parallels with
the Muslim *daman* or tax-farm. The second official was called a *dragoman*,
or *interpres*, which confirms that his name was a corruption of the Arabic
tarjuman (interpreter). He may have been descended from the Muslim
mutarjim, an assistant of the Muslim judge in his dealings with the many
peoples under Muslim rule, and it looks as though his responsibilities were
judicial. In lay fiefs the dragomanate was usually held, like the scribanage,
in fief as a sergeantry.

In the towns too the old taxes and returns continued to be levied,
including a tax in Tyre paid by pork butchers, which must have been a
survival of a Muslim tax on the purveyors of unclean meat. Again, it is not
surprising to find scribes very much in evidence, operating particularly at
the gates, the harbour (in the case of a port) and the markets, where goods
were registered for taxation or taxation was levied. The gates and the
harbour were, of course, points of entry or departure. Goods being ex-
ported were charged an exit tax. Imported goods seem to have been only
registered for taxation, since the entry tax was combined with the sales tax
and levied in the markets. The harbour office (known in Acre as the
Chaine, from the chain that could be raised to close the harbour entrance)
also ran the port and imposed an anchorage tax and a capitation levy on the
crew and passengers in a ship, which in a pilgrim port must have been
profitable. The markets were of various types. Some, such as those in
which products like meat, fish and leather were sold for domestic use, were
independently run, but in large towns the chief markets involved in international trade were administered collectively by an office called the *Fonde*.
In them the goods were weighed by official measurers and the duties were
taken after sale in one of two ways: either, when man-to-man bargains
were being struck by the merchants, charges were levied on the goods'
official value after consulting price lists which were regularly brought up to
date; or there were public auctions conducted by official auctioneers, after
which the duty was taken before the proceeds were divided among the
sellers. Most of these taxes were *ad valorem* – only wine, oil and grain seem
to have been taxed according to quantity – and in Acre the percentages
varied from just over 4 per cent to 25 per cent.

The procedures were typical of Byzantine and Muslim practice and
underline the continuity between the old and new systems. The offices
responsible had sophisticated accounting methods. They not only collected
the taxes but also paid out annual sums in money fiefs and rents to those
individuals granted them by the king or lords. It was even possible for a
man who held a money fief to create rear-fiefs or make alms grants out of

his income, which were paid on his behalf by the office involved. The offices made returns to central and local treasuries, known as *Secretes*, of which the most important was the *Grant Secrete* of the kingdom, an office of record, registration and revenue supervision and collection, which was so like the Muslim central treasury, the *bait* or *diwan al-Mal*, that it was given this name by Muslim contemporaries.

So the old Islamic system continued to function. It was not left un-altered, however; partly, it seems, because the westerners did not come to terms with the fact that in Byzantium and Islam justice and finance were separately administered. In the West these were usually conjoined and it is not surprising to find the European settlers giving at least two of the revenue offices, the *Chaine* and the *Fonde*, additional judicial functions. The *Chaine* in Acre was from at least the mid-twelfth century also a maritime court, concerning itself with the law of the seas and mercantile cases, although all major matters – those involving claims of more than one silver mark – went to the *Cour des Bourgeois*. The *Fonde* also dealt with minor cases of commerce and debt, but in Acre the four native and two Latin jurors, under the presidency of a *bailli*, were also a court for the indigenous. The same concern to reconcile what were irreconcilable western and eastern systems was shown in measures taken to create native courts. In most towns, though not as we have seen in Acre, a special court, the *Cour des Syriens*, was created under the presidency of a *ra'is*, usually a native-born Catholic, to judge minor matters 'according to the customs of the Syrians'. But the establishment of this court, which did not replace the tribunals of the qadis and rabbis but co-existed with them, must have made litigation very confusing for the plaintiffs, because the settlers had imposed a distinction between 'temporal' cases, decided by the *Cours des Syriens*, and 'spiritual' cases, decided by the religious tribunals, which did not exist in Islam or Judaism, but was in accordance with western Christian practice.

Cours des Bourgeois bound the non-feudal judicial system together in the same way as the *Secretes* bound the financial. All major cases concerning men and women who were not vassals went to them, and the minor courts, the *Chaine*, the *Fonde* and even the *Cour des Syriens*, may simply have held preliminary hearings before they were transferred. A *Cour des Bourgeois* was established in every place where there was a European population of a reasonable size. It was a public court with full rights of jurisdiction, including High Justice, the ability to impose the death penalty, over all the non-feudal population and in all issues concerning property held by burgess tenure. It judged according to its own local law. It was presided over by an official appointed by the king, or a lord in his lordship, most commonly called a viscount, who also had police duties, and its decisions were made by burgess jurors; in Acre there were twelve, all men of some standing in the town.

So far we have considered the adaptation of an ancient and fairly sophisticated system to cope with an influx of free European settlers. But just as important were the effects of the super-imposition of feudalism. This process began during Godfrey of Bouillon's one-year reign. Godfrey seems to have kept a tight control over the conquest. It has been suggested that this was a free-for-all and that the existence of allods, free-hold properties, in Latin Palestine is evidence for that. But there is, in fact, no evidence for allods at all; and, although there was certainly some uncontrolled land-grabbing as the crusaders marched on Jerusalem in June 1099, this ended once Godfrey had been elected ruler. Godfrey's own resources were not large enough for him to carry alone the burden of defending what had been taken. We have already seen that Ramle, the key point on the road from the sea to Jerusalem, was held by a bishop. Godfrey granted out two areas, Hebron/Jericho and Galilee, in fief and he may have created a third fief around Nablus. He had, moreover, promised to make a fourth at Haifa before he died. He also began the practice of granting money fiefs. So there is no question but that the feudal system was being imposed on Palestine from the start. The reasons for it are obvious. The number of crusaders who remained in the East were few and Godfrey's household was fully stretched administering Jerusalem and the tongue of land extending from it to the coast. He needed the support and collaboration of individuals who had men at their disposal or were rich enough to recruit them. Tancred, who was put in charge of Galilee, and Galdemar Carpenel, who was given the stretch of south-eastern frontier from Hebron to Jericho, were collaborators with Godfrey in the defence of the settlement, but they naturally needed freedom to reward their own men and provide themselves with secure bases. Only the granting of the territories to them in fief would give them this. The sequence of events is clear in the case of Galilee. Tancred seems originally to have been given the castellany, that is to say an office, not a lordship, of Tiberias, the chief town, but he ran into difficulties trying to extend Christian control east of the Sea of Galilee; a few months later Tiberias (in other words Galilee) was reconstituted as a fief. It is clear that these great fief-holders were permitted considerable latitude in the decisions they made with regard to war with their Muslim neighbours and in the disposal of properties within their territories. This was to be expected since there were few initiatives Godfrey could have taken outside his own domain, where his hands were full enough. There already existed in western Europe precedents for this in the marches in Germany, Spain and Britain, the lords of which always had a more privileged position than fief-holders in more peaceful areas.

We are approaching an explanation of one of the puzzles of the history of the Latin East. The crusaders had conquered an area long subject to centralized government with fairly sophisticated bureaucratic instruments, even if these had recently been disrupted. Under the western Europeans the instruments of government survived, but the state was fragmented. This was less apparent in Antioch, where some sort of provincial system seems to have been imposed, partly because the demesne of the prince was relatively large and comprised all the greater towns. But in the kingdom of Jerusalem the great lordships became palatinates, free of royal control in day-to-day affairs, in which the lords could administer full justice in their seigneurial and public courts with hardly any reservation of cases to the crown. The kings were powerless to intervene as long as feudal services were not threatened. And the lords could conduct their own foreign policy, making peace or war with their Muslim neighbours without reference to the central government. The archives and therefore most of the original charters of the nobles have not survived, but these great privileges for them were in evidence by the late twelfth century. It has been argued that they were gradually accumulated as the nobility stabilized and gained in power from c. 1130 onwards, but there is in fact some slight evidence – references to the title *princeps*, the existence of *Cours des Bourgeois* in their hands, their free-ranging activities with regard to neighbouring Muslims – to suggest that they were enjoyed from the first. It has also been supposed that the settlers, coming on the whole from a decentralized feudal state like France, simply brought with them their understanding of a natural order of things. But contemporaries clearly understood the advantages of centralized government, as the aspirations and performances of the Normans in England and Sicily show. It is much more likely that in a frontier region the only system that was thought to be workable was that of marcher lordships and that this was established at the beginning, when the rulers would anyway have been hard-pressed to find any other solution to their problems.

The workings of feudal law reinforce the image of a frontier feudal society. Among the services required from fief-holders, of course, was military service. In Europe it became common for this to be commuted for money payments, known in England as scutage. Only one example of scutage survives – it is from the county of Tripoli – and there is no evidence that the kings of Jerusalem ever allowed it, in a region, significantly, where the commutation of village-returns for money was common. The kings had, moreover, the right to demand of female fief-holders aged between twelve and sixty the 'service' of marriage, so that suitable men could perform knight's service for their fiefs. It is clear that military service was a precious commodity and its performance could not be done away with. On the other hand, feudal incidents, which assumed such importance in the West, were rarely to be found in the East. There is no evidence for payments of relief, the sums of money rendered to the lord on entry into a feudal inheritance. The lords, including the king, appear to have had no control over inheritance; the customs concerning it were extremely complex and were treated in the finest detail in the lawbooks written in thirteenth-century Palestine. Nor did they, in the kingdom of Jerusalem, have the right to wardship of minors. Obviously nothing was to be allowed to discourage potential fief-holders from taking over their tenancies and the obligations that went with them. When considered alongside early legislation to ensure that fiefs were occupied and not held *in absentia* by heirs living in the West, we can perceive an isolated society, worried about the numbers of fief-holders and concerned to see that fiefs were occupied and military services performed in all circumstances.

The crown and the lords

If, as seems very likely, the kingdom of Jerusalem was fragmented from the start into independent principalities, the lords of which were royal vassals but otherwise exercised full authority as marcher barons in their lordships, the prevailing notion of a pushing, constitutionally strong monarchy in the first two-thirds of the twelfth century cannot be upheld. One of the chief props of the argument for a strong crown, moreover, has been recently shown to be extremely rickety. A law, probably dating from the reign of Baldwin II (1118–31), which was supposed to have given the king the power to disinherit vassals without formal trial in a wide range of cases, was actually, it is now suggested, merely establishing fixed penalties for felonies which would have been subject to trial in the ordinary way. Far from freeing the king from the burdensome need to hear a case formally in his feudal court, it actually presupposed that even open treason would be subject to the ordinary processes of law, which in a case involving the king as lord and his vassal meant the decision of his other vassals advising him in his High Court.

The kings, in fact, presided over what might be called a confederation of lordships in which the ties binding lords to them were not uniform. In the far north, Antioch was legally independent, being a vassal-state not of Jerusalem but of Constantinople. That is not to say that the kings had no authority there. Baldwin I established himself as the arbiter of the affairs of all the Latin East by his intervention in a succession dispute which followed the death of Raymond of St Gilles on 28 February 1105. Raymond's successor in the new county of Tripoli was his cousin William Jordan, Count of Cerdagne, but at the beginning of March 1109 his son, Bertrand of St Gilles, arrived from France with a large army to claim his father's estate. William Jordan called for the support of Tancred, who was now prince of Antioch. In his turn Bertrand appealed to Baldwin, who summoned Tancred in the name of the Church of Jerusalem to treat with him not only on the future of Tripoli, but also on complaints made by the Count of Edessa, against whom Tancred had already been involved in war.

Tancred agreed to recognize the integrity of the county of Edessa in return for the grant of an enormous fief in the kingdom of Jerusalem, comprising all of Galilee, which he had once held, and Haifa, together with proprietary rights over the Temple in Jerusalem. As far as Raymond of St Gilles's territories were concerned, William Jordan was to keep the northern part, consisting of 'Arqah and Tartus, and was to become Tancred's vassal, while Bertrand was to hold Tripoli itself and the region around and was to become Baldwin's vassal. William Jordan died soon afterwards and Bertrand extended his rule over the territory ceded to his cousin. This dispute and its resolution highlighted problems that were always to dog the Latin settlements, since the needs of adequate government and defence in these frontier regions were so acute that the claims of the heir 'apparent', an individual present in person and ready to take over at once, weighed heavily and often in derogation of the legitimate rights of a nearer heir who happened to be in Europe. But it also demonstrated the prestige of the crown of Jerusalem which even the ruler of Antioch, who was not a vassal, could not ignore.

In fact, as long as the princes of Antioch were in conflict with their legitimate overlords, the Byzantine emperors, they would be forced to treat Jerusalem's claims to paramountcy seriously. And Baldwin I was prepared to commit the military resources of the south to the defence of the north in 1110, 1111 and 1115, while the rulers of Antioch and Tripoli in their turn joined him in the defence of Palestine in 1113. No sooner had Baldwin II come to the throne than he had to hurry north to take the regency of Antioch in the name of Bohemond II, the infant son of Bohemond of Taranto, after the disaster that overtook the forces of the principality at the Battle of the Field of Blood in June 1119. His regency lasted for seven years and every year from 1120 to 1123, when he was taken prisoner by Belek of Aleppo, and again in 1124–5 after his release from gaol, and in 1126, he had to campaign in the north, although his withdrawal of armies from Palestine was not popular with his Jerusalemite vassals. He had to intervene in Antioch again in 1130 after Bohemond II's death, and his successor Fulk did so in 1131–2 and 1133. In 1149 Baldwin III had to rush to the north to save the principality and what by then was left of the county of Edessa after another military disaster. He went again in 1150, 1152, 1157 and 1158. These visits were, of course, those of a paramount chief, the head of a confederation, not those of a suzerain.

On the other hand, Edessa and Tripoli were vassal-states, although both had been founded independently of the crown of Jerusalem. In the case of Edessa, the first two counts became kings and ensured the homage of their successors; in the case of Tripoli, homage was given in consequence of Baldwin I's arbitration in the succession dispute of 1109, although Count Pons (1112–37) made determined efforts to break free. Lordship gave the kings rights and obligations in both counties – for instance King Amalric was regent of Tripoli for ten years while the Count was a prisoner of the Muslims – but the circumstances of the establishment of these settlements gave them a large measure of independence. They were not generally regarded as constituent parts of the kingdom, at least in the twelfth century, and it seems that in them the king of Jerusalem was treated as the personal feudal overlord of the counts rather than as king.

The kingdom of Jerusalem proper began at the Nahr el Mu'almetein, just north of Beirut. South of that the lordships were palatinates, as has already been stated. Quite apart from the independence this gave them, the king was extraordinarily dependent on them. Since he had no public courts and therefore no apparatus of public justice outside the royal domain, he could only reach the bulk of his subjects through the mediation of his greater vassals, to whom he had legal obligations in consequence of the feudal contracts between him and them. In particular he had the duty to maintain them in their fiefs unless it could be proved in his court that they had failed in their obligations to him. This court, the High Court, combined the functions of a court for the whole kingdom – although on occasions of national importance it was the nucleus of a much larger gathering, a *parlement* attended by the representatives of other interests in the kingdom – and a seigneurial court of the royal domain. The feudal obligations of the crown meant that power legitimately rested with this body and a result was that constitutional development was stifled: although general taxes were levied by *parlements* in 1166 and 1183 there never developed, as there did in the West, a regular system of national taxation by consent and therefore no Third Estate. The king's central government, superimposed over the sophisticated Arabic bureaucracy, remained primitive, consisting of great officers with traditional titles, seneschal, constable, marshal, butler, chamberlain and chancellor, although in the case of the seneschal, who controlled the *Grant Secrete*, the department concerned was anything but conventional in western terms.

The power of the lords was reinforced by the nature of the feudal system and by developments in feudal society in the twelfth century. In a community in which money fiefs were prevalent, because of the availability of cash-revenues and commutations, it was common for fiefs to be composite rather than uniform in make-up. For instance, only one of the twenty-seven fiefs listed in the lordship of Arsuf in 1261 was held entirely in land and only one other was a pure money fief; the rest were made up of various combinations of money, produce, rations, land and the profits of offices. Similarly, in 1243 a fief-holder near Tyre had three villages and one-third of the revenues of another, two gardens and some land near the city and in Tyre itself a house, an oven and a rent of 60 besants a year. The great fiefs were also composite. Arsuf, which was one of the smaller of them, extended over the coastal plain of southern Palestine from the el 'Auja' river in the south to the Wadi Faliq in the north and reached inland to the foothills of Samaria, but outside it the lord also had lands in the royal domain near Nablus and a house and probably money fiefs in Acre. A large fief built up for the king's uncle in the early 1180s – the only lordship for which we have many of the foundation charters – was a collection of lands and castles in northern Galilee and rents in Acre and Tyre. This diversification of assets gave the magnates some financial stability and helped them to survive the territorial losses of the late 1180s. They were also assisted by the operation of certain laws. One forbade the tenant of a fief owing the service of several knights to subinfeudate a larger proportion of it than he retained himself. The thirteenth-century jurists could not agree whether the value of all rear-fiefs combined should amount to less than half the total value of the fief or whether a lord had simply to hold in his own hands more than the greatest of his vassals. But at any rate this law did mean that seigneurial domains could not be dissipated by alienation and it was supplemented by the custom of allowing what was called *service de compaignons*, by which a fief-holder raised a troop of mercenaries in place of vassals. The expenses of the feudal lords must have been crippling – most of the castles, after all, were in their hands – but after an early period marked by instability and waves of immigrants, in which fiefs rapidly changed hands, the greater lordships settled into the possession of families which held them for several generations. After c. 1130 succession became regular, genealogies became continuous and clear and there began a process of consolidation through marriage and inheritance of the great fiefs into the hands of a few families. By the third quarter of the twelfth century no more than ten families held the twenty-four most important lordships. Stability manifested itself in a consciousness of class and in the gradual whittling away of the prerogatives the kings had enjoyed in the early decades, when their regalian rights had been as follows. Their court had reserved for itself the right to judge minors who were accused of theft and rear-vassals who were accused of stealing from another lord. They could summon a *levée en masse* of all subjects in a moment of crisis. They could legislate, had a large say in the appointment of bishops, alone could mint coins, levy shipwreck and exploit international trading ports and the roads from them into the interior. They perhaps had control of the highways. But already by the time of Baldwin II only the rights of minting and the control of ports and their communications were mentioned as royal prerogatives. And within a few decades even these were challenged: the lords of Haifa and Caesarea were developing their ports; and it is possible that before 1187 the lords of Transjordan and Sidon had begun to mint their own coins. Shipwreck was formally surrendered by King Amalric in the 1160s and by the thirteenth century the magnates seem to have usurped whatever rights the kings had had over their highways.

It would be wrong to think of the twelfth-century kings as powerless. They *were* kings, first of all, and kingship implied more than feudal over-lordship: whatever the realities it suggested a ministry for God, symbolically conveyed through the use of vestments and regalia, a public authority relating to all subjects, whether vassals or not. These kings, moreover, were the possessors of the holiest city in Christendom and sat on the throne of David. This gave them immense prestige. And they were autonomous. Papal approval was sought and given for Baldwin I's assumption of the crown in 1100, but in no sense was Jerusalem a vassal-state of the papacy; and although it is almost certain that in 1171, during a crisis that followed the collapse of his ambitious plans to conquer Egypt, Amalric acknowledged the overlordship of the Byzantine emperor, this meant nothing in practice. The kings were also richer than their vassals. The royal domain was vast in comparison to the fiefs. It consisted of Jerusalem, Acre and Tyre, with the lands around them, and at times it also encompassed Ascalon and Jaffa, Samaria, Beirut, Hebron and Blanchegarde (Tel es Safi), although these were also sometimes apanages, sometimes independent fiefs, and Deir el Balah (Darum). The city of Jerusalem, which had nothing in economic and little in strategic terms to commend it, gave them prestige; Acre and Tyre gave them wealth through the taxes that could be levied on trade. Being richer than their vassals, the kings could always buy mercenaries to supplement their armies and this gave them a certain independence of their subjects, since they were not completely reliant on their services, however important these might be. They could also make great use of money fiefs and therefore could have a large number of direct vassals. This gave them patronage and political power: during the succession crisis of 1186, one claimant, who had pos-session of most of the royal domain and the support of some important magnates, had at her disposal nearly half the feudal knights in the kingdom. As we shall see, they were less affected by the disasters of the late 1180s than their vassals, because the rising prosperity of the ports of Acre and Tyre – a consequence of a change in the Asiatic trade routes which will be described below – led to growing profits that could offset the territorial losses.

Looking at the Latin East at this time, moreover, one clearly discerns a type of society, rapidly disappearing in the West, which depended crucially on a king's personal vigour and military skill. In this exposed frontier region his power as an individual to change events was great and his political position still rested on old-fashioned virtues like military leadership. Baldwin I was a tough personality, a conqueror whose attitude to the granting of fiefs and to the Church was dominated by self-interest. He had ruthlessly exploited the county of Edessa for his own ends and for those of the First Crusade. He greatly extended the area left him by

Godfrey of Bouillon and his prestige was such that he was recognized throughout the Latin East as paramount ruler. But he was probably homosexual and in spite of three marriages, one bigamous and all apparently entered into for material gain, he had no children. His death on 2 April 1118 threw the kingdom into a second succession crisis. His elder brother Eustace of Boulogne was in Europe; his cousin Baldwin of Le Bourcq, the count of Edessa, arrived in Jerusalem on the day of the king's burial. It was decided to send an embassy to Europe to offer Eustace the succession by right of blood, but after the delegation, composed of Eustace's partisans, had left, a meeting of magnates, orchestrated by Joscelin of Courtenay who was to succeed to Edessa, elected Baldwin, who was anointed on 14 April. Eustace was reluctant to travel East and withdrew from the contest when he heard of this. The new king was a nicer man than his predecessor. He was genuinely pious and he was happily married. He was an active and responsible leader of men. But he does not seem to have been very popular and his reign was never a secure one. It was haunted by the problem of succession because he sired only daughters. The nobility of Jerusalem showed discontent at his intervention in Antioch after the catastrophe of the Field of Blood. The Council of Nablus marked, as we have seen, a surrender by him to the Church. In 1122 he had to use force to make Count Pons of Tripoli recognize his overlordship. While he was held prisoner by the Muslims a party in the kingdom may even have offered the crown to Count Charles of Flanders. He probably had to face a revolt from the lord of Transjordan and towards the end of his reign he was in conflict with the patriarch of Jerusalem, who made vast claims on the basis of the promises to Daimbert supposedly made by Godfrey of Bouillon, demanding the town of Jaffa for the patriarchate immediately and the city of Jerusalem itself once Ascalon was conquered. The crown looks as if it was on the defensive.

He did what he could to assure a peaceful succession. Late in 1127 or early in 1128 an embassy was sent to France to find a husband for his eldest daughter Melisende. It landed a great catch, Count Fulk V of Anjou, to whom was promised not only Melisende's hand but also the kingship after Baldwin's death. Fulk came out in 1129 and faithfully served Baldwin until the latter's death on 21 April 1131. By that time a son had been born of the marriage and Professor Mayer has suggested that, no doubt to ensure his inheritance, almost the king's last act was to alter the conditions of future government slightly by conferring the royal power jointly on the three persons involved, Fulk, Melisende and her baby son, another Baldwin. Fulk died in 1143, but the queen remained dominant even after Baldwin III came of age in 1145 and the young king was pushed more and more on to the periphery until he asserted himself in the spring of 1152. He demanded that the kingdom be formally divided with his mother, who in 1150 may even have prevented her own vassals obeying his summons to service in northern Syria; and he then questioned the way the division had been made and moved swiftly to occupy his mother's territories. By the late spring he was in control and his mother was confined to dower land round Nablus. Once in charge he answered an appeal from the north, where the Muslims had taken Tartus. The town was liberated and an assembly of nobles from the kingdom, the county of Tripoli and the principality of Antioch met in Tripoli. This did not accomplish its chief purpose, to persuade Constance, the heiress of Antioch, to marry, but it attested to the young king's strength, not least because he had been able to summon his vassals to a general assembly outside the borders of the kingdom. He proved himself to be another clever and vigorous king, under whom the final coastal conquest, of Ascalon, was made, but he died young, on 10 February 1163, before he had time to complete ambitious plans which included perhaps an alliance of all the Christian powers in the eastern Mediterranean region to conquer Egypt.

He was succeeded by his brother Amalric, who was as able and certainly as energetic. The most striking feature of Amalric's reign, the attempt to take Egypt, will be considered below. But he also tried to find a solution to the main legal impediment to royal control, the impenetrable thickets of privilege which surrounded the great fiefs and shielded them from intervention. His most important legal act, the issuing of a law entitled the *assise sur la ligece*, was a response to a crisis in his predecessor's reign. Gerard, lord of Sidon, had dispossessed one of his vassals of his rear-fief without a judgement in his seigneurial court. King Baldwin had taken steps to redress the vassal's grievance; Gerard had been forced to submit, return the fief and compensate his vassal for the damage done. Now, at a solemn meeting of the High Court, Amalric decreed that in future all rear-vassals were to make liege homage to the king, in addition to the simple homage they made to their own lords, and that the king had the right to demand oaths of fealty from freemen in any fief held in-chief from him. It is true that in the long run this *assise* encouraged solidarity among the feudatories, since those who had made liege homage to the king, great lords and rear-vassals alike, were peers of one another, bound to each other by the common oaths they had taken, and that this solidarity found expression in the use of the *assise* against the crown itself in ways that Amalric could never have envisaged. But at the time the *assise* was an expression of royal strength. In theory the king could now call on the support of rear-vassals if their lord was in conflict with him: after forty days they were bound to come over to his side if their lord was in revolt or was plotting against him or had refused to stand trial in the High Court, on condition that he restored their fiefs to them within another forty days. More important than this, a formal channel of communication to the king was opened, since a rear-vassal was now a member of the High Court itself and could raise an issue of injustice in a lordship directly with the king. Everywhere in Christendom royal jurisdiction tended to operate only at the initiative of plaintiffs and it followed that kings could only realize their potential when they ruled a state in which ordinary men and women could easily take their cases to royal judges through an apparatus of provincial courts. In Jerusalem this was impossible, for the great fiefs were jurisdictionally autonomous and there were no royal courts outside the royal domain. So Amalric took the only action open to him; he made it possible for cases to be brought out of fiefs by plaintiffs and presented to him. Presumably through the oaths of fealty he envisaged similar channels of communication for non-feudal freemen.

But like many strong kings Amalric left his successor a bitter legacy. He had been married to Agnes of Courtenay, the daughter of the last Count of Edessa, and by her he had had two children, Sibylla and Baldwin. On his accession he was persuaded to have this marriage annulled on the grounds of consanguinity and he later married Maria Comnena, the great-niece of the Byzantine emperor. By her he had another daughter, Isabella. There is some evidence that in his reign opinions among the nobility and at court began to polarize between those who sympathized with Agnes and those who supported the king or were building careers under him and his Greek wife, among whom must be included the great historian William, Archbishop of Tyre. On Amalric's death on 11 July 1174 the two sides began to stake out their positions. The new king, Baldwin IV, was a minor. Of the two men entrusted by Amalric with the regency for, and custody of, his son, one was assassinated, the other put aside, and Count Raymond III of Tripoli, Baldwin's nearest adult relative of the royal line, assumed the regency until the king came of age in 1177. Baldwin naturally favoured his mother's adherents and in fact created a great fief for his uncle, Joscelin III of Courtenay, in northern Galilee. Those close to Maria Comnena and many of those associated with the last years of Amalric's rule found themselves deprived of power and influence. But the new king himself was already known to have contracted leprosy. He was assured only of a short life, punctuated by periods of prostrating illness, during which lieutenants would have to be found to rule for him. He was certain to have no children.

In 1176 his sister Sibylla married William of Montferrat in what was the best match yet made by a member of the royal house, because William was related to the German emperors and the French kings. He died in the following year, but left Sibylla with a son, the future Baldwin V. This child, however, was himself sickly. In these circumstances the parties which had already come into existence gathered behind the two heiresses to the throne, Agnes of Courtenay's daughter Sibylla and Maria Comnena's daughter Isabella. The king tended to favour Sibylla and her second husband, Guy of Lusignan, until 1183 when, deeply hurt by Guy's grudging attitude to his desire for adequate revenues while Guy held the lieutenancy on his behalf, and encouraged by Guy's political opponents who were clearly determined to destroy him, he removed Guy from the lieutenancy. He then crowned Baldwin V as his co-ruler, thus passing over Sibylla's rights, gave Raymond of Tripoli the lieutenancy with the expectation of the regency after his own death and sent an extraordinary embassy to the West under the patriarch of Jerusalem which went so far as to offer the over-lordship of the kingdom to the kings of France and England. The king even agreed to a proposal that in the event of his nephew Baldwin V's early demise the pope, the western emperor and the kings of France and Eng-land should decide which of his two sisters was to have the throne; he seems to have had such a hatred of Guy of Lusignan that he even allowed his sister's, and therefore his own, legitimacy to be questioned.

Baldwin IV died in March 1185 and Baldwin V in August 1186. The kingdom, which had always badly needed the rule of strong personalities, had been subjected to twelve years of ineffective government. And it was now split over the claims of the two half-sisters, each with her own party of supporters, precisely at the moment when the Muslims were stronger and more united than they had ever been. To understand this we must look back at the military history of the Christians and Muslims during the previous eighty years.

The defence of the settlements

In frontier societies of this kind the chief attribute required of a ruler was that of war-leader. Life in the Latin settlements was bound to be dominated by military necessity. The Latin occupation of the region does not seem to have been governed by any high strategic principles. Occupation proceeded piecemeal as the opportunity arose for land, or control of a trade route from which tolls could be collected. Effective authority over a district depended on the possession of castles or walled towns from which it could be administered and defended. This factor, and the chronic shortage of manpower, which demanded fortifications so strong that they could be garrisoned with comparatively small bodies of men, led to remarkable programmes of castle-building, the relics of which can still be seen. The countryside was dotted with stone castles of every size, from fortified halls and simple towers, often surrounded by single outer walls, and ridge-top fortresses with large walled enclosures attached to them in which the local inhabitants and their livestock could take refuge, to town citadels and advanced concentric castles, the costs of construction of which have already been mentioned. If faced by counter-invasion, the first objective of which would be to take these strong points, it was important to have an army in the field which could threaten the invader, particularly if he decided to lay siege to one of them. In the same way a long-term aim could be gradually realized by hemming in the approaches to some important goal, such as Aleppo or Ascalon, with fortlets that kept up pressure on its defenders. So the Latin occupation and the Muslim counter-attack were characterized by the occupation of strong points and the building or improvement of fortifications. The haphazard nature of this process can be illustrated by reference to any atlas. Edessa was taken early on, which accounts for this eastern salient to the north of the settlements. By 1153 the whole coast as far south as Deir el Balah had been occupied, but inland the rift valley marked by the rivers Orontes, Litani and Jordan had only been crossed in certain places, particularly the approaches to Aleppo in the north and the great fief of Transjordan in the south, which reached down to the Gulf of 'Aqaba. Elsewhere the settlement was confined to the land along the coast and the absence of any strategic thinking is shown by the fact that all attempts to prove that the Latins had a coherent system of frontier defence have failed: some important passes through the mountain chain to the coastal plain, such as in the neighbourhood of Jisr esh Shughur and around Crac des Chevaliers, contained an unusually large number of castles, but others, like the main routes from Damascus to Tyre and Acre, were for most of the time lightly defended.

For the defence of its territory and for the acquisition of new regions, which was bound to involve siege-works, always a very expensive form of warfare, the Latins were dependent on resources which were never adequate. An incomplete list of knights' services to the kings of Jerusalem of c. 1180 produces 675 knights; we would probably not be far wrong if we assessed the total at c. 700. In its early years the principality of Antioch seems to have been able to raise about the same number, although this must have been reduced by the losses of territory in the middle of the twelfth century. The number of knights in Edessa was possibly 500. Tripoli could certainly raise 100. The total knights' service provided by the feudal system in the whole of Latin Palestine and Syria at its greatest extent was probably no more than 2,000. This is a very inadequate figure for such exposed settlements and there can have been few occasions when even a substantial proportion of it could have been mustered. As we have seen, from a comparatively early date the vassals of Jerusalem showed a marked aversion to service 'abroad', in which they included Antioch; summons to service of this kind had to be preceded by negotiations and it was established that the vassals could not be constriained to serve by unsubstantiated statements of military necessity. Even for service within the kingdom, which theoretically could be demanded for up to a year, no king could ignore the desires or financial capacities of his vassals, while at any given time a number of fiefs would be in the possession of minors or old men who had passed the age of service or heiresses who were not yet married or vassals who were sick. It would be very surprising if Jerusalem could count on putting more than perhaps 500 fief knights into the field.

In addition the kings of Jerusalem could call on the service of sergeants from churches, monasteries and towns. The sum of such service in c. 1180 was 5,025 men, but the fact that they served in contingents mustered only in an emergency suggests that they were not highly trained. A *levée en masse* of the population could also be summoned in a crisis, but little is known about the quality of the force that resulted or the use to which it was put. Far more important, as the twelfth century wore on, was the contribution made by the Military Orders, but we have already seen that the brother knights and sergeants were never very numerous, that they acted more as the commanders of bodies of mercenary troops and that their military obligations often overstretched them.

It is clear enough that the war-resources of the settlers were thin. They were supplemented in four ways. First, increasingly heavy use was made of mercenaries, among whom there was an important group who fought with Muslim equipment and were called turcopoles. The Latin East must have been a prime source of employment for.them, but it was naturally dependent on cash that could be raised to pay them, which was never enough. This is the reason why large sums of money were periodically sent from Europe to Palestine – for instance Henry II of England's monetary expiation for the murder of Thomas Becket – and why there was a national tax in Jerusalem in 1183. Secondly, the pilgrims who arrived from Europe each year to visit the holy places were often called upon to help out in an emergency; the fact that so many of them arrived just before Easter made them a good source of manpower for summer campaigns. Among them were magnates who had engaged themselves in armed pilgrimages or personal mini-crusades, bringing armed contingents with them; for instance, Thierry of Flanders, Henry the Lion of Saxony, Philip of Flanders, Henry of Troyes, later Count of Champagne, and Peter of Courtenay. Thirdly, the Italian merchant communities, especially those of Genoa, Venice and Pisa, would sometimes respond to an appeal, particularly if it involved the reduction of a coastal city. And fourthly, there were the crusaders who will be considered in the next chapter. What is relevant here is that the Latins in the East regularly appealed to Europe for help and very irregularly received it.

They were, of course, isolated, for they had alienated the Byzantine empire, the only strong Christian power nearby. They were also unable truly to influence the course of political events in the Muslim world, on which their existence depended. At the beginning of the twelfth century Near Eastern Islam was fragmented and in turmoil. Antioch and Edessa faced Aleppo and Mosul and, after 1133, a small but fiercely independent enclave established by the Assassins, members of an Isma'ili Shi'ite sect which used murder to further its ends. On the borders of Tripoli were a group of lesser cities and principalities, Seijar, Hama and Homs. Jerusalem faced Damascus to the east and Egypt to the south. After the initial shock of the First Crusade the reaction of most of the petty Muslim states was to reach a *modus vivendi* with the settlers, although not a peaceful one, since the Christians had forced themselves upon an already kaleidoscopic and violent system of local politics and were themselves on the offensive. There were counter-invasions from Egypt immediately and from the Selchükid sultanate in Iraq from 1110 onwards, and there soon began to develop on the Muslim side the idea of *Jihad*, or Holy War, which was at first confined to a few religious leaders in Damascus and Aleppo, but began to spread and came to the surface in the army that faced the Latins at the Field of Blood in 1119. It surfaced again in Aleppo, the key to Muslim Syria, in 1124, at a time when the city was besieged by the Christians. Aleppo was relieved by Aksungur al-Bursuki, the governor of Mosul, and incorporated into the personal state that he was creating for himself before he was murdered by the Assassins in November 1126. On the sudden death of his son Ma'sud in May 1127 the coalition he had created might have broken up had not 'Imad ad-Din Zengi been appointed governor of Mosul. Zengi entered Aleppo in June 1128 and then embarked on a series of conquests, not, incidentally, confined to Christian territory; in fact he was far more occupied in Iraq than in Syria. But in 1135 he cleared the western and south-western approaches to Aleppo of Christian forces by taking el Atharib, Zerdan and Ma'arret. In 1137 he took Ba'rin on the frontier of the county of Tripoli. In 1144, when the Count of Edessa became involved in a defensive alliance against him with a Muslim neighbour, he occupied the eastern fortresses of the county and, taking advantage of Count Joscelin II's absence and the temporary weakness of the garrison, came before Edessa itself on 24 November. He broke into the city on Christmas Eve and sacked it. The citadel fell two days later.

The loss of the capital of the first Latin state in the East made a great impression in the West as we shall see, but there was widespread and spontaneous reaction on the Muslim side as well. In the tumult of praise and propaganda, the concept of the *Jihad*, voiced only intermittently in Zengi's camp before, became prominent. Showered with honours by the caliph, Zengi pressed home his advantage, taking Sürüc and laying siege to Birecik, but he was assassinated by one of his slaves on the night of 14 September 1146 and his territories were divided between two of his sons. The younger of them, Nur ad-Din, received Aleppo. Since he had not succeeded to Mosul, he was not distracted, as his father had been, by the politics of the eastern Fertile Crescent; but on the other hand his resources were fewer. In spite of his inexperience, he showed his mettle at once by rushing to the aid of the garrison at Edessa which was now threatened by the Christians who hoped to gain some advantage from his father's death. He then entered into an offensive alliance against Antioch with the Selchükid sultan of Rum and took Hab and Kefer Lata, which guarded the passage from the Aleppan plain. After the failure of the Second Crusade he renewed hostilities. His army, reinforced by troops from Damascus, utterly defeated an Antiochene army which was inferior in numbers on 29 June 1149. This was a turning-point for him. In his own eyes and in the opinion of his contemporaries he became a champion of the faith. The propaganda of the *Jihad* was exploited by him in every possible way, through poetry, letters, treatises, sermons and inscriptions, and in it two themes stand out: the obligation to reconquer the coastlands, and especially Jerusalem, from the Christians; and the conviction that this could only be achieved through Muslim religious and political unity. This led to a resurgence of what would now be called Islamic fundamentalism. Nur ad-Din took measures against the Shi'ites and others whom he regarded as deviants and he positively encouraged the founding of schools, mosques and Sufi convents.

Unur, the ruler of Damascus, died in the early autumn of 1149; so did Nur ad-Din's brother, the ruler of Mosul. Nur ad-Din was thwarted at Mosul, where another brother was set up as governor – he did not gain the city until 1170 – but he forced Damascus to recognize his suzerainty and, in alliance with the sultan of Rum, he finally took all the remaining territory of the county of Edessa, the last fortress of which, Tilbeşar, surrendered on 12 July 1151. In April 1154 he was at last able to take direct control of Damascus and with the surrender to him of Ba'albek in June 1155 the unification of Muslim Syria was complete. The next few years were spent consolidating his empire, although he also took advantage of Jerusalem's preoccupation with Egypt to raid the northern settlements, laying siege to Harim and in August 1164 inflicting a major defeat on the Christians at Artah, in which Bohemond III of Antioch, Raymond III of Tripoli, the Byzantine *dux* Coloman and the western visitor Hugh of Lusignan were taken prisoner. Harim surrendered a few days later. But in fact he was worried by King Amalric's invasions of Egypt. In 1164, 1167 and 1168 his general Shirkuh marched south to Egypt and became its vizir in 1169. Egypt now recognized Nur ad-Din's suzerainty.

He died on 15 May 1174. Under him the Muslim political scene had been transformed. In place of a confused jumble of petty states there was now a powerful and united Syria, with Egypt under its suzerainty. The Christians had always dreaded the unification of the Muslim Near East, but Nur ad-Din's death led, as might be expected, to a struggle for power among his officers, nominally over the guardianship of his young son. One of these officers was Saladin, who had succeeded his uncle Shirkuh as vizir of Egypt and had, in obedience to Nur ad-Din's orders, abolished Shi'ite Fatimid rule and proclaimed the orthodox 'Abbasid caliphate there in September 1171. In the name of the unity of Islam Saladin occupied Damascus in October 1174 and then marched on Aleppo by way of Homs and Hama. Resisted at Homs and gaining control of Hama only with difficulty, he failed in his first attempt to take Aleppo, but in April 1175 he routed his Muslim opponents at the Battle of the Horns of Hama. Formally invested by the caliph with the government of Egypt and those parts of Syria he now held, he took up the themes of Nur ad-Din's propaganda, the *Jihad* against the Christian settlements and religious and political unity. But in fact he was always a practical and down-to-earth man and his chief aim, the reunification of Nur ad-Din's territories, took a long time to achieve: Aleppo fell only in June 1183; by that time some of Mosul's dependencies were in his hands and Mosul itself recognized his suzerainty in February 1186. Saladin's campaigns against the Christians in these years were frequent, but they do not seem to have engaged his energy and resources to the same extent. In 1177 he planned a large-scale raid on Ascalon and Gaza which was surprised at Mont Gisard on 25 November and thrown back. In the spring and summer of 1179 his forces gained notable victories at Tell el Hara and Marjayoun after which the new Christian fortress of Le Chastellet at Jisr Banat Ya'qub was taken and destroyed. But in 1182 he made an unsuccessful raid on Beirut and in 1183 he failed to bring the kingdom's forces to battle during a razzia into Galilee. Karak in Trans-jordan held out against him in November of that year and again in August and September of 1184, even though he brought with him on the latter occasion the most powerful army he had yet assembled. In fact for in-vasions of the Latin settlements in 1170, 1171, 1173, 1177, 1179, 1180, 1182, 1183 and 1184 all Saladin had to show was the occupation of 'Aqaba on the Red Sea in 1170 and the destruction of Le Chastellet in 1179.

His ambitions, in fact, had set him on an endless road, since the warfare to which he was committed could only be financed out of further conquest: it has been said that he 'used the wealth of Egypt for the conquest of Syria, that of Syria for the conquest of Jazira and that of the Jazira for the conquest of the coast', the 'coast' being, of course, the Latin settlements. He was always in financial difficulties and it goes without saying that his 'empire' was very precariously constructed, resting on the force of his own personality and on uncertain relations with the 'Abbasid caliphate. But it was his good fortune that at the moment his career reached its climax the Christians were exceptionally weak and divided.

The political background to the warfare in the region can, therefore, be summarized as follows. Until 1128 Antioch, Edessa and to a lesser extent Tripoli faced the Byzantine empire, which was never fully reconciled to the Latin occupation of Antioch and parts of Cilicia and entered the region in force in 1099, 1100, 1104, 1137, 1138, 1142 and 1158–9, and a plethora of

Muslim principalities. From out of the chaos emerged the coalition of Mosul and Aleppo, the sultanate of Rum in Asia Minor, and the small, independent and idiosyncratic principality of the Assassins. Until 1169, on the other hand, Jerusalem faced two major powers, Damascus and Egypt. From Nur ad-Din's addition of Egypt to an empire that already included Damascus the Latin settlements faced on their eastern and southern borders a unified coalition which, however precariously bound together, presented them with a real threat.

The Christians' own military activities fall into four phases. The first lasted until c. 1130, ending with the deaths of the two leaders who were survivors of the first generation of settlers, Baldwin II of Jerusalem and Joscelin I of Edessa, and the coming to power of Zengi. It was characterized by Latin advance. At first, of course, the rulers of Jerusalem had to beat off determined attempts by the Egyptians to recover the territory they had lost so lackadaisically. The Christians met invasions from Egypt, which often made use of Ascalon as a forward base, in 1101, 1102, 1103, 1105, 1106, 1107, 1110, 1113, 1115, 1118 and 1123; after 1107, however, most of these irruptions were razzias conducted by Ascalon's garrison. But they also tried to reduce the coastal ports, thus opening the shoreline and its fertile hinterland to settlement and at the same time depriving the Egyptian fleet of bases. Haifa had already fallen shortly after Godfrey of Bouillon's death. Arsuf and Caesarea were taken in 1101, Acre in 1104, Beirut and Sidon in 1110, Tyre in 1124, after which the operating range of the Egyptian fleets was so severely restricted that they became virtually powerless, since their last watering place on the Levantine coast was closed, and finally Ascalon in 1153. And they drove into the interior. Tancred was already pushing to the east of the Sea of Galilee as early as the autumn of 1099. The eastern bank of the Wadi Araba as far as the Red Sea was garrisoned from 1115–16. But some regions close to the coast were reduced slowly: the pilgrim roads to Jerusalem were still insecure in 1118; the hinterlands of Sidon and Beirut were only gradually mastered in the late 1120s. And Latin expansion east to the sea of Galilee aroused the anxieties of Damascus. There was endemic petty warfare on the eastern frontier until 1115 and hostilities were resumed in 1119. Baldwin I sustained a major defeat at es Sinnabra in 1113; and in that year, 1121 and 1124, there were Muslim raids into Galilee. The Latin settlers in the north had to face counter-invasions, organized on behalf of the Selchükid sultanate in Iraq, for five successive years from 1110. In every year, except 1112 and 1114 when the incursions were minor, the Christian rulers combined their forces and then held them back to threaten rather than engage the enemy, although in 1115 Roger of Salerno, the regent of Antioch, was able to surprise the Muslims and gain a victory over them near Tell Danith. This ended the invasions for the time being, but Roger's disastrous exposure of the Antiochene army without its allies to the Muslims in the Battle of the Field of Blood in 1119 was followed by the loss of the Christian strongholds which threatened Aleppo, although some of them were later recovered. Pressure was maintained on the two chief prizes still to be won in the interior, Aleppo, which was threatened in 1100 and besieged in 1125, and Damascus, which was attacked in 1126 and 1129. It says much for the confidence of the Christians in this period that Baldwin I died in 1118 while invading Egypt.

The second phase lasted from c. 1130 to 1153. It was one in which the Christians were on the defensive, although they were still capable of sporadic, opportunist attacks. A feature of this period, it has been pointed out, was their inability to recover what they now lost, in marked contrast to the first phase. Edessa, Ba'rin and Qalaat el Mudiq (Afamiyah) were lost for good; Harim and Baniyas were recovered only for a short time. There were, moreover, only two major offensives, both made possible by foreign aid: against Seijar in collaboration with the Greeks in 1137 and against Damascus, undertaken with the Second Crusade in 1148.

The third phase, from 1153 to 1169, opened with the occupation of Ascalon by Baldwin III of Jerusalem and was characterized by invasions of Egypt by Amalric in alliance with the Greeks. This naturally involved the Christians in sieges: of Bilbeis in 1163, 1164 and 1168, Alexandria in 1167, Cairo in 1168 and Damietta (Dumyat) in 1169. They strained the kingdom's resources and led to serious divisions of opinion among the Christians. From 1164 onwards every invasion was opposed by an army sent to Egypt's aid from Syria and the Christians' failure left the country to Nur ad-Din.

The fourth phase, from 1169 to 1187, was one in which the Latins were back on the defensive. Saladin regularly, if rather half-heartedly, invaded the kingdom and the only major offensive undertaken by the Christians was an assault on Hama and Harim in 1177, taking advantage of the presence of Philip of Flanders and the arrival of a Byzantine fleet. The hero of these years was the young leper king, Baldwin IV, whose powers of military leadership, even in illness, ensured that every attack was met by a Christian army, the duty of which was not to seek battle but to challenge the Muslims' attempts to take castles or towns.

The Battle of Hattin and loss of Jerusalem

Then came Saladin's invasion of 1187. Just before it occurred, the political crisis in Jerusalem had come to a head. After Baldwin V's death in August 1186 Raymond of Tripoli, the regent-elect, lord of Galilee through marriage and leader of the claimant Isabella's partisans, was persuaded to go to Tiberias while the little king's body was sent to Jerusalem in the care of the Templars. Acre and Beirut were siezed in Sibylla's name, while she and her knights hurried to Jerusalem, where they were joined by Reynald of Châtillon, the lord of Transjordan. Sibylla, who also had the support of the master of the Templars and the patriarch, was crowned in the church of the Holy Sepulchre and she herself then crowned her husband, Guy of Lusignan. Isabella's adherents had been outwitted and as they gathered defiantly at Nablus, planning themselves to go as far as crowning Isabella and her husband Humphrey of Tibnine, Humphrey destroyed their position by taking flight and submitting to Guy and Sibylla in Jerusalem. This ended the rebellion, which was over by October. Most of the feudatories made their peace, although Raymond of Tripoli retired in fury to Tiberias, holding out until the following summer, when a disaster for which he was held responsible made his position intolerable. He had, as was his right as lord, made an independent treaty with Saladin and in late April 1187, in accordance with this, he allowed a Muslim reconnaissance force to enter Galilee. At precisely this time a mission sent by Guy, led by Balian of Ibelin, who was Maria Comnena's second husband and lord of Nablus, the archbishop of Tyre and the masters of the Templars and the Hospitallers, was approaching. Ignoring Raymond's warning to stay behind the walls of the castle of 'Afula until the Muslim troops had left the area, the Templars and Hospitallers rashly attacked them and were cut to pieces. The master of the Hospitallers and the marshal of the Templars were killed.

In the meantime Saladin had been looking for a reason to put aside a truce he had made with the Christians in 1185. This was provided by Reynald of Transjordan, who had pursued an extraordinarily adventurous and aggressive policy of his own against the Muslims for some years, launching attacks across Sinai and into northern Arabia as far as Tayma', and even sending a naval squadron into the Red Sea to pillage merchant shipping and to land an invasion force at Rabigh in the Hijaz: it was apparently only stopped a day's march from Mecca. He had now attacked a caravan travelling from Cairo to Damascus and had refused to return the spoil. In late May 1187 Saladin reviewed his troops at el 'Ashtara in the Hauran. It was the largest army he had ever commanded, probably c. 30,000 men, of whom 12,000 were regular cavalry. On 30 June he crossed the Jordan just south of the Sea of Galilee. The Christians made what had become a conventional counter-move, assembling their army at Zippori. This was smaller than Saladin's, but it was much larger than usual. In fact they had stretched the resources of the kingdom to put c. 20,000 men into the field, of whom 1,200 were knights, drawn from Jerusalem and Tripoli and the Military Orders, together with 50 from Antioch. As was customary in times of crisis they had brought with them the kingdom's holiest relic, the fragment of the True Cross discovered in Jerusalem by Arnulf of Chocques in 1099.

Saladin now divided his forces. On 2 July he attacked Tiberias. A tower on the walls was quickly mined and the town was seized, although the garrison, with Raymond of Tripoli's wife Eschiva, withdrew to the citadel. The bulk of Saladin's army was held back from Tiberias at Kafr Sabt, some six miles away. In the Latin camp an anguished debate began. Raymond of Tripoli, by now thoroughly discredited, advised King Guy not to move and even to allow Tiberias to fall. Dr Smail has recently pointed out that quite apart from his obligations as a feudal overlord to a vassal in peril, Guy's experiences four years before may have led him to reject this apparently sensible and disinterested advice. He had been severely blamed, when he was Baldwin IV's lieutenant, for not engaging Saladin in battle when the latter had invaded Galilee in September 1183; and this criticism had marked the start of a ruthless and unscrupulous campaign which had contributed to his fall from favour, his wife's exclusion from the inheritance of the kingdom and the appointment of Raymond of Tripoli as lieutenant in his place and as regent for Baldwin V. At any rate, Guy made the decision to move and the Christian army marched on 3 July, by way of the spring of Tur'an, about nine miles from Tiberias. As it continued its advance it was engaged by the wings of the Muslim army which cut off its retreat, and a chance of returning to the water at Tur'an, while Saladin held the high ground between it and the steep drop from the escarpment down to Tiberias. By evening the Christians had been forced to halt at a spot far from their goal and without water. When, hot and thirsty, they tried to resume their march on the following morning, they were gradually forced off the road on to the rough ground to the north. Raymond of Tripoli and a small party that included the lords of Sidon and Nablus managed to break through the Muslim lines and escape, but most of the Christians gathered round Guy in a hopeless stand on a hill crowned with two peaks, known as the Horns of Hattin. The demoralized survivors of this last stand were taken prisoner. The relic of the True Cross was seized and was paraded through Damascus fixed upside down on a lance.

The results of this disaster were catastrophic. Fortresses and cities had been deprived of their garrisons to swell the Christian army and Saladin could storm through Palestine and Syria with impunity. By September all the important ports south of Tripoli, except Tyre, had fallen to him. Inland from the Palestinian coast only the castle of Beaufort (Qalaat esh Shaqif) remained in Christian hands by January 1189, and it was lost in 1190. In the county of Tripoli, only the city, the town of Tartus, two Templar castles and the Hospitaller castle of Crac des Chevaliers were still Christian; in the principality of Antioch, only the city itself and the castles of Quseir and Marqab. The city of Jerusalem had fallen on 2 October 1187 after a fortnight's siege, for which Balian of Nablus, who had taken charge of its defence, had resorted to the knighting of all noble boys over sixteen years of age and thirty burgesses. Saladin allowed the population, swollen by refugees from the surrounding countryside, to ransom themselves on quite generous terms, so that at least a proportion was freed, although many of these people faced further hardship as they tried to find shelter in the few towns still under Christian control. The Temple area was restored to Islam. The Hospital of St John became a Shafi'ite college. Jerusalem had been lost after an occupation of just over eighty-eight years.

CHAPTER 5

Crusading in Adolescence, 1101–1187

The immaturity of twelfth-century crusading

In the responses of western Europeans to the news of the disasters in Palestine in 1187 crusading came of age. But that was ninety years after the First Crusade and for most of the twelfth century the movement was inchoate. I have already described how around 1107 three intelligent French monks, Robert the Monk, Guibert of Nogent and Baldric of Bourgueil, had taken the crude ideas of the First Crusade's eyewitnesses and had reforged them into a theologically acceptable interpretation of the startling triumph, in which the events were shown to be evidence of God's miraculous interventionary power and the crusaders were portrayed as laymen who had temporarily taken a kind of monastic habit, leaving the world for a time to enter a nomadic religious community, the members of which had adopted voluntary exile in a war for the love of God and their neighbours, were united in brotherhood and followed a way of the cross that could lead to martyrdom. This presentation was to be useful to the Church – the histories of Robert and Baldric were widely read – but it could not be a lasting solution to the theological issue of the rôle of laymen, which required the greater understanding of their particular 'vocation' that developed in the course of the twelfth century: it was no real answer to treat them as if they were not laymen at all. Anyway, this theorizing was on a high plane and when we look at the crusading movement in practice we find confusion. Before 1187 it is hard to distinguish crusades from armed pilgrimages or other expressions of holy, as opposed to crusading, violence in almost any theatre of war. In the early years there was, in fact, a tendency, in the wake of the First Crusade's success, to transfer the ideas and extravagant language to any conflict about which the promoters or the participants felt strongly. Count Helias of Maine, who was devout and had taken the cross, refused to join the First Crusade because King William II of England was threatening his county and he defended it wearing the cross of a crusader, as though engaged in a personal crusade. Advocates of church reform were not slow to adapt the new ideas to the older struggle against simoniacs. Pope Paschal II, for instance, exhorted Count Robert of Flanders, who had just returned from Jerusalem, to aim now to reach the heavenly Jerusalem by fighting on behalf of the reformers against their opponents in Europe. And a remarkable piece of propaganda, composed in Magdeburg in 1108, tried to present the German war against the pagan Wends across the Elbe in crusading terms:

> Follow the good example of the inhabitants of Gaul and emulate them in this also. . . . May he who with the strength of his arm led the men of Gaul on their march from the far West in triumph against his enemies in the farthest East give you the will and power to conquer these most inhuman gentiles (the Wends) who are near by (ed. W. Wattenbach, *Neues Archiv* 7 (1882), pp. 625–6).

At least until the 1140s, moreover, it seems to have been possible for an individual to take the cross at any time, without any pre-condition of papal proclamation and specification of privileges. And the cross could sometimes be considered as creating a permanent rather than a temporary commitment. In 1128, the year the Council of Troyes recognized the Templars, there was a recruiting drive for crusaders in western Europe led by Hugh of Payns, the master of the new Order, which resulted in a crusade and an unsuccessful attack on Damascus in the following spring. At the same time an embassy sent to France persuaded Count Fulk of Anjou to come east to marry Melisende of Jerusalem. Fulk took the cross even though he was not technically making a pilgrimage since he was intending to settle in Palestine.

The early crusades of the twelfth century
The years between the First and Third Crusades can be divided into three periods. The first, from 1101 to 1120, illustrates several of the points I have just made. Spain seems to have inherited the mantle of the First Crusade and was the theatre for two comparatively straightforward crusades, marked by papal letters and privileges; in 1114 against the Muslims in the Balearic Islands, conducted by Catalans and Pisans under Count Ramon Berenguer of Barcelona, which was then switched in 1116 to a campaign down the mainland coast; and in 1118, when Pope Gelasius II proclaimed a crusade, to be led by King Alfonso I of Aragon, against Saragossa (Zaragoza). The city, the most important prize in the peninsula to be seized since Toledo in 1085, fell on 19 December to a large army which included in its ranks the first crusaders Gaston of Béarn and Centulle of Bigorre, and also Alfonso Jordan, the Count of Toulouse, who had been born in Syria, and the Viscounts of Carcassonne, Gabarret and Lavedan. It is noteworthy that this campaign, organized and led by a king who could put the resources of his state at the disposal of the crusaders, was successful not at the expense of some debilitated petty *taifa* kingdom, but against the Almoravids, the formidable North African invaders who had arrived in the

peninsula in 1086 and now controlled most of Moorish Spain; they were routed in battle on 8 December.

There was at least one and possibly two other crusades in this period. It is not easy to decide whether one was a crusade or a pilgrimage. In 1107 a large fleet left Bergen in Norway under the command of Sigurd, who shared the Norwegian throne with his two brothers. After a leisurely journey by way of England, France, Spain, where it may have taken part in a campaign against the Moors, and Sicily, it reached Acre in the summer of 1110. Sigurd was persuaded to help King Baldwin I take the city of Sidon. The other was definitely a crusade, and it was the first to be diverted off course, foreshadowing the Fourth Crusade and the taking of Constantinople. Bohemond of Taranto and Antioch, who had been held prisoner by Danishmend from the summer of 1100 to the spring of 1103, arrived in France early in 1106. After visiting the shrine of St Leonard, the patron saint of captives, at St-Léonard-de-Noblat, at which he fulfilled a vow he had made in jail, he embarked on a triumphant tour of France. He and the papal legate, Bruno of Segni, formally proclaimed a new crusade, with the support of Pope Paschal whom Bohemond had met on his journey, at a council held at Poitiers. They described it in First-Crusade terms as a *via Sancti Sepulchri* with the aims of helping the Christians in the East and also forcing the Muslims to disgorge their Christian prisoners. But it is clear that Bohemond's intentions were already greater: he had travelled to the West to seek aid for his principality of Antioch, which was threatened by the Greeks as well as by the Muslims. We have seen that soon after his release from prison he had had to face Byzantine invasions of Cilicia and Syria, and in June 1104 much of his eastern frontier had fallen to Ridvan of Aleppo. He had held a council in Antioch at which it was decided that the only course open to him was an appeal to the West. The Greeks certainly loomed as large in his thoughts as did the Muslims, and he was accompanied on his tour through France by a pretender to the Byzantine imperial throne with his Greek entourage. In April or May 1106 he married Constance, the daughter of King Philip of France, a match that demonstrated the reputation he now had. On that occasion he himself preached a crusade sermon in the cathedral of Chartres in which he openly urged French knights to join him in an invasion of the Byzantine empire and promised them rich lands. He seems to have been proposing something very similar to the plan of the Fourth Crusade a century later: he would deal with his enemies in turn by engineering by force a change of government in Constantinople on his way to the East, putting a more sympathetic emperor on the throne in place of Alexius. Over the next few months he developed his case. When, on the eve of his departure, he wrote to the pope, he mentioned the usurpation of the Byzantine throne by Alexius as only one issue; he also justified an attack on the Greeks as vengeance for their treatment of the crusaders and as a means of ending schism between the Catholic and Orthodox Churches.

By October 1107 his army, which contained several of his companions from the First Crusade, was mustered in Apulia. On the 9th it landed on the Albanian coast at Valona and then marched for Durazzo, which the Italian Normans had held for a short time twenty-five years earlier. He laid siege to it, but the Greeks cut off his communications across the Adriatic and in the spring of 1108 the Byzantine forces closed around him. As the summer wore on his army became prone to epidemics. In September he surrendered and was forced to sign the Treaty of Devol, to which reference has already been made. Broken by his defeat, he did not return to Syria but retired to his estates in southern Italy, where he died in 1111.

The crusade of Calixtus II

The second period, from 1120 to 1150, was marked by the papacy's attempts to gain control of the movement. It opened with a remarkable but little-known series of events. On 23 January 1120, in an atmosphere of crisis following the catastrophe of the Field of Blood, King Baldwin II and the leaders of the kingdom of Jerusalem decided to send embassies to the pope and to Venice appealing for help. Pope Calixtus II's response was to plan a new crusade on a large scale. He sent letters to Venice and probably also to Germany and France, which suggests that there was a general encyclical summoning the faithful to take the cross. He also decided to promote a crusade in Spain at the same time: one of what must have been a series of general letters survives, dated 2 April 1123, in which he called on crusaders in Spain to fulfil their vows, granted them the same indulgence as that conceded to crusaders to the East, and appointed St Oleguer, archbishop of Tarragona, as papal legate. This letter was issued at the time the First Lateran Council was meeting in Rome; one of its decrees granted the indulgence and the Church's protection to crusaders and imposed sanctions on those who would not have left for Jerusalem or Spain by Easter 1124. So we have here evidence for a crusade, to be fought in Spain as well as in the East, announced by papal encyclicals and reinforced by the decree of a general council of the Church. Nothing on this scale had been seen since 1095–6. But the use by the pope of general letters and his positive planning of two concurrent campaigns, in contrast to Urban II's more negative desire to prevent warriors being drained from Spain, suggests a new approach.

In Venice there was an enthusiastic response. The doge and the leading citizens took the cross and were granted a banner of St Peter by the pope. On 8 August 1122 a large fleet left for the East. The Venetians paused to attack Byzantine Corfu in retaliation for an attempt by the emperor John Comnenus to reduce their privileges in the empire, but they abandoned the siege of the city on hearing that Baldwin II himself had fallen into the hands of the Muslims. They reached the coast of Palestine in May 1123, destroyed an Egyptian fleet off Ascalon, spent Christmas in Jerusalem and Bethlehem and helped besiege Tyre, which fell on 7 July 1124. They were rewarded with a third of Tyre and its territory and with important commercial privileges which had probably been already promised them by Baldwin as inducements to crusade. The Venetians returned home by way of the Aegean, sacking Greek islands and territory as they went. Their pillaging brought the Byzantine government to heel and in August 1126 John Comnenus confirmed and extended their privileges. They were, however, not the only crusaders in the East at the time. They carried others in their ships and there is evidence for men from Bohemia, Germany and France taking the cross. It is also possible that a Genoese squadron participated.

The Spanish crusade was discussed at a council at Santiago de Compostela on 18 January 1125, presided over by Archbishop Diego Gelmírez, who may have been appointed legate alongside Oleguer of Tarragona. Diego issued a stirring summons:

> Just as the knights of Christ and the faithful sons of Holy Church opened the way to Jerusalem with much labour and spilling of blood, so we should become knights of Christ and, after defeating his wicked enemies the Muslims, open the way to the same Sepulchre of the Lord through Spain, which is shorter and much less laborious ('Historia Compostellana', ed. H. Florez, *España sagrada*, vol. 20 (2nd edn, 1791), p. 428).

The crusaders were granted an indulgence 'through the merits of SS Peter, Paul and James'. In fact Léon contributed little in the end. It was Alfonso I of Aragon who in a feat of arms much admired at the time led a major raid into southern Spain in the winter of 1125–6, marching by way of Teruel, Valencia, Murcia, Gaudix, which he tried to take, Granada and Malaga, where he went out in a boat to demonstrate that he had crossed the peninsula. He returned to Saragossa bringing with him 10,000 Andalusian Christians and their families who had decided to emigrate and whom he settled in the Ebro valley.

The pattern of crisis in the East, embassy to the West, and papal response was to be repeated over and over again in the twelfth century. And although the ambitious plans of Calixtus II did not attract much notice from contemporary writers, they were important, for they foreshadowed those of the Second Crusade.

The crusade of 1128–9, the first proclamation of a political crusade, and Gratian's Decretum

In the interim there were three significant events. The first was the preaching in 1128 of the small crusade which attacked Damascus in the following year. The second was the proclamation of what may have been another crusade, of little immediate importance but of great significance for the future. From the late 1120s the papacy was engaged in a struggle against the south Italian Normans, which was accentuated by Roger of Sicily's support for the anti-pope Anacletus, and the papal propagandists resorted to language reminiscent of the reformers a half-century before. Then in May 1135 Pope Innocent II presided over a council at Pisa which decreed that those who fought against the pope's enemies 'for the liberation of the Church on land or sea' should enjoy the same indulgence as that granted by Urban II at the Council of Clermont to the first crusaders. There is no evidence that these fighters had to make crusade vows, but this isolated grant of the crusade privilege to those who fought against political opponents of the papacy provides us with an important link between the struggles of the papal reformers of the eleventh century and the 'political crusades' of the thirteenth. There can be no doubt that it led to discussions and to controversy in the years that followed, with on the one hand an avant-garde, a representative of which was the great abbot of Cluny, Peter the Venerable, prepared to argue that violence against fellow Christians could be even more justifiable than the use of force against infidels, and on the other a body of opinion highly critical of this development. The third was the publication, probably around the year 1140, of Gratian's *Decretum*, the standard compilation of church law. A long section, Causa XXIII, was devoted to warfare and violence. Although on the surface Gratian did not deal with crusading – the Causa's process of argument started with the issue of the suppression of heresy by force – consciousness of it lay behind the armoury of justifications for the Church's authorization of violence provided to clerical readers, who were led inexorably through a panoply of authorities, to the conclusions that war need not be sinful, could be just, and could be authorized by God, and, on God's behalf, by the pope. Gratian provided a source-book for all crusade propagandists. Within twenty years it was being used to provide arguments in favour of the movement and it had a powerful influence in the thirteenth century, as the sermons of preachers show.

The Second Crusade

The capture of Edessa by Zengi on Christmas Eve 1144 has already been described. An embassy from the Latin East, led by Bishop Hugh of Jeble, reached the papal court at Viterbo shortly after the election of Pope Eugenius III in November 1145, to be followed by a delegation of

Armenian bishops. In response, on 1 December the new pope issued a formal crusade encyclical, *Quantum praedecessores*, in which, after touching on the success of the First Crusade and the grave situation now confronting the East, he called for crusaders, granting them an indulgence which was more advanced than that issued by Urban II. He also decreed the protection of crusaders' property, declared a moratorium on the payment of interest on their debts and eased the way, as Urban had done, for the raising of money to cover expenses from the disposal of land.

Although it can no longer be maintained that *Quantum praedecessores* was the first crusade encyclical, because it is now clear that the papal letters for the Spanish Reconquest and those issued at the time of Calixtus II's crusade were precedents for it, there is no doubt that its careful delineation of privileges for crusaders set the tone for all later letters of this sort. It was addressed to France, but there is no evidence that it had arrived there when the next event occurred. The news of the disaster had reached France independently in embassies from Antioch and Jerusalem. The king was one of the most attractive of the medieval French monarchs. Tender-hearted and courteous, pious and serious, Louis VII was a loyal son of the Church, but he was not weak, particularly where royal rights were con-cerned: in many ways he displayed the combination of rectitude and strength which was so marked in his great-grandson, St Louis. It is prob-able that he was already considering making a pentitential pilgrimage to Jerusalem. At his Christmas court at Bourges he presented the bishops and magnates, whom he had invited in larger numbers than was usual, with a plan to go to the aid of the Christians in the East and the Bishop of Langres preached a sermon, calling on all to assist the king in the enterprise. But the response of the court was not enthusiastic and it was agreed that the issue should be discussed again the following Easter after Abbot Bernard of Clairvaux had been consulted.

It was St Bernard who transformed the situation. By this time he was the leading figure in the western Church. He had been primarily responsible for the success and growth of the Cistercian type of reformed Be-nedictinism, the most fashionable monasticism of the age. He had en-gineered the victory of Pope Innocent II (1130–43) over his rival Anacletus and the new pope, Eugenius III (1145–53), had been his pupil. He was the greatest preacher of his day. Fearless and a brilliant speaker and writer, he was at the height of his reputation. No wonder he was consulted by Louis 'as though he were a divine oracle'. He was likely to be sympathetic – he had, after all, already brought his considerable influence to bear in support of the Templars – but he very properly replied that a matter of this importance should be referred to the pope, thereby ensuring that papal initiative was preserved. Eugenius's response was to reissue *Quantum praedecessores* on 1 March 1146, with a few minor changes, and to authorize Bernard to preach the crusade north of the Alps. At Vézelay on 31 March, in a dramatic scene played, as at Clermont, in a field outside the town, St Bernard read the encyclical to the crowd and delivered the first of his crusade sermons with King Louis at his side, wearing a cross sent him by the pope. His audience became so enthusiastic that Bernard ran out of cloth for crosses and had to tear pieces from his own habit to make them. After Vézelay he put his great energy into promoting the crusade by letters and sermons. The letters that have survived are the most powerful crusade propaganda of all time. In them a highly developed concept of the indulgence was combined with a marvellously appealing description of the crusade as an opportunity presented by God to sinful and violent men of redeeming themselves:

> This age is like no other that has gone before; a new abundance of divine mercy comes down from heaven; blessed are those who are alive in this year pleasing to the Lord, this year of remission, this year of veritable jubilee. I tell you, the Lord has not done this for any other generation before, nor has he lavished on our fathers a gift of grace so copious. Look at the skill he is using to save you. Consider the depth of his love and be astonished, sinners. He creates a need – he either creates it or pretends to have it – while he desires to help you in your necessity. This is a plan not made by man, but coming from heaven and proceeding from the heart of divine love (St Bernard of Clarvaux, *Opera*, ed. J. Leclercq and H. Rochais, vol. 8 (1977), p. 435).

Given the attraction of this sort of language, the bitter reactions that followed the crusade's failure are comprehensible.

Bernard's efforts led to great enthusiasm, but he was drawn into northern France and Germany to curb the passions aroused by the unauthorized activities of another Cistercian monk called Radulf, whose preaching bred the same violence against Jews which had marred the First Crusade. In November Bernard reached Frankfurt, where King Conrad III was holding his court. Conrad was another admirable ruler – shrewd, sincere, intelligent, pious, courageous and hard-working – and he had already shown interest in crusading, for he had taken the cross in 1124, but Germany was torn with internal feuding, and powerful interests, which Conrad was never able to overcome, had been opposed to his accession from the start. It is no surprise that he refused to join the crusade and take the leadership of the Germans who were now being recruited in large numbers. It is clear, moreover, that Pope Eugenius, who had been driven out of Rome by a popular uprising, was anxious for Conrad to lead a Germany army into Italy to help him re-enter his city and counter the growing power of the Normans in the south; it had been no part of his crusade plans that German forces should be diverted out of Europe. But enthusiasm for the crusade, which had spread to Italy and England, now had a momentum of its own and Bernard anyway had been carried away by it himself. Following a preaching tour of Switzerland he returned to Conrad's Christmas court at Speyer. After a dramatic sermon, preached during Mass at his own request, in which he directed a personal and highly charged appeal to the German king, drawing attention to his prospects on the Day of Judgement should he fail to answer Christ's summons, Conrad gave way and took the cross.

Although the pope seems to have been not entirely happy with Conrad's decision, the two most powerful rulers in western Europe were now committed to the crusade, which was looking as though it would be a really major expedition. It also began to assume the features of Calixtus II's ambitious enterprise of a quarter of a century before, although this time on an even larger scale. Eugenius responded favourably to a request from King Alfonso VII of Castile for an extension of the crusade to Spain, and he allowed the Genoese and the citizens of the ports of southern France to join that enterprise. Then, at an assembly at Frankfurt on 13 March 1147, about which more below, a section of the German crusaders, mostly Saxons, petitioned to be allowed to crusade against the pagan Wends east of the Elbe rather than against the Muslims. In this request, of course, they were giving expression to ideas current in Saxony since the early years of the century. Bernard agreed to their proposal and persuaded Eugenius, whom he met on 6 April at Clairvaux, to authorize it formally. He justified the new crusade in a startling way, forbidding the crusaders to make any truce with the Wends 'until such time as, with God's help, either their religion or nation shall be wiped out' (St Bernard of Clairvaux, *Opera*, vol. 8, p. 433). This extraordinary statement, which was echoed, somewhat more ambiguously, in Eugenius's formal authorization of the Wendish Crusade, appears to be the proclamation of a missionary war, as such corresponding well with what had for long been a feature of the German drive to the east, and it has never been satisfactorily explained, especially since Bernard expressed opposition to forcible conversion on another occasion. One of the problems we have to face with crusade propaganda, well-illustrated in *Crusade and Mission* by Professor Kedar, is the contradiction between the desire for conversion, or perhaps the conviction that the success of a crusade would establish political conditions favourable to proselytization, and the clear Christian tradition that infidels should not be forced, but only persuaded, to abjure their errors. Faced with the need to arouse an audience which did not appreciate subtlety and hardly comprehended theological nuances, Bernard and Eugenius were not the only propagandists of German crusades who found themselves drawn into making statements of doubtful theology.

Eugenius's encyclical, *Divina dispensatione*, issued at Troyes on 13 April 1147, unfolded the strategy as it was developing, for in it the pope referred to the eastern and Spanish expeditions at the same time as he authorized the German campaign against the Wends. The crusade was now being planned on a huge scale. Eventually five armies converged on the East: those of Louis of France, Conrad of Germany, Amadeus of Savoy, Alfonso Jordan of Toulouse and an Anglo-Flemish force that helped the King of Portugal to take Lisbon on the way. Four more armies took the field in north-eastern Europe: a Danish host which joined another army under Henry the Lion of Saxony and the Archbishop of Bremen, and forces led by Albert the Bear of Brandenburg and a brother of the Duke of Poland. In the Iberian peninsula four campaigns were conducted: by the Genoese against Minorca, by Alfonso VII of Castile against Almeria, by the Count of Barcelona against Tortosa and by Alfonso Henriques of Portugal against Santarem and Lisbon. Contemporaries saw all these expeditions as parts of a single enterprise:

> To its initiators it seemed that one part of the army should be sent to the eastern regions, another to Spain and a third against the Slavs who live next to us (Helmold of Bosau, 'Chronica Slavorum', ed. J. M. Lappenberg and B. Schmiedler, *MGHS rer. Germ.* (1937), p. 115).

At the same time, although not technically part of the crusade, a powerful Sicilian Norman fleet extended Roger of Sicily's rule over the North African coast from Tripoli to Tunis. Nothing on this scale had been seen since the fall of the Roman empire; nor was it often to be seen again.

In many respects great care was taken in the preparation of this massive undertaking. The pope joined Bernard in preaching and recruiting and, although they may have differed slightly in their theologies of penance, the two men proposed a very advanced type of indulgence. We have seen that Urban II's indulgence had been merely a guarantee that the labour of crusading was so unpleasant that it would constitute an entirely satisfactory penance. With Eugenius and Bernard the emphasis shifted from the penitent's self-imposed punishment to God's merciful kindness, confirmed by the Power of the Keys, by means of which the pope could assure sinners of the remission of punishment as a reward for the action undertaken:

> God arranges for himself to be in need, or he pretends to be, so that he can award to those fighting for him wages: the remission of their sins and everlasting glory. . . . If you are a prudent merchant, if you are a man fond of acquiring this world's goods, I am showing you certain great markets; make sure not to let the chance pass you by. Take the sign of the cross and you will obtain in equal measure remission of all the sins

which you have confessed with a contrite heart. If the cloth itself is sold it does not fetch much; if it is worn on a faithful shoulder it is certain to be worth the kingdom of God (St Bernard of Clairvaux, *Opera*, vol. 8, pp. 314–15).

Eugenius appointed Cardinals Theodwin of Porto and Guido of San Chrysogono to be legates of the French army, to be assisted by Bishops Arnulf of Lisieux, Godfrey of Langres and Alvis of Arras. Bishop Anselm of Havelberg was made chief legate for the Wendish Crusade, to be assisted by Bishop Henry of Olmütz, who had originally been appointed legate for Conrad of Germany's army, and Wibald of Stavelot, the abbot of Corvey. Eugenius and Louis of France wrote to the kings of Hungary and Sicily and the Byzantine emperor Manuel Comnenus, informing them of their plans and asking for provisions and passage. Manuel replied cautiously, suggesting in one letter to the pope that the crusaders take the same oaths of homage to him as their predecessors had made to Alexius and asking in another for guarantees from the French that they would not harm the empire and would return to it cities which had once been under its control. Louis adopted a practical measure to cope with the problem of the expenses of crusading, which so affected participants, by raising a levy, perhaps the imposition of feudal aids, which was the first example of the subsidies and taxes that were to transform crusading in the thirteenth century. Conrad saw to it that roads to the East through Germany were improved and bridges were repaired. There were splendid and solemn assemblies in France and Germany at which plans were discussed. But from all this planning there was a glaring omission. There was no consultation with the Latin rulers in the East: twelve years later Pope Adrian IV was to remind Louis forcefully of this, pointing out the harm that resulted. The only possible explanation is that, although of course they planned to end their crusade with a pilgrimage to Jerusalem, Louis and Conrad were intending to march directly across Anatolia to Edessa, by-passing even the principality of Antioch.

This was obviously in the minds of those who took part in the French assembly at Étampes on 16 February 1147, which had to make the final choice of a route to the East. It had before it two options: to follow the overland route by way of the Balkans, Constantinople and Asia Minor, or to travel by sea from Sicily. Conrad of Germany, who was on very bad terms with Roger of Sicily, had apparently only considered the overland journey, which anyway made sense if the prime target was Edessa. At Étampes there were divisions of opinion and a heated debate – it seems that one party, with the support of an embassy from Roger of Sicily, warned the King of France against putting himself at the mercy of the Greeks by going to Constantinople – but the overland route was decided upon and departure was set for 15 June. The German assembly at Frankfurt on 13 March was informed of the French decision, announced an itinerary through Hungary and set the middle of May as the date for departure, so as to march a few weeks ahead of the French. The two armies which, like those of the First Crusade, contained many unarmed pilgrims as well as crusaders, were to join forces at Constantinople.

The Germans left on the appointed date and passed through Regensburg and Vienna into Hungary, the king of which had been persuaded that their passage would be more peaceful if he paid Conrad a large sum, levied from his Church, with which to buy provisions. This measure, which must have been insisted on by crusaders who knew of the experiences of their predecessors, ensured that there was no trouble. The Germans then came to the frontiers of the Byzantine empire. Manuel was on good terms with Conrad, with whom he was bound by an alliance against the South Italian Normans; he had, moreover, recently married Bertha of Sulzbach, Conrad's relative and, it seems, his adopted daughter. He does not appear to have feared and distrusted the Germans as he did the French and his emissaries merely demanded an oath from the Germans that they would not harm his interests in any way. When they had given this assurance the Germans were promised provisions and they marched by way of Niš, Sofia, Plovdiv and Edirne to Constantinople, which they reached after a journey free from major incident, although there were some instances of plundering and a few brushes with the imperial forces.

On good terms with Conrad Manuel might be, but he was not careless. Like his grandfather Alexius he was determined to deal with the crusade leaders separately by shipping them and their armies across to Asia as soon as possible after their arrival. He had even wanted Conrad to by-pass Constantinople and to cross the Dardanelles at Sestus. Conrad had demurred when this was first put to him, probably because he did not want to miss his rendezvous with Louis, but at the end of September, after about three weeks at Constantinople, he agreed to be transported across the Bosporus, perhaps because the Byzantines had asked him to help them against Roger of Sicily, who had now invaded Greece, a request that put him in an embarrasing position. At any rate his army, supplemented by a force from Lorraine which had now arrived, crossed the straits and pressed on into Asia Minor. At Nicaea it gathered provisions for an advance on Konya. But it was so large – Conrad's followers had rejected his sensible suggestion that the non-combatants should be sent separately to Jerusalem – and its advance was so slow that supplies were soon exhausted. Somewhere near the site of the victory at Dorylaeum in 1097 it was ambushed and defeated. The German retreat became a rout, with the Turks harrying the columns at will, and the shattered army reached the relative safety of Nicaea at the beginning of November. Most of the crusaders now tried to return home, leaving Conrad and a much reduced force to send messengers begging Louis of France for aid.

Louis had taken splendid leave on 11 June when, at the great abbey church of St Denis and in the presence of the pope, he had venerated the relic of St Denis, under whose patronage he was to believe himself to be throughout the crusade, had received the oriflamme, the sacred war-banner of his kingdom, and had been presented with his pilgrim's purse by Eugenius himself. From Metz, which had been chosen as the French mustering-point, his army marched by way of Worms to Regensburg, where it found boats ready to carry the baggage down the Danube as far as Bulgaria and where it began to follow the road already taken by the Germans. It was amply supplied by the Hungarians, with whose king Louis was on good terms, and, greatly to his personal cost, Louis was able to keep his army provisioned in Byzantine territory until it reached Con-stantinople on 4 October; like Conrad he refused to by-pass the city. Throughout the march, however, he was forced to conduct negotiations with Manuel, whose ambassadors had met him at Regensburg. Manuel obviously feared and distrusted the French. He knew there had been negotiations with Roger of Sicily – in fact a party of French crusaders did travel to Constantinople by way of southern Italy – and he must have been very conscious of the ties of sentiment and nationality that bound the French and the settlers in the Latin East. The prince of Antioch, moreover, was the Queen of France's uncle. His representatives may well have informed him of the statements made by members of a party within the crusade headed by Bishop Godfrey of Langres, which was bitterly hostile to the Greeks. So it is not surprising that he made more stringent demands of the French than of the Germans. Louis's advisers were pre-pared to agree not to seize any town or castle in Byzantine territory, but they were not ready to promise to return to the empire any place which had once belonged to it, which is understandable given that their intention was to recover Edessa, which in the distant past had been within the empire. And the crusaders were bewildered by the news, which reached them when they were a day's march from Constantinople, that Manuel had made a treaty with the Turkish sultan at Konya, through whose territory they would have to pass. In their camp before Constantinople, the fortifications of which Manuel had strengthened, the Bishop of Langres's party even proposed launching an attack upon the Byzantine capital. The French waited for a fortnight for the armies they knew were coming from the West, but rumours of German successes ahead of them, which turned out to be false, made them restive and Louis had to agree to a crossing of the Bosporus; further negotiations with the Greeks then held him up on the Asiatic side until the reinforcements arrived. In the end his agreement with Manuel did not specify the return of all past imperial territory. The crusaders made homage and promised not to take any place under imperial jurisdiction; in return they were promised guides and supplies and the Greeks recognized that they would have to plunder where provisions were not made available.

At Nicaea they heard of the rout of the Germans and they were joined by Conrad and the remnants of his army. At Esseron they turned for the sea, hoping for an easier and better-supplied passage if they marched through Byzantine lands along the coast, although this meant the abandonment of their strategy. At Ephesus Conrad, who was ill, left for Constantinople, but the French pressed on, ignoring a warning that the Turks were gathering to oppose them. By the time they reached Eskihisar on 3 or 4 January 1148 they were desperately short of provisions and the march to Antalya, which they reached on 20 January, was a terrible one: they suffered severely from Turkish harassing attacks which the Greek inhabitants and garrisons were unwilling to hinder, until the Templars who were with them were put in charge of order on the march. At Antalya, on the edge of Byzantine territory, the French found little in the way of supplies, particularly for their horses which were now being decimated by starvation. A fleet promised by the Greeks to transport them all to Antioch proved to be so small that it could only take a fraction of them. In the end Louis embarked for Antioch having tried, as far as he could, to ensure that the bulk of his force was fitted out for the overland journey; in fact only a small number of those unfortunate crusaders managed to get through. It must be stressed that although for most of his march Louis had been leading his army through a region supposedly under Byzantine control, it had received little support from the population, the government or its officers, and the survivors can only have remembered the frustration and broken promises. The most recent historical judgement is that Manuel's fear of the French was so great that he connived at their destruction. The French had been distrustful of the Byzantines before they had left France. Their experiences in the Balkans and Asia Minor had borne out the complaints of their predecessors and left them with an abiding bitterness.

Louis reached Antioch on 19 March. Refusing to take part in any campaign in the north he wished only to press on to Jerusalem to fulfil his vow. Conrad and other German crusaders were already there, together with new arrivals from the West, and a council-of-war, held in Acre on 24 June and attended by a galaxy of Christian rulers and nobles from East and West, decided to try to take Damascus. The proposal, which was only one of several discussed, was not as foolhardy as it is often supposed to have been. The destruction of the crusading armies in Asia Minor had put an end to any hope of re-taking Edessa. Damascus had already been attacked by the forces of the kingdom of Jerusalem in 1126 and 1129, on the latter occasion with the aid of crusaders from Europe. There were strong religious and strategic reasons for occupying the chief city in Syria and there were sound political arguments as well. Zengi's career had shown how dangerous a united Muslim Syria could be; it could only be a matter of time before his son, Nur ad-Din, who had just married the governor of Damascus's daughter, took it over unless he was forestalled.

In the middle of July the largest army yet put into the field by the Latins assembled at Tiberias under the command of Louis, Conrad and King Baldwin III of Jerusalem. The leaders decided to attack Damascus from the west, where the suburban orchards would assure supplies of timber, food and water, and they advanced on the city, which had sent appeals for help to Nur ad-Din and his brother. Driving the Muslims back from the banks of the Barada river on 24 July, the Christians occupied a good position from which to launch an assault. But now they made an extraordinary decision. Knowing that the eastern wall was less well fortified and conscious that the impending arrival of Muslim armies of relief made a rapid capture imperative, they shifted their camp on 27 July to an exposed site with no water and little food on the eastern side of the city. They were trapped as a result: the eastern walls may not have been recently improved but they were strong enough to hold them up; they could not return to the western side which was quickly reoccupied by the Muslims; they had placed themselves in a position from which they could only withdraw, which is what they did.

This ended the crusade and there were bitter recriminations and accusations of treachery, especially against individuals and institutions in the Latin East. The Greeks, of course, were roundly condemned for their treatment of the crusaders in Asia Minor and hostility towards them was fanned when a Sicilian squadron, in which the French king and his entourage were returning home was attacked by a Byzantine fleet, which was still at war with Roger of Sicily. Louis narrowly escaped capture; his wife Eleanor of Aquitaine, whose behaviour at Antioch during the crusade had been atrocious enough to start the train of events which would lead to the annulment of the marriage a few years later, was in another ship and was detained by the Greeks for a time. On his arrival in Italy Louis began to plan a new crusade with Roger of Sicily and Pope Eugenius, which, like Bohemond of Taranto's, would wreak vengeance on the Greeks on its way to the East.

Meanwhile in north-eastern Germany a large army under Henry the Lion had set out from Artlenburg in the middle of July 1147 and had laid siege to the Wendish stronghold of Dobin, before which it had been joined by the Danes. The siege, marked by a Wendish sortie that routed the Danes, had ended inconclusively with a peace treaty according to which the Wends renounced idolatry and the Wendish prince Niklot became an ally and tributary of Count Adolf of Holstein, with whom he had had good relations before the crusade had disrupted them. Early in August the main force under Albert the Bear, which was certainly massive, had left Magdeburg and, crossing the Elbe, had raided enemy country before dividing, with one part laying siege unsuccessfully to Demmin and the other marching to Szczecin (Stettin), which was in fact already Christian. More had been achieved in Spain. The first party of crusaders to leave home, men from the Low countries, the Rhineland, northern France and Britain, had set sail from Dartmouth and had arrived at Porto (Oporto) in Portugal in June 1147. The Portuguese, who had taken Santarem from the Moors three months before, had persuaded the crusaders to participate in the siege of Lisbon, which fell to them on 24 October. In the east of the peninsula, Almeria, the chief Andalusian port for trade with Africa and the Near East, had fallen to a combined Castilian, Aragonese, south French, Genoese and Pisan force on 17 October. At the end of 1148 the Aragonese, south French and Genoese had gone on to take Tortosa and in the autumn of 1149 they occupied Lérida, Fraga and Mequinenza, the last Muslim outposts in Catalonia.

But the Spanish crusade was the only success, as contemporaries, particularly English ones who were proud of their compatriots, were quick to point out. Elsewhere this huge burst of activity had had nugatory results and the effect of this fiasco on Catholic Christian morale was severe. The crusading movement plumbed depths of despair it did not reach again until the fifteenth century and a strategy on this scale was never to be attempted again. Two German commentators, the Würzburg annalist and Gerhoh of Reichersberg, even took the view that the whole enterprise had been accursed. To the Würzburg annalist it had been the work of the devil, a revolt against God's righteous punishment, inspired by

pseudo-prophets, sons of Belial and witnesses of Anti-Christ, who by stupid words misled the Christians and by empty preaching induced all sorts of men to go ('Annales Herbipolenses', *MGHS*, vol. 16, p. 3).

To Gerhoh of Reichersberg there was link between the disasters and the presence in this world of Anti-Christ. The Latin settlers had displayed avarice and the crusaders, who had deviated from rectitude, had been allowed by God to be deceived by preachers and false miracles to perish in the East. Others, echoing the interpretations of the disasters of 1101, explained the failures in the East as a punishment meted out on the crusaders themselves, whose wicked behaviour had led God to withdraw his favour; and they tended to attribute the successes in Spain to the humility of the crusaders there. In this storm of protest and obloquy the dignity and forbearance of two leading Cistercian participants stand out. Bishop Otto of Freising, Conrad's half-brother and the leader of one of the

German armies in Asia Minor, attributed failure to the mysterious but always benevolent ways of God:

> 'Although our expedition was not good for the extension of boundaries or for the comfort of our bodies, it was good for the salvation of many souls' (Otto of Freising, *Gesta Friderici imperatoris*, ed. G. Waitz, *MGHS rer. Germ.* (1912), p. 93).

So did St Bernard, the 'pseudo-prophet' on whom, most woundingly but expectedly, the opprobrium fell. In response he was inspired to write one of the finest expositions of resignation to the will of God in Christian literature:

> How can human beings be so rash as to dare to pass judgement on something that they are not in the least able to understand? It might perhaps be a comfort for us to bear in mind the heavenly judgements that were made of old. . . . For . . . it is true that the hearts of mortal men are made in this way: we forget when we need it what we know when we do not need it. . . . The promises of God never prejudice the justice of God (St Bernard of Clairvaux, 'De consideratione', *Opera*, vol. 3 (1963), pp. 411–12).

Low morale

The failure of the Second Crusade ushered in the third period, in which for nearly forty years Christian demoralization was reflected in a low level of crusading. Papal authority had now been established, but its benefits must have seemed doubtful to the popes. The planning of a new crusade after Louis of France's return to the West came to nothing. Crises in the East continued to occur and they were invariably followed by embassies to the West begging for help. In response, as in 1120 and 1145, the popes issued encyclicals, formally summoning the faithful to crusade in the East, in 1157, 1165, 1166, 1169, probably in 1173, in 1181 and 1184. It would be wrong to say that these had no effect: in 1166 Henry II of England and Louis VII of France, towards whom most of the appeals were directed because of his known piety and commitment, planned the levying of an income and capital tax, similar to the Saladin tithe of 1188; some money was eventually sent to Jerusalem. And several small expeditions, like that of Philip of Flanders in 1177, did reach the East. But on the whole these papal appeals fell on deaf ears and with good reason. While Jerusalem and most of the territory conquered in the first half of the century was still in Christian hands, crusades, that is to say large armies of temporary soldiers who would return home once their vows had been fulfilled, were not the answer to the Latin settlers' predicament, because they required not the conquest of new land, but an increase in the forces permanently garrisoning the territory already held. This is why there was so much emphasis in these years on measures to increase the standing defence, for instance Henry of England's promise in 1172 to maintain 200 knights in Jerusalem for a year as part of his penance for the murder of St Thomas Becket. Furthermore, until 1170 the kingdom of Jerusalem must have appeared quite strong to the European public, since it had been prepared to embark on its own campaigns of territorial aggrandisement.

The popes who tried vainly to rouse Christians to service in the East made few efforts to intervene in other theatres, where warfare continued spasmodically, whether dignified with the title of crusade or not; in fact historians are faced with great problems, and often run the risk of appearing to be pedants, when they try to distinguish crusades from the other engagements in this chronic violence. Indulgences, for instance, were still occasionally granted without formal papal authorization: for instance, papal legates in Spain, and even Spanish bishops, issued them on their own initiative and in 1166 the council of Segovia was prepared to offer the same indulgence as that granted to pilgrims to Jerusalem to those who would defend Castile against, apparently, Christian invaders; and the high point in Spain in these years, the defence of Huete in 1172, was indulgenced but not apparently preceded by an encyclical. In the north the Danes under King Valdemar I, often in alliance with Henry the Lion of Saxony, were particularly active, stung by raids on their coastline by Wendish slave-traders, and their efforts culminated in the capture of Rügen in 1168. They then began to attack the peoples living at the mouth of the Oder. The conquest of Pomerania was accompanied by the foundation of monasteries as centres of active missionary work. In Spain Almoravid power collapsed and gave way to representatives of another North African religious movement, the Almohads, who seized Morocco in 1145, crossed into Europe and occupied Cordoba, Jaén, Malaga and Granada. They retook Almeria in 1157, together with Ubeda and Baeza. During fifty-five years of bitter warfare, from 1157 to 1212, the Christians were forced on to the defensive. Against this background the scarcity of papal encyclicals is striking and is perhaps another sign of demoralization. There was only one papal letter authorizing crusading in northern Europe. It was issued by Pope Alexander III, probably in 1171. It offered only a limited indulgence and its wording suggests that the pope thought the conflict with the Slavs was over and that the next enemies to be dealt with were the Finns and Estonians further east, although it was not until 1184 that the Danes began to think seriously of carrying war to the eastern Baltic and even then their plans did not materialize. And with regard to Spain there were only three papal crusade authorizations, written in 1153, 1157–8 and 1175.

The most significant development in the peninsula in this period was the establishment of national Military Orders, drawing their inspiration partly from the Templars and Hospitallers, partly from short-lived societies founded by Alfonso I of Aragon to defend Saragossa in 1122 and Monreal del Campo c. 1128. The first Spanish Military Order came into existence when in 1157 the Templars returned the exposed frontier castle of Calatrava to King Sancho III of Castile. At the king's court in Toledo was Raimundo, abbot of the Cistercian abbey of Fitero. One of his monks, Diego Velázquez, who had been a knight, persuaded him to ask for the castle and volunteers were summoned to defend it. Many of these men were formed into a confraternity and in 1164 they were admitted into the Cistercian Order and were given a modified Cistercian rule. The foundation of the Order of Calatrava was followed by those of Santiago in 1170, San Julian del Pereiro shortly before 1176 – this was affiliated to Calatrava and in the thirteenth century took the name of Alcántara – Evora, later known as Avis and also affiliated to Calatrava, soon after 1166, and Montegaudio, founded c. 1173 and absorbed by Calatrava c. 1221. These Orders flourished in Castile, Léon and Portugal, but not in Aragon, where the Templars and Hospitallers were predominant. They were used to defend the invasion routes leading from Almohad territory, but they also undertook military campaigns, ransomed prisoners and actively settled the frontier regions under their control with Christian peasants. Their emergence signalled a developing feature of the crusading movement in Spain, its national character. Half a century before, the Spaniards had been joined by many volunteers from across the Pyrenees, but now these came less, partly because the Spaniards themselves resented them. In February 1159 Pope Adrian IV had to discourage Louis of France and Henry of England from campaigning in the peninsula unless they had the permission of the Spanish kings and he made it clear that they would not be welcome without prior negotiations; he reminded Louis how he and Conrad had gone on the Second Crusade without consulting the Latin settlers in the East and he drew attention to the damage caused by that failure. The Spanish Reconquest was becoming a war of national liberation and the Spanish crusades were with a few exceptions to be nationalistic and under the control of the local rulers.

In the papal letters of this period, whether for crusades to the East or in the Baltic region or in Spain, there is further evidence of the lack of morale. In 1157, 1165 and 1166 Popes Adrian IV and Alexander III resorted to variations of the very advanced formulation of the indulgence to be found in Pope Eugenius III's *Quantum praedecessores*. This must have worried the papal curia, because in 1169 the decision was made to return to the more old-fashioned concept of Pope Urban II, that the crusade was merely a satisfactory penance. In Alexander III's appeal of that year this was stressed by referring to the indulgence explicitly as that remission of penance imposed by the priestly ministry which Urban and Eugenius are known to have established (Alexander III, 'Epistolae et Privilegia', *PL*, vol. 200, col. 600).

For the next thirty years the papacy was to stick to this conservative formulation in spite of the vast strides in penitential theology that had been made by contemporary theologians. As late as 1187 and the great encyclical *Audita tremendi* which launched the Third Crusade it was still being firmly expressed:

> To those who with contrite hearts and humbled spirits undertake the labour of this journey and die in penitence for their sins and with right faith we promise full indulgence of their faults and eternal life; whether surviving or dying they shall know that through the mercy of God and the authority of the apostles Peter and Paul, and our authority, they will have relaxation of the satisfaction imposed for all their sins of which they have made proper confession ('Historia de expeditione Friderici imperatoris', ed. A. Chroust, *MGHS rer. Germ.* NS, vol. 5 (1928), p. 10).

A contemporary propagandist, Peter of Blois, explained that this was merely a declaration of the worth of the exercise as a satisfactory penance:

> By the privilege of the apostle Peter and the general authority of the Church the Lord had intended in this sign (of the cross) a means of reconciliation; so that the assumption of the commitment to journey to Jerusalem should be the highest form of penance and sufficient satisfaction for sins committed (Peter of Blois, 'De Hierosolymitana peregrinatione acceleranda', *PL*, vol. 207, col. 1061).

The development of traditions

The years from 1101 to 1187, therefore, witnessed an extraordinarily ambitious fiasco and then a period in which the movement was at a low ebb in spite of activity in all the theatres of war. Crusading still lacked maturity, but it was developing all the time. It diversified to include wars against pagans beyond the north-eastern frontiers of Christendom and at least the threatening of papal enemies in the interior of Europe; and in Spain it began to develop individual features. There were the first steps in organizing adequate financing. European rulers began to take part. The indulgence was formulated and reformulated. The popes established their right to authorize the wars and got into the habit of issuing crusade encyclicals. However unsuccessful many of these were in recruiting crusaders, they gave the draftsmen at the curia practice in drawing up the privileges of protection, legal immunity and spiritual benefits which came to be so precisely expressed in the thirteenth-century letters. And a stream of pilgrims, unarmed and armed, and of little parties of crusaders, flowed to Palestine, demonstrating that although Christians had been demoralized by the failure of the Second Crusade and were not inspired to mount a major expedition, their faith and commitment to the Holy Land were not shaken. It was during the twelfth century that the European noble and knightly families built up traditions of military service to Christ which were to benefit the movement in the thirteenth. Countless examples are to be found. For instance, Count Thierry of Flanders, a nephew of the Count Robert who had played a distinguished rôle in the First Crusade, took part in the Second Crusade and also visited the East in 1139, 1157 and 1164; his wife, Sibylla of Anjou, King Fulk of Jerusalem's daughter by his first marriage, ended her days as a nun at Bethany; his son Philip led an armed company to the East in 1177 and died during the Third Crusade; his grandson Baldwin was a leader of the Fourth Crusade and became the first Latin emperor of Constantinople. The careers of the ancestors of John of Joinville, one of the most attractive thirteenth-century crusaders who accompanied St Louis to the East in 1248, demonstrate how an example set before 1187 bore fruit in commitment later, although it should be remembered that these men were seneschals of the Counts of Champagne, a line of men obsessed with crusading. Geoffrey III of Joinville had taken part in the Second Crusade. Then, Geoffrey IV died on the Third Crusade. Geoffrey V, who had accompanied his father on the Third Crusade, took the cross again for the Fourth and died on it. Simon, John's father, took the cross for the Albigensian Crusade and again for the Fifth. In the development of these traditions European laymen, who from the first had rebuilt the message of the preachers to their own specifications, were appropriating crusading for themselves at a time when churchmen were expressing a growing respect for the idea of a lay vocation. We have seen that theologians working just after the liberation of Jerusalem in 1099 had been concerned to monasticize the movement and to treat crusaders as temporary quasi-monks. Echoes of this attitude can still be found at the time of the Second Crusade, which is not surprising in view of the influence on it of the Cistercians Eugenius and Bernard, but by the Third Crusade the movement's character was much more clearly that of a lay devotion; the element of religious profession had anyway been channelled into the ethos of the Military Orders. The family traditions built up before 1187 meant that crusading was now part of the secular concerns of lineage, reputation and domestic custom. In this, as in other respects, western Europe had been unconsciously preparing itself for its response to the loss of Jerusalem to Saladin.

CHAPTER 6

Crusading at its Height, 1187–1229

The Third Crusade

The news of the catastrophe at Hattin and the fall of Jerusalem reached the West in the early autumn of 1187. The old pope, Urban III, died, it was said of grief, on 20 October. Within ten days his successor, Gregory VIII, was sending out an appeal for a new crusade. This encyclical, *Audita tremendi*, is one of the most moving documents of crusading history. It must have been drafted by Urban before his death, since the eight days that elapsed between Gregory's election on 21 October and the date of the earliest surviving versions of it is too short a time for such an important letter to have been composed, approved, corrected and copied. *Audita tremendi* opened with a lament over recent events in Palestine and then in a profoundly theological passage explained the disasters as a punishment for the sins not only of the Latin settlers but also of all Christians, whom it summoned to acts to penance:

> Faced by such great distress concerning that land, moreover, we ought to consider not only the sins of its inhabitants but also our own and those of the whole Christian people. . . . It is, therefore, incumbent upon all of us to consider and to choose to amend our sins by voluntary chastisement and to turn to the Lord our God with penance and works of piety; and we should first amend in ourselves what we have done wrong and then turn our attention to the treachery and malice of the enemy.

The letter went on to appeal to Christians to be mindful of the transitory nature of this world and to 'accept with an act of thanksgiving the opportunity for repentance and doing good' by going to the aid of the Latin East 'according to the will of God who taught by his own action that one ought to lay down one's life for one's brothers'. It ended with a conventional list of privileges for crusaders, including an old-fashioned indulgence, and a sumptuary clause. ('Historia de expeditione Friderici imperatoris', ed. A. Chroust, *MGHS rer. Germ.* NS, vol. 5 (1928), pp. 6–10).

This beautiful letter was echoed in the preaching of the crusade, which was everywhere characterized by calls to repentance. It also marked an important stage in the development of crusading thought, for the papacy was now associating success in war directly with the spiritual health of all Christianity. This train of thought manifested itself until the sixteenth century in the way general councils, summoned to reform Christendom, were convoked at the same time as crusades were proclaimed.

The news had been brought to Rome by Genoese merchants. Hard on their heels came Joscius, the Archbishop of Tyre, the only city on the Palestinian coast still in Christian hands. It was being energetically defended under the leadership of Conrad of Montferrat, the younger brother of Sibylla of Jerusalem's first husband, who had arrived in Palestine in the wake of the disaster and himself showered the West with appeals for aid. Archbishop Joscius sailed in the late summer and arrived in Sicily. King William II of Sicily responded at once by despatching a fleet, which in the spring and summer of 1188 saved Tripoli and provisioned Antioch and Tyre, making an important contribution to the survival of the settlements. Joscius must have reached Rome in the middle of October. He then travelled in winter-time to France and on 22 January 1188 met King Henry II of England and King Philip II of France at Gisors, on the frontier between the duchy of Normandy and the royal domain, where the kings were meeting to discuss the drafting of a truce between them. Presented with his appeal, the kings, Count Philip of Flanders who was with them and the other magnates present took the cross and began to make plans. Following a practice begun on the Second Crusade, when the Wendish crusaders had worn distinctive crosses, it was decided that the crusaders of each nation would wear crosses of different colours: the French red, the English white and the Flemish green. Henry and Philip agreed to levy a general tax for the crusade, the second, in fact, of the decade and known as the Saladin Tithe.

But then the vicious politics of western Europe intervened. War broke out between Henry's eldest surviving son, Count Richard of Poitou, and the Count of Toulouse. The kings of England and France became embroiled in the summer and autumn, and relations between them reached a low point when Richard switched support to the king of France. By the summer of 1189, worried by Henry's preference for his younger brother John, he was in open rebellion. Henry died on 6 July, very shortly after reaching a settlement on the crusade with Philip, and Richard was crowned king of England on 3 September. A storm of protest had blown up at the delays, and the reasons for them, not only from ecclesiastics but also from troubadours and trouvères: there can be no doubt that public opinion was scandalized. Richard had, in fact, taken the cross earlier than his father had done and the force of public pressure was such that he could no longer put off the expedition, even had he wanted to. In November he agreed to join forces with Philip at Vézelay on 1 April 1190. The date of mustering was later put back to 1 July, but the English and French crusades were at last in train.

The vacillation of the English and French kings looked very bad when compared to the response in Germany. The Emperor Frederick I was now nearly seventy and had governed Germany for thirty-six years. He was a vigorous old man – his physical stamina was tremendous – and he was intelligent and adaptable, with a strong personality and a penchant for flamboyance that had sometimes led him into scrapes. He had been on the Second Crusade forty years before and his mind had occasionally turned to crusading in the interim: he had discussed it in 1165 and 1184. How far his commitment to the movement was conventional piety, or speculative and associated with conceptions of the duty of emperors to defend Christendom, or even eschatological and influenced by the idea of the last Christian emperor who would rule Jerusalem before the advent of Anti-Christ, is now hard to tell. But he certainly was in the mood to respond to Cardinal Henry of Albano, who was sent by Pope Gregory VIII to preach the cross in Germany. Frederick was deeply moved by a crusade sermon preached by Bishop Henry of Strasbourg in December 1187 although, being the man he was, he took a few months to make up his mind that Germany could survive his absence. In a typically dramatic gesture he then summoned a special court, a *curia Jesu Christi*, to be presided over not by himself but by Christ, and on *Laetare* Sunday (27 March 1188), when the introit of the Mass begins 'Rejoice Jerusalem!', he and many members of the German nobility took the cross in Henry of Albano's presence. The date of departure was set for the feast of St George, 23 April 1189, and the land route was again chosen. The Hungarians, Serbians, Greeks and even the Turks of Konya were told of the plans. The Greeks received the assurance that there would be a peaceful passage through the empire and they in turn promised to provide guides and supplies. Final arrangements were made at Regensburg, where the crusaders gathered on the appointed date, and on 11 May 1189 the army began its march.

It contained many leading figures in the German Church and nobility and it was very large; the estimate of 100,000 men made by contemporaries was certainly an exaggeration, but it must have been one of the largest crusading armies, if not the largest, ever to take the field. It was very well-organized and discipline was strictly maintained. But it began to be harassed by brigands as it passed through regions of the Balkans under Byzantine control, while the markets which had been promised were not opened; there was no evidence of preparations for the Germans' arrival. In fact the Byzantine Emperor Isaac Angelus had made a pact with Saladin in which he had agreed to delay and destroy them, and so obstacles were deliberately, though not very effectively, put in their way. Isaac, moreover, foolishly tried to bring pressure to bear by arresting Frederick's ambassadors in Constantinople and holding them as hostages, while his officers' vain attempt to use regular troops to block the advance was brushed aside. By the time the Germans occupied Plovdiv on 26 August they were in no mood to be thwarted, and Isaac's refusal of passage across the Dardanelles until Frederick sent him more hostages and promised to surrender to the Greeks half his conquests from the Muslims was ignored. The Germans resorted to plundering and Frederick, who was negotiating with Serbian and Vlach-Bulgarian rebels against Byzantium, also began to think seriously of attacking Constantinople itself: on 16 November he wrote to his eldest son Henry, asking him to persuade the Italian maritime cities to raise a fleet to join him before Constantinople in the following March to lay siege to the city.

Isaac had been forced to return the German ambassadors at the end of October, but the next few exchanges were sourced by his refusal to address Frederick by his proper title, another issue on which he had to climb down. Frederick moved his winter quarters to Edirne and now held a large area of Thrace, while negotiations with an increasingly panic-stricken Byzantine government continued. On 14 February 1190 Isaac at last agreed to furnish ships for transport across the Dardanelles from Gallipoli (Gelibolu) – at least, unlike his predecessors, he had persuaded the Germans to by-pass Constantinople – to provide markets, supplies and hostages, to release the Catholic prisoners he held, to pay reparations and to accept that the Germans would expect to forage in those regions where provisions were not supplied.

The Germans left Edirne on 1 March and crossed the Dardanelles between the 22nd and the 28th. In Byzantine Asia Minor, however, they met with the same harassment and non-cooperation that they had experienced in Europe. Leaving Alaşehir on 22 April, they entered Muslim territory and made straight for Konya. On the march they suffered as their predecessors had done – their horses and pack-animals died and they ran out of food – but Konya fell to them on 18 May. Refreshed by the stores they found there and promised adequate supplies by the Turks, who were now anxious to let them through in peace, they reached Karaman, on the borders of Cilicia, on the 30th. Here they were again in Christian territory and they were greeted with friendliness by the Armenians, but on 10 June Frederick, who had proved that it was still possible to march an army through Asia Minor and was exuberant and hot, succumbed to the temptation of one last *coup de théâtre*, this time fatal for him. He tried to swim the river Göksu, which is deep and wide. In mid-stream he got into difficulties; perhaps he had a heart-attack. At any rate he was dead or drowned by the time his nobles reached him.

The German crusade, which had done so well, brushing the Byzantines aside with icy efficiency and marching in a disciplined fashion across

Turkish Asia Minor, was broken by his death. Some crusaders left at once for home. The rest divided into those who sailed to Antioch and Tripoli and those who marched overland to Syria, losing many of their number in the process. At Antioch the army was further decimated by an epidemic. It began its journey down the coast in late August and early in October arrived before Acre, which had been besieged by the Christians for eighteen months. King Guy of Jerusalem had been released by Saladin in the summer of 1188, but in the following spring Conrad of Montferrat, who denied his right to the kingship, had refused him and Queen Sibylla entry into Tyre, the only Palestinian city in Christian hands. Guy's reaction had been courageous; he had marched south with very few troops to lay siege to Acre. His action had forced his leading vassals, who had remained neutral or had sided with Conrad, to join him and by the following autumn many of them were with him. This so weakened Conrad that in September 1189 he was persuaded to take part in the siege and by the spring of 1190 he had made peace with Guy in return for the promise of a fief in northern Palestine, including Tyre. Guy had been joined over the months by various parties of crusaders, among them a large contingent of Germans, Netherlanders and English in September 1189, and a major French army under the counts of Champagne, Blois and Sancerre in July 1190. It might be supposed that the arrival of the main German force would have strengthened the besieging host. But the Germans, demoralized and dis-eased, continued to sustain heavy losses, among them the old emperor's son, Duke Frederick of Swabia, who died on 20 January 1191. By the following spring most of them had left for home.

Meanwhile Philip of France, who before setting out had solemnly re-ceived the oriflamme in the church of St Denis like his father forty-three years before, and Richard of England had met at Vézelay. On 4 July 1190 they began their march to the Mediterranean coast. Richard was nearly thirty-three years old. His courage, resourcefulness and real administrative ability showed up best on the battle-field and on campaign: he was, in fact, the finest crusade commander since Bohemond of Taranto, and possibly the best of all. But he was also vain, with a love of pomp and display – he was very good-looking – and he was devious and self-centred. He had inherited an efficient and energetic apparatus of government, which had thrown itself into making preparations from the moment of Henry II's agreement to crusade. The Archbishop of Canterbury had organized systematic preaching throughout the country and in spite of bitter opposition the Saladin Tithe had been collected. To supplement it Richard had sold everything that could be sold and had ruthlessly exploited every relationship for cash and every opportunity to raise enormous sums of money. He therefore found himself in fairly comfortable circumstances and his superior financial resources were apparent throughout the crusade.

Philip was a younger man, still only in his mid-twenties. He was not impressive to look at – he had already lost the sight of one eye – and ten years of government of France had made him cautious and distrustful, cynical and nervous. He was not clever or well-educated, but he was sharp and intelligent in a practical way and he had a capacity for hard work and taking pains, combined with self-control, a disposition towards equity and fairness and a prudence that made him a great king. Ruthless he might be but he was usually ruthlessly fair. He ruled a far less centralized country than Richard did and he could not override the opposition to the Saladin Tithe. He was forced to state publicly that it would never again be levied; and outside the royal domain it was collected by his great magnates for their own crusading needs. So he was much less well off than Richard although he led a larger army: about 2,000 mounted men to 800 at the most.

Richard had expected to find an English fleet at Marseille, but it had stopped off in Portugal and had not yet arrived. He had to hire other ships, in which he reached Messina in Sicily on 22 September to find his fleet from England and Philip of France already there. Richard had business to transact in Sicily which would help him to raise even more cash for his crusade. His sister Joan was the widow of King William II and he wanted her dowry back from Tancred, count of Lecce, who had seized the throne, together with a legacy left by William to his father Henry II. He resorted to violence, seizing the Calabrian town of Bagnara, across the straits from Messina, and on 4 October Messina itself, which was sacked by his troops. Tancred was forced to pay 40,000 gold ounces, half for Joan's dowry and half as a marriage portion for his daughter who was betrothed to Arthur of Britanny, Richard's heir, although Philip managed to get one-third of the gold for himself on the basis of an agreement made by the two kings at Vézelay to share their acquisitions.

Philip sailed for the East on 30 March, 1191. Richard, who had stayed to meet his new fiancée, Berengaria of Navarre – his betrothal was a delicate issue since he had been engaged to Philip's sister Alice – sailed on 10 April. His fleet cruised by way of Crete and Rhodes to Cyprus, which he reached on 6 May. The Greek ruler of the island, Isaac Comnenus, who had declared his independence of Constantinople in the 1180s, had imprisoned some English crusaders whose ships, including one of the royal treasure-ships, had been wrecked in a storm off the southern coast; and the great ship carrying Berengaria and Joan was hove to offshore, fearful of making a landing. Richard at once demanded the return of his men and goods. When Isaac refused, Richard invaded the island and by 5 June, when he left for Acre, it was in his hands. It was to remain under Latin control for nearly four hundred years.

Philip reached Acre on 20 April and Richard on 8 June. They found the city blockaded. Forces had continued to arrive during the autumn, winter and spring of 1190–91, including an English advance party under the Archbishop of Canterbury. But, like all crusades, the army was a confederation of contingents under different leaders and it was deeply divided over political developments in the kingdom of Jerusalem. Sibylla and the two daughters she had borne Guy had died in the autumn of 1190. This meant, of course, that although Guy was the anointed king, the heiress to Jerusalem was now Isabella, Sibylla's younger half-sister who was married to Humphrey of Tibnine. It will be remembered that it had been Humphrey's defection that had destroyed the baronial rebellion in 1186. A group of leading nobles, including Balian of Ibelin, lord of Nablus and the husband of Isabella's mother Maria Comnena, and the lords of Sidon and Haifa, planned to have Isabella's marriage to Humphrey annulled so that she could be wed to Conrad of Montferrat, who was well-connected and had proved his ability and the strength of his personality. Isabella was abducted from her tent in the camp before Acre and an ecclesiastical court, dominated by the papal legate, who was a supporter of Conrad, and by Conrad's cousin, the Bishop of Beauvais, ruled that her marriage to Humphrey had been invalid, much to the disgust of the Archbishop of Canterbury, who represented the sick patriarch of Jerusalem at the hearings. Isabella was hurriedly married to Conrad: a marriage that was later considered to have been technically incestuous, since Conrad's brother had been married to Isabella's half-sister, and bigamous. She then formally required the kingdom from the High Court. She was accepted and homage was paid to her. It looked as though Guy of Lusignan was being put aside.

It was certain that the two European kings would be asked to arbitrate in this affair – Richard had been met in Cyprus by Guy, Humphrey of Tibnine and their supporters – and it was also certain that their responses would be different, because each was entangled in the skeins of western feudal and family relationsips: Guy's family, the Lusignans, were feudatories, although extremely difficult ones, of Richard's county of Poitou; Conrad was Philip of France's cousin. But they agreed to adjudicate and the course of events now strengthened their hands. Acre capitulated on 12 July, in spite of a last-minute attempt by Saladin to save it, and Philip and Richard divided the city between them in accordance with their agreement on the division of spoils. This meant that their decisions on the allocation of what had been royal property could effectively decide the winner in the conflict over the kingdom of Jerusalem. On 28 July they announced a compromise: Guy was to have the kingdom for the rest of his life, but after his death Isabella and Conrad would inherit it. All royal rents were to be shared, and apanages were to be created in the south – Jaffa and Ascalon – for Guy's brother Geoffrey, and in the north – Tyre, Sidon and Beirut – for Conrad.

Philip then gave Conrad his half of Acre, against Richard's wishes, and left for home on 31 July. A large body of French crusaders, under the leadership of the Duke of Burgundy, remained in Palestine and was to play an important part in the events that followed.

The terms of the agreement for the surrender of Acre had been that the garrison was to be spared and released on the promise of a ransom of 200,000 dinars; the relic of the True Cross, lost at Hattin, was to be returned; and a large number of Christian prisoners were to be set free; hostages were to be held by the crusaders pending the fulfilment of the conditions. But negotiations with Saladin broke down when the first instalment of the ransom became due and in a fit of rage Richard ordered the massacre of most of the hostages, some 2,700 men, in the sight of the Muslim army that was still encamped near Acre. He then decided to strike for Jerusalem, which meant first marching to the port of Jaffa, seventy miles down the coast. His army set out on 22 August with the Christian fleet sailing alongside and regularly supplying it. The knights were organized in three divisions, marching in column. Inland from them, on their left flank, there was a protective screen of foot-soldiers, who had to ward off most of the attacks; half of the infantry were periodically rested by allowing them to march with the baggage-train that trundled between the knights and the sea. The army kept a steady disciplined progress in spite of being continually harassed by Muslim skirmishers and light cavalry. The self-restraint displayed by the infantry was remarkable for the time and in so far as it was a response to Richard's leadership, demonstrated that he was a military commander of the highest calibre. On 7 September Saladin managed to bring him to battle north of Arsuf, where the road passed through a gap between a forest and the sea. He used conventional tactics, seeking to weaken the Christian formation by archery and by attacking its flank and rear. The Hospitallers in the rearguard, maddened by their horses' injuries, launched into a charge too early and Richard had to order a general advance before he was ready, but he was able – and this is further evidence of his quality as a commander – to halt the charge once it had achieved its purpose and to reform his line to meet a Muslim counterattack. The Muslims eventually retired, leaving Richard's army, which had sustained comparatively light losses, in possession of the field.

Three days later the crusaders reached Jaffa and began to restore its fortifications. There were three options open to Richard: a treaty with Saladin; an immediate advance on Jerusalem, which was dangerous while there was a large Muslim army in the vicinity; or the occupation and refortification of Ascalon, the walls of which the Muslims were in the process of destroying, since this would limit Saladin's ability to bring up reserves from Egypt. At first Richard did not abandon any of these alternatives. He began to concentrate all the troops he could at Jaffa, but he also entered into negotiations with Saladin for the cession of Palestine to the Christians; it was during these that he was supposed to have suggested his sister Joan as a wife for Saladin's brother. By late October he had decided to advance on Jerusalem, although he proceeded very cautiously: by 23 December he had only reached Latrun, half-way from Jaffa to the holy city. By 3 January he had reached Beit Nuba, only twelve miles from Jerusalem, but then, on the advice of the local Christian leaders, he decided to withdraw and refortify Ascalon. On the 20th he reached the place and work on its walls went on until early June; on 23 May the fortress of Deir el Balah further south was taken by storm. He then decided to try for Jerusalem once more. His army marched on 7 June and on the 11th again reached Beit Nuba. It halted there until late in the month, but because his line of supplies back to Jaffa was threatened and he realized that his force was not large enough to hold Jerusalem, Richard again withdrew, after a debate during which the option of an invasion of Egypt was raised. On 26 July he returned to Acre.

Richard's withdrawal gave Saladin his chance. On the 27th he launched an attack on Jaffa, which was still weakly fortified. By the 30th the garrison was seeking terms, but Richard was already on his way by sea to relieve it. He arrived the following day to find the Muslims in possession of the town and the garrison in the process of surrendering the citadel. Wading ashore and supported by a sally from the citadel, in which the garrison had rallied, he drove the demoralized Muslims out of the town. And an attempt on 5 August by Saladin to surprise Richard's tiny force, including perhaps fifty knights of whom no more than ten had horses and a few hundred crossbowmen, faltered as soon as his soldiers saw the Christians drawn up in a solid defensive formation.

Richard's military achievements were impressive even though he had not been able to liberate Jerusalem. He was, however, not nearly as successful in local politics as he was on the battlefield. His support of Guy of Lusignan, to whom he was prepared to surrender his conquests, was frustrated by Conrad of Montferrat, the French crusaders and the local barons, who had never really accepted the compromise of 28 July 1191. They set out to undermine his military efforts since they knew that the territory he gained would be handed over to Guy, and they negotiated directly with the Muslims in the hope of getting grants of land directly from Saladin. In February 1192 there was an unsuccessful attempt to seize Acre for Conrad. Richard came to realize that Guy's political situation was hopeless and c. 13 April he summoned a council of his army and accepted the advice that Conrad should be king. He compensated Guy with the lordship of Cyprus; he had sold the island to the Templars but after a revolt in April 1192 they were anxious to return it. Within a fortnight, however, Conrad was dead, struck down in Tyre by Assassins. It was never known who had employed them, but the seizure of Richard as he returned from the crusade by Leopold of Austria, who had taken part in the siege of Acre, and his imprisonment by the emperor Henry VI demonstrates that they, who were both Conrad's cousins, believed that he had been responsible. At any rate Isabella was now married, with Richard's consent if not on his initiative, to the crusader Count Henry of Champagne, who ruled the kingdom until his death in 1197.

By mid-August 1192 Richard had fallen very ill. His crusade had lost impetus and he was worried by news of events in Western Europe. On 2 September his representatives signed a truce with Saladin which was to last for three years and eight months. The Christians were to hold the coast from Tyre to Jaffa. Ascalon's fortifications were to be demolished before it was returned to Saladin. Christians and Muslims were to have free passage throughout Palestine. Many of the English crusaders visited the shrines in Jerusalem, although Richard did his best to prevent the French crusaders, whom he had not forgiven for frustrating his campaign, from going as well. He sailed from Acre on 9 October.

The crusade of 1197

The Third Crusade had as an epilogue another crusade. Frederick I of Germany had been succeeded by his eldest son, Henry VI, whose ambitions in Europe, to turn the German empire into a hereditary monarchy and to pacify Sicily, which he claimed by right of his wife and had to occupy by force, may well have led him to consider the advantages to his international standing of crusading to the East as soon as Richard's truce with Saladin expired. He must also have shared the enthusiasm for crusading that was almost universal at the time and he may have felt some obligation to fulfil his father's vow, left uncompleted by his death. He took the cross in Holy Week 1195 and on Easter Day summoned his subjects to crusade at a solemn diet at Bari, promising to supplement the crusaders with 3,000 mounted mercenaries. In June he left for Germany to promote the enterprise and on 1 August Pope Celestine III published a new crusade appeal and called on the German clergy to preach the cross. In October and December, at Gelnhausen and Worms, Henry personally witnessed the enrolment of the German nobility. At Gelnhausen he also agreed to a proposal from Cyprus that the island should become a vassal-kingdom of the empire, and soon afterwards the negotiations began which were to lead to the ruler of Cilician Armenia also becoming a vassal-king. At the diet of Würzburg in March 1196 the arrangements for the crusade were completed and a year later an impressive Germany army, probably almost as large as that led by Frederick, was assembling in the ports of southern Italy and Sicily. It was led by the Archbishop of Mainz, for Henry, who had not been well and had to deal with renewed unrest in southern Italy, had probably now given up all hope of leading it himself. On 22 September 1197 the main German fleet reached Acre. The Germans occupied Sidon and Beirut, which had been abandoned by the Muslims, and laid siege to Tibnine, but then news from home caused their crusade to disintegrate. Henry VI had died at Messina on 28 September leaving a baby son, and the kingdom of Germany and the empire were bound to be disputed. On 1 July 1198 a truce was made with the Muslims in which the Christian possession of Beirut was recognized and by the end of the summer most of the leading crusaders had left to protect their lands and rights at home.

The Third Crusade and the crusade of 1197–8 demonstrated what enthusiasm the movement could command in Europe when there was a real crisis in the East and what large forces could be put into the field at such a time. The record of these years, if judged in terms of the men and matériel channelled to the East, is remarkable. And, after rather a slow start, the crusaders' achievements were outstanding. In 1188 the Christians had been left only with the city of Tyre and one or two isolated fortresses inland; by 1198 they held nearly the whole of the Palestinian coast. But Jerusalem had eluded them, which helps to explain the obsessive concern with crusading which continued to be displayed at all levels of society.

Pope Innocent III

By the time the Germans were withdrawing from Palestine there was a new pope, for on 8 January 1198 Lothario dei Conti di Segni had been elected and had taken the name of Innocent III. He was then aged thirty-seven or thirty-eight and so was a comparatively young man. Vigorous and quick-witted, his judgements upon others and his decisions, even on points of law in which he had been well-trained, could be hasty. He had an exceptionally high view of his office as a vicariate for Christ, with authority over all aspects of Church business and a final say in secular affairs, although it is important to stress that his concerns were primarily pastoral and his decisions were therefore often pragmatic. His ideas and temperament drove him to take far more interest in the management of crusades than had his predecessors, who had been content to leave the planning and conduct to the laity once they had preached them. During the twelfth century leadership of the movement in the field had been assumed by kings: Louis VII of France and Conrad III of Germany; Philip II of France, Richard I of England and Frederick I of Germany. It has often been suggested that Innocent deliberately tried to exclude kings from the management of crusades. This is misleading; rather he positively set out to manage crusades himself. It happened that the time was right for him to do so, since Henry of Germany had recently died and Richard of England and Philip of France were not anxious to reassume the cross after their recent involvement. But events were to demonstrate that the papacy had not the ability in law nor the organizational powers to direct crusades successfully.

Innocent nevertheless contributed more to the movement than any other individual except Urban II. He could not expect to lead a crusade himself – as early as August 1198 he was admitting that his office was too demanding for him to go to the East in person – but crusading was something that appealed to both the speculative and political sides of his nature. No other pope seems to have devoted quite so much time to the movement. No other pope preached as many crusades as he did. Perhaps no other pope would have subordinated a fundamental principle of canon law to the needs of crusading as rashly as he did when in 1201 he decreed that the Holy Land was in such dire straits that a man could take the cross without his wife's consent. He justified this violation of the natural right of married women and the principle of the parity of both partners in a marriage contract in a ruling about which canon lawyers, who never denied its validity, were always uncomfortable, by reference to analogies with the secular world, arguing that since the objections of wives could not overrule the demands of earthly kings for military service they could not be a hindrance to the commands of the heavenly king. In this he developed a theme found in his letters: that, although by its nature voluntary, the vow to crusade was a moral imperative. It was demanded of qualified Christians by God and could not be set aside with impunity:

> To those men who refuse to take part, if indeed there be perchance any man so ungrateful to the lord our God, we firmly state on behalf of the apostle Peter that they . . . will have to answer to us on this matter in the presence of the Dreadful Judge on the Last Day of severe Judgement (Lateran Council IV: *Conciliorum oecumenicorum decreta*, ed. J. Alberigo et al. (1962), p. 244).

It was this conviction that led him not just to invite the clergy to support the crusade he preached in 1198; he strictly ordered them to do so. On the other hand it would be wrong to suppose that the movement dominated his thinking to the exclusion of everything else. He was one of those enthusiasts with a capacity for concentration on whatever problem he was facing and his pontificate reveals plenty of other examples of major issues in which his guiding hand and individual approach can be discerned. It has been pointed out that he did not come to the papal throne with any preconceived plan for a crusade; it was only in the summer of 1198, six months after his election, that the first signs of one appear, probably in reaction to an appeal from the East which followed the collapse of the German crusade.

The Fourth Crusade

In August 1198 he issued his first crusade encyclical, addressed directly to all prelates, counts, barons and Christian people. In this he was not passing over kings, whom he wanted to participate – he called upon Richard of England and Philip of France to make a truce for five years – but he was implying that they would have no greater say in planning than any other crusader. Authority over the crusade in its early stages was to be entirely in his hands. Crusaders were summoned to be ready for two years' service by the following March. Two legates would go ahead to Palestine to prepare for their arrival. Prelates of the Church were ordered to send armed men or to contribute their equivalent in cash. The encyclical also contained a new formulation of the indulgence. Innocent had opted for the new theology of penance and a remission of the type foreshadowed in the writings of St Bernard and Eugenius III and in doing so he definitively established the indulgence as it has been known to Catholics ever since: only very rarely were the old formulae used thereafter. No longer was the indulgence merely a declaration that a penitential act would be satisfactory; it was now a promise on God's behalf of the remission of the penalties that were the consequence of sin, whether imposed by the Church itself or by God in this world or the next. The emphasis was to be no longer on what the sinner did – it was doubtful if there was anything he could anyway do that would outweigh his sins – but on the loving willingness of a merciful God to make good any deficiency by rewarding the devout performance of a meritorious work:

> We, trusting in the mercy of God and the authority of the blessed apostles Peter and Paul, by that power of binding and loosing that God has conferred on us, although unworthy, grant to all those submitting to the labour of this journey personally and at their expense full forgiveness of their sins, of which they have been moved to penitence in voice and heart, and as the reward of the just we promise them a greater share of eternal salvation (Innocent III, *Register*, ed. O. Hageneder and A. Haidacher, vol. 1 (1964), p. 503).

This unequivocal formulation made a great impression on contemporaries. Geoffrey of Villehardouin, who played a leading part in the crusade, wrote:

> because the indulgence was so great the hearts of men were much moved; and many took the cross because the indulgence was so great (Geoffrey of Villehardouin, *La conquête de Constantinople*, ed. E. Faral (1961), vol. 1, p. 4).

It soon became clear, however, that Innocent had characteristically taken the bold step of issuing a major encyclical without considering its consequences. There was enthusiasm for the crusade as the popular response to the sermons of the crusade preacher Fulk of Neuilly, commissioned by the pope in November 1198, soon showed, but it would require more than enthusiasm to galvanize knights. The experiences of crusaders for a century had shown what financial difficulties even the best-prepared could get into and the fact was that warfare was becoming more and more expensive. It had already become the practice, as we have seen, for kings to raise cash to help crusaders and it is probable that knights were becoming reliant on the participation of their rulers and the back-up they alone could provide. Without it they were reluctant to commit themselves. But the kings of France and England were again at each other's throats and a truce made between them in January 1199 was nullified by King Richard's death two months later. The papal legate Peter Capuano, moreover, was forced out of France after he had placed the kingdom under an interdict because of King Philip's disavowal of his queen, Ingeborg of Denmark. March 1199 came and went without any large-scale response from the nobles and knights. Innocent's reaction was typical of him. He redoubled his efforts and at the end of the year took a step even bolder than his original one. He announced the first direct taxation of the universal Church, the raising of a fortieth of all revenues for one year; grants to crusaders were to be made out of this in each province by a committee of churchmen and laymen, including members of the Military Orders. The trepidation with which he approached this controversial innovation is shown by the way he opened his letter of instruction with a commitment to tax his own church of Rome at the higher rate of a tenth and the care he took to stress that his measure was not intended to create a precedent. Of course it did, and the taxation of the Church was to become a regular method of raising money for crusading, which it transformed by providing proper funding. It gave future popes an authority over the movement more real than that of their predecessors, because they became its bankers. But in 1199 the measure was probably a sign of Innocent's desperation. His appeal had not provided enough volunteers and he must have understood that without the kings' support the costs were now too high for many, even in the military classes. The only alternative was for him to subsidize crusaders himself. He also hoped, it is clear, to supplement them with mercenaries. In fact this first attempt at taxation was not particularly successful. There was resistance to it, as one might expect, and it took a long time to collect. Some English assessments were only collected in 1217; by 1208 it had still not been raised even in parts of Italy.

Even before Innocent had promulgated this measure, but perhaps in response to rumours that it was impending, the nobles and knights were beginning to show more interest. If the contemporary Geoffrey of Villehardouin is to be believed – and he is by no means always trustworthy – the first evidence of this came on 28 November 1199 in a way that was characteristic of their class. During a tournament held at Écry (today Asfeld-la-Ville) the young Counts Thibald of Champagne and Louis of Blois took the cross, together with many of their vassals and two important lords of the Île-de-France, Simon of Montfort and Reynald of Montmirail. On 23 February 1200, Ash Wednesday, Count Baldwin of Flanders, who was Thibald's brother-in-law, also vowed to crusade, as did his brothers Henry and Eustace and many of his vassals. The three counts, from families with long traditions of crusading, were the natural leaders of the movement and they acted together. A meeting at Soissons decided to delay planning until the number of recruits had grown. Two months later another meeting, held at Compiègne, decided on the sea route to the East and gave six men, two of whom were chosen by each count, plenary powers to negotiate the best terms they could with one of the maritime cities.

The six delegates, two of whom were the famous trouvère Conon of Béthune and the future historian of the crusade, Geoffrey of Villehardouin, decided to approach Venice. Crossing the Alps in mid-winter they put their case in February 1201 to the ducal council and the doge Enrico Dandolo, who was extremely old – he must have been getting on for ninety – and partially blind, but shrewd and indomitable. The response must have exceeded all their hopes. The Venetians promised transport, which would naturally have to be paid for, but they added fifty armed galleys to the fleet, committing themselves to crusade as equal partners with, of course, an equal share in the spoil. The fleet, it was settled, must be ready by 29 June 1202 and it was secretly agreed that its destination would be Egypt, a sign of the conviction, which had been developing for fifty years, that the Holy Land could only be secured by taking war to the centres of Muslim power in the region, although this could not possibly have been decided upon by the six envoys alone, even with their plenipotential powers; it must have been suggested to them by their masters in France, who would have known that the kingdom of Jerusalem had made a five-year truce with the Muslims in 1198. At this stage, however, the French delegates made an error which was to change the course of events, for, in providing the Venetians with an estimate of the size of the crusade, they wildly exaggerated it, multiplying by at least three times the number of crusaders actually enrolled by late 1200. The agreement specified an army of 4,500 knights and their horses, 9,000 squires and 20,000 foot, for whom a sum of 85,000 marks of Cologne – not an excessive price – would have to be paid in instalments by April 1202. The treaty was solemnly ratified at an assembly in the church of St Mark and a copy of it was sent to the pope for his confirmation.

It is remarkable, given the efforts he had put into the proclamation of the crusade, that Innocent only reappeared on the stage at this juncture. An army was being raised in France and its leaders had sent delegates to conclude a treaty with Venice with apparently no thought of consulting him beforehand. There is some evidence that he was worried by the course events were taking and that he was distrustful of Venice, which was in dispute with Hungary over ports on the Dalmatian coast: there was already the danger that Venice might take advantage of the presence of a large army to restore her influence in that part of the Adriatic. But there was little the pope could do other than approve the treaty and throw his weight behind the plan for the crusade's departure in the summer of 1202.

The envoys returned to France to find Thibald of Champagne dying. Since he had been one of a triumvirate the first reaction was to try to replace him. But after the Duke of Burgundy and the Count of Bar-le Duc had refused to take his place, an assembly, meeting towards the end of June 1201 at Soissons, decided to offer the Marquis Boniface of Montferrat the command of the whole army. Boniface had not crusaded before, but we have already come across one of his brothers, William, marrying Sibylla of Jerusalem and another, Conrad, marrying her half-sister Isabella. A third brother, Renier, had married a Greek princess and had ranked as a Caesar in the Byzantine empire before being murdered in 1183. So there were strong links with the East. It has already been pointed out that members of the Montferrat family were very well-connected, being cousins of the French and German royal houses: in fact King Philip of France may have suggested Boniface for the leadership of the crusade. Boniface was one of the best-known military commanders of his day and his court was a centre of chivalry. He was also a personal friend and subject of Philip of Swabia, the younger brother of the dead Emperor Henry VI. Philip was a contestant for the empire, to which he had been elected in April 1198, and was therefore in conflict with the pope, who now favoured his rival Otto of Brunswick. He was allied by marriage to the Byzantine imperial house, for his wife was Irene Angelus, whose father, the Emperor Isaac, had been deposed, blinded and imprisoned with her brother Alexius by her uncle, Alexius III. Boniface came to Soissons in the late summer of 1201, accepted the command of the army and took the cross. He then went, by way of Cîteaux where an important cross-taking ceremony coincided with a meeting of the Cistercian general chapter, to Germany to attend Philip of Swabia's Christmas court at Hagenau.

To that court also came the young Alexius Angelus, Philip's brother-in-law, who had escaped his uncle's surveillance and fled to the West to appeal for help on his father's behalf. It is possible that the use of the crusade as a means of forcing a change of government in Constantinople was discussed at Hagenau and was raised with the pope by

Alexius in the following February and by Boniface in the middle of March. But if so Innocent certainly rejected any such idea and no decision can have been made by the time the crusaders began to reach Venice in the middle of the summer of 1202.

Too few of them came. Some of those who had taken the cross did not fulfil their vows. Others decided not to travel by way of Venice but to make their own arrangements and go directly to Palestine from other ports. Many others simply did not exist, being figments of the delegates' imaginations when the year before they had grossly overestimated the numbers expected. At any rate in the early autumn of 1202 it was found that only about one-third of the projected 33,500 men had turned up and the result was that, in spite of every effort and the generosity of the leaders who contributed what they could from their own pockets, the crusaders were left owing the Venetians 34,000 silver marks for shipping which had already been built. The Venetians, who had involved themselves in a massive ship-building enterprise to prepare a fleet of about 500 vessels at a cost to their own commercial interests, were determined to get payment and even threatened to cut off supplies to the crusaders, who were encamped on the Lido, the large island closing the lagoon from the Adriatic. Winter was approaching and with it the end of the sailing season. Without even leaving Europe the crusaders had already fallen into the most characteristic trap of crusading, a desperate shortage of cash, in spite of Innocent's revolutionary measure of taxing the Church which by now, in fact, can have produced little. It was at this stage that the doge suggested a postponement of the payment of their debt until it could be settled out of plunder, on condition that they helped him recapture the port of Zadar on the Dalmatian coast from the Hungarians. They naturally accepted and found themselves committed to start their crusade by attacking a Christian town which was subject to a fellow-crusader, since King Emeric of Hungary had himself taken the cross. Whatever the rights or wrongs of Emeric's occupation of Zadar the Church was bound to maintain him in possession of it, just as it was bound to protect the properties of Zadar's assailants while they were away from home. And because the crusaders began their enterprise anxious about their debts to the Venetians, which would have to be repaid out of profits, the leaders were in the mood to open negotiations with the young Alexius Angelus, whose envoys came to ask for their aid in his cause. At the same time many crusaders were worried by the course of events, all the more so since the Venetians refused to accept the credentials of the papal legate, Peter Capuano, which forced him to return to Rome. There were many defections and before he left Venice Peter Capuano, who seems to have been prepared at least to turn a blind eye on the attack on Zadar, had to insist that some leading churchmen, including Bishop Conrad of Halberstadt and Abbot Martin of

Pairis, swallow their doubts and remain with the army to assure it of some spiritual direction. Even Boniface of Montferrat felt it prudent to leave the crusade and travel to Rome; he did not rejoin it until after Zadar had fallen.

Once their terms had been accepted Enrico Dandolo and many leading Venetians took the cross. A fleet of over 200 ships, including 60 galleys, left Venice in early October 1202 and sailed slowly down the coast in a show of force designed to impress other subject cities before appearing off Zadar on 10 November. The army landed, but it now received a letter from the pope forbidding it to attack any Christian city and referring to Zadar by name. Several important crusaders, led by the Cistercian abbot Guy of Vaux-de-Cernay and Simon of Montfort, voiced their opposition to the siege in the pope's name and even sent messages to Zadar's defenders encouraging them to resist. They then withdrew some distance and played no further part in the action. On 24 November the city fell and was sacked, the spoil being divided between the crusaders and the Venetians. The decision had already been taken to winter at Zadar, since it was now too late in the year to continue the voyage, and it was there that Boniface of Montferrat found them in the middle of December. Close on his heels came envoys from Philip of Swabia proposing, on behalf of Alexius, that if on its way to the East the crusade would restore him and his father to the Byzantine throne the patriarchate of Constantinople would be made to submit to the papacy, 200,000 silver marks would be handed over for division between the crusaders and the Venetians, and the host would be provisioned by the Greeks for an additional year. Alexius would himself join the crusade if his presence was desired and he would anyway contribute an army of 10,000 Greeks to it and would maintain a force of 500 knights in Palestine at his expense for the rest of his life. These terms were accepted by the Venetians and by most of the greater leaders, for whom they must have presented an opportunity to repay their debt and at the same time get the benefit of whole-hearted Byzantine participation in a campaign in the East. But they involved flagrant disobedience to the pope and this weighed heavily with large numbers of their confrères, many of whom appear only to have accepted them because the alternative, the dissolution of the army, was unthinkable. It is clear that there was general dissatisfaction and anxiety and there were more defections, including that of Simon of Montfort.

The crusaders had incurred automatic excommunication for their insubordination. The bishops in the army were prepared to give them provisional absolution while a delegation visited Rome to explain their action and ask for forgiveness. Innocent found himself caught in a trap. The crusade he had hoped for had at last departed and inflexibility on his part might lead to its dispersal. So he was prepared to absolve the crusaders provided they restored what they had taken illegally and did not invade other Christian lands. He refused, however, to absolve the Venetians and he issued a formal letter of excommunication of them.

Men who were supposed to be directly under the pope's control had flatly disobeyed him. They went on to disobey him again in every particular. Zadar was not restored to Hungary. Boniface of Montferrat refused to publish the bull of excommunication of the Venetians on the grounds, he explained, shrewdly playing on Innocent's fears, that he did not want the crusade to break up; he would only deliver it to the Venetians if the pope insisted. And by the time Innocent replied in June 1203, insisting that the bull be published and repeating that the crusaders were not to attack any more Christian territory, referring specifically this time to the Byzantine empire, the fleet was approaching Constantinople.

The crusaders had sailed from Zadar late in April 1203. Although there was still controversy among them over the course they were taking they were joined at Corfu by Alexius. Leaving Corfu on 24 May they passed before the sea-walls of Constantinople before disembarking on 24 June across the Bosporus at Kadiköy. They then marched north to Usküdar (Scutari). On 5 July they crossed the Bosporus and landed at Galata, just across the Golden Horn, the enormous creek that was Constantinople's chief port. On the 6th they stormed Galata's main defence work, a great tower, while the Venetians broke the chain that stretched across the entrance to the creek. The French crusaders now marched up the shore of the Golden Horn, rounded the end of it and pitched camp outside the north-western stretch of the city's land-walls, in the angle between them and the water. The Venetian fleet occupied the harbour and prepared to storm the shore defences. On 17 July there was a general assault during which the Venetians occupied about a quarter of the length of these walls, but they abandoned them on hearing of a sortie made by the Greeks against the French, a sortie which, in fact, withdrew again without major engagement. Although the attack on the city had failed, the Emperor Alexius III fled that night and the blind Isaac Angelus was released from prison. He reluctantly agreed to the terms his son had negotiated and on 1 August the young Alexius was crowned his co-emperor.

By August 1203, therefore, the crusaders had every reason to hope that the prologue to their crusade was nearly over. They wrote to the pope and the western kings explaining what they had done and announcing the postponement of their journey to the East until the following March: they had agreed to stay at the expense of Alexius, who wanted them to prop up his régime in its early months. At the same time Alexius assured Innocent of his intention of submitting the Greek Church to Rome. Innocent hesitated again and did not reply until the following February, when he did no more than reprove the crusaders and the Venetians for their actions and order them to continue with the crusade; he also told the French bishops in the army to see that the leaders did penance for their sins. But during the winter of 1203–4 the situation at Constantinople had gravely deteriorated. Alexius had paid the first instalments of the money he had promised, but the Greek people and clergy bitterly resented the Catholic presence and rioting and faction-fighting erupted in the city. Alexius began to cool towards his patrons and the payments dried up. In November, after a delegation of crusaders and Venetians had presented him with an ultimatum, hostilities broke out. Then late in January 1204 a *coup d'état* removed Alexius and his father and a wave of anti-Catholic xenophobia elevated to the throne a great-great-grandson of Alexius I, who took the title of Alexius V.

The crusaders could afford neither to proceed to the East nor return to the West. They were in a hostile environment and were short of provisions and forced to forage. In March they decided that there was only one move left for them to make, the capture of Constantinople itself and the subjugation of the Byzantine empire, although this worried and distressed many of them: on the eve of the assault on the city elaborate justifications, based on the Greeks' sin in abetting the murder of their emperor and their schismatic condition, were concocted by the clergy in the army to give some relief to the crusaders' consciences. Enrico Dandolo, representing Venice, and Boniface of Montferrat, Baldwin of Flanders, Louis of Blois and Hugh of St Pol, representing the other crusaders, concluded a treaty to govern the division of spoil once Constantinople was theirs. The Venetians were to have three-quarters of all booty up to the amount still owed them; over and above that there was to be equal division. Venice was assured of all the privileges previously granted her by the Byzantine emperors. Twelve electors, six from either side, were to choose a Latin emperor, who was to have one-quarter of the empire, including the two imperial palaces in Constantinople. The remaining three-quarters were to be equally divided between the parties. The clergy of the party that failed to get the emperorship would have the right to nominate a cathedral chapter for St Sophia in Constantinople, which would choose a Catholic patriarch. Clergy would be appointed by both parties for their own churches, which would be endowed only with enough to enable them to live decently; the residue would be treated as spoil. Both sides agreed to remain in the region for a year to help to establish the new Latin empire and a joint commission was to be set up to distribute titles and fiefs, which would be heritable through the female as well as the male line, and assign services. The doge would not personally owe military service to the emperor, but fief-holders in the Venetian territories would perform it. No citizen of a state at war with Venice would be admitted to the empire. The emperor was to swear to abide by the terms of the treaty and a commission consisting of the doge,

Boniface of Montferrat and six councillors from either side would adjust the terms if need be; both parties agreed to petition the pope to make violations of them punishable by excommunication. It has often been pointed out that this treaty, which established the constitution of the Latin empire, assured it of a weak emperor and over-powerful Venetian presence.

The assault began at daybreak on 9 April against the harbour wall: the land-walls had proved themselves to be very strong the previous year, while the Venetians had been more successful attacking from the waters of the Golden Horn. It failed, but it was resumed on the 12th, with floating freighters grappling the tops of the towers with flying bridges, while other troops landed and scaled the walls. By evening the crusaders were in control of a section of the wall and had begun to penetrate the city. Dusk brought the fighting to a close and the crusaders slept by their arms in the flickering light of a fire started by Germans and raging through the wooden buildings in the nearby quarters of the city, expecting renewed resistance in the morning. But there was none, for the emperor had fled. For three days Constantinople was systematically and ruthlessly sacked. This was, of course, the usual fate of cities taken by assault, but on this occasion the pillaging seems to have been particularly thorough. The Greeks have not yet forgotten or forgiven it, but it was a consequence of the obsession with loot that had been engendered by the failure of the crusaders to meet their debts to the Venetians. In it there was also another element. Constantinople was most famous in the West for being the greatest storehouse of relics in Christendom. Western Christians, as we have seen, were obsessive about relics and there had grown up among them traditions of *furta sacra*, sacred thefts, in which the stealing of the bones of saints had been justified, if successful, by the proven desire of the saints to have their relics transferred to other places. The sack of Constantinople was a massive *furtum sacrum*, made against the background of the hysteria that had swept Europe following the loss of the relic of the True Cross of Jerusalem at the Battle of Hattin in 1187. It is no coincidence that Constantinople's collection included another famous piece of the True Cross.

Once the spoil had been divided the crusaders could proceed to the election of a new emperor. Boniface of Montferrat, who had occupied the imperial palace of the Boukoleon and was betrothed to Margaret of Hungary, the widow of the emperor Isaac, must have expected the title. But he found himself baulked in the choice of the six non-Venetian electors, for in the end six churchmen were chosen, only three of whom favoured him. This made it certain that he would not be successful, since the Venetians opposed his candidature. After long debates the electors unanimously announced their choice of Baldwin of Flanders at midnight on 9 May. Baldwin was crowned on the 16th by the assembled Catholic bishops, because there was as yet no Latin patriarch.

The diversion of the Fourth Crusade to Constantinople has led to endless and rather pointless historical argument. Was it the result of a conspiracy and, if so, who was involved? Enrico Dandolo, Philip of Swabia, Boniface of Montferrat, even Innocent III, have been named as candidates. In fact the capture of Constantinople seems to have been the result of a series of accidents. From fairly early on the pope knew of an element in the crusade which wanted to take Byzantine territory, but the intention of the leaders in 1203 seems to have been merely to engineer a change of political control in Constantinople – a plan not unlike that proposed by Bohemond of Taranto in 1106 – so that their debts would be paid and a friendly government left in the Byzantine empire. There is no need even to explain the crusade in terms of the long history of bad relations between crusaders and Greeks; it was a response to a request from a Byzantine prince, made when the crusaders were heavily in debt because of an error of judgement on the part of the six delegates who had negotiated on their behalf with Venice. The inclusion of Innocent's name among those responsible for the diversion is particularly unkind. He certainly determined to make the best of things after the event and instructions flowed from Rome with the aim of taking advantage of the fall of the Byzantine empire to bring about, even to enforce, Church union. From the start, however, the crusade proceeded in a way that was galling for him. One act of disobedience led to another. Most of the crusaders, however divided and personally distressed, ignored his advice and prohibitions; and the crusade ended in a way that was bound to make the unification of the Catholic and Orthodox churches, so dear to his heart, harder.

> How is the Greek Church, so afflicted and persecuted, to return to ecclesiastical union and a devotion for the Apostolic See when she sees in the Latins only an example of perdition and the works of darkness, so that with reason she already detests them more than dogs? (Innocent III, 'Opera Omnia', *PL*, vol. 215, col. 701).

The Baltic crusades

Innocent preached two other crusades while the Fourth Crusade was being prepared, although one of them was quite small. The first was the Livonian Crusade in the Baltic region, which he inherited from his predecessor. It had its origins in a mission to the Livs on the river Dvina patronized by Archbishop Hartwig of Bremen, who saw in the creation of a bishopric at Üxküll the chance of extending his province. The mission made little progress, although it had the personal support of Pope Celestine III. In 1193 and 1197 Celestine was persuaded to grant indulgences to those who crusaded in the service of the new Livonian church, but in 1198 there was a set-back and the bishop was killed. In the bishop's place the archbishop appointed his own nephew Albert of Buxtehude. This remarkable, energetic and rather brutal man, who was to dominate the Baltic crusading movement for thirty years and was to carve a church-state, directly dependent on Rome, out of the pagan communities around Riga, recruited more crusaders and sought authorization from the new pope. Innocent summoned the Christians of northern Germany to the defence of the Livonian church on 5 October 1199: he justified the use of force as defence of Christian converts persecuted by their pagan neighbours. The crusaders, however, do not seem to have been granted the full indulgence and only those who planned to make pilgrimages to Rome were allowed to commute their vows to participation in the campaign. In 1204 Innocent issued a more important letter in which he permitted Albert to recruit priests, who had vowed to go to Jerusalem, to work on his mission instead, and authorized laymen who could not go to Jerusalem 'on account of poverty or bodily weakness' to commute their vows to fight the barbarians in Livonia with the full indulgence; and he licensed Albert's representatives to open churches once a year throughout the province of Bremen even where there was an interdict. The effect of this letter was to initiate a 'perpetual crusade', which was thenceforward to be a feature of the northern wars, although it was not to be fully developed for another forty years. Albert transferred the capital of his see down river from Üxküll to Riga, which could be reached by cogs (roundships) sailing from Lübeck, and fostered the cult of Our Lady of Riga and of the idea of Livonia as Our Lady's dowry, which was adopted presumably to justify pilgrimages to it. He returned to Germany every year until 1224 to recruit crusaders for summer campaigns. These were supplemented by the brothers of a small Military Order, the Sword-Brothers, which he established in 1202. There were probably never more than 120 of these, living in six convents, but they organized the crusaders during the summer and garrisoned strongholds in the winter: the Christians used a strategy that made maximum use of fortified religious communities and small castles. By 1230 Livonia had been conquered in a series of grim annual campaigns against peoples superior in numbers but inferior in the techniques of war.

So had Estonia to the north in campaigns begun by the Danes during Innocent's pontificate. We have already seen that the Danes' eyes were turning to the eastern Baltic in 1184. Although before 1216 they were concentrating on the conquest of the Pomeranian coast from Lübeck to Gdańsk (Danzig), their fleets attacked Finland in 1191 and 1202, Estonia in 1194 and 1197, Saaremaa (Ösel) in 1206 and Prussia in 1210. Of these campaigns, the attack upon Saaremaa was certainly presented as a crusade and crusading ideas, distorted by the northern concept of the missionary war that we have already seen in statements by St Bernard and Eugenius III, are also to be found in a letter from Innocent to King Valdemar II of Denmark in 1209, in which Valdemar was exhorted.

to root out the error of paganism and spread the bounds of the Christian faith . . . Fight in this battle of the war bravely and strongly like an active knight of Christ (Innocent III, 'Opera', vol. 216 col. 117).

In letters to Otto of Brunswick and to the Danish Christians, written on the same day, Innocent referred to Valdemar's activities as 'so holy a pilgrimage' and mentioned an indulgence. Like Bernard he was sailing close to the wind when he tried to reconcile crusading and the north European missions. It was not until 1219, however, in response to appeals from Albert of Buxtehude at Riga, who had been alarmed by an incursion from Russian Novgorod, and Pope Honorius III, who had promised him that he could keep the land he conquered from the heathen, that Valdemar invaded northern Estonia and established a presence at Tallinn (Reval). In the following year the Danes, together with the Sword-Brothers, subjugated northern Estonia, but this led to competition with the Germans, who were advancing into Estonia from Livonia to the south, and the Swedes, who were occupying the north-western coast. Valdemar ruthlessly used his naval control of the Baltic and the threat he could pose to shipping out of Lübeck to force his fellow-Christians to agree to his control of northern Estonia, although the settlement there was in fact far more German than Danish.

By the 1220s the idea of a perpetual crusade was taking root. The crusaders were signed with the cross, were referred to as *peregrini* and *crucesignati* and enjoyed the full indulgence. Measures were taken to tax the Church on their behalf. Their crusades were justified as defensive aid to missions and were privileged in much the same ways as crusades to the East, although Pope Honorious III, like Innocent, seems to have been always careful to stress that the goal of Jerusalem had precedence over them.

The crusade against Markward of Anweiler

The other early crusade of Innocent III was that preached against Markward of Anweiler, an imperial officer who had tried to maintain a presence in Italy after Henry VI's death. Dr Housley has pointed out that in the light of the policies of Honorius II and Innocent II towards the Sicilian Normans and in particular the precedent established by Innocent II at the council of Pisa in 1135, the enterprise was not radical; but it was certainly extreme. Innocent, determined to recover the papal patrimony in central Italy and acutely sensitive about southern Italy and Sicily, where he was regent for the child Frederick, was galvanized by the activities of Markward and his German followers, who were trying to establish themselves in the south. On 24 November 1199, having heard that Markward had crossed into Sicily, he wrote to the people there referring to him as 'another Saladin' and 'an infidel worse than the infidels'. He claimed that he was allied to the Muslims of Sicily, who have recently been shown to have been a powerful body of people, and that he was threatening the preparations for the Fourth Crusade. All who resisted him were granted the same indulgence as that enjoyed by crusaders to the East, since the ports of Sicily might be essential to the coming crusade. It is clear from other evidence that for nearly a year the pope had been envisaging a crusade against Markward as a last resort, but in fact the plans came to very little. Only a few men, the most important being Count Walter of Brienne, who was more concerned to assert the rights he claimed to the fief of Taranto, were enlisted – incidentally it was in this crusade that the young St Francis seems briefly to have enrolled – and Markward's death in 1203 ended the reason for the enterprise. But the letter of November 1199 was a straw in the wind, as were Innocent's fulminations at the end of his life against the English barons, 'worse than the Muslims', who by rebelling against King John, who had had the political sense to take the cross, were hindering the Fifth Crusade, which was in preparation. Dr Lloyd has suggested that by the early weeks of Honorius III's pontificate the defence of the English kingdom against the rebels in league with Louis of France had indeed become a kind of crusade and that it was for this that the nine-year-old Henry III took the cross at the time of his coronation on 28 October 1216.

The Albigensian Crusade

Innocent was thinking seriously about another crusade to the East in 1208 and sent appeals to France and northern and central Italy, although the only discernible response came from that passionate crusader Duke Leopold VI of Austria, who had been on the Third Crusade, had taken the cross for the Fourth and was in the future to crusade in Spain, Languedoc and Egypt. Innocent responded with one of those deflating letters with which he liked to put high men who were doing their best in their place:

> There is much more merit in the gibbet of Christ's cross than in the little sign of your cross. . . . For you accept a soft and gentle cross; he suffered one that was bitter and hard. You bear it superficially on your clothing; he endured his in the reality of his flesh. You sew yours on with linen and silken threads; he was fastened to his with hard, iron nails (Innocent III, 'Opera', vol. 215, col. 1340).

But in the meantime events in south-western France were leading to a crisis there. For decades the Church had been worried by the growth of heresy in that region. Since a heretic denied the God-given function of the Church as the custodian of revelation he was believed to be a rebel who had deliberately turned from truth and had chosen to disturb the order established by Christ.

Heresy was, therefore, treated as an active, not a passive, force, and it came to be associated in many minds with the *routiers*, bands of mercenaries who were already disturbing a region in which it was strong and against whom sanctions, which incorporated crusade ideas, had already been proposed. The Church was particularly worried by the increasing numbers of Cathars, the followers of a type of neo-Manichaeism who believed in two principles, or Gods, of the spiritual and material worlds and saw it as their duty to free their souls from the matter in which they were imprisoned; they renounced as far as was possible everything of this world, including marriage and the eating of meat, milk and eggs, that was considered to be material or procreative in origin. To them the order and life of the Church was vain and belief in the Trinity an error, since Christ had had no material reality. In place of the Church they set up their own hierarchy and liturgy. The demands made by their religion were so extreme that only an inner core, the 'perfects' (*perfecti*) were fully initiated; the majority were 'believers' (*credentes*), who committed themselves to undergo initiation before death. By the late twelfth century the Cathars, together with the Waldensians, were the most numerous sectaries the Church had to face and their presence was especially strong in northern Italy and south-western France, both areas, it should be noted, where there was no strong central political authority.

That last point is crucial to an understanding of Innocent's thinking. Since the fourth century the Church had normally looked to secular authority to use force and breed the fear which had proved itself to be the most effective remedy to heresy, and it is no accident that in the central Middle Ages nations with strong rulers had very few problems with heretics. The Counts of Toulouse, the nominal lords of most of the region with which we are concerned, had very little control over an area which was one of the most backward in France in terms of political cohesion. Whatever power they did enjoy was further limited by the conflicting allegiances they themselves owed, since they were vassals of the king of France for many of their lands, but also of the king of England in the west, the king of Aragon in the south and the German emperor in the east. The claims and ambitions of these rulers, embroiling themselves in internal conflicts in Languedoc, had led to savage and debilitating wars. The Count of Toulouse was in no position to take effective measures. Nor were his overlords. The king of France, in particular, was far too enmeshed in war with the English kings in northern France to cope with heresy in the south, even if he had been capable of tackling it. Innocent was faced by a classic dilemma. Heresy presented a serious challenge. In Languedoc it was permeating all levels of society, including the nobility, and with every year that passed it would be harder to eradicate. Although there were probably fewer than 1,000 perfects in the region between 1200 and 1209 a high proportion of them were from noble families: of those known by name to us 35 per cent were nobles; and it is also significant that a large majority, 69 per cent, were women, preponderantly noblewomen. The sister of the Count of Foix was a perfect and another sister, his wife and daughter-in-law were believers. Catholic abbots and bishops had heretical relatives. And the secular powers on which the pope relied could do nothing.

In the course of the twelfth century the Church had resorted to various measures. A series of preaching missions had been despatched to Languedoc. The 27th canon of the Third Lateran Council in 1179 had called on all Christians to go to the aid of their bishops, if these decided to resort to the use of force. They would enjoy a limited indulgence for doing this, but would be granted the full indulgence if they were killed. They would have the same protection of their lands in their absence as had pilgrims to Jerusalem. This was followed in 1181 by a little military campaign in Languedoc under the command of a papal legate; and it is worth noting that a fierce critic of the Third Crusade, Ralph Niger, argued in the winter of 1187–8 that knights should not be sent overseas because they were needed at home to resist heresy. In 1184 the bull *Ad abolendam*, issued by Pope Lucius III after a conference at Verona with Emperor Frederick I, set up episcopal inquisitions, abolished all privileges of exemption from episcopal authority in this matter and stressed the need for collaboration between Church and State in the suppression of heretics who, if contumacious, were to be handed over to the secular arm for punishment.

Innocent tackled the problem with his accustomed energy. He sent a succession of legates to southern France. He took measures to reform the local church, which was in a bad way – between 1198 and 1209 he deposed seven bishops – and he encouraged the preaching mission of Diego of Osma and Dominic which was to lead to the foundation of the Dominicans. But gradually he came round to the view that the use of force was needed. In May 1204 he called on King Philip of France to bring the power of the kingdom to bear in aid of spiritual authority and he went further than any pope had gone before in attaching to this exercise of secular power the full crusade indulgence. This inclusion of the most important crusade privilege in a summons to a king merely to do his duty had no effect. Neither had renewed appeals to Philip in February 1205 and November 1207, the last of which repeated the grant of the indulgence and added the promise to protect the warriors' properties in their absences. Innocent also sent copies of this letter to the nobles, knights and subjects of France; it was as though he was calling upon the whole French political community to protect the Church, while at the same time making the task more attractive through the granting of crusade privileges. But Philip's reply made much of the difficulties he was experiencing in his conflict with John of England and set conditions for his intervention in the south which the pope was in no position to meet.

Then, on 14 January 1208, Peter of Castelnau, one of the papal legates in Languedoc, was assassinated in circumstances which led the pope to suspect the complicity of Count Raymond VI of Toulouse, already excommunicated for his failure to deal effectively with heresy. As soon as he heard the news Innocent solemnly proclaimed a crusade against the heretics and their abettors, in powerful letters sent to all parts of France and probably to other regions of western Europe as well. He called for men to take vows, although at this stage he granted them, it is interesting to note, rather an old-fashioned indulgence, expressed in terms of satisfactory penance for sin: perhaps he was not yet entirely certain of his ground. Three legates were appointed to organize the preaching of the crusade and lead it, and the pope decreed the abolition of usury and a delay in the repayment of debts, the usual way of enabling crusaders to raise money for their campaign. Measures were also taken to tax the churches in the regions from which the crusaders came in order to help finance their expeditions.

The novelty of Innocent's proclamation of the Albigensian Crusade did not lie in his encouragement of the use of force against heretics; after all that was the issue already comprehensively justified, with reference to historical precedents and authorities stretching back to the fourth century, in Gratian's *Decretum*. It was the use of a crusade in this way that was new, even if its long pre-history had made it almost inevitable. It came about in 1208 because the secular authorities were unwilling or unable to do their duty as the Church saw it. Heresy posed a threat to Christendom as a whole, a threat worse than that from the Muslims, as Innocent put it. That it was an internal rather than an external threat did not alter the fact that in the name of Christendom the army of the universal Christian republic could be called upon to confront it. But of course the fact that it was an internal war gave this crusade unusual features. Southern France was not Palestine, nor even Spain or Livonia, which is why crusaders to Languedoc came to take vows to serve there for only forty days. This short and comfortable period of service must have diluted the penitential nature of the enterprise; and although the crusaders sometimes called themselves 'pilgrims', the goal of their pilgrimage has never been identified and was perhaps a fiction. The Albigensian Crusade illustrates how crusading was coming to flourish independently of some of the elements, like the penitential pilgrimage, that had combined to make it.

The response to Innocent's appeal was enthusiastic, even fervent, and by the spring of 1209 a large force was gathering to attack the south. Raymond of Toulouse hastened to make terms and on 18 June 1209 was reconciled to the Church in a dramatic scene on the steps of the abbey of St Gilles, in front of the great western façade on which the Passion of Christ, in a manifestation of Catholic orthodoxy, is sculpted in stone. He then underwent a penitential whipping inside the abbey church and, because the crowd was so great, had to be led out by way of the crypt, past the new tomb of Peter of Castelnau. The crusade invaded the lands of Raymond Roger of Trencavel, viscount of Béziers and Carcassonne and lord of the Albigeois and of Razès, where the heretics were numerous. Béziers fell on 22 July and large numbers of citizens, both Catholic and Cathar, were massacred in conditions which suggest that the army, which contained many poor people from northern France, had got out of hand – Carcassonne, which held out for two weeks, was treated much more lightly – although the ferocity was exemplary and led to a collapse of resistance.

The time had now come for a secular leader to be appointed to administer the Trencavel lands and set up a permanent base for future operations. The choice fell on Simon of Montfort, who had opposed the attack upon Zadar and the diversion of the Fourth Crusade on principle seven years before. Simon was now in his late forties. Lord of Montfort and Epernon since 1181, he had inherited the earldom of Leicester in 1204 on the death of a maternal uncle. Courageous, tenacious and devout, he was a great military commander and a model husband. He was also ambitious, obstinate and capable of horrifying acts of cruelty. Until his death in the summer of 1218 he had a thankless and lonely task. Every summer parties of crusaders from France and Germany would descend on Languedoc for the campaigning season. Once their forty days' service was completed they would return home, often at most inconvenient times, and during each winter Simon would be left almost entirely alone, trying desperately to hang on to the gains he had made in the previous summer. In a decision, moreover, that must have prolonged the agony by more than a decade, Innocent abolished most of the indulgences for the Albigensian Crusade early in 1213 in favour of his plans for a new crusade to the East. He therefore cut the ground from under Simon's feet and made his position even more precarious.

In 1210 Simon mastered the rest of the Trencavel lands and King Peter II of Aragon, who had earlier refused to acknowledge him, now accepted his offer of homage for them. Raymond of Toulouse had still not fulfilled the promises he had made at the time of his reconciliation with the Church in 1209 and, although he seems to have pursued no consistent policy in the interim, the legates were convinced that he was not to be trusted. Simon, therefore, prepared to attack Toulouse and Raymond's other lands. Throughout 1211 and 1212 he followed a strategy of the encirclement of Toulouse itself by taking nearby strongholds, although towns which had adhered to him would defect to the count when autumn and the end of the campaigning season came. In the winter of 1212–13 Peter of Aragon, his prestige enhanced by the part he had played in the victory of Las Navas de Tolosa, approached the pope directly on behalf of his vassals in Languedoc and his brother-in-law the Count of Toulouse, and this certainly provided Innocent with the pretext to abolish crusade privileges for outsiders on the grounds that Simon had over-reached himself, although it is clear that the pope had decided to concentrate Christian resources on a new crusade to the East. In the summer of 1213 Peter marched to Raymond of Toulouse's assistance, but on 12 September he was killed and Aragon's expansionist policy north of the Pyrenees was checked, when his army was decisively defeated by Simon's greatly inferior forces at the Battle of Muret. By the end of 1214 Simon was in control of most of Raymond's lands and the expedition to the south of Louis of France, King Philip's heir, in the early summer of 1215 was a triumphal procession. In November the Fourth Lateran Council assigned to Simon those of Raymond's territories which he had taken; the remainder were to be held in trust by the Church for the Count's son.

This was the high point of Simon's career, but it was also a turning-point, because the nobility and towns of the region began to rally to the dispossessed count and his son. In September 1217 Raymond entered Toulouse and on 25 June 1218 Simon was killed before the city by a stone thrown by a mangonel. Leadership was assumed by his son Amalric, then twenty-six years old, but he could not reverse the decline, in spite of the fact that in 1218 the crusade had full privileges restored to it by Innocent's successor, Honorius III. Even Raymond's death in August 1222 did not assist Amalric: his son Raymond VII was more popular than he had been. Amalric was at the end of his resources and the situation was saved only by the intervention of the French crown. In January 1226 King Louis VIII vowed to crusade in the south. On 9 September the royal army took Avignon after a three-month siege and almost all the region east of Toulouse declared for the king, who left the administration of his conquests to a new lieutenant, Humbert of Beaujeu. Although Louis died on 8 November in the course of his journey home, Humbert embarked on a policy of ruthless and systematic destruction in response to Raymond's VII's attempts to regain his territory, and the end of the crusade came with the Peace of Paris of 12 April 1229. Raymond received the western and northern parts of the domains held by his father at the start of the crusade, with the proviso that Toulouse could be inherited only by his daughter Joan, who was to be married to King Louis IX's brother Alphonse of Poitiers, and their heirs; otherwise it would revert to the king. The Peace also contained clauses dealing with the issue of heresy, of which the most interesting was the endowment of a fund to establish the salaries for ten years of four masters of theology, two decretists, six masters of arts and two masters-regent of grammar at Toulouse, which marked the origins of the university there.

The clauses of the Peace of Paris and the decrees of a council held at

Toulouse in November 1229 demonstrated that twenty years of crusading had not been very effective, since heresy was as much a concern as ever. The fact was that crusading, particularly when as episodic as this type was, could not eradicate deep-rooted heresy. It required the establishment of the inquisition in Toulouse in 1233 and the persistent pressure that such an instrument could bring to bear for headway to be made: from 1250 the Cathar leaders were withdrawing to Lombardy; by 1324 southern French Catharism was dead.

Crusading in Spain

Innocent also proclaimed a new crusade in Spain. In spite of persistent warfare, the only crusading activity in the peninsula since the late 1170s had been in 1189, when two fleets of Frisian, Danish, Flemish, German and English crusaders bound for the East had helped Sancho I of Portugal to take Silves and Alvor, and in 1193 and 1197, when Pope Celestine III had issued crusade encyclicals. In the second of these the pope had decreed that residents of Aquitaine might commute to Spain their vows for Jerusalem; presumably these had been made at the time of the Third Crusade and were still unfulfilled. This was in response to the great victory of the Almohad caliph Ya'qub over Alfonso VIII of Castile at Alarcos on 19 July 1195, a defeat which horrified Christian opinion. Ya'qub was seen as a new Saladin. But by 1210 Alfonso felt strong enough to renew the offensive and raiding began, fortified by crusade privileges from Innocent and probably based on the Calatravan castle of Salvatierra, well within Muslim territory. The caliph Muhammad an-Nasir resolved to take action and after a siege of ten weeks took Salvatierra in early September, although this success came too late in the year for him to exploit it.

The news of the loss of Salvatierra caused anxiety throughout western Europe and inspired the pope to proclaim a new crusade in the spring of 1212 in letters written to France as well as Spain: in Rome itself fasting and special prayers were ordered for a Christian victory. Although only one northern Frenchman of importance, Bishop Geoffrey of Nantes, seems to have taken the cross, the response was strong in southern France, perhaps as a by-product of the Albigensian Crusade. In June 1212 a large army was mustering around Alfonso of Castile at Toledo: knights from France, Léon and Portugal; King Peter of Aragon with a strong force; and, of course, the great Castilian nobles, knights and city militias. It set out on the 20th. Alfonso made the extraordinary decision to seek engagement and gamble on a decisive battle. Malagón and Calatrava were taken, but on 3 July most of the French deserted, upset by the heat and possibly by the generous terms allowed to the garrison of Calatrava when it surrendered; only Archbishop Arnold of Narbonne and some 130 French knights stayed to share in the triumph that was to follow. The army went on to capture a string of fortified places and was joined by King Sancho VII of Navarre before hurrying to meet the advancing Muslims at the Despeñaperros Pass. The Almohad army was encamped on the plain of Las Navas de Tolosa, blocking the pass, but the Christians took a secret path through the hills before appearing to face it on the plain. On 17 July battle was joined and the Muslims were routed after an engagement in which the scales were turned by a heroic charge led by the king of Castile. After the victory the Christians took the castles of Vilches, Ferral, Baños and Tolosa, opening Andalucia to invasion, and Baeza and Ubeda, which they destroyed.

Like Hattin twenty-five years before, the battle was the result of deliberate risk-taking, but this time the gamble came off. The news of the victory was greeted in Rome with euphoria and inspired one of the finest of Innocent's letters, a paean of triumph and thanks to God:

> God, the protector of those who hope in him, without whom nothing is strong, nothing firm, multiplying his mercy on you and the Christian people and pouring out his anger on races that do not acknowledge the Lord and against kingdoms that do not invoke his most holy name, according to what had been foretold long ago by the Holy Spirit, has made a laughing-stock of the races which rashly murmured against him and a mockery of the peoples thinking empty thoughts by humbling the arrogance of the strong and causing the pride of the infidels to be laid low.

Innocent characteristically refused to congratulate Alfonso of Castile himself on the success. Victory was to be attributed not to the crusaders but to God, just as defeat was never a failure on God's part but a commentary on the wickedness of crusaders:

> It was not your highness's hands but the Lord who has done all these things. . . . For that victory took place without doubt not by human but by divine agency. . . . So do not walk proudly because those who work wickedness have fallen there, but give glory and honour to the Lord, saying humbly with the prophet *the zeal of the Lord of Hosts* has done *this*. And while others exult in chariots and horses you ought to rejoice and glory in the name of the Lord your God (Innocent III, 'Opera', vol. 216, cols. 703–4).

Las Navas de Tolosa was a turning-point in the Reconquest, although this would not have been apparent to contemporaries, for its fruits were slow in ripening. The Spanish Crusade, like the Albigensian, was set aside, at least as far as outsiders were concerned, by Innocent in 1213 and on several occasions his successor Honorius III expressed the opinion that the

Reconquest should not divert resources from the crusade to the East, although shiploads of Dutch and Rhineland crusaders on their way to Palestine helped the Portuguese take Alcácer do Sal in 1217. Honorius was prepared to grant a partial indulgence to fighters in Spain in 1219, but even then he stressed that this was only to be granted to those who could not travel to Egypt for some good reason. After the capture of Damietta by the Fifth Crusade his attitude changed and he renewed indulgences in 1221 for an enterprise to be led by Alfonso IX of Léon-Castile and in 1224 for one to be led by Ferdinand III of Castile, although this indulgence, in accord with Innocent's decree of 1213, was confined only to Spaniards. The full renewal of indulgences for the Spanish crusades came in 1229 in a letter from Pope Gregory IX and there were southern Frenchmen on James I of Aragon's crusade of that year to the Balearic islands.

The Children's Crusade and the preaching of the Fifth Crusade

The picture we have of crusading in 1212 is again a panoramic one, if not on the scale of 1147–50. War was being waged on three fronts – along the Baltic coast, in Languedoc and in Spain – but there was relative peace in the East where in 1211 the kingdom of Jerusalem had made a six-year truce with the Muslims. During the previous winter northern France and the Rhineland had been in a ferment as the preaching of men like William of Paris and James of Vitry for the Albigensian Crusade fired popular enthusiasm and gave rise to upheavals of a type to be found occasionally for the next century. A spontaneous movement arose among children, two of whose leaders were Nicholas, a young boy from Cologne, and a French shepherd boy called Stephen, who claimed to have had a vision of Christ and led crowds of children and shepherds to Paris, chanting, 'Lord God, exalt Christianity! Restore the True Cross to us! They were accompanied by many adults, several of whom were diverted by churchmen into the Albigensian Crusade. The largest band travelled up the Rhine and across the Alps into Lombardy. There many of them dispersed, although a group under Nicholas's leadership reached Genoa, where they broke up: some seem to have reached Rome, where Innocent dispensed them from their vows, which were not technically valid anyway; others may have travelled west to Marseille where, the story goes, they were deceived by two merchants into embarking on ships from which many of them were sold into slavery in North Africa.

With the enthusiasm for crusading that seemed to be prevailing it is not surprising that Innocent's mind should have been turning again to the idea of a crusade to the East once the truce made there ended in 1217. In the middle of January 1213 he told his legates in Languedoc that he was planning such a crusade and in the following April he proclaimed it, at the same time demoting the crusades in Spain and Languedoc:

Because . . . aid to the Holy Land would be much impeded or delayed . . . we revoke the remissions and indulgences formerly granted by us to those setting out for Spain against the Moors or against the heretics in Provence, chiefly because these were conceded to them in circumstances which have already entirely passed and for that particular cause which has already for the most part disappeared, for so far affairs in both places have gone well, by the grace of God, so that the immediate cause of force is not needed. If perchance it were needed, we would take care to give our attention to any serious situation that arises. We concede, however, that remissions and indulgences of this kind should remain available to the people of Provence and to Spaniards (G. Tangl, *Studien zum Register Innocenz' III* (1929), pp. 93–4).

In the following September he explained to one of his crusade preachers in Germany exactly what this meant:

Those who have taken the cross and have proposed to set out against the heretics in Provence and have not yet translated their intention into action must be diligently persuaded to take up the labour of the journey to Jerusalem, because this is an action of greater merit. If perhaps they cannot be persuaded, they must be compelled to carry out the vow they have not yet fulfilled (Innocent III, 'Opera', vol. 216, col. 905).

This delayed the resolution of the Albigensian Crusade for years, as we have seen, and it caused dismay in Spain. At the Fourth Lateran Council in 1215 the Spanish bishops as a body begged the pope to restore full crusade status to the Reconquest. The pope seems to have assured them that according to the terms of his decision indulgences were available, but only to Spaniards. Even the crusade along the Baltic shore, already isolated and self-contained, appears to have come under threat for a time, and Albert of Buxtehude was reported making an impassioned and successful plea to the pope during the council, using an argument based on his idea of Livonia as Our Lady's dower:

Holy Father, just as you take care to concern yourself with the Holy Land of Jerusalem, which is the land of the Son, so you ought not to ignore Livonia, which is the land of the Mother. . . . For the Son loves his Mother and just as he would not wish his land to be lost, so he would not wish his Mother's land to be endangered (Henry of Livonia, 'Chronicon Lyvoniae', *MGHS*, vol. 23, p. 293).

The fact was that the Roman curia was not happy with the dissipation of effort involved in the waging of war on several fronts concurrently and this was the first example of a kind of decision that became common in the thirteenth century. The popes, who oversaw the whole range of crusading activity, could decide which theatre of war needed their support most at a given moment. And the fact that crusaders were increasingly dependent on them for financial subsidies through the taxation of the Church meant that as the century wore on their readiness to intervene grew.

Innocent and his advisers planned the new crusade with great care. *Quia maior*, the new encyclical and possibly the greatest of them all, was sent to almost every province of the Church in the second half of April and early May 1213. It opened with an exposition of crusading thought and dwelt on themes that preachers had been putting to their audiences for a long time. Crusading was an act of Christian charity. The summons to crusade was a divine test of an individual's intentions and also a chance to gain salvation; in this respect Innocent went about as far as it was possible to go theologically, referring to the crusade not only as 'an opportunity to win salvation', but also as 'a means of salvation'. The Holy land was the patrimony of Christ. Innocent had never hesitated to exploit the concept of the crusade as a quasi-feudal service to God, which was recognized by churchmen as being rather a dangerous one in that it implied mutual obligations between God and man along the lines of those between lord and vassal – God, of course, was not obliged to anyone – and he repeated it here. He included the formulation of the indulgence he had already introduced and also an important new statement on the enforcement of vows. He had already ruled that as pope he could grant deferment, commutation (the performance of another penitential act in place of that vowed) and redemption (dispensation in return for a money payment, theoretically equalling the sum that would have been spent on crusade), but he had formerly allowed these only in the context of a strict enforcement of most of the vows made. But *Quia maior* revealed a change of policy, which was a measure of the need felt to raise money. Everyone, whatever his or her condition, was to be encouraged to take the cross, but those who were not suitable could then redeem their vows for money payments:

> Because in fact it would mean that aid to the Holy Land would be much impeded or delayed if before taking the cross each person had to be examined to see whether he was personally fit and able to fulfil a vow of this kind, we concede that anyone who wishes, except persons bound by religious profession, may take the cross in such a way that this vow may be commuted, redeemed or deferred by apostolic mandate when urgent or evident expediency demands it (Tangl, *Studien*, pp. 93–4).

A few months later Innocent explained this to a puzzled preacher:

> You can deduce clearly from the encyclical what you ought to do about

women or other persons who have taken the cross and are not suitable or able to fulfil the vow. It states expressly that anyone, except a religious, may take the sign of the cross at will in such a way that when urgent need or evident expediency demands it that vow may be commuted or redeemed or deferred by apostolic mandate (Innocent III, 'Opera', vol. 216, col. 905).

The implementation of this policy by his legates in France caused a scandal and the abuses to which it was liable led to sporadic criticism throughout the thirteenth century.

Like *Audita tremendi*, *Quia maior* laid great stress on the need for repentance. It decreed monthly penitential processions throughout Christendom and introduced a new intercessory rite to be inserted into the Mass after the Kiss of Peace and before the reception of communion. And Innocent's passion for organization, and perhaps also his experience of the difficulties of recruitment in 1198–9 and 1208, led him to introduce an elaborate system for the preaching of the cross, which resulted in the production in England, France and Germany of handbooks for preachers. He personally oversaw preaching in Italy. In Scandinavia and France papal legates were charged with organizing recruitment. In every other province of Latin Christendom the pope appointed small groups of preachers, many of them bishops, with legatine powers, who were permitted to delegate the task of recruitment to deputies in each diocese. The pope laid down detailed rules for their behaviour and clearly took a great interest in the way they carried out their duties.

The penitential sections of *Quia maior* underlined the conviction that crusading could only be successful if accompanied by a spiritual reawakening of Christendom. Innocent carried the belief of his predecessors in the necessity for general reform to its logical conclusion. *Quia maior* was issued in conjunction with a summons to a general council, the Fourth Lateran Council, the proceedings of which were permeated with crusading themes. It was opened on 11 November 1215 with a sermon from Innocent in which he stressed the twin aims of crusade and renewal. Among the decrees there was one, *Excommunicamus*, which justified, and laid down rules for, crusades against heretics and led some canonists like Raymond of Peñafort to be concerned lest it would be treated as a standing authorization for crusading of this type. Even more important was an appendix to the decrees, entitled *Ad liberandam*, which was approved by the council on 14 December and carried the planning of the Fifth Crusade further, giving the date for its departure as 1 June 1217, when the truce between the kingdom of Jerusalem and the Muslims would have ended. This, Professor Brundage has pointed out, was 'the most extensive and ambitious catalogue of crusader rights and privileges promulgated by the papacy up to that time and . . . its provisions were repeated verbatim in most papal letters throughout the rest of the Middle Ages'. It legislated for priests in the armies and their enjoyment of their benefices *in absentia*. It included Innocent's classic formulation of the indulgence. It declared the immunity of crusaders from taxes and usury and a moratorium on their debts and it assured them of the Church's protection of their property. It prohibited trade with the Muslims in war-materials and banned tournaments for three years. It decreed peace in Christendom for the duration of the crusade. Most of these provisions had appeared in *Quia maior* and other papal letters, but *Ad liberandam* also instituted another tax on the Church. Although in *Quia maior* Innocent had called on churchmen to endow fighting men, he had refrained from reintroducing the tax provisions of 1199, perhaps because they had been so unsuccessful. Now he ordered a three-year tax of a twentieth of all Church income, six times more onerous than the earlier one, and he put papal commissioners in charge of raising it: in 1199 he had left the collection of the tax to the bishops, but their lack of cooperation had very soon persuaded him to send officials from Rome to oversee it. Unlike 1199, there was no guarantee in *Ad liberandam* that the tax would not create a precedent: indeed this time it was imposed with the approval of a general council and the principle was thereby established that a pope had the right to tax the clergy. The ratification of this tax by the general council did not enhance its popularity. It met with fierce opposition in Spain, where churchmen were upset by the demotion of the Reconquest, and resistance in France, Italy, Germany and Hungary.

Innocent died on 16 July 1216, just after preaching the cross in central Italy and at a time when he was preparing to embark on a tour of northern Italy in the interests of the crusade. With him the various formulae and definitions reached their mature forms and his letters became exemplars for future popes. He extended the use of crusading within a traditional framework of thought which few expressed as lucidly and beautifully as he, or his draftsmen, did. He was the first pope to tax the Church for crusades, the first to exploit redemptions and the first to build up an elaborate system for preaching the cross. And yet, as with so much else in his pontificate, his policies were not successful because his ideas were too ambitious and his actual power far too restricted. The Fourth Crusade, in particular, had demonstrated the intrinsic weakness of his position. Canon law prohibited priests from military command and the pope was a priest; in spite of his desire to control the greatest instrument at his disposal as 'papal monarch', he had to rely on secular magnates, who were all too fallible and were often thoroughly incompetent.

The course of the Fifth Crusade

Innocent's successor, Pope Honorius III, was an elderly man, but he pressed forward with preparations for the Fifth Crusade, trying to cope with the obstacles that so often obstructed the launching of expeditions of this type. Frederick II, the young king of the Romans, had taken the cross at the time of his coronation in Aachen in July 1215, but was unlikely to be able to go while his throne was contested by Otto of Brunswick. The papal legates in France, Robert of Courçon and Archbishop Simon of Tyre, had aroused great enthusiasm among the poor, but the Fifth Crusade was not popular with the French nobles and was to be unusual in that it was not dominated by them: they had perhaps been too deeply involved in the Albigensian Crusade. The indifference of so many of the French knights worried thoughtful churchmen, but this lack of commitment was more than made up for elsewhere, particularly in Hungary, Germany and the Netherlands, where the success of one of the best of the preachers, Oliver of Paderborn, was said to have been literally phenomenal, being accompanied by miracles.

King Andrew of Hungary, who had taken the cross in 1196 but had been granted a series of postponements by the popes, was the first to move. His representatives negotiated with the Venetians for a fleet to meet him at Split, but when his army, containing contingents led by the dukes of Austria and Merano and the archbishop of Kalocsa and many bishops, abbots and counts from the empire and Hungary, mustered there in late August 1217, it was found that the king's envoys had fallen into exactly the opposite trap to that which had ensnared the ambassadors of the Fourth Crusade. Too many troops arrived for the ships available and the main body had to wait for several weeks before embarkation. Many knights returned home or made plans for sailing in the following spring.

A large army of crusaders gathered at Acre in the autumn: too many, in fact, for the food to hand, because a poor harvest had led to famine conditions in Palestine. Crusaders were even being advised to return home. Before they had come the King of Jerusalem, John of Brienne, and the masters of the three Military Orders of the Temple, St. John, and St Mary of the Germans, had been considering plans for two separate but simultaneous campaigns: one to Nablus with the intention of recovering the West Bank lands and the other to Damietta in Egypt. Now a council-of-war met and, putting both of these aside for the time being, decided to promote a series of small-scale expeditions to keep the enemy, and doubtless the troops in Acre, occupied until the rest of the crusade arrived. In early November a reconnaissance-in-force pillaged Bet She'an and crossed the Jordan south of the Sea of Galilee on the 10th, before marching up the eastern shore of the lake and returning to Acre by way of Jisr Banat Ya'qub. After a brief rest the crusaders marched against Mount Tabor in Galilee, which the Muslims had fortified; the threat from it had been referred to by Innocent III in *Quia maior*. On 3 December they advanced up the mountain in a mist, but their attack failed, as did a second assault two days later. On 7 December they returned to Acre. A third expedition, of not more than 500 men, set out not long before Christmas to attack brigands in the mountainous hinterland of Sidon, but it was ambushed and destroyed.

Meanwhile the King of Hungary, who had played no part in operations after the first reconnaissance-in-force, was making preparations to return home. He left for Syria early in January 1218 and travelled overland to Europe through Asia Minor, taking many of his subjects with him. The crusaders who remained in Acre occupied themselves with the refortification of Caesarea and the building of a great new Templar castle at 'Atlit until fresh reinforcements arrived. These began to sail into Acre on 26 April. With large numbers of Frisians, Germans and Italians now assembling and, just as importantly, with an impressive fleet at their disposal, the leaders decided that the time had come to invade Egypt. On 27 May the vanguard of the invasion force arrived at Damietta. Meeting little resistance, the crusaders chose a site for their encampment, which they fortified with a moat and wall, on an island opposite the city, bordered by the Nile and an abandoned canal. It was to be eighteen months until Damietta fell. During this period the besiegers were to be reinforced by Italian, French, Cypriot and English crusaders, although there were, of course, also departures: for instance Leopold of Austria left in May 1219. There was obviously the need felt for some structure of command and King John of Jerusalem was given the overall leadership, although that seems to have meant little more than the presidency of a steering committee. In September 1218, moreover, the papal legate Pelagius of Albano arrived. Pelagius had a strong personality and he was prepared to challenge John's assumption that Egypt would be annexed to his kingdom if it was conquered. His voice became dominant on the committee and John slipped more and more into the background.

In the first stage of the siege the Christians strove to take the Chain Tower, an impressive fortification on an island in the middle of the Nile, from which iron chains could be raised to halt river traffic. Various measures were tried before a floating siege-engine designed by Oliver of Paderborn himself, a miniature castle with a revolving scaling-ladder incorporated into it, was built on two cogs lashed together and was sent against the tower on 24 August 1218. After a fierce fight the crusaders gained a foothold on the tower, the surviving defenders of which surrendered on the following day. The sultan of Egypt was said to have died of shock after hearing the news of this reverse.

The crusaders did not immediately press home their advantage and the Muslims countered the loss of the tower by blocking the Nile with sunken ships. In October the crusaders had to fight off two determined attacks on their camp. And they laboured to dredge the abandoned canal that bounded it so that they could by-pass Damietta and bring their ships up above it. The canal was open by early December, but the winter was exceptionally severe and they suffered intensely from floods which destroyed their provisions and tents and carried over to the Muslim bank of the Nile a new floating fortress, built this time on six cogs, which they had been constructing. In early February 1219, however, the Muslim army facing them abandoned its encampment near the city on hearing of the flight of the new Egyptian sultan, who had uncovered a plot to depose him, and order was restored too late to prevent the Christians crossing the Nile and occupying the same bank as Damietta, together with large stocks of provisions. They now held both sides of the river and built a bridge between them.

At this point the Egyptian government sued for terms, proposing to surrender all the territory of the kingdom of Jerusalem except Transjordan and to adhere to a thirty-year truce in return for the crusaders' evacuation of Egypt. The king of Jerusalem was in favour of acceptance, but Pelagius and the Military Orders were not, even after the Egyptians added to their offer a rent of 15,000 besants a year for the castles of Karak and Shaubak in Transjordan. They had, meanwhile, been reinforced by an army from Syria. Throughout March, April and May they launched attacks on the new Christian camp. The crusaders built a second pontoon bridge, resting on thirty-eight vessels, below the city and from 8 July they made a series of direct assaults on Damietta until the drop in the level of the Nile made it impossible for them to reach the city's river walls with their scaling-ladders. The Muslims outside the city, who had responded with counter-attacks, penetrated deep into the Christian camp on 31 July before being driven out. On 29 August the crusaders decided to launch an attack on the Muslim encampment, but, drawn into a trap by a feigned withdrawal, they were badly mauled when their advance faltered. The sultan at once reopened negotiations, adding to his previous proposals the promise to pay for the rebuilding of the walls of Jerusalem and the castles of Belvoir, Safad and Tibnine. He also offered the relic of the True Cross which had been lost at Hattin. The king of Jerusalem, the French, the English and the Teutonic Knights were for acceptance, but Pelagius, the Templars and Hospitallers were adamantly against. In fact the garrison of Damietta was now so weakened by starvation that it could not defend the city properly and on the night of 4 November four Christian sentries noticed that one of the towers appeared to be deserted. Scaling the wall, they found it abandoned and the crusaders quickly occupied the city. The Egyptian army stationed nearby withdrew hastily to El Mansura and by 23 November the Christians had taken the town of Tinnis along the coast without a fight.

The latent discord between Pelagius of Albano and John of Jerusalem now came to a head. John left, depriving the crusade of its chief military leader, and the tensions at the top manifested themselves lower in the ranks in riots, exacerbated by disputes over the division of the rich spoil found in the city. Rather surprisingly, the Christians made no further move for nearly twenty months, allowing the sultan to turn his camp at El Mansura into a formidable stronghold. Again he renewed, and in fact raised, his offer to them; again they turned it down. Pelagius and the crusade were awaiting the arrival of the emperor Frederick II who at his coronation on 22 November 1220 promised to send part of his army on the next spring passage and to go to Egypt himself in the following August. The German troops arrived in May 1221 and at last preparations were made for an advance into the interior. On 7 July John of Jerusalem, strictly ordered by the pope to rejoin the crusade, returned and on the 17th the crusaders began to march down the east bank of the Nile. On the 24th, against John's advice, they moved into a narrow angle of land, bounded by two branches of the Nile, opposite El Mansura and then halted. The river began to flood in August and the Muslims made use of a small canal to bring ships into the main branches, blocking the river route back to Damietta. This unexpected move forced the Christians to withdraw, but the Muslims sent their land forces round behind them, cutting off their retreat, and broke the dykes to flood the land. The crusaders were trapped and had to sue for peace. On 30 August they agreed to leave Egypt in return for a truce of eight years and the True Cross, which they were never given; perhaps the Egyptians did not have it.

The crusade of Frederick II

Reinforcements sent by Frederick had arrived in the middle of this débâcle and their leaders bitterly opposed the terms which had been agreed. Indeed, when Frederick heard of them he was furious. He had not fulfilled his pledge to crusade in the autumn of 1221 and he was being as severely criticized for his failure to depart as the kings of England and France had been thirty years before. This does not mean that he was not serious about crusading. He was still in his twenties. He could certainly be ruthless, but, in spite of the scandalous stories told about him in his lifetime – his was a career that somehow bedazzled contemporaries as well as his recent biographers – there is no doubt that he was conventionally pious and that he felt deeply committed to the crusading movement. The long civil war in Germany and the anarchy he found on his return to southern Italy explain his delay in fulfilling the vow he had made in 1215. Pope Honorius, however, who had himself been criticized for the failure of the Fifth Crusade, could not refrain from venting his feelings and rebuking the emperor for his delay. At Ferentino in March 1223 Frederick renewed his vow in the presence of King John, the patriarch of Jerusalem and the masters of the Military Orders. The date of 24 June 1225 was set for his departure and he was betrothed to the heiress of the kingdom of Jerusalem, for whom John was now regent. He offered free transport and provisions to crusaders, but in spite of these generous financial inducements the response was not great, partly because it had been decided to employ mendicant friars for the first time as preachers: they were inexperienced and were despised by their audiences. The emperor was forced to suggest a postponement to allow the preaching to have more effect. At San Germano on 25 July 1225 he agreed to depart on 15 August 1227 and he accepted some severe conditions imposed on him by the pope. He promised to maintain 1,000 knights in the East at his expense for two years, and to pay a fine of 50 marks for every man less than that figure, to provide 100 transports and 50 armed galleys and, to meet his war expenses, to send 100,000 ounces of gold in advance in five instalments to the leaders of the settlement in Palestine, to be returned to him when he arrived in Acre.

Frederick married Yolande (Isabella) of Jerusalem in Brindisi on 9 November and took the title of king of Jerusalem, having himself crowned in a special ceremony at Foggia. This led to the goal of his crusade being switched from Egypt to Jerusalem. Meanwhile quite heavy recruitment was occurring in Germany and England and by mid-summer 1227 large numbers of crusaders were assembling in southern Italy; they sailed from Brindisi in August and early September. Although many of them dispersed when the news reached Palestine that the emperor was not joining them after all, the main body marched down the coast to Caesarea and Jaffa to restore their fortifications, while others occupied and fortified the city of Sidon in its entirety – half of it had been controlled from Damascus – and built the castle of Montfort, north-east of Acre.

Frederick, meanwhile, who had fallen ill, put into the port of Otranto and decided to wait until he was better. Pope Gregory IX responded by excommunicating him. It is hard to decide whether Gregory acted in this way because he was exasperated by yet another delay, which was what he claimed, or whether he was preparing the ground for his invasion of Frederick's south Italian possessions, which would have been impossible had Frederick been a legitimate crusader, since the Church would have been bound to protect his property. At any rate, when Frederick at last sailed for the East on 28 June 1228 he was an excommunicated and unrecognized crusader. On reaching Acre on 7 September, after an interlude in Cyprus which will be described later, he found himself in no position to fight a campaign. His army was small, because so many of the crusaders of the previous year had returned home, and divided, because many elements did not want to be associated with him now that he was excommunicated. But since 1226 he had been exchanging embassies with al-Kamil, the sultan of Egypt, who wanted to enter into an alliance with him against his brother, al-Mu'azzam of Damascus. By 1228 al-Mu'azzam was dead, but al-Kamil, who does not seem to have realized how weak Frederick was, was prepared to use Jerusalem as a bargaining counter to ensure Egypt's security.

Negotiations began at once. In a show of what force he had Frederick marched from Acre to Jaffa in November and on 18 February 1229 a treaty was signed by which al-Kamil surrendered Bethlehem and Nazareth, a strip of land from Jerusalem to the coast, part of the district of Sidon, which had already been occupied by the Christians, the castle of Tibnine and, above all, Jerusalem itself, although the Temple area was to remain in Muslim hands and the city was not to be fortified. In return Frederick pledged himself to protect the sultan's interests against all enemies, even Christians, for the duration of a truce of ten years; in particular, he would lend no aid to Tripoli or Antioch or to the castles of the Military Orders of Crac des Chevaliers, Marqab and Safita. This treaty is evidence that the Fifth Crusade had given the Egyptian government a severe shock, but it was unlikely that Jerusalem would be defensible. On hearing of it the patriarch of Jerusalem imposed an interdict on the Holy City. Frederick entered it on 17 March and the following day went through an imperial crown-wearing ceremony in the Church of the Holy Sepulchre, echoing the ancient prophecy of the last German emperor in occupation of Jerusalem before Antichrist, which had been an element in crusading thought from the start and may have motivated his grandfather. Jerusalem was to remain in Christian hands for fifteen years, but it does not seem to have been reincorporated into the kingdom and was treated by Frederick as a personal possession.

On 19 March he left Jerusalem and returned to Acre, where he faced resistance from the patriarch, the nobles, whose relations with him will be discussed later, and the Templars; Acre was in a state of disorder, with armed soldiers roaming the streets. News of the invasion of Apulia by papal armies forced him to leave hurriedly for home. He tried to go secretly in the early morning of 1 May, but his departure was discovered and he was pelted with tripe and pieces of meat as he passed the meat markets on his way down to the port.

So the Fifth Crusade had a curious postscript. Jerusalem was recovered in a peace treaty negotiated by an excommunicate, whose crusade was not recognized and whose lands were being invaded by papal armies. The Holy City itself was put under an interdict by its own patriarch. Its liberator left Palestine not in triumph but showered with offal.

CHAPTER 7

Crusading reaches Maturity, 1229–c. 1291

Crusading thought in the mid-thirteenth century

One hundred and fifty years after its birth crusading thought was given a classic, if rather uninspiring, expression in the writings of Pope Innocent IV (1243–54) and his pupil Henry of Segusio (better known as Hostiensis). Both men stressed that the pope was the sole earthly authority for crusading, the expression of his power being the indulgence, which only he could grant. The Holy Land, consecrated by the presence and suffering of Christ and once part of the Roman empire, was rightfully Christian and the occupation of it by the Muslims was an offence in itself for which the pope, as vicar of Christ and heir of the Roman emperors, could order retribution. Crusades could also be waged defensively against threats from infidels and by extension against those who menaced Christian souls within Christendom: Hostiensis echoed Peter the Venerable's opinion that crusades against heretics, schismatics and rebels were even more necessary than those to the Holy Land. He was, in fact, much more radical than Innocent on relations between Christians and infidels. Innocent was prepared to argue that the pope had a *de jure*, but not *de facto*, authority over infidels, with the power to command them to allow missionaries to preach in their lands and a right in the last resort to punish them for infringements of natural law, but he stressed that Christians could not make war on them for being infidels; nor could they fight wars of conversion. Hostiensis, on the other hand, supposed that the pope could intervene directly in affairs of infidels and that their refusal to recognize his dominion was in itself justification for a Christian assault upon them. He even suggested that any war fought by Christians against unbelievers was just, by reason of the faith of the Christian side alone. This went too far and Christian opinion since has tended to follow Innocent rather than Hostiensis.

By the middle of the thirteenth century crusading had become commonplace and many committed families could look back on four or five generations of crusaders. The privileges which regulated crusader status had become formalized. The greatest of them, the indulgence, has already been described. To it were added rights which were elaborations of those traditionally enjoyed by pilgrims: the protection of property and dependants in a crusader's absence; a delay in the performance of feudal service and in judicial proceedings to which he might be a party while he was away, or alternatively a speedy settlement of court cases before his departure if he should wish it; his ability to count the crusade as restitution of theft; a moratorium on the repayment of debts and freedom from interest payments until his return; exemption from tolls and taxes; for a cleric the freedom to enjoy his benefice though not resident and to pledge it to raise cash; and for a layman the freedom to sell or mortgage fiefs or other property which was ordinarily inalienable. A further group of rights gave him a privileged legal position in the extraordinary circumstances in which he found himself: release from excommunication by virtue of taking the cross and the ability to count a crusade vow as an adequate substitute for another not yet fulfilled; licence to have dealings with excommunicates and freedom from the consequences of interdict; a guarantee against being cited for legal proceedings outside his native diocese; the privilege of having a personal confessor, who was often permitted to dispense him from irregularities and to grant pardon for sins, like homicide, which were usually reserved to papal jurisdiction.

The machinery for preaching, though never again as systematic as that proposed by Innocent III in 1213, was well-established and with the proclamation of indulgences and the appointment of legates to supervise recruitment it would swing into action, making increasing use of the mendicant friars at the lower levels. The Church, moreover, was now regularly taxed. Usually apportioned at a tenth, the levies were demanded of the whole Church or of the clergy in particular provinces for periods varying from one to six years. Settlement was usually expected in two equal instalments a year and the money raised was supposed to subsidize crusaders. There is evidence of grants to a wide range of individuals from kings to petty lords; very often a grant consisted of the cash raised from churches in a magnate's own territories and in those of his relatives if they had taken the cross. I have already pointed out that this gave the popes a directing power that they could never have hoped for in the twelfth century, because, with crusading so expensive and crusaders patently in need of funds, they could divert their grants and therefore a large part of crusade resources in the direction dictated by their policy at a particular time. In practice, however, their control was never as effective as the theory would suggest. If a grantee failed to fulfil his vow his subsidy, which had been deposited in the meantime in religious houses, was supposed to be sent to Rome, but particularly where kings were concerned the popes seldom got all they should. And the taxation, which tended to become cumulative as new subsidies were demanded while old ones were still in arrears, was extremely unpopular and was strongly criticized on grounds of principle. Papal envoys were greeted with hostility and resistance was such that the returns were often slow in coming and were sometimes not paid at all.

The crusades of 1239–41

The truce that Frederick II had made with the sultan of Egypt was due to end in July 1239 and in anticipation Pope Gregory IX issued a new crusade proclamation in 1234. He gave a special commission to preach the cross to the Dominicans, who were much more successful then their predecessors had been ten years before. In contrast to the Fifth Crusade, the response in France was enthusiastic; indeed in September 1235 Gregory had to order the French bishops to see that crusaders did not leave before the truce in the East expired. He himself had been considering a more ambitious, and far more useful, plan to maintain an army in Palestine for ten years after the ending of the truce, but he had put forward a quite unrealistic proposal, which was to be modified by Gregory X in 1274 and must have been based on the crusade taxes of the twelfth-century kings: every Christian, male and female, cleric and lay, who did not take the cross was to contribute one penny a week to the cause – a sum that was quite beyond the means of most – and out of this crusaders to, and building works in, the East were to be subsidized. The contributors would be rewarded with a two-year indulgence (Gregory IX, *Registre*, ed. L. Auvray (1896–1955), nos. 2664–5). It is not surprising that this tax does not ever seem to have been collected.

It had been hoped that the French crusaders would be in the Holy Land before July 1239, but the insistence of Frederick II, on whose ports in southern Italy they might have to relay for shipping and supplies, that no army should set foot in Palestine until after the truce expired, meant that their departure was postponed until August 1239. And much more seriously, the pope changed his mind. The desperate needs of the Latin empire of Constantinople, which will be described in the next chapter, led him in the late summer of 1236 to propose switching the crusade, under the leadership of Peter of Dreux, the Count of Britanny, to Constantinople. He asked Count Thibald of Champagne, who had taken the cross for Palestine, to help the Latin Empire. He told the Archbishop of Reims, who was Peter of Dreux's brother, to finance Count Henry of Bar if he decided to go to Constantinople and he ordered the Bishop of Sées to commute his vow to the aid of the Latin empire and authorized the Bishop of Mâcon to allow Humbert of Beaujeu, the hammer of Languedoc in 1226, to commute his; the pope is supposed, in fact, to have commuted the vows of 600 northern French knights. He also wrote to Hungary to encourage Christians there to assist Constantinople. But in France there was resistance to this change of goal – in the end even Peter of Dreux and Henry of Bar went to Palestine – and by late May 1237 Gregory seems to have become reconciled to the fact that there were now going to be two crusades. Owing to the efforts of the Latin emperor Baldwin II who led it, the crusade for Constantinople was quite large when it left in the late summer of 1239, although the only great French nobles known to have taken part were Humbert of Beaujeu and Thomas of Marly. It took Çorlu in Thrace in 1240 and its presence bought Constantinople a breathing-space.

Meanwhile the French crusaders for the Holy Land, who mustered at Lyon, comprised the most glittering crusading army recruited in France since 1202 and were headed by two peers, Count Thibald of Champagne, who was also king of Navarre and was the son of the early leader of the Fourth Crusade, and Duke Hugh of Burgundy; two great royal officers, the constable Amalric of Montfort, Simon of Montfort's son and inheritor in Languedoc, and the butler Robert of Courtenay; and the Counts of Britanny, Nevers, Bar, Sancerre, Mâcon, Joigny and Grandpré. Most of them sailed from Marseille in August and reached Acre around 1 September. News soon reached them of a Muslim attack on Jerusalem, but their arrival coincided with a widening of divisions among the leading settlers over whether to launch an attack on the ruler of Damascus or the sultan in Cairo, who were at odds with one another and could therefore be tackled separately. In the end it was decided to take on both at once. The army would march down the coast to refortify the citadel of Ascalon before campaigning against Damascus. On 12 November a very strong army of c. 4,000 knights reached Jaffa, where they learnt that there was a large Egyptian force at Gaza. Ignoring the warnings and even the veto of Thibald of Champagne, Peter of Dreux and the masters of the Military Orders, a force which included the Duke of Burgundy, the Counts of Bar, Montfort and Brienne, the last of whom had custody of Jaffa, and the lords of Sidon and Arsuf and Odo of Montbéliard, the constable of Jerusalem, pressed on through the night and camped on the frontier beyond Ascalon. Perhaps its plan was not as rash as it appears to have been: it included nobles of the kingdom of Jerusalem, who might be expected to know their enemy. But the leaders neglected to post sentries and were surrounded and, although the duke of Burgundy and lords of the settlement deserted, Henry of Bar and Amalric of Montfort refused to do so. In the engagement that followed they were tricked into leaving their position to charge after a feigned retreat. Henry was killed. Amalric and some eighty knights were captured.

The main body of the Christian army learnt of the ambush on reaching Ascalon, but the Egyptians retired without further engagement. The crusaders did not start to rebuild the citadel at Ascalon as they had planned, but withdrew back up the coast to Acre; and there they stayed, even after an-Nasir Da'ud, the lord of Transjordan, took Jerusalem and destroyed the Tower of David. In the spring of 1240 Thibald led his forces north to Tripoli, tempted by an offer of conversion to Christianity from the lord of Hama which does not seem to have been serious and stemmed from a desire for aid against his fellow Muslim princes. Nothing of course came of this venture and Thibald was back in Acre in May. He then negotiated an alliance with as-Salih Isma'il of Damascus, who was worried by a turn of political events that had brought his nephew and predecessor as ruler of Damascus the sultanate of Egypt and promised to return Beaufort and the hinterland of Sidon, Tiberias, Safad and all Galilee to the Christians, together with Jerusalem, Bethlehem and most of southern Palestine, once the coalition between Damascus and the Latins had gained victory over Egypt. The treaty was naturally resisted by Muslim religious leaders – as-Salih Isma'il even had to besiege Beaufort before handing it over – and within the Latin kingdom by the party which was still in favour of a treaty with Egypt. But Thibald led his army to a rendezvous with the Damascene forces at Jaffa. As the Egyptians advanced on Palestine large numbers of the Damascenes, who were anyway demoralized, deserted, leaving the Christian force isolated. So Thibald was persuaded to enter into negotiations with Egypt., Again there was opposition within the Christian ranks, and on the face of it his crusade had been somewhat absurd. He had begun by making war on both Egypt and Damascus and he had proceeded to negotiate two mutually contradictory peaces. Nevertheless he secured from the Egyptians the promise of the lands in southern Palestine, including Jerusalem, already granted to the Christians by Damascus: that is to say more territory for the settlers than they had held since 1187. After visiting Jerusalem he departed for the West in September 1240, leaving the Duke of Burgundy and the Count of Nevers to rebuild the fortress at Ascalon. No sooner had he left than a second wave of crusaders arrived.

There had been a significant response in England to Pope Gregory's appeal. Richard, Earl of Cornwall, King Henry III's younger brother, had taken the cross in 1236. He had to resist attempts by his brother and the pope to keep him in England; in 1239 Gregory had even suggested that he send to Constantinople the money he would have spent crusading and he had only reluctantly agreed to his spending on his crusade the cash which had been collected in England for the Latin empire. He left England on 10 June 1240, accompanied by William, Earl of Salisbury, and about a dozen nobles. Simon of Montfort, the Earl of Leicester and Amalric's younger brother, who also crusaded at this time, seems to have travelled to the East separately. There were c. 800 English knights in the two parties. Richard reached Acre on 8 October. He found the leadership of the settlement still bitterly divided over relations with Damascus and Egypt, but he decided to follow the advice of the majority, who were for the treaty with Egypt. Marching down to Jaffa, he met the Egyptian envoys and then proceeded to Ascalon to complete the building of the citadel, which he handed over to the emperor Frederick's representatives, ignoring the claims of the baronial opposition which will be described in the next chapter. On 8 February 1241 the truce with Egypt was formally confirmed and on the 13th the prisoners-of-war taken at Gaza were returned. On 3 May Richard sailed for home.

The first crusade of St Louis

Much of the territory gained by Thibald and Richard was lost in 1244 when yet another switch in alliances led to the capture of Jerusalem by the Khorezmians and the disastrous defeat of the Latin settlers at the Battle of Harbiyah (La Forbie). It is possible that the news of the fall of Jerusalem contributed to King Louis IX of France's decision to take the cross in the following December. But there were also other reasons for his vow. He was seriously ill at the time. It may be that psychologically his decision was an act of rebellion against the tutelage of his able and domineering mother, Blanche of Castile, who had held the regency during his minority and had been a great influence upon him even after his coming of age: he was now thirty. She was very upset, and with the Bishop of Paris's help persuaded him that a vow made during an illness was not binding: his response was to take the vow again once he was well and nothing his mother could say would deter him. It has been pointed out that this defiance of his mother's wishes in a sacred cause echoed the action of his sister Isabella, to whom he was very close, when, eighteen months before, she had rejected the offer of marriage to the emperor's heir – an alliance that had the support of Blanche, Frederick II and the pope – and in the course of a dangerous illness had vowed herself to perpetual virginity. She did not enter a convent but lived at home like a nun, dressing very simply and devoting herself to the care of the poor. The parallels – illness, vow, rejection of their mother's plans for them – may not be coincidental.

Louis's choice of the vehicle for this defiance was a perfectly natural one for a man of his station and inclinations. He lived in a world suffused with crusading fervour and he had already shown a commitment to the movement by contributing large sums to the financing of the crusade to Constantinople led by the Emperor Baldwin, and that to Palestine led by Thibald of Champagne. He was, of course, the inheritor of a powerful family tradition. On his father's side almost every generation had produced a crusader since 1095; his great-great-great-grandfather's brother had taken part in the First Crusade; his great-grandfather and grandfather had been leaders of the Second and Third Crusades respectively; his father had died returning from the Albigensian Crusade, which made it natural for Blanche to be so very apprehensive. But through Blanche herself Louis was the heir of another line of dedicated crusaders. The kings of Castile had been leaders of the Spanish Reconquest and Blanche's father had been the victor of Las Navas de Tolosa. By this time the weight of family traditions of crusading was bearing heavily on many shoulders and the weight on Louis's was as heavy as any; he was to be accompanied on crusade by three brothers.

Once he had made the decision he threw himself into preparations. Like his great-grandfather he had taken the initiative in advance of a papal proclamation of war. What is more, Pope Innocent IV, embroiled in conflict with Frederick II, was very little help to him. Innocent had to flee from Italy and, after Louis had refused him asylum at Reims, he took up residence in Lyon to which a council was summoned in the summer of 1245. On 17 July Frederick was deposed. This division of Christendom on the eve of the crusade was bad enough – in 1248 it was even rumoured that Frederick was thinking of marching on Lyon – but the situation was made worse by the dispersal of crusading effort, since the pope now authorized the preaching of a crusade against Frederick in Germany and Italy as well as promulgating another in Spain. It says much for Louis's forbearance that he remained on good terms with both the emperor and the pope. But in these circumstances he could expect little help from western Europe beyond the French frontiers. Eastern Europe, moreover, had been shattered by a Mongol invasion of 1241. He was going to have to rely on his own resources. He worked hard for order in France – he had suppressed serious baronial uprisings between 1241 and 1243 and seems to have decided to persuade as many of the former rebels as possible to accompany him to the East – and in a way that was typical of any departing crusader and pilgrim anxious not to leave behind ill-feeling or cause for complaints he hit upon a new method of enquiring into the state of the royal administration and its bearing on the ordinary people throughout the royal domain and the apanages held by his brothers. In the early months of 1247 he sent out investigators (*enquêteurs*), mostly Franciscan and Dominican friars, to inquire into grievances against him or his administrators. These men uncovered a great deal that was wrong and their findings shocked the king. The consequences were drastic. There were at least twenty new appointments in the higher ranks of the provincial administration, although the evidence suggests that Louis did not put in new men but made use of experienced and trustworthy officials. A similar attitude towards departure was shown by John of Joinville who went with him:

I said [to my men and my vassals], 'Lords, I am going overseas and I do not know whether I will return. Now step forward; if I have wronged you in any way I will make amends to each of you in turn' . . . I made amends to them according to the judgements of all the men of my land and so that I would not influence them in their decisions I rose from the court and accepted whatever they decided without questioning it. Because I did not want to take with me a single penny to which I had no right, I went to Metz in Lorraine to raise a mortgage on a large part of my land (John of Joinville, *La Vie de Saint Louis*, ed. N. L. Corbett (1977), p. 106).

Preaching the crusade had begun in France early in 1245. Odo of Châteauroux, the cardinal-bishop of Tusculum, was given charge of it as legate, while preachers were also sent to England, western Germany and Scandinavia. The army that eventually departed was probably of c. 15,000 men, of whom there were 2,500–2,800 knights. Most of the crusaders were French, although there were also some Norwegians, Germans, Italians, Scots and c. 200 Englishmen. A feature of this crusade was Louis's attempt to solve the perennial problem of costs by underwriting the expenses of the nobles and by subsidizing a substantial number of knights. He lent money to leading crusaders, including his brother Alphonse of Poitiers, and he continued to lend cash during the crusade. He also arranged for transport and in 1246 he contracted for thirty-six ships from Genoa and Marseille, although the lesser leaders also hired ships on a smaller scale. He concerned himself with port facilities and supplies. Aigues-Mortes, which had already begun to be developed as a royal port, was improved by the construction of an artificial canal and a magnificent tower, to be his residence before departure. Vast stores were sent ahead to Cyprus and it is a measure of the care he took that in spite of the endemic corruption and pilfering of the time his army was nearly always well-supplied. When one adds to this catalogue the cost of his ransom in 1250 the expenses borne by him were enormous. It is remarkable that he seems to have remained solvent until 1253, when he was forced to borrow from Italian merchants; this was probably due to the effect on the fiscal arrangements in France of the death of his mother and regent in 1252.

It is known that Louis spent over 1,500,000 pounds *tournois* on his crusade at a time when his annual income was c. 250,000 pounds. Steps were taken to reduce royal expenditure, but in fact the money mostly came from sources other than his ordinary revenues, which increased markedly under the new administrators. In 1245 the Council of Lyon granted him a twentieth of ecclesiastical revenues for three years, which the French clergy voluntarily increased to a tenth; additional tenths for two years were granted in 1251. It is true that for reasons already given very little reached Louis from outside France, apart from dioceses in Lorraine and Burgundy bordering on his kingdom. But it is estimated that the French Church itself contributed 950,000 pounds, in other words about two-thirds of his expenses. To church taxation and royal revenues were added cash realized on the properties of heretics – there was a sustained drive to confiscate these – money extorted from Jews, particularly as a result of a campaign against usury, and profits accruing from royal licences to certain chapters and monastic communities to elect their bishops and abbots and the enjoyment of part of the revenues of some vacant benefices. And there were 'voluntary' benevolences which towns in the royal domain were expected to contribute, not once but several times, and which have been estimated to have brought in c. 274,000 pounds.

The king's departure was preceded by a tour of the royal domain early in 1248, the central act of which was the dedication of the Sainte Chapelle in Paris to house the relics of the Passion from Constantinople, about which more below. A solemn exposition of these relics was followed by the reception by Louis of the pilgrim's scrip and staff in Notre-Dame and a walk barefoot to St Denis, where, like his predecessors, he took possession of the oriflamme. After visiting religious houses around Paris he left for the south, embarked at Aigues-Mortes on 25 August and reached Cyprus on the night of 17 September. He spent eight months on the island while his army, supplemented by troops from Latin Greece and Palestine, gradually mustered. It seems that he was determined not to repeat past mistakes but to invade Egypt with maximum force. His crusade sailed at the end of May 1249, reaching the mouth of the Nile by Damietta on 4 June. The landing began on the 5th – it is a sign of the care he had taken that the crusaders had a large enough number of shallow-draughted vessels to put ashore a strong force at once – and the Muslim opposition was brushed aside. The defenders of Damietta itself, thoroughly demoralized, abandoned the city, which the Christians entered on the following day.

Louis must have been expecting a long siege, since, after all, Damietta had held out against the Fifth Crusade for over a year. And the Nile was soon to flood. It is not surprising that his initial success was followed by a long delay, although the possibility of moving in the meantime along the coast to take Alexandria was seriously discussed. It was not until 20 November that the march into the interior began, an advance that coincided with the death of the sultan and near panic among the Egyptians. It took the crusaders a month to reach the bank of the Nile opposite the main Egyptian defensive works at El Mansura. On 7 February 1250 the existence of a crossing-place was revealed by a local inhabitant and an advance guard under the king's brother Robert of Artois crossed on the 8th. Without waiting for the rest of the army it charged through the Muslim camp and into El Mansura itself, where it was trapped in the narrow streets and destroyed. Robert was killed. Louis, who had crossed with the main body, fought a dogged battle with the Muslim army for the whole day before the Egyptians withdrew to El Mansura, leaving him in possession of the field. But they had not been broken and were no longer leaderless, for the new sultan reached El Mansura on 28 February. The crusaders, exposed and isolated and now ravaged by disease, were harassed constantly, while the Muslims, transporting ships on camel-back around the Christian position and launching them downstream, cut them off from Damietta and their supplies. At the beginning of April the crusaders recrossed the Nile to their old camp and on the night of the 5th began their retreat to Damietta. They had managed to struggle only half-way when they were forced to surrender. The most carefully prepared and best organized crusade of all had been destroyed and its leader was a prisoner of the enemy.

On 6 May Louis was released, but his ransom had been set at 400,000 pounds (800,000 besants), half of which was paid immediately. Damietta, in which his queen had just given birth to a son, was surrendered. Most of the French returned to Europe, but Louis sailed to Acre: he wanted to see that his fellow-crusaders gained their freedom from the Egyptians and he was determined to help defend the Latin settlements against any new Muslim offensives that might result from his failure. He stayed in Palestine for nearly four more years and effectively took over the government of the kingdom of Jerusalem, negotiating a treaty with Egypt in 1252 which included the prospect of an offensive alliance against Damascus – it came to nothing – and in 1254 a two-year truce with Damascus and Aleppo. He refortified Acre, Caesarea, Jaffa and Sidon on a massive scale. He sailed for home on 24 April 1254, leaving a force of 100 knights to garrison Acre at his expense: this was the origins of a French regiment which was to remain until 1286 and was to play an important political rôle there. He reached Hyères in Provence early in July, a changed man. The disaster of 1250 was interpreted by him as a personal punishment for his sins. His devotions became more intense and penitential. He dressed and ate simply. He dedicated himself to the poor. He desired death. He sought to make good kingship a kind of expiation for his offences which, he believed, had brought shame and damage on all Christianity.

Crusading in Prussia and Livonia

Competing all the time with crusades to the East in the thoughts and planning of the popes were those in Europe. Along the shores of the Baltic there had already developed, as we have seen, a kind of perpetual crusade, justified as defensive aid to the little churches growing up in the wake of missionary work among the heathen and, although not entirely confined to Germans and Scandinavians, very much their enterprise. Until 1230 the main thrust had been in Livonia and Estonia, where the foundations of Christian control had now been laid. Although crusading continued in Livonia and in the middle of the century was extended by the Swedes to Finland, it came to be concentrated in Prussia, to the west of those regions. It was again a missionary bishop who got the movement going. Christian, a Cistercian monk of the Polish abbey of Lekno, whose early successes as an evangelist had won the support of the Polish nobles Duke Conrad of Masovia (Mazowsze) and Bishop Goslav of Plock, as well as that of Pope Innocent III, had been consecrated Bishop of Prussia in 1215. But with his success there came growing hostility from the natives and after several expedients, including the foundation of a new German Military Order, the Knights of Dobrzyn, had failed, Conrad of Masovia stepped in and in 1225 offered the Teutonic Knights, with whom the subjugation and rule of Prussia was henceforward to be associated, a substantial holding in the region.

Their Order, that of the Hospital of St Mary of the Germans of Jerusalem, had its origins in a German field-hospital at the siege of Acre in 1189–90, which was reconstituted in 1198 as a German Military Order. Like the Hospitallers, the Teutonic Knights had the twin functions of fighting and caring for the sick, but their Rule drew especially on that of the Templars. Until 1291 their headquarters were in Palestine and they were primarily concerned with the defence of the East: they had a large estate near Acre, centred on a castle, Montfort, the building of which has already been mentioned, and important holdings in the lordship of Sidon and in Cilician Armenia. Like the Templars and Hospitallers, however, they were also endowed with properties in Europe and found themselves involved in campaigns there. In 1211 King Andrew of Hungary gave them a stretch of his eastern frontier to defend against the Kipchak Turks. But they made themselves unpopular. They insisted on exemption from the authority of the local bishop and gave the Holy See proprietary rights over their territory. They seem to have increased their holdings by dubious means. They introduced German colonists. The king, who did not want to have an autonomous German religious palatinate on his frontier, abrogated their privileges and when they resisted expelled them by force.

It was at this point that Conrad of Masovia's invitation arrived, and it came to a master, Hermann of Salza, who was exceptionally able and a close adviser of the Emperor Frederick II. He wanted a training-ground for his knights before sending them to the East – Dr Christiansen has written that 'the Prussian venture was training for further Jerusalem crusades as cubbing is to foxhunting' – and he was determined to establish the kind of ecclesiastical state which the Order had wanted to create in Hungary. The first step was to get authorization from the emperor and in the Golden Bull of Rimini of 1226 Hermann received the status of an imperial prince for the province of Kulmerland (Chelmno) and all future conquests in Prussia. The Teutonic Order, therefore, was the first of the Military Orders to be given what would later be regarded as semi-sovereign status. The next was to make the new territory a papal dependence. In 1234 Gregory IX took it into the proprietorship of St Peter and the special protection of the Holy See, returning it to the Knights as a papal fief. Meanwhile Hermann sent his first detachment to the Vistula in 1229 and the conquest began. Potential conflict with the missionary activities of Bishop Christian were resolved when Christian was captured by the Prussians in 1233; he was held for six years, after which, in spite of his protests that the Order was more interested in making subjects than converts and was positively hindering conversion, it was too late for him to reverse the subordination of the Church in Prussia to it. He died in 1245, an embittered and disillusioned man.

Under the leadership of the Teutonic Knights the features of the Baltic crusade we have already discerned became more pronounced. Their Order was nearly exclusively German and their policies of settlement developed out of those already to be found in the *Drang nach Osten*. Each district was colonized by knights and burghers, the latter being generally given customs for settlement based on those of German Magdeburg, which provided a satisfactory means of establishing the Order's lordship and a basis for cooperation with the new German towns. And, perhaps because the masters spent so much time in Europe and could liaise directly with the papacy, unlike their opposite numbers in the Temple and the Hospital, the Knights were able to formulate more clearly the concept of a perpetual crusade. From the early 1230s a stream of crusaders was flowing into the region. In 1245 Pope Innocent IV granted plenary indulgences to all who went to fight in Prussia, whether it was in response to a specific papal appeal or not:

> We concede the same indulgence and privileges that are granted to those going to Jerusalem to all in Germany who, in response to the appeals of the Teutonic Knights and *without public preaching*, put on the sign of the cross and wish to go to the aid of the faithful against the savagery of the Prussians (J. Voigt, *Codex Diplomaticus Prussicus*, vol. 1 (1836), pp. 59–60).

So, unlike those Spanish bishops who had occasionally issued indulgences on their own authority in the twelfth century, the Teutonic Knights were empowered by the very pope who stressed that indulgences could only be granted by him the right to issue them without any reference to papal proclamations of war. In fact churchmen in northern and central Europe were repeatedly instructed to preach the crusade in the Baltic region.

The strategy employed by the Order was based on the building of castles, using forced Prussian labour, alongside which the settlements of German burghers were founded, while Dominican friars under its control christianized the countryside around. It seems to have planned an advance down the Vistula from Kulmerland to the Zalew Wiślany (Frisches Haff) and then eastward along the shore in the direction of Livonia, where from 1237 the Sword-Brothers were placed under its rule; after this the conquest of the interior would begin. The Zalew Wiślany was reached in 1236 and by 1239, with most of the shore in its hands, it began to penetrate the interior.

But in the first Prussian revolt of 1242 the Order lost much of the territory it had gained and had to fight a ten-year war of recovery. A land-bridge linking Livonia and Prussia became a reality with the foundations of Memel (Klaipéda) from Livonia in 1252 and Königsberg (Kaliningrad) by an impressive crusading expedition from Prussia led by King Ottakar II of Bohemia, Rudolf of Hapsburg and Otto of Brandenburg in 1254. Then came the second Prussian revolt of 1260, following the defeat of the Livonian Teutonic Knights at Durbe by the Lithuanians. Many of the garrisons and colonies established in Prussia were destroyed and the first group of crusaders marching to their relief was annihilated. Pope Urban IV, who had been planning a crusade against the Mongols, urged all those who had taken the cross to go to the Knights' assistance, offering plenary indulgences for any length of service. A series of German crusades took place, particularly in 1265, 1266, 1267 and 1272, but the revolt was only crushed in 1283 after warfare of such ruthlessness that it left half of Prussia a wilderness. Civil liberties which had been promised to all converts after the first revolt were now forgotten and most Prussians became serfs on the estates of the Knights and German immigrants and a few collaborators. By the end of the thirteenth century large-scale German colonization of Prussia could begin.

An invasion of Lithuania by the Sword-Brothers from Livonia had been bloodily repulsed in 1236 and the territory south of the Dvina lost at that time was only won back by 1255. The union of the Teutonic Knights and the Sword-Brothers, however, led to proposals for expansion eastwards against the Russian principalities which culminated in the capture of Pskov in 1240. This drive was halted by Alexander Nevski, prince of Novgorod, who retook Pskov and on 5 April 1242 defeated the Order in the Battle on Lake Peipus. The Order's ambitions were already bringing it into conflict with the forces which were to engage much of its attention in the fourteenth century, the Russians, the Poles and the Lithuanians, but at this time more concern was expressed about the Mongols.

The Mongol empire had its origins in an expansionary movement among a group of Turkish and Turco-Mongol tribes north-west of China under a chieftain called Temüjin, who in 1206 took the title of Genghis Khan, or universal emperor, and set out to conquer the world. In 1211–12 northern China fell to his men. The regions east of the Caspian Sea were conquered in 1219–20, after which raids were launched across southern Russia. His death in 1227 did not disturb the rhythm of conquest. Between 1231 and 1234 the Kin dynasty of northern China was liquidated, Korea was annexed and Iran was occupied. From 1237 to 1239 central Russia was conquered and in 1240 the Ukraine. In 1241 Poland and Hungary were invaded and a German army was defeated at Legnica (Liegnitz), although the death of Genghis Khan's successor, Ögödai, in 1242 interrupted the invasion of central Europe and may indeed have saved it. Faced with this appalling danger Pope Gregory IX proclaimed a crusade against the Mongols in 1241. This was confirmed in 1243 by Pope Innocent IV and resistance to the Mongols was on the agenda of the First Council of Lyon in 1245. In 1249, when the danger again appeared to be acute, Innocent allowed crusaders to the Holy Land to commute their vows to war against the Mongols. By then he had empowered the Teutonic Knights, to whom he had given the virtual direction of the north-eastern front of Christendom, to grant plenary indulgences to all taking the cross against them.

Crusading in Spain

The second traditional area of crusading activity in Europe can be clearly distinguished from that along the Baltic. There never was a perpetual crusade in Spain, even though there were constant petty wars there against the Muslims. The Almohad empire was now weakening and for over twenty years after 1228 the Spanish Muslims had no help from Africa and had to face the Christians alone. Under two great leaders, James I of Aragon and Ferdinand III of Castile, Christian Spain experienced some of its greatest triumphs. But it is fair to say that this extraordinary period has never been studied enough from the point of view of crusading: we can identify particular Spanish crusades and we can trace their developing features, but we cannot yet reach firm conclusions about them. Crusade privileges were granted to those assisting the Spanish Military Orders, the activities of which, particularly in the occupation in the 1230s of the region of Badajoz and the Campo de Montiel and Sierra de Segura, are reminiscent of those of the Teutonic Knights. James of Aragon led crusades which took Majorca, 1229–31, and the kingdom of Valencia, 1232–53, reaching a line of demarcation between Aragon and Castile that had been optimistically laid down in 1179. The Portuguese reconquest was completed by 1250. In 1230 Badajoz was taken and in 1231 St Ferdinand led a crusade which was marked by his brother Alfonso's victory over Ibn Hud, the paramount Muslim king, at Jerez. The way was now open for Ferdinand's conquest of Cordoba, the ancient Muslim capital, on 29 June 1236 and Seville, one of the greatest cities in western Europe, on 23 November 1248. Ferdinand was easily the most successful Christian warrior against Muslims of his day. English public opinion maintained that he

> alone has gained more for the profit and honour of Christ's Church than the pope and all his crusaders . . . and all the Templars and Hospitallers (*Flores Historiarum*, ed. H. R. Luard (1890), vol. 2, p. 355).

His career demonstrated, moreover, that the Reconquest was now largely a national enterprise; the crusade against Seville was even authorized by the pope in 1246 at the time St Louis's crusade to the East was being prepared. Few crusaders now came from abroad and the popes recognized Spanish crusading as a royal responsibility, which explains why Ferdinand was able to exploit the Spanish Church for his wars, especially in the form of the so-called *tercias reales*, the third of tithes which should have been spent on the upkeep of church buildings and was increasingly directed his way or seized by him. In fact, as Dr Linehan has pointed out, the Reconquest had a cost and that was the impoverishment of the Spanish Church, partly because it had to bear the expenses, partly because the drift of population south into the conquered lands reduced its revenues. This made it very dependent on kings like Ferdinand, who reimbursed himself at its expense, and it also made it insular, reluctant to finance crusades elsewhere.

But now for nearly a century, from 1252 until 1340, the pace of recon-quest slowed as new masters of Morocco, the Marinid dynasty, poured troops into what remained of Moorish Andalucia. At first Christian ambitions were high and between 1252 and 1254 a crusade was even being preached to invade Africa; King Alfonso X of Castile tried to recruit King Henry III of England and later King Hakon of Norway for it. In the end the city of Salé, which had rebelled against the Marinids, was held only for a fortnight in1260. Alfonso had to face a large-scale Muslim revolt in 1264. In response to it he had a crusade preached on the basis of out-of-date papal authorizations and he expelled all Muslims from Murcia, the source of the uprising, when it came into his hands. He was, however, unable to take Granada, partly because Castile was not strong enough to occupy it single-handedly, partly because the Marinid sultan Ya'qub (Abu Yusuf) entered Spain and put the Christians on the defensive.

Crusades against heretics

The Baltic and Spanish crusades deprived the East of recruits and diverted resources, since the local churches contributed and the papacy generally allowed them to do so. In Germany the development of a perpetual crusade, something that even the defence of the Holy Land had never been, meant that there was a permanent diversion of effort. In Spain the power of the kings meant that they could, if they so wished, frustrate the transmission of resources to the East. There were other local crusades. There was a small one authorized by the pope in 1232 against the Stedinger peasants in Germany whom the Archbishop of Bremen had accused of heresy. The Bishops of Minden, Lübeck and Ratzeburg were ordered to preach the cross in the dioceses of Pæderborn, Hildesheim, Verden, Münster, Osnabrück, Minden and Bremen and the campaign, in which crusaders from the Low Countries as well as Germany took part, was waged early in 1234. In the same category were crusades authorized in 1227 and 1234 by Popes Honorius III and Gregory IX against Bosnian heretics, for which there was also the commutation of crusade vows, and in 1238 against John Asen of Bulgaria's alliance with Byzantine Nicaea, which was ordered to be preached in Hungary. These crusades do not seem to have attracted much criticism or to have created many problems for the papacy, perhaps because they were local.

Political crusades

But in quite another class were the crusades in Italy. In a sense the opening campaign had been that conducted by papal armies under John of Brienne in the mainland territories of the kingdom of Sicily from 1228 to 1230. This attack on the emperor's lands while he was in Palestine had been justified by Pope Gregory IX as a war in defence of the Church against a man who had oppressed Sicilian churchmen and had dared to invade the papal states. The soldiers had been promised 'remission of sins' in general terms and had been financed by an income tax levied on the clergy: the churches in Sweden, Denmark, England and northern Italy all paid a tenth in 1229 and French bishops were asked to send to Rome the final payments of a five-year tenth which had been imposed on their dioceses in 1225 in support of the Albigensian Crusade. But full crusade indulgences were not granted and it is noteworthy that the soldiers wore the sign of Peter's Keys, not the cross. The campaign looks more like a thirteenth-century version of a war of the Investiture Contest than a crusade. In 1239–40, however, the crisis was such that a recognizable crusade was preached. Pope and emperor were again in conflict. Frederick had control of southern Italy and he was close to achieving dominance in northern Italy as well. The organization of the crusade began in 1239 and preaching was authorized in northern Italy and Germany. By early 1240 Frederick's army was threatening Rome itself. Gregory preached the cross in Rome and in February 1241 he went so far as to allow his legates in Hungary to commute the vows of crusaders to the East to the war against the emperor. He asked for aid, although not at first linked to crusading, from the universal Church and money was raised, in spite of much reluctance, in England, Scotland, Ireland and France. This crusade achieved little other than checking Frederick's advance on Rome, but it started a train of events that were to dominate Italian politics for almost a century and a half.

The crusade against Frederick was renewed by Pope Innocent IV in 1244 and from 1246, the year after the Council of Lyon had deposed the emperor, a stream of letters from the pope, addressed particularly to Germany where anti-kings were being set up, urged crusade-preaching. The army which took the old imperial capital of Aachen for the anti-king William of Holland in October 1248 had many crusaders serving in it, but in Germany there were short bursts of enthusiasm for the wars rather than sustained commitment. Innocent collected large sums of money from the

Church, especially from Italians beneficed in trans-Alpine countries and from dioceses in England, Poland, Hungary and Germany, most of which seem to have gone to finance the German struggle. On the other hand, the papal cause was relatively weak in Italy and a lack of cash seems to have been part of the reason why an invasion of Sicily in 1249 failed.

Frederick died on 13 December 1250. The crusade in Germany was renewed in the following February against his heir Conrad IV and preaching was again ordered there in 1253 and 1254. But with the great emperor dead the eyes of the papacy turned to the kingdom of Sicily which was, after all, a papal fief. Its invasion would require a large, well-organized and well-financed army, which is one reason why the Italian crusades came to be run on the same lines as those to the East. It would also need a leader of weight and distinction and papal policy in the 1250s was directed towards finding one. Richard of Cornwall was approached; then Charles of Anjou, one of St Louis's brothers; then King Henry III of England, who had taken the cross in March 1250, on behalf of his younger son, Edmund of Lancaster. When the negotiations with Henry broke down – Henry had agreed to an impossible condition of underwriting all the papacy's war expenses and had had to suffer the imposition of baronial government in England – the pope turned again to Charles of Anjou and between 1262 and 1264 the terms for the transfer of the crown of Sicily to him were hammered out.

The first crusade against Manfred, Frederick's illegitimate son and the upholder of the Staufen cause in southern Italy, was preached early in 1255 in Italy and England. An army under the Florentine cardinal Octavian degli Ubaldini marched against Lucera and to defeat, after which Manfred achieved such dominance that he was crowned king of Sicily in August 1258. Preaching continued while crusading warfare spread into northern Italy – between 1255 and 1260 a crusade in the March of Treviso overthrew the Ghibelline despots Ezzelino and Alberic of Romano – and to Sardinia. Meanwhile Pope Urban IV granted Charles of Anjou's request that a crusade to conquer the kingdom of Sicily should be preached in France, the empire and northern and central Italy. This crusade set out from Lyon in October 1265. On its march it was joined by Italian contingents and it reached Rome in the middle of January 1266, a few days after Charles had been crowned king of Sicily in St Peter's. Charles, who was very short of money, began his campaign at once and on 26 February defeated and killed Manfred in the Battle of Benevento. The whole kingdom of Sicily was soon under his control, although the crusade had to be revived in April 1268, when Conrad IV's young son Conradin descended on Italy to regain his inheritance. In August he was defeated at the Battle of Tagliacozzo and he was executed in Naples in October. The surrender of the last Staufen garrison at Lucera in August 1269 ended the first phase of the struggle.

The rise of Charles of Anjou in the Mediterranean political world was meteoric. Already in 1267 William of Villehardouin, the prince of Achaea and Latin ruler of the Peloponnese (the Morea), recognized him as his overlord – on William's death in 1278 Charles took over the government of Achaea directly – and the Latin emperor of Constantinople granted him suzerainty over the Greek islands and the Latin holdings in Epirus. William was to lead 1,100 knights of the Peloponnese to reinforce Charles's army at Tagliacozzo. In 1277, after long negotiations, a claimant to the throne of Jerusalem sold him the crown, with the papacy's connivance and support, and in September of that year his vicar took up residence in Acre. It is clear that the hopes of the papacy for the survival of the Latin settlement in Palestine rested on the fact that it was now integrated into a huge eastern Mediterranean empire which might, with the active support of Charles's close relative the king of France, provide it with the permanent defensive capability that crusades, of their nature *ad hoc* and temporary, could never give. But on 30 March 1282 the island of Sicily rose against Angevin-French domination in a revolt known as the Sicilian Vespers and the islanders called in King Peter of Aragon, who was married to Manfred's daughter Constance and had the best navy in the Mediterranean. Peter's landing at Trapani on 30 August aroused the indignation of Pope Martin IV. The pope was a Frenchman who as legate had concluded the curia's negotiations with Charles in 1264 and had been helped to the pontifical throne by Charles's political intriguing, but any pope, claiming the feudal overlordship of Sicily, would have looked on the Aragonese action as a challenge to his authority, and beyond that Martin must have recognized the danger to the papacy's carefully constructed scheme for the preservation of the Christian presence in the East. On 13 January 1283 a crusade was declared against the Sicilians, but preaching was at first restricted to the kingdom of Sicily itself and was only extended to northern Italy in April 1284. In November 1282 Peter of Aragon was excommunicated and in March 1283 he was deprived of his kingdom, which was claimed to be another papal fief. A legate was sent to France to organize a crusade against him, while Charles of Valois, the second son of King Philip III, was promised Aragon on terms very similar to those under which his great-uncle Charles of Anjou held Sicily. A four-year tenth was levied on the French clergy and on the dioceses bordering on France to finance the crusade. Preaching in France began in the early months of 1284 and in February King Philip accepted the crown of Aragon for his son.

The crusades in southern Italy and northern Spain were fiascos. In fact in the spring of 1283 the Aragonese themselves carried war on to the Italian mainland and they demonstrated their supremacy at sea, capturing Charles of Salerno, Charles of Anjou's heir, in a naval engagement off Naples in June 1284. Charles of Anjou's death in January 1285, which was followed by that of Martin IV on 28 March, weakened the cause. Charles of Salerno only obtained his liberty and came into his own in October 1288, on terms that involved a commitment from him to work for peace between Aragon, France, Sicily and Naples. Meanwhile Philip III had invaded Spain with an army of at least 8,000 men in the spring of 1285. The Aragonese in Gerona held the crusade up all summer. In the early autumn their fleet was recalled from Sicilian waters and it destroyed the navy servicing the French and deprived the crusade of its supplies. Philip was forced to retreat and he died during the withdrawal at Perpignan on 5 October.

With the Aragonese advance into mainland Italy held at a defensive line south of Salerno everyone seems to have wanted peace, especially after the loss of Palestine and Syria in 1291, which made the diversion of resources look selfish and foolhardy. The papal curia itself was divided, but the election of Pope Boniface VIII in 1294 marked the success of the war-party there. In the summer of 1295 Boniface persuaded King James II of Aragon to withdraw from Sicily, but the king's younger brother Frederick, the governor of the island, rebelled and was crowned king at Palermo in March 1296. So crusading against the Sicilians was renewed in 1296, 1299 and 1302, while it was also proclaimed in 1297–8 against the Colonna cardinals, a faction in Rome composed of personal enemies of Boniface and allies of Frederick. With the help of James the Angevins cleared Calabria in 1297–8 and won a naval victory at the Battle of Cape Orlando in 1299. But the island was too strong to be reoccupied and the treaty of Caltabellotta in August 1302 recognized Frederick's rule over Sicily; although according to the treaty he was to hold it only for life, the island was destined to remain in Aragonese hands.

These 'political' crusades were justified in traditional ways by the popes, who showed themselves to be acutely aware of the criticism that they were misusing the movement for their own ends at a time when the Christians in the East were in dire straits. They stressed the need to defend the Church and the faith; they compared their enemies in Italy to the Muslims and they argued that these were hindering effective crusading to the East. They also went to great lengths to build up an efficient machinery for preaching and getting their message across. There was, in fact, a fairly large response, although all armies were made up of both crusaders and mercenaries. Crusade-preaching in France in the years 1264 to 1268 was particularly successful and the armies of 1265–6 and 1268 contained not only men who had taken the cross for the first time, but also experienced crusaders from the eastern wars like Érard of Valéry, who drew up the battle plan for Tagliacozzo.

I have served [wrote Peter Pillart, an old knight, to Philip III of France] you and your ancestors in the year they went to Damietta and to Sicily and at the siege . . . of Tunis (É. Berger, 'Requête adressée au roi de France', *Études d'histoire du Moyen Âge dédiées à Gabriel Monod* (1896), p. 349).

In Italy itself the greatest response came, as might be expected, from the Guelf areas that traditionally supported the papacy. Dr Housley, the most recent historian of these crusades, is surely right in maintaining that there was enough response to make one doubt the common belief that they had little ideological appeal. The ethos in the armies, moreover, was typically crusading. The papacy diverted to them a large part of the resources, particularly from clerical taxation, that were available for crusading in the East. Moneys from England, France, the Low Countries, Provence and the imperial dioceses financed Charles of Anjou's campaigns in the 1260s. Between 1283 and 1302 Christendom from the British Isles to Greece was frequently taxed to restore Angevin rule in Sicily. The heavy taxation led to important innovations such as the organization of Christendom into collectorates by Pope Gregory X in 1274, the increasing reliance of the popes on credit and banking facilities and, in the fourteenth century, to the institution of new taxes to reduce this reliance; and it extended the curia's control over the movement. But it was understandably unpopular and was resisted, particularly in England in the 1250s and France in the 1260s; there can be no doubt that it had a bad effect on the relations between the papacy and the Church at large.

The development of the 'political' crusades raises questions that are being hotly debated. Were they perversions of the movement preached simply to further papal policies in Italy? Did they arouse such hostility among the faithful that they damaged the papacy in the eyes of its subjects? The first of these questions is particularly controversial because there is a group of historians who maintain that these were not true crusades; indeed some of them refuse to give the title of crusade to any war not fought in the East for the recovery of Jerusalem or the defence of the Holy Land. They maintain that, whatever the popes and canon lawyers may have said – and they are prepared to admit that the papacy took a broad overall view of crusading – the ordinary faithful did not regard crusades in Europe in the same light as crusades to the East. Their answer to the first question is, therefore, bound up with their answer to the second, since they assume that public opinion was hostile to these diversions.

There can be no doubt that crusades to the East carried the most prestige and were the most appealing. Nor can there be any doubt that expressions of hostility to crusading in Europe can be found. Harsh words were written by Languedociens, not surprisingly, but also by men in northern France and England against the Albigensian Crusade. And in Germany, Italy, France, Spain and the Holy Land there was quite widespread criticism of crusades against Catholic Christians like Frederick II and his descendants. The strongest element in it was that such crusades diverted resources and manpower from the Latin East. Christians in Palestine, Cyprus and Greece kept up a barrage of complaints, summed up in a rebuke apparently delivered in 1289 by a Templar messenger to Pope Nicholas IV after the fall of Tripoli:

> You could have succoured the Holy Land with the power of kings and the strength of the other faithful of Christ . . . but you have armed kings against a king, intending to attack a Christian king and the Christian Sicilians to recover the island of Sicily which, kicking against the pricks, took up just arms (Bartholomew of Neocastro, 'Historia Sicula', *RISNS*, vol. 13, 3, pp. 108–9).

When Pope Innocent IV was tactless enough to order the preaching of his crusade against Conrad IV at a time when St Louis's crusade was in shreds and Louis himself was in Palestine, the French government and people united in fierce opposition to it. The depth of feeling in France also manifested itself in the Crusade of the Shepherds, an extraordinary reaction to the news of Louis's defeat and imprisonment in Egypt. Its leader was a demagogue called the Master of Hungary, who carried in his hands a letter he claimed to have been given by the Blessed Virgin Mary. His message was that the pride of the French nobles and churchmen had been punished in Egypt and that just as shepherds had been the first to hear the news of Christ's Nativity so it was to them, the simple and the humble, that the Holy Land would be delivered. His army of the poor reached Paris, where it was well received by Queen Blanche; after this it fragmented into different companies and became progressively more violent until, outlawed by Blanche and with the Master killed, it disintegrated. Against this background it was not likely that the French would take kindly to the diversion of resources to Germany or Italy. Blanche took measures to prevent the preaching in France of the crusade against Conrad and threatened to confiscate the lands of any who took the cross for it.

Examples of this sort of reaction have been collected by historians, and they were taken seriously by experienced preachers like the Dominican Humbert of Romans in the early 1270s. But they do not in themselves demonstrate that people in general made a distinction in kind between crusading to the East and in Europe; it should not be forgotten that crusading to the East also attracted a measure of criticism. Nor can one create out of them the picture of widespread disillusionment. Dr Siberry has recently noted that the critics were on the whole either long-standing opponents of the papacy, who would be expected to be critical anyway, or individuals who had particular reasons for expressing opposition to specific diversions of resources from the East. For instance, the French government, which had bitterly opposed the crusade against the Staufen in 1251, was brought to support Charles of Anjou's crusade of 1265 into Sicily. St Louis, who was a most moral man, cannot have been opposed to 'political' crusades in principle. There were some signs of disillusionment and there were a few root-and-branch pacifists, horrified by the whole tradition of Christian violence. How numerous they were is open to question; it is likely that there were very few indeed. Dr Siberry has pointed out, moreover, that criticism in the thirteenth century never reached the heights of vituperation that had been scaled in the aftermath of the débâcle of the Second Crusade.

In fact the most striking thing about the movement, wherever it manifested itself, was its continuing popularity. Crusades were waged in all theatres of war and they could not have been fought without crusaders. On the whole the papal arguments for particular crusading ventures, whether in Europe or in the East, were received sympathetically enough for there to be recruits. It is impossible to show, and it is hard to believe, that the prestige of the papacy was diminished by the Italian crusades. The popes genuinely perceived the threat to their position in Italy to be so great that they had no option but to preach them. They also believed that the future of the Latin East depended on the integrity of the kingdom of Sicily and therefore on the crusades that followed the Sicilian Vespers. But that is not to argue that the Holy Land did not suffer in reality from these diversions. It must remain an open question whether the Latin settlements in Palestine and Syria would have survived longer had the popes felt able to make more resources available. The fact is that at the very time when revenue from commerce in the Latin kingdom of Jerusalem declined because of a change in the Asiatic trade routes, which will be discussed in the next chapter, it was deprived of money and matériel that could have passed to it from Europe because of crusading in Italy and against Aragon.

The second crusade of St Louis

It would be wrong, however, to suppose that the period from 1254 to 1291 was one in which the Latin East was starved of European resources. The French crown poured money across the Mediterranean, mostly into the hands of the regiment it maintained in Acre: it was later estimated by the French treasury that the king spent an average of 4,000 pounds *tournois* a year between 1254 and 1270, and funding at much the same level continued until 1286. King Edward I of England also gave substantial support. The papacy organized a series of small expeditions, transmitted large sums of cash and through its representative the patriarch of Jerusalem paid for mercenaries to supplement the French regiment. And it continued to plan crusades.

In the aftermath of the fall of Constantinople to the Byzantine Greeks in 1261 Pope Urban IV seems to have been thinking of a crusade to recover it for the Latins, but there was soon a change of plan and in 1263 the pope was again thinking of aid to the Holy Land. Until 1266 the crusade of Charles of Anjou into southern Italy had precedence, but in the meantime the Mamluk armies from Egypt had begun the systematic reconquest of Palestine. At this Louis IX of France took the initiative, as he had done in 1244. Late in 1266 he informed Pope Clement IV of his intention, incidentally ruining the project for a small expedition which was due to leave hurriedly for the East in the following spring, and on 24 March 1267 he took the cross at an assembly of his nobles. This time the response in France was not enthusiastic – the French, after all, had just been involved in Charles of Anjou's campaigns – and the force that eventually left was smaller than that in 1248. But Louis planned this crusade as carefully, if not even more carefully, than he had his first. He was promised a three-year tenth from the French Church and a three-year twentieth from the dioceses bordering on France in 1268; that is from the year the Sicilian tax ended. The towns were again asked for aid. His brother Alphonse of Poitiers raised well over 100,000 pounds *tournois*, mostly from his own domains. Louis made contracts with Genoa and Marseille for shipping, specifying that the vessels were to be at Aigues-Mortes by the early summer of 1270. And crusaders were recruited elsewhere in Europe, particularly in Aragon and England, where the kings wanted to crusade. Charles of Anjou, perhaps somewhat reluctantly, also agreed to join his brother.

The Aragonese left first. On 1 September 1269 King James I sailed from Barcelona, but his fleet was so damaged by a storm that he and most of his crusaders returned home. A squadron under two of his bastard sons, the Infants Ferdinand Sanchez and Peter Fernandez, reached Acre at the end of December. Their force, however, was not strong enough to engage the Mamluk sultan Baybars of Egypt when he appeared before the city at the head of a raid and they soon returned to the West with little achieved. In England, in the aftermath of the civil war between Henry III and Simon of Montfort, crusade-preaching from 1266 had led to the formation of a substantial body of crusaders, among them Henry III's eldest son Edward, who took the cross in June 1268 after winning over his father, who had intended to go himself in fulfilment of a vow he had made in 1250, and the pope, who had agreed with Henry that Edward should remain in England. Edward may well have been under the influence of his relative St Louis; the two men were in touch by late 1267 and in August 1269 Edward went to Paris to attend a council-of-war. He promised to join Louis's expedition in return for a loan of 70,000 pounds *tournois*. He made widespread use of similar contracts of service to those used by Louis, binding to himself the crusaders in his following in return for subsidies. It has even been suggested by Dr Lloyd that his crusade was 'an extended household operation in all its essentials', but this of course made it expensive and the crown used every measure open to it to raise cash, including a general tax of a twentieth in 1269–70; the Church contributed the grant of a two-year tenth in 1272. Edward left England in August 1270, but by then the crusade was already set for failure.

Louis had sailed from France on 2 July, a month later than he had intended. His original plan of campaign had been to sail to Cyprus, but over the previous year a new one had been formulated, involving a preliminary descent upon Tunis in North Africa before proceeding to the East. It has been suggested that he had been persuaded to adopt this course of action by Charles of Anjou, who might benefit from a demonstration against the Hafsid ruler of Tunis, but the details of Charles's preparations suggests that he was not *au fait* with the plan to attack Tunis, which must have been decided at the French court. It may be that Louis believed that Tunisia was a major supplier of Egypt, which would be indirectly weakened by such an attack. If so, he was wrong; the Egyptian government was greatly relieved when it heard what he had done. Professor Richard, however, has recently proposed that we look again at the explanation given by the king's own confessor, Geoffrey of Beaulieu. Geoffrey stated that Louis was attracted by the chance of converting the ruler of Tunis, who had let it be known that he would be baptized provided that he had the support of a Christian army to persuade his subjects to accept it; there had, in fact, been a Tunisian embassy in Paris in the autumn of 1269.

The fleet gathered off Cagliari in southern Sardinia and the crusaders landed in Tunisia without serious opposition on 18 July, encamping round a fort built on the site of ancient Carthage. They settled down to wait for the arrival of Charles of Anjou, but in the summer heat dysentery or typhus swept through the insanitary camp. The king's eldest son Philip was dangerously ill. His youngest, John Tristan, who had been born at Damietta, perished. Louis himself succumbed to sickness and on 25 August he died, stretched out penitentially on a bed of ashes. On the night before he died he was heard to sigh, 'Jerusalem! Jerusalem!' Charles of Anjou arrived on that very day and soon decided that the crusade should withdraw. On 1 November he ratified a treaty drawn up with the Tunisian ruler, from which he personally derived most benefit – one-third of a war indemnity the Tunisians were forced to pay, together with a renewal and augmentation of tribute and of Sicilian trading rights and the promise of expulsion from Tunisia of Staufen exiles who were fomenting trouble – and on 11 November the crusaders left for Sicily.

Edward of England reached North Africa the day before the crusade left and, although he was not happy with what he found, he sailed with Charles of Anjou and Philip of France to Sicily, through a storm off Trapani which did great damage to the fleet. He voyaged on to the Holy Land at the end of April 1271, accompanied by only 200–300 knights and c. 600 infantry, and disembarked at Acre on 9 May. The English remained inactive while the Egyptians took the Teutonic Knights' castle of Montfort, but on 12 July they raided into Galilee and in November, together with local troops and another body of crusaders under Edward's brother Edmund, who had reached Palestine in September, they tried to take the Mamluk castle of Qaqun near Caesarea. They surprised a large Turkoman force nearby, but withdrew at the approach of a Muslim army and any further action was prevented by a ten-year truce, agreed between Egypt and the kingdom of Jerusalem in April 1272. There was little Edward could now do. His brother left Acre in May. On 16 June he was severely injured when one of his native servants tried to assassinate him. For a time he was too ill to move, but he eventually left for home on 22 September.

Pope Gregory X

The second crusade of St Louis, which accomplished so little, was the last full-scale crusade before the fall of the Latin settlements in 1291, but that was not for want of enthusiasm. Tedaldo Visconti, who had taken the cross and had gone directly to Acre in the summer of 1270, was elected pope in the following year by a body of cardinals who expressed the hope that he would do all in his power to save the Holy Land. He adopted the name of Gregory X. Before leaving Palestine to take up office he preached a sermon on the text

> If I forget thee, O Jerusalem, let my right hand forget her cunning. If I do not remember thee, let my tongue cleave to the roof of my mouth; if I prefer not Jerusalem above my chief joy (Psalm 136 (137): 5–6).

In a letter to Edward of England, who was still in Acre, he told how he had hurried directly to the papal curia at Viterbo, not even stopping at Rome, so as to begin work on bringing aid to the Holy Land immediately; and before he had been consecrated he sent a letter to Philip of France with a proposal for fitting out an expedition. He felt, in fact, as obsessively about the movement as Innocent III had done. His first act at Viterbo was to summon a conference of cardinals and of men familiar with conditions in the East and it was in this gathering that he decided to convoke a new general council with the two-fold aim of reforming Christendom and promoting a crusade, which he would lead himself. He tried to prepare carefully for this, the Second Council of Lyon, by calling for written advice from the clergy and during it, on 18 May 1274, he issued the *Constitutiones pro zelo fidei*, the most imposing crusade document since the *Ad liberandam* constitution of 1215. The *Constitutiones* contained many elements found in earlier decrees, especially *Ad liberandam*, but there was much in it that was new, in particular on the raising of funds. A six-year tenth was to be levied on the whole Church, with exemptions only granted on the strictest conditions. Christendom was to be divided into twenty-six districts staffed by collectors and sub-collectors. Every temporal ruler was to be asked to impose a capitation tax of one silver penny *tournois* a year within his dominions: this was obviously influenced by Gregory IX's attempted levy of 1235. Gregory X's aim was to build up a huge reserve and had he lived a really major enterprise might have been mounted. As it was, his preparations were heroic. Tremendous efforts culminated at the council in the formal reconciliation of the Latin and Greek churches and the promise from the Byzantine emperor to do all in his power to help the coming crusade. In 1275 the kings of France and Sicily took the cross. So did Rudolf of Hapsburg in return for Gregory's agreement to crown him emperor. The plan was for the pope to crown Rudolf in Rome on 2 February 1277; then on the following 2 April pope and emperor would leave together for the East; there was even discussion with the Greeks about their proposal for the crusade to follow the path of the First in order to reconquer Asia Minor on its way to the East. It is clear that Gregory was planning an eastern crusade on a more ambitious scale than had ever been dreamed of before. But on 10 January 1276 he died. To a despairing contemporary.

> It does not seem to be the divine will that the Holy Sepulchre should be recovered, since the great number attempting it are seen to have laboured in vain (Salimbene of Adam, 'Chronicon', *MGHS*, vol. 32, 494–5).

The failure to launch a great crusade after 1276

Gregory's crusade never departed and the huge sums collected for it were dissipated on the Italian crusades. Although proposals for large-scale expeditions were still put forward – Edward of England bombarded the papacy with them from 1284 to 1293 – it was small parties that sailed to help the kingdom of Jerusalem in its last years. On 18 June 1287 Countess Alice of Blois landed at Acre with a little crusade which included Count Florent of Holland; it was followed in 1288 by a force under John of Grailly and in 1290 by others of Englishmen under Odo of Grandson and of north Italian crusaders under the Bishop of Tripoli.

One reason for the failure to mount a large-scale crusade after 1272 was the increasing complexity, viciousness and cost of inter-state disputes in western Europe. Another was the prevalence of the view that great crusades were counter-productive. They were difficult to raise, provision and control and could be expected to do little long-term good, since they would conquer, but not occupy, territory, the defence of which would put additional strains on the already over-stretched resources of the Latin East once the crusaders had returned home. What was needed, of course, was a strengthening of the permanent garrison, and this explains the money sent to Palestine in these years by the papacy, France, and to a lesser extent England, to maintain bodies of troops there. In this respect the popes had pinned their hopes on Charles of Anjou and the integration of the kingdom of Jerusalem into an eastern Mediterranean empire which would theoretically be able to defend it, especially since it had the backing of France. The gamble failed. Given Charles's much greater interest in the conquest of Albania and even the Byzantine empire it would probably have failed anyway. But reality dawned in 1286 with the war against the Sicilians and Aragonese going badly, Charles dead and his heir a prisoner of the Aragonese. By then the Latin settlements in Palestine and Syria had only five more years of existence left.

CHAPTER 8

The Latin East, 1192–c. 1291

In the third decade of the thirteenth century the western settlers in Palestine and Syria were probably more secure than their ancestors had been before 1187. It is true that even after Frederick II's treaty with al-Kamil of Egypt in 1229 they ruled much less territory than their great-grandfathers in the middle of the twelfth century. They held the coast from Jaffa to Beirut, with a tongue of land extending through Ramle to Jerusalem and a somewhat wider salient reaching Nazareth in Galilee. North of Beirut the county of Tripoli remained much as it had been in 1187, but the principality of Antioch was now confined to the area immediately around Antioch itself and a strip of the coast in the south, from Jeble to the Hospitaller castle of Marqab and the border with the county of Tripoli. But these settlements were no longer lonely Catholic outposts in the Levant.

Cilician Armenia

North of the principality of Antioch the Cilician Armenian ruler Leo had accepted a crown from the western emperor in 1198, together with a form of submission to Rome which was never very real and has been already described. Cilicia nevertheless was latinized in all sorts of ways. Leo took as his second wife Sibylla, the daugher of Aimery of Cyprus and Isabella of Jerusalem, and his daughter and heiress Zabel was therefore the first cousin of the queen of Jerusalem and the king of Cyprus. Leo gave castles and territories to the Hospitallers and Teutonic Knights and privileges to Genoese and Venetian merchants. His court was transformed: offices changed their character at the same time as they adopted Latin functions and titles; the system of landholding and the relations of the 'barons' with the crown were modified in imitation of western feudalism; westerners held some of the fiefs; and the authority of western law gradually grew until the *Assises of Antioch*, translated into Armenian, were adopted as their own by the Armenians in the 1260s. In the 1250s King Hetoum entered, as a subject power, into an alliance with the Mongols, but that did not affect Cilicia's relationship with the Latins, which grew even closer. King Toros (1292–4) married Margaret of Cyprus. His sister Isabella married Amalric, the King of Cyprus's younger brother, and in the fourteenth century the

Armenian crown passed into the hands of this cadet branch of the royal house of Cyprus until Cilician Armenia was finally destroyed in 1375.

Cyprus

Off the Levantine coast there was now Latin Cyprus. We have already seen that the island was conquered in 1191 by Richard I of England and was sold to Guy of Lusignan, the rejected king of Jerusalem, in 1192. Guy died late in 1194 and was succeeded by his brother Aimery, who married Isabella of Jerusalem in October 1197, after the death of Henry of Champagne. At about the same time he paid homage to representatives of the western emperor and received a crown from them, so that from that date he was king of Cyprus in his own right and of Jerusalem by virtue of his marriage. After his death in 1205 the crowns went their separate ways: Cyprus passed to Hugh I, Aimery's son by his first wife Eschiva of Ibelin; Jerusalem was inherited by Maria, Isabella's daughter by Conrad of Montferrat. Hugh of Cyprus married Isabella's third daughter Alice of Champagne and the crowns were reunited in their grandson, Hugh III of Cyprus and I of Jerusalem, who succeeded to Cyprus in 1267 and to Jerusalem in 1269.

Guy of Lusignan had established a feudal system in Cyprus, peopling it largely with immigrants from Palestine, particularly from those families which had supported him in his struggle to retain the crown of Jerusalem. They were later joined by many of the leading nobles from the mainland – King Hugh I's mother, after all, was an Ibelin, a member of the most prominent feudal house in Palestine – and by 1230 many of the great nobles had estates in both kingdoms. The Latin settlers introduced feudal customs from the mainland, and in 1369 a particular interpretation of them, John of Ibelin-Jaffa's great work of jurisprudence, became an official work of reference in the High Court of Nicosia.

There were, however, differences. Cyprus *was* a separate realm, as a representative of its nobility, himself a titular Count of Jaffa, stressed in 1271 when he argued that the Cypriot knights were not bound by their feudal contracts to serve outside it, in this case in Palestine. It had, moreover, a different constitutional status, for it was a fief of the western empire, whereas Jerusalem was an independent state. In certain important respects the system of agriculture on which Cypriot feudalism rested was different from that on the mainland. Before the Latin conquest Cyprus had been exposed to the processes of 'manorialization' which had begun to affect Byzantine rural life and many Cypriot villages were markedly more 'manorial' than their Palestinian counterparts, with demesne lands in the possession of landlords and heavy labour services demanded of many of the peasants. And the Catholic church, at least after 1222, adopted a more interventionist attitude towards the indigenous Greek population and clergy, although the situation was closer to that in Palestine and Syria than to that in Greece. The number of Orthodox dioceses was drastically reduced from fourteen to four and the Orthodox bishops became coadjutors to the four Catholic bishops, with responsibilities for the churches of the Greek rite. There was resistance from the Greeks, occasional brutal countermeasures from the Latins and periods of hostility between the Churches, but these were relatively rare. On the other hand, the Greeks were poor and deprived of patronage, which helps to explain the cultural influence of the Latins upon them, manifested most strikingly in the building of a new Orthodox cathedral in Famagusta in the Gothic style in the fourteenth century.

Greece

North-west of Cyprus, across the Cretan and Aegean seas, was the Latin empire of Constantinople, bounded by the Greek splinter states of Nicaea and Epirus and the Vlacho-Bulgarian empire. The treaty between the Venetians and the other crusaders drawn up before the capture of Constantinople had been modified by two further treaties of October 1204 and October 1205, by the way the Greek territories had been conquered and by private arrangements made between individual leaders. The Latin emperor had a triangular block of land in eastern Thrace, together with the north-western edge of Asia Minor and some islands in the Aegean. Venice had part of the European coast of the Sea of Marmara and a corridor of land inland to Edirne, the Ionian islands, where the county of Cephalonia (Kefallinia) was eventually forced to recognize Venetian suzerainty, Methóni and Koróni in the southern Peloponnese, the island of Euboea off the eastern coast of Greece, the island of Crete and the Cyclades and northern Dodecanese and other islands, assembled by Marco Sanudo into a duchy of the Archipelago centred on Naxos, which was recognized as a fief by the Latin empire. Western Thrace, part of Macedona and Thessaly made up the kingdom of Thessalonica (Thessaloniki) ruled by Boniface of Montferrat, whose suzerainty extended over Thebes and Athens. South of them lay the Peloponnese, which the Latins began to conquer over the winter of 1204–5 and where William of Champlitte, a grandson of Count Hugh I of Champagne, had been recognized as Prince of Achaea, subject to the Latin empire.

The settlement of a western super-stratum, drawn not only from Europe but also from Palestine, from whence many sought the relative security of Greece, proceeded along the already well-tried lines of the granting of fiefs. The feudal system that resulted is best illustrated by evidence from the Peloponnese, where the settlement lasted longest and gave rise to a legal collection, the *Assises of Romania*, the final redaction of which was written in French between 1333 and 1346 and was later translated into Venetian Italian, in which language it survives. Below the Prince of

Achaea were his direct vassals, divided into liege vassals, who were entitled to have vassals of their own, and simple vassals, men not of the knightly class, such as sergeants, who were not. Among the liege vassals were the barons of the principality who enjoyed a special status and were referred to as 'peers of the prince'. They had the right to exercise both high and low justice in their courts, whereas other liege vassals had only low justice and simple vassals had jurisdiction only over their peasants. This colonial society was, like that of Latin Jerusalem, highly class-conscious, but the lords in Greece, unlike those in Jerusalem, did not on the whole live down in the cities but above them in the acropolises or in isolated castles or fortified manor-houses: the remains of 150 strongholds have been identified in the Peloponnese alone, mostly thrown up in the early thirteenth century. This, of course, underlined the distinction between them and the Greeks – intermarriage was rare – and it was reinforced by their chivalric culture, the most glittering of the time, expressed in the tournaments they loved and in the histories and French romances they enjoyed: the French spoken at the court of Achaea at Andravidha was reputed to be as pure as that spoken in Paris.

Most of the Greeks sank into subservience, and this was exacerbated by the conquerors' policy towards the Orthodox church. In 1204 the Venetians, in accordance with the treaty between them and the rest of the crusaders, had nominated the cathedral chapter of St Sophia, which then elected Thomas Morosini, of a noble Venetian family and at that time only a sub-deacon, to the patriarchate of Constantinople. Pope Innocent III had to confirm this uncanonical appointment and Thomas's promotion through the clerical orders to priest and bishop, but he also began the long process of wresting the chapter of St Sophia from Venetian control. The Greeks naturally found it hard to recognize the new patriarch, especially after 1208 when the Byzantine emperor in exile in Nicaea assembled a synod to elect a new Orthodox patriarch. Most Orthodox bishops deserted their sees or refused to recognize Thomas or, in the few cases in which recognition was given, objected to a reconsecration of themselves according to Catholic rites which implied that their previous consecration had been uncanonical. The Latins embarked on a policy of substituting Catholic bishops for Orthodox ones, although they could not afford to reproduce the complex Byzantine hierarchy of metropolitan sees with suffragan bishops and autocephalous archbishoprics without suffragans. They also introduced western monastic and religious orders. But everywhere Orthodox monasteries and local married clergy survived *in situ*, although the Greeks were forced to pay thirtieths to the Catholic clergy in place of full tithes.

Most of them, moreover, were regarded by their western overlords as technically unfree. The chief exception was a class of *archontes*, great landlords or imperial officials before the conquest, whom the Latins tried to conciliate by promising the maintenance of the Orthodox clergy and the Byzantine legal and fiscal systems, although, in fact, the use of Byzantine law ceased in the public sphere and the transference of rights of jurisdiction and taxation to private feudal landlords meant the disappearance of the old public system of taxation. The *archontes*, however, ranked as simple vassals, along with the western sergeants, and by the middle of the thirteenth century some of them were receiving proper fiefs and were beginning to be dubbed knights, thus qualifying for liege vassalage. This paved the way for the occasional Greek who had not been an *archon* to be raised to the highest feudal class. By the fourteenth century Greek liege vassals were to be found and there were latinized Greeks like the translator of the Chronicle of Morea who, writing just before 1388, criticized the Greeks of Constantinople and Epirus and accused the Orthodox of being schismatics.

By the treaties of 1204 the Venetians had acquired three-eighths of the empire. They elected their own *podestà*, who was assisted by an administration modelled on that of Venice, although the mother city soon took steps to see that his powers were limited. The treaty with the empire of 1205 laid down a procedure for collectively deciding the scale of potential military threats that demanded service from all, whether Venetians or not. A council, made up of the *podestà*'s council together with the barons of the empire, would do this and it could also require the emperor to follow its advice; it was to supervise any judges appointed to arbitrate between him and those from whom he desired service. Every time a new Latin emperor was crowned he had to swear to uphold the conditions of the treaties of March and October 1204 and October 1205, which to the Venetians formed the empire's constitution and which gave them a powerful political position, although they would have had great influence anyway, given the size of their holdings. On the other hand the treaties imposed severe limitations on the emperors from which they were never able to escape.

This was particularly unfortunate because in the first half of the thirteenth century they were the most insecure and exposed of all the Latin rulers in the East. They had to face threats from the Vlacho-Bulgarians and the Byzantine Greeks who had established the three *emigré* states of Epirus, Trebizond (Trabzon) and Nicaea, the last under Theodore Lascaris, the son-in-law of the Emperor Alexius III. Over and over again the Latins had to fight on at least two fronts. In spite of early successes in Asia Minor, in which the last Byzantine emperor Alexius V had been taken – he had already been blinded by his rivals and was now forced to jump to his death from the top of the column in the forum of Theodosius in Constantinople – the ruler of Bulgaria, Ioannitsa, invaded Thrace early in 1205 and ravaged it for nearly a year. He captured the Emperor Baldwin, whom he may well have murdered. At any rate Baldwin died in captivity and his brother and regent Henry was crowned emperor on 20 August 1206. A man of remarkable powers of tenacity and leadership, Henry faced an appalling situation, not only in Thrace but also in Asia Minor where by the beginning of 1207 the Latins had only a toe-hold. But Ioannitsa died that summer and on 1 August 1208 Henry defeated the Bulgarians who were anyway divided over the succession. In 1211 he drove them back and then defeated Theodore Lascaris; and the treaty of Nymphaeum that followed gave the Latins the entire Asiatic shore of the Sea of Marmara and a stretch along the Aegean.

He died, aged only forty, on 11 June 1216 and his successor Peter of Courtenay, the husband of his sister Yolande, was captured by Theodore of Epirus before he ever reached Constantinople. Peter's son, Robert of Courtenay, came to the throne on 25 March 1221 and soon had to face war on two fronts. Theodore of Epirus was pushing into Thessaly: in 1222 he took Sérrai, in 1224 Thessaloniki and in 1225 Edirne – it is indicative of the situation that he took the last city not from the Latins but from Nicaean Greeks who had crossed the Dardanelles – and he threatened Constantinople itself. In the meantime warfare had again broken out with Nicaea, where John Ducas Vatatzes had succeeded to the Byzantine throne. By 1226 the Latin settlers had lost all of Asia Minor except Izmit, which they held only until 1235. Probably the only factor that saved Latin Constantinople at this time was the insistence of John Asen of Bulgaria, Ioannitsa's nephew and successor, who wanted the empire for himself, that Theodore of Epirus allow Robert to hold his lands undisturbed.

After a cruel revolt by his own knights at what they regarded as his shameful marriage to a French woman of humble birth – they mutilated her and drowned her mother – Robert fled to Rome. He died in 1228 on his way back to Constantinople. His heir was his brother Baldwin II, who was only eleven years old. Spurning John Asen's attempt to secure Constantinople by a marriage alliance between his daughter and the young emperor, the barons of the empire called in that experienced trouble-shooter, John of Brienne. John had been born c. 1170, the third son of the Count of Brienne, and he had spent most of his life in relative obscurity as a vassal of Champagne before being selected in 1210 to be the husband for Maria, the young heiress of Jerusalem. He had proved himself to be an effective king, although we have already seen him being outmanoeuvred by the papal legate in Egypt during the Fifth Crusade. His wife had died in 1212 and he had ruled as regent for his daughter Yolande until she was married to the Emperor Frederick II in 1225. Frederick had refused to permit him to keep the regency and, it was rumoured, had seduced one of his nieces who was in his daughter's entourage. John's fury was such that he had become a commander of the papal forces that invaded Frederick's southern Italian territories while the emperor was in Palestine, but now the barons of the empire offered the hand of their emperor to another of his daughters, by his most recent wife Berengaria of Castile, if he would consent to be crowned co-emperor, to rule for life. John had arrived in Constantinople by the summer of 1231 with 500 knights and 5,000 men-at-arms to whom the pope had granted crusade indulgences. The military and political situation, which was already bad, was worsening. In 1230 Theodore of Epirus had been defeated and captured by John Asen, who had swept through Thrace, Thessaly and a large part of Albania. John Asen, who wanted an autonomous Bulgarian patriarchate, opened negotiations with the Nicaeans, with whom resided the exiled Orthodox patriarch of Constantinople, and in 1235 concluded a pact with John Vatatzes according to which his daughter was betrothed to John Vatatzes's son and Bulgaria gained its own patriarchate. John Vatatzes crossed the Dardanelles, sacked Gallipoli and joined forces with the Bulgarians before being utterly defeated outside the walls of Constantinople by John of Brienne, who had with him only 160 knights.

But Latin Constantinople was now doomed. John of Brienne died on 23 March 1237 and the settlers were saved for a time only by the launching of the crusade from the West in 1239 which has already been described and because the Nicaean Byzantines, now established in Europe, were engaged in consolidating their bridgehead in the Balkans and were anxious about the Mongols, who were now threatening them from the East. Baldwin II, by now heavily dependent on French subsidies, made several fund-raising tours of western Europe. The last great relics in Constantinople had to be disposed of for cash: the Crown of Thorns was mortgaged to the Venetians, from whom it was redeemed by St Louis; it found its resting-place in the Sainte Chapelle in Paris, which was specially built for it, as we have seen. Baldwin engaged in complex monetary transactions, even resorting to the mortgaging of the person of his only son, Philip, who spent his childhood and youth in Venice in the custody of his father's creditors. He was redeemed, thanks to King Alfonso X of Castile, in the first half of 1261, but by then Latin Constantinople had only a few months left. On 25 July, while most of the garrison was away on a Venetian expedition to attack the island of Kefken in the Black Sea, a Byzantine force from Nicaea infiltrated into the city and occupied it with very little resistance. Baldwin fled and the Venetian fleet was able to save only the wives and children of Venetian residents. On 15 August the Nicaean emperor Michael VIII made his ceremonial entry into the city and was crowned Basileus in St Sophia.

French and Venetian settlers still held southern Greece and the islands in the Aegean. In the middle of the thirteenth century Achaea in the Peloponnese was the most brilliant of all the Latin states in the East, with the princely court at Andravidha famous as a school of chivalry. The knights gathered round the princes, William of Champlitte, Geoffrey I, Geoffrey II and William of Villehardouin, and the lords of Athens, Othon and Guy of la Roche, engaged in a constant round of chivalric enterprise, including petty war with the Byzantines to the north. The heyday of Latin rule and prosperity was the early 1250s, but a dispute with Venice and Guy of la Roche gradually engulfed the peninsula and no sooner had that ended when William of Villehardouin was defeated by the Nicaean emperor Michael VIII at the battle of Pelagonia in the summer of 1259. William was imprisoned by the Greeks and in 1261 was forced to surrender to them the strongholds of Monemvasia, Mistra (Mistrás) and Mani in a treaty which was ratified by a parliament composed mainly of the wives of the imprisoned lords. William was dispensed by the pope of the promises he had made under duress, but the two-year war that followed decimated and exhausted the settlers and devastated the principality. Conscious of his insecurity William ceded Achaea to Charles of Anjou, the new king of Sicily, on 24 May 1267, in return for the right to hold it for life. By the terms of the agreement his daughter Isabel was to wed one of Charles's sons, who would succeed him, but if that son died childless Achaea would revert to Charles or his heir. Three days later, as we have seen, the Latin Emperor Baldwin confirmed the cession and added to it suzerainty for Charles over the Archipelago, Corfu and the Latin possessions in Epirus, in return for the promise of 2,000 mounted men to help him recover his empire.

So Latin Greece became subject to the kingdom of Sicily. Charles certainly seems to have wanted to go further and to conquer Constantinople, but at first he committed resources to the principality's defence as well as trying to maintain a presence in Albania, where he was recognized as king in 1271. In February 1277 William of Villehardouin's son-in-law and heir presumptive, Philip of Anjou, died and William himself followed him to the grave on 1 May 1278. The principality now passed directly under Charles's rule, but took second place in his strategic thinking to Albania and especially to his designs on Constantinople. After the Sicilian Vespers in 1282 Latin Greece was left to fend for itself. One of the first acts of Charles II was to restore the government of the principality to Isabel of Villehardouin, on the occasion of her marriage to Florent of Hainault, a great-grandson of the Emperor Baldwin I, in 1289; he later gave his favourite son, Philip of Taranto, immediate over-lordship of Florent and Isabel and all Latin Greece. Florent died in January 1297, leaving a three-year-old daughter, Mahaut, and in 1301 Isabel married her third husband, Philip of Savoy, Count of Piedmont. He was deposed five years later by Charles for refusing to pay homage to Philip of Taranto and for pursuing policies against Angevin interests. In spite of Isabel's protests, Philip of Taranto took over the direct government of Latin Greece.

For twenty years the Angevins had been struggling to recover the island of

Sicily from the Aragonese. Now, by an extraordinary turn of events this conflict was extended into southern Greece. In 1309 Thessaly had been invaded by a band of mercenary adventurers, the Catalan Company, composed of Catalans and other northern Spaniards who were the survivors of various mercenary bands that had been employed in the south Italian wars by the Aragonese princes. The Company had hired itself to the Byzantine emperor Andronicus II to fight the Ottoman Turks, who were making almost their first appearance on the historical scene, but it had quarrelled with him and had pillaged its way through Thrace and Macedonia, for a time serving the French prince, Charles of Valois, the brother of King Philip IV, who was married to a grand-daughter of the Latin Emperor Baldwin II and wanted to stake a claim to the empire. Edged by the Greek ruler of Thessaly towards Athens, the Catalans took service with the duke, Walter of Brienne, in 1310, but when he refused them land and would not pay the wages due to them they turned against him. Walter assembled an army from all over Latin Greece and brought them to battle on 15 March 1311 at Halmyros in Thessaly. The result was a sensation. In an engagement typical of a period in which the old chivalry was being overtaken in expertise by new professional soldiers Walter led a charge directly into a swamp which he mistakenly believed was a green meadow. He and almost all his knights were slaughtered. The Catalans themselves took over Thebes and Athens which were lost to the French. The knighthood of the Peloponnese was depleted by about a third of its members. An era had ended.

The Italians

In the twelfth century the Latin East had been isolated. In the thirteenth it had expanded to comprise several states scattered over a large part of the eastern Mediterranean seaboard. It was no longer only a question of safeguarding a lifeline to the West, which had been important enough; now the maintenance of continual trans-marine contacts over a large area was essential. The Latin settlers had always been dependent on the sea-power provided by western merchants, particularly from the Italian ports of Venice, Genoa and Pisa. In the thirteenth century these Italians still provided the sea-power, but with their territorial gains in Greece and the Greek islands they were themselves politically integrated into the framework they helped to bind together. Thenceforward the histories of east Mediterranean trade and east Mediterranean settlement and crusading become virtually indistinguishable.

Italians had been engaged as traders in the region before the crusades. Pisa and Genoa had had few contacts with the great centres of commerce there, for on the whole their activities had been confined to the western Mediterannean, but Amalfi and particularly Venice were already active.

The Venetians had gained privileges from the Byzantines, partly because to the Byzantine government they were still subjects of the empire, and the charter issued by the Emperor Alexius I to them in 1082, with its granting of freedom from customs and market taxes in a number of specified ports, was a prototype for the rights later given to Italian merchants by the rulers of the Latin settlements. The Italians shared in the conquest of Palestine and Syria. The Genoese took part in the First Crusade, the Pisans arrived in 1099 and the Venetians in 1100. At a rather later date they were joined by merchants from Languedoc, Provence and Catalonia.

In the twelfth century the stronger trading cities, Venice, Genoa and Pisa, had gained rights that may be summarized as follows. First, they were given property, usually quarters in cities, which included administrative buildings, churches, public baths and ovens, although the Venetians were also given a third of the city-territory of Tyre in 1124, in which they settled some of their compatriots as fief-holders, and the Genoese family of Embriaco got personal possession of the town and fief of Jubail in the county of Tripoli. Secondly, they acquired jurisdictional rights, the ability to judge their own nationals and in some cases those living in their own quarters. Thirdly, they were granted commercial privileges: rights of entering, remaining in or leaving certain ports, the reduction or abolition of entry, exit and sales dues and sometimes the possession of their own markets. These privileges enabled them to establish their own *comptoirs* or factories (in the old-fashioned sense of this word): quarters in which their merchants could stay when they arrived with the fleets from the West. These were deserted out of season, with only a small resident community – c. 300 persons in the Genoese quarter in thirteenth-century Acre – left to service them.

Although the Italian merchants were highly privileged, this meant less than it might have done until the 1180s, because the bulk of the spice trade from the Far East, by far the most profitable and attractive commerce, did not pass through the Palestinian and Syrian ports but through Alexandria in Egypt, the most important port in the eastern Mediterranean. There was, however, enough of it, together with commerce in local products like sugar and cotton and the importation for oriental markets of western manufactures such as cloth, to encourage them to build up their *comptoirs* and to create administrative structures, establishing in each of them consuls or viscounts or both. These administrators had to cope with the fact that the kings of Jerusalem soon began to adopt a tougher stance towards them with the aim of at the very least keeping them to the letter of the charters of privilege issued to them. The kings insisted that the Italian courts could only deal with their nationals who were visitors; if any Italian settled permanently he was to become answerable to royal justice. And they maintained that they had only jurisdiction in low justice: high justice, the justice of blood, was reserved to the crown. They tried to prevent their vassals alienating fiefs to the Italians and some of them even tried to cut back their privileges. The pressure became at times so intense that Genoa and Venice ceded some of their *comptoirs* and properties to their own vassals, who would fight their battles for them; the Embriaco fief of Jubail developed in this way.

In the last quarter of the twelfth century, however, the situation altered. The Asiatic trade routes changed course for reasons that are still not clear. After 1180 spices from India and the Far East were increasingly by-passing Egypt and being brought to Syria, where Damascus, Aleppo and Antioch were major centres. Damascus was becoming especially important and its chief ports, Acre and Tyre, were in Christian hands. Acre came to rival and even overtake Alexandria as the chief market in the eastern Mediterranean seaboard and there the western merchants were already ensconced and privileged. The resulting growth in the volume of trade benefited the crown. It will be remembered that customs and sales duties were totted up and taken in a single lump sum in the markets, usually expressed as a percentage of the commodity's value. This was, of course, payable by both buyer and seller, so that even if one party to a transaction was exempt from taxation the other, usually a Muslim merchant from the interior, was not. A government, therefore, could never lose more than half the customs and sale tax even if it granted total exemption to one party. The hope was that an increase in traffic, which would never have taken place had not merchants been on hand to carry the goods away, would more than compensate for any losses incurred by granting privileges in the first place. Oriental merchants, in fact, never seem to have been privileged, and they were charged additional exit taxes as they left by the city gates for home. And the rights gained by the Venetians and Pisans in Acre to have their own markets, which could have led to the government losing the right to levy taxes even from those with whom they had dealings, meant in practice only that they could sell in them the goods they had brought from Europe; to fill the holds of their ships for the voyage home they had to buy in the royal markets, where the vendors had to settle their share of the duty. The government, moreover, seems to have strictly enforced the payment of dues by those residents who bought in the Italian markets, and they took measures to prevent the Italians circumventing the restraints upon them by themselves travelling to and trading in the Muslim interior. A consequence was that the kingdom of Jerusalem in the first half of the thirteenth century was quite rich; one sign of the size of its revenues from trade is that it was able to make up much of the feudal service lost with the territorial fiefs in 1187 through the granting of additional money fiefs.

But if the crown was relatively richer, so were the Italians, and their response to increased business and the large number of their merchants now in the East can be seen in the way they centralized the control of their eastern *comptoirs*. In the 1190s Venice appointed a *bajulus Venetorum in tota Syria* to be stationed in Acre. At about the same time Genoa and Pisa each appointed two consuls for all Syria, also to be resident in Acre, and in 1248 Pisa put authority into the hands of a single *consul communis Pisanorum Accon et totius Syriae*. Between 1187 and 1192, moreover, Guy of Lusignan and Conrad of Montferrat were prepared to grant more privileges in return for support in their struggle for the crown. The Pisans gained rights of jurisdiction, including high justice, over all those living in their quarters and the Genoese were given the privilege that cases involving high justice would be decided by their own and royal judges sitting together. Henry of Champagne tried, not very successfully, to cut back these immunities again, and he began to exert a pressure on the Italians that was to be applied sporadically in the thirteenth century, although the long period in which the kings were absent and the fact that in times of financial crisis the Italians had great influence as shippers, money-changers and lenders – John of Brienne was at the mercy of the Genoese Lucchino Corsali – meant that it was not consistent.

The Aiyubids

The prosperity of the Latin East in the first half of the thirteenth century and the range and depth of the Latin settlements around the shores of the eastern Mediterranean gave the settlers in Palestine and Syria in many ways greater security than they had ever had. They faced, moreover, much less aggressive Muslim neighbours. Saladin had died on 4 March 1193 and the provinces of his empire – Egypt, Aleppo, Damascus, the Jazira, Transjordan, Hama, Homs and Ba'albek – held together only by his personality, became independent principalities under his relatives and descendants, one of whom assumed a precarious paramountcy over each generation: al-'Adil (1200–1218), al-Kamil (1218–38), as-Salih Aiyub (1240–9). The Aiyubids, of course, had other frontiers to concern them, besides that with the western settlers. This was also a period of great prosperity for them and for their subjects, partly because of the receptivity of western Europe to Asiatic goods; and that depended on the transit of those goods through the Christian ports. Although ideas of the *Jihad* survived and even flourished, the emphasis was on co-existence and the period was marked by a succession of truces. Jerusalem and Antioch-Tripoli, now almost integrated into Near Eastern politics, engaged in alliances and counter-alliances like any of the petty states in the region. But one of these alliances and the consequences of it provided evidence that appearances were deceptive. In 1244 a party in the kingdom overturned the truce with as-Salih Aiyub of Egypt, which has already been described, and entered into an offensive alliance against him with as-Salih Isma'il of Damascus and an-Nasir Da'ud of Transjordan, which allowed the Christians to extend their control over the Temple area in Jerusalem. Egypt turned to the Khorezmians, the survivors of a state north of Iran which had been broken by the Mongols in 1220. They had been serving as mercenaries in northern Iraq and they now swept down from the north and burst into Jerusalem on 11 July; on 23 August the Tower of David surrendered to them. On 17 October at the Battle of Harbiyah (La Forbie), north-east of Gaza, the Franco-Damascene alliance was shattered by them and the Egyptians. The bulk of the Christian army, possibly comprising 1,200 knights and the largest since Hattin fifty-seven years before, died on the field.

Before 1244, however, the relatively undisturbed conditions had allowed the leading settlers to indulge in the involved political disputes which seem to have interested them so much. In every case the issues were important ones, stemming from problems of inheritance and the unique situation in which they found themselves.

Antioch-Tripoli

The principality of Antioch and the county of Tripoli came to be united under a single ruler, although, of course, each continued to have its own administration and customary law, after a war of succession in the early years of the thirteenth century. Raymond III of Tripoli had died in 1187 leaving no direct heirs. Passing over the claims of his relatives in the West, he had designated his godson Raymond, the eldest son of Prince Bohemond III of Antioch, to succeed him, although the prince managed to substitute for him his younger son, the future Bohemond IV. Raymond of Antioch predeceased his father, leaving as his heir his young half-Armenian son, Raymond Roupen, who had the support of his great-uncle, King Leo of Cilician Armenia. Prince Bohemond III, however, sent him back to Cilicia with his mother, although Archbishop Conrad of Mainz, who had brought Leo the crown from the western emperor, put pressure on Bohemond to make his vassals swear to uphold Raymond Roupen's succession. This was not popular and the young Bohemond, now Count of Tripoli and determined to take over the principality himself, entered Antioch and deposed his father, with the support of the Templars who were in dispute with Leo over his retention of their march around Bağras on the borders of Antioch and Cilicia, and a commune which had already been proclaimed in the city to resist the growing threat of Armenian supremacy. The revolt was short-lived, but after Bohemond III's death in 1201 Bohemond IV regained Antioch with the commune's support and held it until 1216, in the face of a series of invasions from Cilicia, a party of opposition within the principality and the peace-making efforts of the leaders of the kingdom of Jerusalem and the pope, who excommunicated both him and Leo. The struggle gave rise to extraordinary incidents which indicate how integrated Antioch was into the Near Eastern scene. In 1201 Bohemond called in az-Zahir of Aleppo and Sulaiman of Rum to help him against Cilician Armenia and in November 1203 a force, comprising troops from Antioch and Aleppo supplemented by Templars, plundered Armenian villages near Bağras. In 1209 Kai-Khusrau of Rum invaded Cilicia on Bohemond's behalf. Meanwhile Bohemond, who depended on the support of the commune of Antioch, which had a strong Greek element within it, was on bad terms with the Catholic patriarch, Peter of Angoulême. Early in 1207 he connived at the enthronement of the titular Orthodox patriarch and in 1208 he entered into an alliance with the Nicaean emperor Theodore Lascaris. When Peter of Angoulême led a revolt in the city, Bohemond threw him into prison and deprived him of food and water. Peter died in agony after drinking oil from the lamp in his cell.

By 1216 Bohemond had become estranged from his Muslim ally in Aleppo and was unpopular in Antioch because of his long absences in Tripoli. A party favouring Raymond Roupen was growing among the nobility, which included Acharie of Sarmin, the commune's mayor. On the night of 14 February Leo of Cilician Armenia entered the city and within a few days was in possession of it. Raymond Roupen was consecrated prince and since at that time he was regarded as Leo's heir there was the prospect of the union of Antioch and Cilicia. But he proved to be unpopular and in 1219 the city rose against him. Bohemond took it over without resistance and held it thereafter, although he was reconciled with the Church only on his deathbed in 1233. There was an uneasy peace with Cilicia, broken in 1225 when Bohemond invaded it in alliance with Kai-Qobad of Rum after his son Philip, who had married Leo's heiress Zabel, had been murdered in an Armenian revolt.

After 1233 the new prince, Bohemond V, preferred, as his father had done, to live in Tripoli, and Antioch was isolated under its commune of Latins and Greeks. Large parts of Christian territory, around Bağras, Marqab, Tartus, Safita and Crac des Chevaliers, were in the hands of the Military Orders which maintained their own fairly agressive policies with regard to the petty Muslim states in their vicinity. The domains of Bohemond V give the impression of being a splintered confederacy, only surviving because of differences between the Aiyubid princelings and their desire for peace.

Constitutional conflict in the kingdom of Jerusalem

There were also serious problems of succession to the throne of Jerusalem. The conflict between Sibylla and Isabella and their husbands had, as we have seen, ended in 1192 with Isabella on the throne. She married four times but was survived only by daughters. The eldest of these, Maria, married John of Brienne, but this only produced another daughter, Yolande, the wife of the Emperor Frederick II, and she died giving birth to a son, Conrad, on 1 May 1228. Neither he nor his son Conradin ever set foot in Palestine. From 1186 to 1268, therefore, the kingdom was in the hands of heiresses, for whom husbands had to be found, or absentee rulers, for whom regents or lieutenants had to be found. If this was not bad enough, the laws of inheritance and the customs governing the appointment of regents and lieutenants were complicated by the succession of minors and by the way a litigious and clever baronial opposition invented new laws and manipulated existing ones when it suited them to do so. While she lived Yolande, as queen regnant, could legally be represented by lieutenants. After her death her son was a minor and the laws of regency came into operation. The child's father had the first call on the regency as long as he came to the East to be formally accepted in office, and so Frederick II was regent from September 1228, when he arrived in Acre, with the right to appoint his own lieutenants on his return to Europe. His regency aroused great opposition and the approach of Conrad's majority was made an excuse for the invention of a legal fiction: that a king who had come of age but did not come to the East to be crowned should be treated as though he was entering a new minority. Frederick's regency having lapsed according to this interpretation, the regency was judged to have devolved on Conrad's nearest heir apparent, who was the dowager Queen Alice of Cyprus, Isabella of Jerusalem's third daughter. On her death in 1246 the regency passed to her son King Henry I of Cyprus, but he himself died in 1253, leaving a minor heir, Hugh II, who was granted the regency of Jerusalem on behalf of the new minor king, Conradin. Being a minor himself, Hugh needed a regent for his regency and this office was taken by his mother, Plaisance of Antioch, until she died in 1261. The complications of the regency and succession, with all the opportunities they provided for legal chicanery, were compounded by the fact that the Cypriot regents were themselves often absentees and so appointed their own lieutenants in Acre, while the interstices between these regencies of the kings' relatives were filled by vassal regents. In the 1260s, moreover, the regency and then, after the execution of Conradin, the throne, were disputed by various claimants: Hugh of Brienne, the son of Alice of Cyprus's eldest daughter; Hugh of Antioch-Lusignan, the son of Alice's younger daughter; and Maria of Antioch, Alice's niece through her younger sister Melisende.

The crown of Jerusalem carried with it, of course, immense prestige. Until the middle of the thirteenth century, while the trade routes ran favourably, it was also quite a rich prize, which explains the interest taken in it by foreigners like Frederick II and even Charles of Anjou. Frederick's policies in Palestine, however, and the residual strength of the crown caused the resident nobility to fear for what they perceived to be their liberties.

The issues were given an additional dimension by the emergence among them of a remarkable school of jurists. This had come into existence partly as a result of two features of Jerusalemite and Cypriot law. The first was a usage whereby the king or a lord, as president of a feudal court, could appoint a vassal to help him or another vassal with *conseil* and could demand the acceptance of this duty as a feudal service. A counsellor of this sort, called a pleader, was not an advocate so much as an adviser; and so complicated were the procedures in the feudal courts that it was essential for anyone engaged in litigation to make use of an adviser of this sort:

> The master of pleaders . . . has very great authority (wrote one of them), for by employing a clever pleader one can sometimes save and preserve in court one's honour and body, or one's inheritance or that of a friend; and through the lack of a clever pleader, when he is needed, one can lose one's honour, body or inheritance (Philip of Novara, 'Livre de forme de plait', *RHC Lois*, vol. 1, p. 569).

It followed that those who were skilled in law were greatly in demand, as much by lords as by vassals. It seems to have been common for a man with a reputation of this kind to be granted fiefs in several lordships, which gave him the opportunity of rendering *conseil* in as many feudal courts as were involved. And since the second feature of the law was the *assise sur la ligece* which, it will be remembered, had given the king the right to demand liege-homage from all rear-vassals, a liege vassal could obviously also plead in the king's own court. Although there is evidence that in the thirteenth century many vassals did not make liege-homage to the crown as they should, the openings for a semi-professional class of legal counsellors are clear. For instance James Vidal, a French knight who was a fief-holder in Palestine by April 1249 and regularly attended the High Court until 1271, also had at one time or another fiefs in the lordships of Caesarea, Arsuf, Iskanderuna and perhaps Nazareth.

The pleaders had prestige before 1187, but the disasters of that year increased it immeasurably. In the thirteenth century it was maintained that the laws of Jerusalem, or at least some of the more important ones, each written on a separate piece of vellum and sealed by the king, the patriarch and the viscount of Jerusalem, had been kept in a chest in the church of the Holy Sepulchre. When Jerusalem had fallen to Saladin the chest and its contents had been lost. At one stroke the character of the law had been changed, since it was no longer based on a corpus of written material – or at least had an important written element – but had become customary.

The kingdom's lawyers, therefore, had now to depend for their knowledge on custom and hearsay:

> The usages and laws of the kingdom . . . are not written down, nor are they made into canons, nor are they authorized by agreement, nor have they been since the land was lost (Philip of Novara, p. 536).

So it was to the pleaders, above all to those who moved in circles in which the old laws were remembered and discussed, that vassals sitting in judgement would turn. One of the oddest developments in these exposed frontier marches in the thirteenth century was this appearance of a group of pedantic and highly prestigious lawyers; indeed it is probable that knowledge of the law and the ability to plead were more highly regarded, and a more certain way to prominence, than military skill.

The men with legal reputations came from many different groups. Two were rulers, Aimery of Cyprus and Jerusalem and Bohemond IV of Antioch-Tripoli. Others were, at least at times, supporters of Frederick II. Others raised themselves from the burgess class to knighthood through their legal abilities. But the most important circle comprised members of the higher nobility or men closely associated with them and in the early thirteenth century three men were dominant in it, 'the three wisest men that I have ever seen this side of the sea' (Philip of Novara, p. 559). Ralph, lord of Tiberias, was unquestionably the greatest of them, his prestige enhanced by his personal experience of procedures before 1187. John of Ibelin, 'the Old Lord' of Beirut, was the head of the family that now dominated Palestine and Cyprus and, as the son of Balian of Ibelin's marriage to King Amalric's widow Maria Comnena, was Queen Isabella's half-brother. Balian, lord of Sidon, was the head of the oldest-established noble family, the Greniers, and he was also John of Beirut's nephew through his mother Helvis of Ibelin. These three great magnates, at the centre of a circle of lesser lords, knights and burgesses, gave way to another generation of jurists, most of whom were Ibelins or their relatives: John of Arsuf, John of Beirut's son, John of Jaffa, his nephew and the author of the best of the law-books, and Philip of Novara, a vassal of John of Beirut and of his son Balian. In its turn that generation was replaced by another, led by John of Arsuf's son Balian and John of Jaffa's son James.

We have evidence for the direct transmission of ideas. John of Beirut admitted his debt to Ralph of Tiberias, Philip of Novara his to Ralph of Tiberias, John of Beirut and Balian of Sidon, John of Jaffa his to John of Beirut and Balian of Sidon. So here was a school of law largely, it is true, confined to relatives and dependants. At the centre of the web of relationships were the Ibelins, who by the middle of the century held, or were closely related to the possessors of, the lordships of Beirut, Arsuf, Sidon,

Caesarea, Tyre and Jaffa. They and the royal house of Jerusalem, moreover, were descended from a common ancestress, Maria Comnena, while the royal house of Cyprus was descended from John of Beirut's cousin Eschiva of Ibelin, Aimery of Lusignan's first wife; the relationship was cemented by the marriages of Kings Hugh II and III to Ibelins and by that of Hugh III's sister Margaret to John of Montfort-Tyre, who had an Ibelin grandmother. It is noteworthy that the leaders of the first generation of jurists had been associated with the baronial opposition to Guy of Lusignan in the 1180s and 1190s. Ralph of Tiberias was the stepson of Raymond III of Tripoli. John of Beirut was the son of Balian of Nablus. Balian of Sidon was the son of Reynald of Sidon. Since legal ability and political influence went together it is not surprising to find so many members of this school expressing political ideas in opposition to the crown.

Their written output, including four law-books and several histories, was remarkable for the time. In it were to be found the outlines of a political theory which was closely related to others thrown up elsewhere by baronial movements and, typically, rested on a mythical reading of the past, on a legendary golden age, in this case immediately following the First Crusade. The starting-point appears to have been a historical interpretation of the conquest of Palestine in 1099. To the jurists Palestine had been conquered by the First Crusade and was therefore held by the most absolute of rights, that of conquest. But it did not belong to the pope, nor even to the kings: the crusade was regarded as a mass migration over which there had been no acknowledged leader.

> When this land was conquered it was by no chief lord, but by a crusade and by the movement of pilgrims and assembled people.

So it belonged by right to God and to the people who, they maintained, had elected their ruler.

> They made a lord by agreement and by election and they gave him the lordship of the kingdom ('L'Estoire de Eracles empereur et la conqueste de la Terre d'Outremer', *RHC Oc.*, vol. 2, p. 389).

This did not necessarily mean that the rulers were limited by this contract for government thereafter; the jurists themselves stressed that Godfrey of Bouillon's successors held their kingdom from God and by hereditary right. But there were constitutional consequences. The jurists believed that after his election Godfrey had appointed a commission to look into the customs of other lands and on the basis of its reports, together with the results of regular enquiries made later, had compiled a body of legislation, by which he and his vassals and his people . . . should be governed, kept, held, maintained, tried and judged (John of Jaffa, 'Livre des Assises de la Haute Cour', *RHC Lois*, vol. 1, p. 22).

This corpus had been established by the decisions of his court. In a remarkable passage John of Jaffa suggested a comprehensive body of law drawn up in writing with the agreement of ruler and ruled, in other words a kind of written constitution. The jurists maintained, moreover, that the rulers of Jerusalem had always, or should have always, sworn not only to uphold their ancestors' laws, but also, in accordance with these, only to make judgements through their courts. And it was this last belief that provided them with their point of reference for limitations on the crown.

It is clear that they were prepared to treat kingship only in its feudal and hardly at all in its public aspect. To them the king was, above all, their *chef seigneur*, their feudal overlord, contractually bound to them in the same way as they were bound to him. It followed that disputes between him and them, which obviously would involve their contractual relationship, could only be properly decided in his court, the arena in which such matters should be discussed. And since equity in feudal custom demanded that a party could not be judge in his own suit, judgement in such cases belonged to the court, where the king's vassals, their peers, sat and gave him counsel, rather than to the king himself. This above all applied to the penal element in judgement that might involve bodily punishment or the confiscation of a fief.

The lord cannot put a hand, or have a hand put, on the body or fief of his vassal unless it is by the judgement (the *esgart* or *conoissance*) of his court (John of Jaffa, p. 315).

Such a doctrine was, of course, to be found wherever there was feudal resistance to kings, but its strict implementation would have made government impossible. No western king ever kept strictly to the letter of feudal custom and the kings of Jerusalem were no different from others in this respect. Their opponents were cleverer than most, but when it came to putting their ideology into practice they were not very effective, largely because they were blinded by their own ideas.

What they chose to do was to exploit the *assise sur la ligece*, which was originally a law issued by the king for his own benefit. To them the *assise*, which had come into existence because of an act of wrongful dispossession by a lord of Sidon, underlined the condition of the feudal contract that there were no occasions on which any lord, even the king, could take action against a vassal without the formal decision of his court. If a king failed to abide by his contractual obligations the wronged vassal could demand justice according to the law from him; he could withdraw his own service; or he could ask his peers to aid him. They would first call upon the king to hear the case properly; if he refused they could use force to release their peer from jail or reoccupy his fief, provided this did not entail raising their hands against the king's person; or they could solemnly 'all together and each individually' withdraw their services from him. This sounds very impressive and in a frontier state like Jerusalem where there was a heavy reliance on the military services of the vassals it should have been effective. But it had a fatal flaw. It could only be effective in a dreamland in which all the feudatories acted in unison and the ruler was totally dependent on their services. In a perfect feudal world – the world constructed in the law-books – it might have worked. In the reality of the first half of the thirteenth century the feudal class was never really united, while the wealth accruing from commerce enabled the rulers to survive, at least temporarily, without its services.

This was apparent the first time the feudatories resorted to their interpretation of the *assise sur la ligece*. In 1198 King Aimery, convinced that Ralph of Tiberias had something to do with an attempt on his life, arbitrarily banished him from the country. Ralph responded by asking his peers to demand on his behalf judgement in the High Court. When the king would not be moved they solemnly threatened to withdraw their services to no effect whatever. Ralph remained out of Palestine until Aimery's death.

This fiasco does not seem to have affected the jurists' belief in the efficacy of the *assise*, perhaps because on one later occasion it was successfully used. In July 1228 the Emperor Frederick II reached Cyprus over which, as the young king's overlord, he had been demanding wardship and its profits during the minority. This impinged directly on John of Beirut, who had succeeded his brother Philip as guardian of the king on his mother's behalf. Frederick renewed his demands in person in a dramatic scene, in which he surrounded his guests at a banquet with armed men. In the name of the crown of Jerusalem he also ordered John to surrender the fief of Beirut which he maintained was held illegally. The wrangle was patched up before the Emperor sailed on to Palestine, but in the following May he farmed the regency of Cyprus to five leaders of a party of Cypriot nobles who were hostile to the Ibelins and ordered them to disinherit his opponents without reference to the High Court. This was to lead to civil war.

Frederick reached Acre in September 1228 and assumed the regency. Once he had gained the city of Jerusalem by treaty he returned to Acre, determined to restore to the crown the authority he believed it had lost since the middle of the twelfth century and he took two measures which he could not uphold; he dispossessed the Ibelins and their supporters of their fiefs in the royal domain round Acre; and he tried to enforce the claims of the Teutonic Knights, who were his staunchest backers, to the lordship of Tibnine, ignoring the rights of the hereditary claimant. In a turbulent few weeks the feudatories adopted the procedures they believed were open to them. They reoccupied the Ibelin fiefs by force and they threatened to withdraw their services, compelling the Emperor to back down from his judgement in favour of the Teutonic Knights. In their euphoria at their success they forgot that Frederick, still excommunicated, without troops, worried by the invasion of southern Italy by papal forces and anxious to return home, was in an exceptionally weak position.

After his departure from Palestine civil war broke out in Cyprus, where the Ibelin partisans refused to recognize the rule of the five imperial 'regents' who had seized their fiefs. John of Beirut fitted out an expedition from Palestine which defeated the imperial forces outside Nicosia on 14 July 1229; the last of the castles in imperial hands surrendered in the following summer. The Emperor prepared a strong force under his marshal, Richard Filangieri, whom he had appointed his lieutenant in Palestine, which sailed for the East in the autumn of 1231. It did not attempt a landing on Cyprus, but occupied the town of Beirut on the mainland and laid siege to its citadel. Richard demanded the submission of Tyre, which he got, and appeared before an assembly of knights and burgesses of Acre, which probably recognized him as a duly appointed lieutenant of an absent regent. But it was pointed out to him that at Beirut he was trying to dispossess a vassal of his fief by force, which was against the law. Since he ignored the request to withdraw, John of Beirut led a force from Cyprus to relieve his fortress early in 1232, but by that time a commune, based on a confraternity already in existence, had been established in Acre, the purpose of which seems to have been to act as a focus of resistance to the Emperor and to ensure that Acre, the most important part of the royal domain, did not fall into his hands. In fact the establishment of the commune and its survival for a decade is a commentary on the failure of the elaborate mechanism provided by the baronial interpretation of the *assise sur la ligece*. John himself did appeal to his peers in accordance with the *assise*, but this time the response was in pathetic contrast to the grandiose pretentions of the theory: only forty-three of his peers rode north to his aid. They did not, in fact, engage the imperial forces. John had to return to Acre, where he was appointed the commune's mayor and he collected a large enough body of men to threaten Tyre. This drew Richard away from Beirut, although a small baronial force left north of Acre was surprised and defeated by him on 3 May. Meanwhile John's absence from Cyprus and his failure to dislodge the imperialists in Palestine encouraged Frederick's supporters on the island to seize control again and they were joined by Richard Filangieri. The Ibelins destroyed them at the Battle of Aghirda on 15 June and with the capture of Kyrenia in April 1233 the civil war on Cyprus was over.

For the next nine years the region settled into an uneasy peace. Cyprus was firmly in the hands of the Ibelins. So was Beirut and many of the fiefs in Palestine. Of the royal domain, Acre was under the control of its commune; Tyre and Jerusalem were in the hands of the Emperor. The years 1232 to 1241 witnessed long and fruitless negotiations between the emperor, the pope and representatives of the Jerusalemite nobility. In 1242 support for Frederick, which seems to have been growing and included the Hospitallers, led to a *coup* that very nearly acquired Acre for him, but the fiction was invented by the baronial party that the young King Conrad, who would come of age in the following year, would need a new regent. Alice of Cyprus was appointed and the baronial party at last took Tyre and occupied Jerusalem soon afterwards. The regency of Alice's successor, Henry of Cyprus, was remarkable for grants of the royal domain to the greater magnates in the Ibelin faction – Jaffa to John of Ibelin-Jaffa, Achzib to Balian of Ibelin-Beirut, Tyre to Philip of Montfort – and for the way Pope Innocent IV, who deposed Frederick from all government in 1245, supported the regent, confirmed charters, some of them fraudulent, on his own authority and freed Cyprus from imperial suzerainty.

The Mamluks, and changes in the Asiatic trade routes

In the 1250s the situation of the Latins in the East changed decisively for the worse because of events beyond their control. The Mongols arrived on the scene. They defeated the Selchükids of Rum at Kös Daği in 1243, after which Anatolia became a Mongol protectorate. In 1256 they destroyed the Assassins' headquarters at Alamut in Iran. In 1258 they took and sacked Baghdad and they then occupied upper Iraq. In 1260 they invaded Syria. They pillaged Aleppo, destroyed the petty Aiyubid principalities in the north and terrorized Damascus into submission.

The Mongols were stopped in September of that year at the Battle of 'Ain Jalut in Palestine by the Mamluks of Egypt. Mamluks, specially trained slave-soldiers from the frontiers of Islam, particularly at this time Kipchak Turks from southern Russia, had long been a feature of Islamic armies and they had become powerful in Egypt, where they had formed a picked bodyguard, the *Bahriyah*, of the sultan as-Salih Aiyub. The *Bahriyah* played a distinguished part in the defeat of St Louis's crusade in spite of as-Salih Aiyub's death on 22 November 1249. But the new sultan, Turan-Shah, distrusted them and wanted to replace them in the offices of state with members of his own military household. They assassinated him on 2 May 1250 and proclaimed as 'queen' as-Salih's concubine, Shajar ad-Durr, who had been a Turkish slave like themselves and had held the reins of power between as-Salih's death and Turan-Shah's arrival. A Turkoman Mamluk emir, Aybeg, became commander-in-chief and Shajar ad-Durr's husband, while a little Aiyubid prince called al-Ashraf Musa was made sultan and was temporarily associated with their rule for the sake of form.

An attempt by the other Aiyubid princes to invade Egypt in the name of legitimism was thrown back. Aybeg's rule, punctuated by violence and revolt, ended on 10 April 1257, when he was murdered in his bath by Shajar ad-Durr, who was herself disposed of soon afterwards. Aybeg was succeeded by his son 'Ali, but this, in a way that was to be typical of the Mamluk sultanate, was a shadow hereditary succession lasting only long enough to allow one of the emirs to emerge as the next ruler, after which the heir by birth was allowed to retire into obscurity. In the face of the threat from the Mongols 'Ali was deposed and the senior of his father's Mamluks, Kutuz, was proclaimed sultan on 12 November 1259. It was Kutuz who defeated the Mongols at 'Ain Jalut, but on his way back in triumph to Egypt he was stabbed to death on 24 October 1260 by a group of emirs under his chief general, Baybars, who had also been a leader of Turan-Shah's assassins. Baybars then usurped the Egyptian throne. Within three months he had secured Damascus and he then extended Mamluk rule over Syria and into northern Iraq. He installed a member of the 'Abbasid family as caliph in Cairo in 1261, making Egypt the seat of the caliphate. And he began to whittle away the Latin settlements.

After 'Ain Jalut the Latins found their hinterland in the possession of two powerful forces, the Mongols and the Mamluks, with the borderlands between them in northern Iraq. Baghdad was in ruins. The trade routes of the Arab world were in chaos. At the same time the unification of central Asia under the Mongols provided the opportunity for the development of new routes from the Far East. Two of them were to be important until late in the fourteenth century. One route passed from the port of Hormuz (Hormoz) on the Persian Gulf through Iran to Tabriz, after which it branched, with one road going to Trebizond on the Black Sea, the other bending south to Ayas in Cilicia, which in the late thirteenth century became an important port with direct links with Famagusta in Cyprus. The other passed through central Asia north of the Caspian Sea to a group of ports at the northern end of the Black Sea: Azov (Tana) Feodosiya (Kaffa), Sudak (Soldaia) and Balaklava (Cembalo).

The consequences of this second shift in Asiatic trade routes within a century were even more profound than those of the first had been. The eyes of Italian merchants began to turn from the eastern Mediterranean to the Black Sea. And, as was bound to happen in any period of change, tension rose among them. Constantinople, which controlled the narrow channel from the Black Sea into the Mediterranean, took on a new importance and with its loss to the Byzantine Greeks in July 1261 the Venetians, who had been active in the Black Sea since 1204, suffered a major reverse. Earlier in the year the Byzantine emperor Michael VIII had signed a treaty with Genoa which gave the Genoese much the same privileges as the Venetians had had in the Latin empire. In fact the

Genoese never enjoyed to the full the rights they had been promised – in 1264 they were temporarily banished from Constantinople – but they got a quarter at Pera, across the Golden Horn from the city, and they gained access to the Black Sea. Their war fleets were now regularly sent to the Aegean and in the 1260s naval warfare between the Italian cities spread throughout the eastern Mediterranean. Peace was only made in 1270, mainly because St Louis insisted on having a fleet for the crusade he was planning. But Genoa was embarking on a period of expansion and this meant further warfare: with Pisa, which spilled into the East in the 1280s, and with Venice, which broke out towards the end of the century.

An early manifestation of this bitter rivalry was a civil war that tore through the streets of Acre from 1256 to 1258, known as the War of St Sabas because it was sparked off by conflict between the Venetians and Genoese over some property belonging to the monastery of St Sabas. Venice and Genoa, and also Pisa which began by supporting Genoa but went over to Venice in 1257, sent out fleets and soldiers. Siege engines were set up in the streets and several of the fortifications built by the Genoese at the entrances to their quarter can be seen to this day. The residents of the city found themselves drawn on to one side or the other. The feudatories were divided. Most, under John of Arsuf who became regent in 1256, favoured the Genoese; but an important party under John of Jaffa, who had been regent when the war broke out, favoured the Venetians and engineered another change of regencies, bringing in the child Hugh of Cyprus whose mother Plaisance took over the government and swung it on to Venice's side. Professor Mayer has recently suggested that behind these political manoeuvrings there was a long history of differences, although this has been questioned by Dr Edbury. What is unquestionable is that the tensions between the Italian merchant communities came to divide the leadership of the kingdom of Jerusalem. The war was only settled in June 1258 when a sea battle between enormous Venetian and Genoese fleets ended with the Genoese losing half their galleys and c. 1,700 men dead or taken prisoner. They decided to abandon Acre and concentrate in Tyre. The Venetians took over part of their quarter, building round their new possession a wall, stretches of which still stand.

The changes in the pattern of Levantine trade also meant a sharp decline in the volume of goods passing through the Christian ports on the coast. And that meant poverty. Clear signs of financial strain are evident. In the late 1250s Julian, lord of Sidon, began to give away parts of his lordship to the Teutonic Knights and 1260 he leased the rest of it to the Templars. He was a heavy gambler, but his territory had suffered greatly from the Muslims and the last straw seems to have been a Mongol raid before 'Ain Jalut which penetrated Sidon itself and destroyed the town walls; he could not afford to have them rebuilt. In 1261 Balian of Arsuf leased his lordship to the Hospitallers. The costs of fortification and garrisoning were, as we have already seen, enormous. In fact it is surprising that so many lords held on to their fiefs for so long.

The Mamluk conquests

Once he had established control over the Muslim regions of Syria the new Mamluk sultan Baybars began systematically to reduce the territory in Christian hands. Like Saladin, who was a Kurd, Baybars was a foreigner, a Kipchak Turk, but unlike Saladin he did not come from old Islamic territory and he remained very much a Turkish warrior chieftain. He was a treacherous and ruthless man, but he was a good administrator and a fine general – a much better one than Saladin had been – and his methodical approach to the reconquest of the coast made it possible for his successors to drive the Latins out of their settlements. He began with a devastating raid into Galilee in 1263, in the course of which he destroyed the cathedral of Nazareth. In 1265 he took Caesarea and Arsuf and temporarily occupied Haifa. In 1266 he seized the Templar castle of Safad, in 1268 Jaffa, the Templar castle of Beaufort and Antioch, in 1271 Templar Safita, Hospitaller Crac des Chevaliers and Montfort of the Teutonic Knights. By the date of his death on 30 June 1277 the Latin settlers were confined to a strip of coastline from 'Atlit to Marqab, with an enclave further north at Latakia. The Muslim campaigns were not indiscriminately destructive. Baybars seems to have been concerned on the one hand to make it hard for the westerners to establish bridgeheads on the parts of the coast he had conquered, but on the other to provide Egyptian shipping with the watering-places of which it had been deprived since 1197. Arsuf, Caesarea, Antioch and Montfort were partially or totally destroyed, but Jaffa survived and estates in the lordships of Arsuf and Caesarea were assigned to his emirs and given a centre at the castle of Qaqun, although the countryside between them and the sea was abandoned to nomadic tribesmen. Crac des Chevaliers, Beaufort and Safad were repaired and garrisoned, as were Hunin and Tibnine; in fact a ring of fortresses encircled Acre like a tightened noose. But Baybars never seems to have made a serious attempt to take Acre itself. He made several surprise descents on the city, but these were really only impromptu raids; a feature of his serious military moves was their careful planning and equipping. He seems to have been conscious of the fact that his empire's prosperity still depended to a large extent on Acre as an outlet for goods and he may have been reluctant to endanger the economic well-being of a large part of his dominions by too hasty an assault on it.

The destruction of the settlements in Palestine and Syria

Among the westerners a kind of paralysis, excusable in the circumstances, set in. They were seriously divided over the policy to adopt towards their enemies. Bohemond VI of Antioch-Tripoli, who had succeeded Bohemond V in 1252, joined his father-in-law Hetoum of Cilician Armenia in seeking an alliance with the Mongols and entered Damascus with the Mongol army in March 1260; he was able to increase his holdings in Syria as a result. On the other hand, the government in Acre, considering, probably rightly, that the immediate threat from the Mongols must be countered at whatever the cost, allowed the Mamluk sultan Kutuz to camp outside the city for three days before 'Ain Jalut and provisioned his army. Even within the kingdom individual fiefs would go their own way. In the 1250s John of Jaffa appears to have had his county excluded from a truce with Damascus to allow him to conduct a series of raids on the Muslims from it. In 1261 and 1263 he, John of Beirut and Hospitaller Arsuf made their own truces with Baybars; John of Jaffa was even prepared to allow Jaffa to be used as a supply point for the Egyptian field army. In 1269 Isabella of Beirut made an independent treaty with Baybars and this enabled her to defy a demand from the king for *service de mariage* in 1275. Separate truces with the sultan Kalavun were made by the Templars in 1282, by the government of Acre and the Templars of Sidon in 1283 and by Margaret of Tyre in 1285.

In fact the settlements were hopelessly split into factions. The county of Tripoli was divided into parties, one of which, made up of Italian immigrants and known as the 'Roman faction', had been introduced by Bohemond V's wife Lucienne of Segni, Pope Innocent III's great-niece, and was headed by her brother, Bishop Paul of Tripoli. It had grown in influence during the rule of her son Bohemond VI. When Bohemond VII came from Cilicia to take over the government in 1277 he found his rule opposed by this faction and the Templars; they were soon joined by Guy Embriaco, the lord of Jubail, who had been estranged by Bohemond's refusal to permit the marriage of his brother to a local heiress. For six years the county suffered a civil war, which ended only when Bohemond immured Guy of Jubail, his brothers John and Baldwin and a relative called William in a pit and left them to starve to death.

The accession to the throne of Jerusalem of Hugh of Antioch-Lusignan in 1269 – he was the first resident king of the blood-line since Baldwin V in 1186 – did not go unchallenged. His aunt, Maria of Antioch, a granddaughter of Isabella of Jerusalem, claimed the throne as the nearer heiress to Yolande, the last ruler actually present in the East. Maria's case was better in law than Hugh's, but it seems that the High Court, which decided on these conflicting claims by virtue of its corporate decision on the lord to whom homage should be paid, preferred to overlook them in favour of those of a younger man who was already king of Cyprus. Maria appealed to Rome, where her case was being heard in 1272, and on the advice of the Templars, and probably with the pope's support, she offered to sell the crown to Charles of Anjou. The case was withdrawn from the Roman curia in 1276 and in March 1277 the sale of the crown to Charles was completed.

Hugh, meanwhile, had found government of what remained of the kingdom of Jerusalem almost impossible. He tried to act with authority. He may have insisted on the right of his court to deal with cases concerning Italian property outside the communal quarters. He was determined not to sanction automatically those alienations of fiefs or parts of the royal domain made during the years of regency. There are even signs of administrative development: the emergence of an inner council and the use of a privy seal. But at the same time he faced insubordination – I have already referred to Isabella of Beirut's refusal to perform *service de mariage* – and hostility from the Templars. And he must have known that Charles of Anjou, whose strength in the eastern Mediterranean region was now formidable, was preparing to enforce his claims and was backed by the papacy, the Templars, the Venetians and, very importantly, by the French regiment in Acre on which the kingdom had come increasingly to rely since it had been established in 1254. Charles's strength must have seemed to many of the settlers to be providing a lifeline for them; and that was probably how it seemed to the papacy.

In October 1276 Hugh left Palestine precipitately, stating that the kingdom was ungovernable. Eleven months later, in September 1277, Charles of Anjou's vicar, Roger of San Severino, arrived and claimed the government on behalf of his master. This could have been met with the defiant appeals to law and custom that Frederick II had encountered, particularly as Roger threatened to exile and disinherit those feudatories who resisted him. In the event there was very little resistance from the vassals of Jerusalem, perhaps because they knew the mind of Rome. The baronial movement, which had given rise to such splendid theories and had put up such dogged opposition in the past, ended with a whimper.

The kingdom of Jerusalem was now part of an eastern Mediterranean empire which could be expected to have the resources to support it. But Angevin government was not accepted everywhere and in the period from 1277 to 1286 Christian Palestine was more divided than ever. John of Tyre and Isabella of Beirut went their own way: King Hugh, hoping to recover his kingdom, paid visits to Tyre in 1279 and 1284 and to Beirut in 1283. He died in Tyre on 4 May 1284 and was succeeded first by his eldest son John, who lived for only a year, and then by his second son Henry. Meanwhile the Sicilian Vespers were followed by Charles's death and the Angevin empire began to crumble. Opinion in the Holy Land veered back in favour of the Cypriot royal house; even the Templars seemed to support a change of government. On 4 June 1286 King Henry landed at Acre and the French regiment, now isolated, was persuaded to withdraw from the citadel. On 15 August Henry was crowned in the cathedral of Tyre, which had become the traditional place for coronations, and the court returned to Acre for a fortnight's feasting, games and pageants: scenes from the story of the Round Table and the tale of the Queen of Femenie from the Romance of Troy.

This was the last festival in Acre, for the Mamluks had begun to advance again. In 1285 the great Hospitaller castle of Marqab and the town of Maraqiyah (Maraclea) fell. In 1287 Latakia was taken. In 1289 the sultan Kalavun, who had usurped the Mamluk throne in 1279 and had been supporting dissident elements in the county for some years, marched against Tripoli, which was still split by the bitter divisions left by its civil war. Bohemond VII had died on 19 October 1287 and his sister Lucy's rights of inheritance had been resisted by a commune with the support of the Genoese; she had only been admitted after long negotiations. As the siege of Tripoli began the Venetians and Genoese deserted and a general Muslim assault on 26 April met with little organized resistance. The countess escaped with Amalric, the younger brother of King Henry who had come with some Cypriot reinforcements, but most of the defenders were massacred. The Mamluk army moved on to occupy Enfeh and Batroun. All that was left of the county were the important Templar fortress of Tartus in the north, and Jubail under John of Antioch, who had married the lord's daughter. He and the Latin residents of Jubail were allowed to remain there under Muslim supervision until perhaps 1302.

The Christians in Acre sent urgently to the West for help. Reinforcements arrived in August 1290: twenty Venetian and five Aragonese galleys bringing a force of north Italian crusaders of poor quality. A truce for ten years had been arranged with Kalavun, but the Mamluks were now presented with a justification for breaking it when the Italian crusaders rioted and massacred some Muslim peasants who had come into Acre to sell local produce. Kalavun died on 4 November, but his son al-Ashraf Khalil continued with the preparations. In March 1291 his army left Egypt, to be joined on its march by contingents from all over the Mamluk dominions. On 5 April the huge army, with an impressive siege-train, arrived before Acre. By 8 May the outer fortifications were becoming so damaged that they had to be abandoned and a general assault on the 18th overwhelmed the defenders. King Henry, who had reached the city on the 4th, and his brother Amalric escaped by ship to Cyprus, as did several nobles and their families, but large numbers of Christians perished. By the evening the only part of Acre still in Christian hands was the Templar fortress-convent by the sea. An agreement to surrender it broke down when Muslim soldiers began molesting Christian women and boys who had sought refuge there. The Mamluks mined the building and on the 28th it collapsed, burying defenders and attackers alike in its fall.

Tyre had already been abandoned on 19 May. Sidon was taken at the end of June, although its sea-castle held out until 14 July. Beirut surrendered on 31 July and Tartus and 'Atlit were evacuated by the Templars on 3 and 14 August. Apart from a Templar garrison on the island of Arwad, two miles out to sea from Tartus, which held out until 1302, and the shadowy rule of the Embriaci in Jubail, the Latin Christian presence in Palestine and Syria had ended, although in the fourteenth century it was rumoured among the Muslims that the kings of Cyprus would secretly cross over to Tyre by night to undergo a silent coronation in the ruins of the cathedral.

CHAPTER 9

The Variety of Crusading, c. 1291–1523

The range of options

In the last few years our understanding of the crusading movement in the fourteenth century has changed radically. The old picture of decline has given way to one of many enthusiasts being presented with the same variety of options their ancestors had had in the thirteenth century. For instance, Humbert of Vienne took part in the Smyrna crusade in 1345 after showing interest in the proposal for one to the Canary Islands. John Boucicaut, the marshal of France, joined the Prussian *reysen* three times as a young man. He took the cross for King Peter of Cyprus's crusade to Alexandria in 1363 and for Louis II of Clermont's crusade to Mahdia in 1390, although the French king forbade him to go on the second of these; he went to Prussia instead. He was on the Crusade of Nicopolis in 1396 and around 1400 he was an active crusader in the eastern Mediterranean region. Henry Grosmont, Duke of Lancaster, was reported to have crusaded to Granada, Prussia, Rhodes and Cyprus. Dr Keen, in fact, has drawn attention to the many English noblemen and gentry involved in a wide range of enterprises, among them, at the lower end of the scale, Nicholas Sabraham, who had been to Alexandria, Hungary, Constantinople and Nesebŭr, and has pointed out that it is against this background that one should place Chaucer's Knight, who had 'reysed' in Prussia, Livonia and Russia and had crusaded in Spain, Egypt and Asia Minor.

> Ful worthy was he in his lordes werre,
> And therto hadde he riden, no man ferre,
> As wel in cristendom as in hethenesse,
> And evere honoured for his worthynesse.
> At Alisaundre [Alexandria] he was when it was wonne.
> Ful ofte tyme he hadde the bord bigonne
> Aboven alle nacions in Pruce (Prussia);
> In Lettow [Livonia] hadde he reysed and in Ruce [Russia],
> No Cristen man so ofte of his degree.
> In Gernade [Granada] at the seege eek hadde he be
> Of Algezir [Algeciras], and riden in Belmarye [Morocco].
> At Lyeys [Ayas] was he and at Satalye [Antalya],
> Whan they were wonne; and in the Grete See
> At many a noble armee hadde he be.

It is probable that by the middle of the century enthusiasm was confined to nobles, knights and the caste of professional soldiers, who were living by a fully developed chivalric code in which crusading ideals played an important part: we hear much less of ordinary people. But as in the thirteenth century there was scarcely a year in which there was not crusading somewhere. Work has only just begun on the fifteenth century, but it is already apparent that the papal curia was as committed as ever and there were plenty of enthusiasts still around, although now the complexity of European politics, and particularly the politics of the Italian peninsula, made it almost impossible to present the Turks with a united front.

Crusade theoreticians

Crusading thrived, of course, on disasters. It was typical that with the news of the loss of Acre in 1291 there was a revival of fervour. In 1300 a rumour swept the West that the Mongols had conquered the Holy Land and had handed it over to the Christians. Pope Boniface VIII sent 'the great and joyful news' to Edward I of England and probably to Philip IV of France as well. He encouraged the faithful to go at once to the Holy Land and he ordered the exiled Catholic bishops of Palestine to return to their sees. All over Europe men hurriedly took the cross and in Genoa several ladies sold their jewelry to help pay for a crusading fleet, although in the end the project was dropped.

The fall of Acre also inspired the writing of a spate of crusade treatises, which continued to appear at intervals throughout the fourteenth century. The authors all had to face up to the obvious problem that a major effort would now be required, since it was no longer the case of reinforcing a beach-head but of organizing a full-scale invasion. Although there was naturally a wide range of proposals – Ramon Lull revived the ancient Spanish argument that the Reconquest would lead to a liberation of Jerusalem by armies marching overland through North Africa – four ideas, which were already being bruited on the eve of the fall of Acre, appear over and over again. The first was the suggestion that the Military Orders should be united and out of them a new super-Order should be created. This was partially achieved when the Templars were suppressed. The second concerned the government of a future kingdom of Jerusalem. A group of theoreticians put forward the idea of a warrior king, a *Bellator Rex*, the master of the Military Order that would wage the crusade and then rule Palestine; for one of them, Peter Dubois, this post should always be held by a son of the king of France. These first two ideas climaxed in the dream of the Cypriot chancellor and tutor to Charles VI of France, Philip of Mézières, of the foundation of a new Order, the *Nova Religio Passionis Jhesu Christi*, the members of which would take vows of obedience and poverty but of conjugal fidelity rather than celibacy, since the Order itself would be responsible for colonizing, ruling and defending the Holy Land. Between 1390 and 1395 Philip, who also worked tirelessly for peace between England and France as a prelude to a crusade, recruited the support of over eighty nobles, especially in England and France, but also in Scotland, Germany, Spain and Lombardy, including Louis II of Clermont and John Boucicaut. The third idea was the conviction that the Muslims' ability to resist invasion could only be impaired if their economy was damaged by means of the imposition of an embargo on trade with Egypt, the richest Muslim nation and the reoccupier of Palestine. The fourth distinguished two kinds of crusade, the *passagium generale*, a great international expedition of the traditional kind, and the *passagium particulare*, a preliminary strike on a smaller scale to enforce the embargo, weaken the enemy or gain some specific advantage. It is remarkable how far these ideas were put into practice: in Prussia and on Rhodes order-states came into existence, ruled by the masters of the Teutonic Knights and the Hospitallers of St John; there was an embargo on trade with Egypt; and there were *passagia particularia*.

The fall of the Templars

The Order-states were established in reaction to one of the most sensational events in late medieval history, which would probably never have occurred had not the rôle of the Military Orders already been the subject of critical discussion. Early in the morning of 13 October 1307 nearly every Templar in France was arrested on the charge of heresy. Such a cloud of rumour and scandal was thrown up by this cataclysm that it was impossible then and it is impossible now to establish whether they were guilty of any of the charges laid against them, some of which were bizarre in the extreme. They were rich and King Philip IV's government was short of cash. Most historians have treated their destruction as a good example of what the developing state machinery could do at a time when the crown controlled the inquisition and the papacy was on the defensive. Some have considered Philip to have been mad, his fevered brain buzzing with lurid suspicions. Very few have believed that the Templars were guilty of the crimes of which they were accused. The Templars were closely interrogated and many of them were tortured. The results were startling. Confessions to some or all of the charges were extracted from the vast majority of them: all but four of 138 Templars questioned in Paris for instance. Most of them were not fighting knights, but even the knights were rather simple and uneducated men, who did not have the intellectual training or confidence to stand up to experienced interrogators: the grand master James of Molay later claimed to be 'a knight, unlettered and poor'. Those original confessions hung like a cloud over the rest of the story.

For Pope Clement V their arrest was an attack on the Church, an unprecedented denial of the right of religious to ecclesiastical justice, particularly since they were members of an Order under the protection of the Holy See. But his situation was a delicate one. The pontificate of Boniface VIII had ended only four years previously with the pope dying of shock after being kidnapped by a force led by a minister of the French king. The curia had been trying to appease France in the intervening years but Clement, a Gascon and therefore born a French-speaking subject of the king of England, was having to fight off the determined efforts of the French government to have Boniface condemned posthumously. Rome was considered too insecure for residence and after his election in June 1305 Clement lived at Poitiers before moving his court to Avignon in 1309. Meanwhile he tried to seize the initiative in the case of the Templars by establishing an official Church enquiry into the allegations and in November 1307 he ordered the arrest of all the Templars outside France. In the following February he suspended the activities of the French inquisition. This led to conflict and then to compromise with the French crown: throughout Christendom there would be episcopal investigations of individuals while concurrently church commissioners would look into the performance of the Order as a whole. The results of the work of these enquiries and commissions were inconclusive and a majority at the Council of Vienne in 1311 wanted to give the Templars themselves at least a hearing, but under pressure from France Clement suppressed the Order on 3 April 1312 and on 18 March 1314 James of Molay and Geoffrey of Charney, the Templar preceptor of Normandy, having retracted everything they had confessed, were burnt at the stake.

It is important to remember that the Templars were not alone in being severely criticized at this time. All three major Military Orders active in the East were blamed for the reverses there. By 1291 the proposals for a union of the Templars and Hospitallers, which had been raised as early as the Second Council of Lyon in 1274, were convincing enough for Pope Nicholas IV to order them to be discussed in all provincial synods; and this was an encouragement to general debate. The Teutonic Knights and the Hospitallers must have felt themselves very exposed, and rightly so, for serious charges were being brought against them as well. In Livonia the clergy, over whom the Teutonic Knights did not have the control they had in Prussia, were voicing bitter complaints about their behaviour, including their despoliation of the Church, their brutal treatment of the archbishop and citizens of Riga, their failure to defend Livonia properly, their hindering of missionary work – indeed it was claimed, not for the first time, that they alienated the heathen by their cruelty – and their internal corruption. By 1300 the papal curia was concerned about these allegations and in 1310 Clement ordered a full investigation, particularly of the charge that the Knights were allying themselves with pagans against their fellow-Christians. The Teutonic Knights did not come at all well out of the Livonian scandal – they had almost certainly behaved far worse than the Templars ever did – and the final verdict of the Church in 1324 was highly critical of them. The Hospitallers of St John were also in a bad way, although it is true that at the same time as he was pressing for the dissolution of the Templars King Philip of France was backing a crusade to be led by their master. The fourteenth century was punctuated by demands from the popes for their reform – in 1355 Pope Innocent VI even went as far as to threaten to reform the Order himself if the Hospitallers would not – and internal enquiries in the 1360s and 1370's revealed a very unsatisfactory state of affairs. It is clear that both the Teutonic Knights and the Hospitallers recognized that they must be seen to be doing something positive and it is no coincidence that in the same year, 1309, the grand master of the Teutonic Knights took up residence at Marienburg (Malbork) in Prussia and the Hospitallers moved their headquarters to Rhodes.

The Teutonic Knights in Prussia and Livonia

To understand the first of these moves something must be said about the continuing crusade in the Baltic region which was, of course, not confined to the Teutonic Knights. In the far north the frontier in Finland between the Catholics and the Russian Orthodox was unstable and in the 1320s, when enthusiasm for crusading was general, a movement got under way in Sweden and Norway to protect these Catholics from the Orthodox schismatics. In 1323 Pope John XXII had a crusade proclaimed in Norway and although war with Novgorod petered out in the mid-1330s, crusading was revived in the 1340s by King Magnus of Sweden and Norway, who was under the influence of his cousin St Bridget, a strong adherent of the movement. He led a crusade to Finland in 1348 which achieved very little. He campaigned again in 1350 and another crusade was preached on papal authority in the following year. That expedition never materialized and in 1356 there began the internal political convulsions that put paid to Magnus's ambitions. Norway and Sweden passed into the hands of alien rulers for a century and they thwarted at least two papal attempts, in 1378 and 1496, to have new crusades preached against the Russians. Further south crusading had had to respond to the arrival of the Mongols and the emergence of the powerful state of Lithuania, the creation of a prince called Mindoug who by the time of his death in 1263 had unified his people, a peasantry under the domination of a warrior mounted class, into a strong and comparatively prosperous nation. Mindoug had accepted baptism and for a short time had professed Christianity, even receiving a crown from Pope Innocent IV, but he had reverted to paganism after the defeat of the Livonian Christians at Durbe. Lithuania was a heathen society and an expansionist and aggressive one at that. Of its neighbours, Poland, which was reunited under a king in 1320 after nearly two centuries without one, was firmly committed to crusading, in spite of almost constant strife with the Teutonic Knights. Its efforts were concentrated in the northern Ukraine, where it campaigned against both Lithuanians and Mongols until the latter were decimated by the Black Death. Papal crusade letters were sent to Poland in 1325, 1340, 1343, 1351, 1354, 1355, 1363 and 1369. The Hungarians were also involved in this struggle and were sent crusade letters by the popes in 1314, 1325, 1332, 1335, 1352 and 1354.

This was the political stage on which the Teutonic Knights already stood and where they decided to concentrate their forces. It will be remembered that in 1226 their master had been confirmed in his possession of a march in Prussia and had received from the western emperor the title of imperial prince. After the fall of Acre they had moved their headquarters to Venice, half-way between Palestine and the Baltic. Then in September 1309 the grand master Siegfried of Feuchtwangen took up residence at Marienburg in West Prussia, which henceforth was to be his Order's central Convent. He came, of course, to the region where the Order was most deeply involved militarily, but he also came to a divided and de-moralized body of men who were smarting under the Livonian scandal; an attempt by his predecessor Gottfried of Hohenlohe in 1302 to make them live in stricter conformity to the Rule had aroused such opposition that he had been forced out of office. Siegfried's response and that of his brothers was to withdraw into their Baltic shell and to extend and reinforce their authority over their semi-sovereign state, while vigorously prosecuting the crusade and attracting to their little wars as many crusaders as they could. The transference of the headquarters was preceded by the acquisition in 1308–9 of eastern Pomerania and Gdańsk by ruthless methods. In Prussia the Order built up an efficient economy based on the management of its demesne lands and it dominated the secular Church. The popes remained suspicious of its motives, but it had the right to wage a perpetual crusade, as we have seen, and did not have to seek papal authorization every time it granted indulgences. It could, therefore, recruit lay knights for periods of short service with the Order.

Throughout the fourteenth century a stream of crusaders from all over Europe came to fight with the Teutonic Knights in campaigns, known as *reysen*, which took the form of raids through a frontier wilderness into the areas of Lithuanian settlements: for instance Bohemians in 1323, Alsatians in 1324, Englishmen and Walloons in 1329, Austrians and Frenchmen in 1336. John of Bohemia made three trips. Henry of Lancaster went in 1352. Henry, Earl of Derby, the future King Henry IV, went in 1390 and 1392. In 1377 Duke Albert of Austria came with 2,000 knights for his 'Tanz mit den Heiden' (Dance with the Heathen). In the following year the Duke of

Lorraine joined the *winter-reysa* with seventy knights; shortly after this Albert of Austria turned up again with the Count of Cleves and they had a special *reysa* laid on for them so that they could fulfil their vows before Christmas. The *winter-reysa* was a *chevauchée* of between 200 and 2,000 men with the aim simply of devastating a given area as quickly as possible. There were usually two of these a year, one in December, the other in January or February, with a gap between for the Christmas Feast. The *sommer-reysa* was usually organized on a larger scale with the intention of gaining territory by destroying an enemy strongpoint or building a Christian one, although plundering was a feature too. These *reysen* were not unlike sports, subject to the weather conditions in much the same way as horse-racing is today. Those who took part had the right to leave shields painted with their coats-of-arms hanging in Marienburg or other fortresses; and sometimes before, sometimes after, a *reysa* a solemn feast would be held at Marienburg, with a Table of Honour for the ten or twelve most distinguished knights present. In 1375 the grand master Winrich of Kniprode, under whose magistracy this chivalric theatre became most magnificent, presented each of the twelve knights at the Table with a shoulder badge on which was written in gold letters *Honneur vainc tout*. The Order of the Tiercelet, a Poitevin Order of knights, had a special augmentation of its insignia, the claws of its emblem of a falcon gilded, for a member who had been on a *reysa*.

Were it not for the brutality and the very real hardships that were part of them, one is tempted to write of the *reysen* as packaged crusading for the European nobility, and their popularity demonstrated how attractive this package could be when wrapped in the trappings of chivalry. But they depended on the existence of a frontier with paynim and an infidel enemy which could be portrayed as being aggressive. Their *raison d'être* vanished in 1386 when the Lithuanian Grand Duke Jagiello, who accepted baptism, married the Polish Queen Jadwiga in Cracow and took the name of King Vladislav II of Poland. Christianity made slow progress in Lithuania after this dynastic union, but the Lithuanians were now subject to Christian government. A condition of the union, moreover, was that Jagiello would recover for Poland eastern Pomerania and Kulmerland. At Tannenberg (Grunwald) on 15 July 1410 the Order's forces were destroyed by a Polish and Lithuanian army which also contained Czech, Moravian, Vlach and Crim Mongol mercenaries. The grand master, the chief officials and c. 400 Teutonic Knights lay dead on the field. Marienburg held out and the First Peace of Thorn (Toruń) of 1 February 1411 enabled the Order to keep most of its territory. But it was never again to be the force it had been, not least because simmering discontent among its subjects, Germans, Prussians and Poles, who were losing their separate identities and evolving into a self-consciously Prussian society, came to the surface. The gentry and townspeople formed themselves into a Union to protect their interests in the face of the Order's ruthless attempts to restore control: in the 1450s this Union rejected the Order's overlordship and turned to Poland. Meanwhile Prussia, which had been ravaged by invading armies in 1414, 1422 and 1431–3, was partitioned in the Second Peace of Thorn of 19 October 1466, which ended the Thirteen-year War with Poland. The Order lost Marienburg and was left only with eastern Prussia which it held as a Polish fief. Although it survived until 1525 in Prussia and 1562 in Livonia, crusading along the Baltic was coming to an end. The last time non-German crusaders came to Prussia seems to have been for the *reysa* of 1413. The crusading rôle of the Order was debated, and defended, at the Council of Constance in 1415–18, when the Teutonic Knights appealed to the assembled prelates against Poland. In Livonia a certain number of knights still took part in *reysen* against the Russians and Walter of Plettenberg, the Livonian master, organized a heroic defence against Russian invasion in 1501–2. But it is significant that although his proctor in Rome begged for a crusade encyclical he never got it: Pope Alexander VI was hoping that the Russians would ally themselves with the Catholics against the Turks.

The Hospitallers of St John on Rhodes

The Teutonic Knights brilliantly exploited their independent situation in the far north to create a type of crusading that was fashionable and gained them public recognition while at the same time exposing themselves to the minimum of interference from the Holy See. The Hospitallers' experience was very different, but their task was much more formidable. On 27 May 1306 their master, Fulk of Villaret, whose headquarters were now at Limassol in Cyprus, came to an agreement with a Genoese admiral called Vignolo de' Vignoli, who claimed rights in the Dodecanese, for the joint conquest of Rhodes and its archipelago. On 23 June a Hospitaller squadron of two galleys and four other vessels, carrying a small force that included thirty-five brothers of the Order, left Cyprus and, joined by Genoese galleys, began an invasion of Rhodes which took much longer than anticipated: the city of Rhodes probably did not fall until the middle of 1308 and the island was not completely subjugated until 1310, although the central Convent had already been moved there in the previous year. By the bull *Ad providam* of 2 May 1312 the pope granted most of the Templars' estates and properties to the Hospitallers. In the long run this greatly enriched them, although it took them a long time to get control of even a proportion of the lands to which they were now entitled: they took over most of those in France on the payment of huge indemnities only in 1317; in England they had still not taken full possession of them by 1338. Nevertheless by 1324 their estates had doubled and the Templar properties helped to finance the defence of Rhodes and their active rôle in military engagements in the eastern Mediterranean region. Even so, the costs of conquering, fortifying and establishing an administration on Rhodes saddled the Hospitallers with crippling debts. The central Convent was not solvent until the 1330s and even then its finances were precarious, which helps to explain the comparative efficiency with which the Hospitallers had to manage their European estates; they were driven to exploit them in the most effective way. This, and the fact that Rhodes was far less secure than Prussia, led the papacy to intervene much more frequently in their affairs than in those of the Teutonic Knights, whom they must sometimes have envied.

Rhodes is a large and fertile island, nearly 50 miles long and 20 miles wide, only 12 miles off the south-western coast of Asia Minor. It dominated one of the most important sea-routes in the eastern Mediterranean and it had a fine harbour. It had a population of c. 10,000 Greeks, now joined by western colonists who were offered land on favourable terms. The Hospitallers also held a few neighbouring islands, of which the most important was Cos, and on the mainland after 1408 they built a large castle at Bodrum to replace the one they had lost at Smyrna (Izmir) which will be referred to below. Their relations with the Greek population appear to have been good, but the city of Rhodes, at the centre of which was the enclosure for the Convent, also came to have a large west European community. It had been strongly fortified by 1346 and the Hospitallers continued to improve its defences and those of other strongpoints throughout the archipelago. By the early fifteenth century Rhodes was one of the most heavily fortified places in the world and the consequent security meant that its commercial importance increased. It had also become a major part of call for pilgrims travelling to the Holy Land. To it, in much the same way as to Prussia though in fewer numbers, came lay knights to campaign with the Order and, as they did in Marienburg, they hung their coats-of-arms in a *Maison d'honneur* in Rhodes.

After the loss of the Palestinian mainland the Order began to build up a navy and in the centuries that followed this was the most distinctive feature of its contribution to crusading, which became as much a naval as a military enterprise since it involved the defence of scattered Christian settlements around the Aegean. The Hospitallers usually had a fleet of seven or eight war galleys, the maintenance of which was a heavy expense. Rhodes was well-situated for offensive operations, particularly against the Turkish emirates of Menteshe (Muğla) and Aydin on the mainland, which in the first half of the fourteenth century threatened Christian shipping, but the Hospitallers were always a significant component in crusade-planning and made an important contribution to the defence of all the Latin settlements in the area. They also played a major rôle in the capture and defence of Smyrna from 1344 to 1402; indeed from 1374 they were responsible for it. Rhodes was recognized by the Muslims as a threat to their interests and it was attacked by the Egyptians in 1440 and 1444. The most striking demonstration of its reputation throughout Christendom can be seen today on the face of the English Tower, at the south-eastern corner of the *enceinte* at Bodrum: a line of English coats-of-arms sculpted in stone, at the centre of which are the royal arms of King Henry IV and six other members of his family and then a further nineteen shields; no less than seventeen of the individuals represented here were Knights of the Garter. It is likely that the shields record contributions to the building of the tower, probably c. 1414.

It is not surprising that as Turkish power increased the threat to Rhodes grew. By the late 1470s the Hospitallers were expecting to have to meet invasion sooner or later and were making the best preparations for it they could. From 23 May to late August 1480 the Turks laid siege to the city of Rhodes with a large force before withdrawing exhausted. The successful defence of Rhodes did wonders for the Hospitallers' prestige – in France *Te Deums*, processions and the ringing of church bells were decreed; an account of the siege in English was in print within two years – and the respect with which they were regarded was enhanced when the Turkish prince Jem, Sultan Bayazid's younger brother, fled to Rhodes two years later; he was to be a prisoner first of the Order and then of the papacy until his death in 1495. But the Ottoman sultanate under great conquerors like Selim I and Suleiman I was not going to permit this Christian outpost, insignificant in comparison with the territories they had subdued, to exist indefinitely. In July 1522 a large armada under the command of Suleiman himself began to disembark troops on the island. By the 28th Turkish batteries were bombarding the city. The invasion was well-planned and was on a very large scale. After months of bombardment, mining and assaults the walls were no longer tenable, the Hospitallers' stock of munitions was low and the Greek inhabitants were anxious to give up. On 18 December the grand master Philip of l'Isle Adam surrendered and, permitted to leave with honour, sailed from Rhodes on 1 January 1523.

Cyprus

Rhodes was, of course, only one of the many Latin settlements throughout the eastern Mediterranean region. To the south-east was the kingdom of Cyprus, governed by a succession of rulers of the Lusignan dynasty – Henry II, Hugh IV, Peter I, Peter II, James I, Janus, John II, Charlotte and James II – until in 1489 it was taken over by Venice in consequence of an extraordinary manoeuvre by which King James II's Venetian queen Catherine Cornaro was adopted by Venice so that in the event of the deaths of both her husband and her heir it would pass to the Republic. In its heyday before 1369, the year in which King Peter I, one of the most spectacular figures in the fourteenth-century crusading movement, was assassinated, it was very prosperous and the city of Famagusta, linked to the Asiatic trade routes through the smaller ports of northern Syria and especially the Cilician port of Ayas until the latter was occupied by the Mamluks in 1337, was a hub of commercial activity. The island was now the cultural centre of the Latin East: the royal palace in Nicosia was described by travellers as being the finest in the world. Some of the luxury and splendour is still discernible in the surviving churches and other ecclesiastical buildings. The cathedral of Nicosia dates from the thirteenth century, but the cathedral of Famagusta, the churches of St Catherine in Nicosia and St Mary of Carmel in Famagusta, where the great Carmelite Peter Thomas was buried, and the Premonstratensian abbey of Bellapaise are among the most beautiful buildings of the Latin East. Many of the survivors of the mainland settlements were now in Cyprus: of the assassins of Peter I, two, Philip of Ibelin titular lord of Arsuf and Henry of Jubail, had names already familiar to us, and the third, John of Gaurelle, seems to have been a descendant of a Poitevin follower of Guy of Lusignan; Raymond Babin, who was an associate, came from a family settled in Jerusalem in the twelfth century. The feudal system, represented at the apex by the High Court in Nicosia, was, as we have seen, strongly influenced by Latin Jerusalem and it overlay, as on the mainland, a previous administration, in this case Byzantine. The traditions of the mainland were maintained and at first were strong, manifesting themselves in a remarkable display of constitutional ingenuity, in which the Ibelins played a large part, when in 1306 King Henry II was removed from government and replaced by his brother Amalric, who ruled as governor for four years. But the traditions gradually faded and by the time Venice took over the island the High Court was practically moribund; the Venetian senate imposed its own administrators, who had no legislative powers and from whose courts appeals could be lodged in Venice.

In fact after 1369 a succession of disasters struck the kingdom. In 1373 war broke out with Genoa and a squadron of Genoese galleys burnt Limassol, took Paphos and besieged and captured Famagusta, seizing the person of the king; later the Genoese also took his uncle James. In October 1374 Cyprus was forced to agree to pay annual tribute and an enormous indemnity against the return of Famagusta. An attempt to take Famagusta by force failed in 1378 and the city, with a zone of two leagues around it, was transferred to Genoa in return for the release of James, who had now inherited the crown. Intermittent hostilities with the Genoese continued off and on for decades, punctuated by Genoese victories after which more indemnities were extracted from the wretched Cypriots. Then in 1425

Mamluk Egypt, responding to Cypriot raids on the Egyptian and Syrian coasts, launched a large-scale attack on the island during which the shoreline between Larnaca and Limassol was pillaged and many Cypriots were enslaved. With the island's weakness revealed, a powerful Egyptian invasion force, probably with the connivance of the Genoese, landed on the southern coast on 1 July 1426. On the 7th, in the Battle of Khirokitia, the Cypriot army was routed and King Janus was taken alive. Nicosia was sacked and Janus was paraded before the crowds in Cairo. He was ransomed for 200,000 ducats, an annual tribute of 5,000 and the acknowledgement of the sultan of Egypt's suzerainty. In 1448 Corycus, the last Cypriot holding on the Cilician mainland, was lost.

Greece

West and north-west of Cyprus was Venetian Crete, the duchy of the Archipelago and the other island-lordships in the Aegean, of which the most important were Venetian Euboea, Lesbos, granted to the Genoese by the Byzantines in 1354 and ruled by the Genoese family of Gattilusio, and Chios, the world centre for the production of mastic, which had been seized by the Genoese in 1346 together with Foça (Phocaea) on the mainland, which was a major source of alum. In continental Greece the Latin settlements mirrored the political divisions in southern Italy, some recognizing the Angevin kings of Naples, others the Aragonese kings of Sicily.

The overlords of the principality of Achaea in the Peloponnese were, as we have seen, the kings of Naples. In 1315–16 the principality was the scene of armed conflict between two pretenders, Louis of Burgundy, who had married the heiress Mahaut with the support of the French crown and had paid homage to the Angevin Philip of Taranto – himself now married to the Latin empress – and Ferdinand of Majorca, the younger son of King James I of Majorca, who had married a granddaughter of William of Villehardouin. Ferdinand landed near and occupied Killini (Glarentsa) in advance of Louis's arrival, but he was killed in the Battle of Manolada on 5 July 1316. The victor was himself dead within a month and Mahaut was forced to surrender the principality in 1322 when it was discovered that she had secretly married a Burgundian knight without her overlord's consent. King Robert of Naples arranged for his youngest brother, John of Gravina, to hold the principality directly from Philip of Taranto. By this time it was a shadow of its former self. In the north the Catalans in Athens posed a constant threat. In the south the Byzantine Greeks at Mistra were expanding the area under their control, so that John of Gravina was recognized only in the western and northern coastal regions where the great lords had nearly independent powers anyway. His suzerainty was also acknowledged by the duchy of the Archipelago, but the islands of

Cephalonia and Zante (Zákinthos) remained virtually autonomous under the rule of the Orsini.

Philip of Taranto died in 1331 and was succeeded as overlord by his son Robert, for whom Philip's widow the Empress Catherine acted as regent until her death in 1346. John of Gravina, who did not like the idea of performing homage to his own nephew, surrendered the principality, which therefore passed directly into its overlord's hands. But as the threat to it from the Turks grew the absentee Angevins, Robert, then another Philip of Taranto, then Queen Joanna of Naples herself, could do little to help their subjects in southern Greece, who were increasingly isolated and anarchic. In 1376 the Latin Peloponnese was leased for five years to the Hospitallers, who found its defence a heavy burden, not least because their master, Juan Fernandez of Heredià, was captured and sold to the Turks when he tried to take the Epirote city of Arta in 1378. The rule of Joanna's successors, Charles III and Ladislas of Naples, was shadowy in the extreme, while the claims of a succession of pretenders to the principality were more shadowy still. Effective power came to be exercised by a company of Navarrese and Gascon knights, who had first been employed by the Hospitallers and took control of a large part of the Peloponnese, including the princely domain. In 1396 King Ladislas of Naples recognized the situation by conferring the title of prince on this company's leader, Peter Bordo of St Superan. After his death the head of the oldest and richest of the baronial families, Centurione Zaccaria, persuaded Ladislas to confer the title on him. Centurione, who was able and resourceful, managed to preserve the Latin Peloponnese for a generation, but the *coup de grâce* was delivered by the Byzantine despot of Mistra, Thomas Palaeologus, who forced Centurione to betroth his daughter to him, Thomas, in 1429. Centurione continued to bear the title of prince until 1432, after which Thomas took over the whole principality, except for the Venetian possessions in the south-west and the north-east.

To the north, the Catalan Company which had taken over the duchy of Athens in 1311 after the Battle of Halmyros sought and accepted overlordship from Frederick, the Aragonese king of Sicily, who appointed his younger son Manfred duke. Under a series of able vicar-generals Athens and Thebes were divided among and run by members of the Company. Manfred's line held the dukedom until the 1350s, when it passed directly to the throne of Sicily. But internal disputes began to tear the Catalan settlement apart and they were intensified after 1377 by a dispute within the Aragonese royal family for the Sicilian throne. From 1379 Athens was annexed to the crown of Aragon itself, but in that year the Navarrese Company, with the connivance of the Hospitallers, took Thebes. Then in 1385 Nerio Acciajuoli, the lord of Corinth and a member of a Florentine banking family which had risen in Angevin service in the Peloponnese, entered the duchy and in 1388 occupied the acropolis of Athens, thus ending Catalan rule. When Nerio died in 1394 he left no legitimate male heirs. His son-in-law, the Byzantine despot, Theodore of Mistra, seized Corinth. Venice held Athens for a time until forced out by Nerio's bastard son, Antonio Acciajuoli, who ruled the duchy from 1403 to 1435, a period that was comparatively peaceful and prosperous. The government of Antonio's successors was ended when the Turks occupied Athens on 4 June 1456.

The history of the Latins in the eastern Mediterranean region in the fourteenth and fifteenth centuries is one of squabbling petty states, some under absentee dynasties, bound together by religion and by little else. Active at every stage one can find Italians, whose commercial concerns gave them an interest in the maintenance of the settlements – indeed they can be seen gradually taking them over – and whose shipping provided the means of communication, and the Hospitallers of St John, who were the trouble-shooters of the area. These anarchic and weak lordships, moreover, were faced by a growing threat from the Ottoman Turks.

Crusading in Spain and Italy, 1302–78

From the point of view of the papacy, however, the same conflicts of interest prevailed as in the thirteenth century. Crusading continued in Spain as well as in the Baltic region; and threats from political opponents in Europe were at times believed to pose a greater danger to Christendom than the lengthening shadow in the East.

Although in 1309–10 the kings of Castile and Aragon waged an unprofitable crusade against the Moors, which certainly impeded, as was intended, a *passagium particulare* to the East, and there was some activity in 1318–19, there was a stalemate in Spain in the early fourteenth century, in spite of regular grants of money and authorizations of crusade-preaching. The popes were highly suspicious of the Spanish kings, who seemed to be cynically manipulating crusade appeals for their own purposes. But in 1312 Alfonso XI, who was to prove himself to be the best military leader in the peninsula since St Ferdinand, inherited the throne of Castile. From 1328 a series of papal grants concerning crusade-preaching and the collection of tenths and *tercias* evidenced a revival of activity on the frontier with Granada. This attracted interest from across the Pyrenees and in 1326–7 and 1331 King Philip VI of France (in 1326 still Count of Valois), in 1328–9 King John of Bohemia and King Philip of Navarre and in 1330 Count William of Jülich were enthusiastic enough to plan to lead parties of crusaders to Spain. The period was one in which crusading fervour was at a high level in western Europe and outsiders had not shown so much interest in the Reconquest for a century, although it subsided on the news of a short-lived truce made with Granada in 1331. Then in 1340 the Marinid sultan 'Ali began to move troops across the straits from Africa and a Marinid army of c. 67,000 men besieged Tarifa. Alfonso, leading about 21,000 men, mostly Castilians and Portuguese, took the same sort of gamble by seeking engagement that his ancestor had taken at Las Navas de Tolosa. On 30 October he won a major victory on the banks of the little river Salado, returning to Seville with so much booty that in Paris the price of gold and silver fell. In August 1342 he laid siege to Algeciras with soldiers from all over Europe, including Genoese and nobles from France, Germany and England, King Philip of Navarre, Gaston of Béarn, Roger Bernal of Castielbon and the Earls of Derby and Salisbury among them. The city fell in March 1344, the straits of Gibraltar were won and the flow of African invaders into Spain was dammed. But in 1350 Alfonso died of the Black Death while besieging Gibraltar and thereafter the Reconquest flagged for a century. Christian Spain, riven by internal disputes, was not strong enough to take Granada. Realism gave way to dreams, like Peter I of Castile's proposal to crusade in Africa in 1354, which had been foreshadowed by the planning of a crusade to the Canary Islands in 1344.

The Italian crusades in support of the Angevin rulers of Naples had ended in 1302. After that date they were directed against the 'Ghibelline' supporters of imperial claims, which had been revived in northern and central Italy, although in fact the first significant crusade of the new period was preached in 1309 against Venice, not a Ghibelline city at all, after a dispute over the succession to Ferrara, a place of strategic importance to both sides. Venice submitted in 1310, but Ferrara, which from 1317 was under a regime hostile to the papacy, was also involved in the next crusade, which was proclaimed in December 1321 against its Estensi rulers, Matthew Visconti of Milan and Frederick of Montefeltro and his brothers and supporters in the march of Ancona and the duchy of Spoleto. Frederick of Montefeltro was defeated and the Visconti regime in Milan went under, but the continuing resistance of the Ghibellines meant that papal authority was not restored in the region. The crusade was extended to cover Mantua as well in 1324, but the resulting campaigns, although enormously costly, only achieved a precarious balance of forces which was broken in 1327 by King Louis IV of Germany's *Romzug*, his descent on Italy. Louis's initial success, his deposition of the pope and appointment of an anti-pope and his occupation of Rome led to a crusade being declared against him in 1328, but lack of money and supplies forced him to leave Rome and Italy, the Ghibelline coalition collapsed and many of its leaders, including Azzo Visconti and the Estensi, changed sides. But now Pope John XXII lent his support to a plan to establish a kingdom in Lombardy for John of Bohemia, the son of the former emperor Henry VII and a committed crusader, to hold as a papal fief. In September 1332 the League of Ferrara was formed to oppose this and the pope's desire to dominate northern and central Italy was thwarted.

The papacy tried again in 1353, when Pope Innocent VI sent Cardinal Gil Albornoz, who as Archbishop of Toledo had celebrated Mass before the Battle of Salado, to Italy to regain control of the papal state. Gil Albornoz was successful in the western provinces, but he could not overcome the Romagna. In October 1354 Francesco Ordelaffi of Cesena and the Manfredi of Faenza were declared to be heretics and in the winter of 1355–6 a crusade was proclaimed against them. Gil Albornoz completed the reconquest of the Romagna in 1357 at a huge cost. In 1360, however, the Church went to war with the Visconti of Milan and in 1363 declared Bernabò Visconti to be a heretic. The crusade was renewed and, although peace was concluded in 1364, it was again revived in 1368 when preaching was organized in Italy, Germany and Bohemia. A feature of these wars of the 1350s and 1360s was the use by both sides of mercenary companies, against which crusades were also preached when they got out of hand; they provided models for further crusading activity against *routier* bands in France in the 1360s. For almost the whole of the pontificate of Gregory XI (1371–8) the Church was at war in Lombardy and Tuscany, although Gregory, who commuted vows, resorted to crusade terminology and transferred certain crusade taxes, does not seem to have launched fully privileged crusades in Italy, preferring to grant limited indulgences which were applicable only in case of death.

This endemic crusading in Italy was given impetus by the exile of the popes in Avignon from 1309 to 1378. Under strong pressure to return to Rome, yet reluctant to do so until order had been restored in the papal state, fearful of the emperors, particularly in the light of Louis IV's *Romzug*, they pressed on when they could. They could not avoid criticism for this, particularly in France, swept by crusading fever in the 1320s, where it was not acceptable that a crusade to recover the Holy Land should be postponed in Italy's favour. In 1319 Pope John XXII even diverted to his Italian wars a Franco-papal fleet of ten ships intended for the eastern crusade, and in response King Philip V of France went so far as to take the Visconti and the Ghibelline league under his protection. Nor could the popes avoid having to pay for these enormously expensive wars; nearly two-thirds of John's revenue was spent on them. It is remarkable how the papacy managed to meet the bills and remain solvent; to do so it drew on its experiences in the thirteenth century and elaborated a system of extraordinary taxes, especially caritative subsidies ('voluntary' donations), annates (taxes on the first year's income of the new holder of a benefice) and intercalary fruits (income from benefices during vacancies) to supplement the crusade income taxes it was levying on the clergy. This led to the system of clerical taxation that prevailed to the end of the Middle Ages.

The fourteenth-century popes tended to associate Ghibellinism with heresy, or at least with schism, and this featured alongside traditional references to the defence of the rights of Christendom's mother church in their justification of the Italian crusades. Charges of heresy were not usually made heedlessly, but by the 1320s they were being levelled forcefully and elaborately, backed by references to the Ghibellines' denial of papal authority and their association with known heretics like the Franciscan Spirituals. In fact the popes were at that time deeply worried about heresy and schism and in this respect the crusades against the Ghibellines were large-scale versions of a type of crusading which included a savage little war against the followers of Fra Dolcino in Piedmont in 1306–7, the proclamation of a crusade against Cathars in Hungary in 1327 – cancelled when it was realized that it encroached on the authority of the inquisition – and a minor campaign against heretics in Bohemia in 1340.

Crusading to the East, 1291–1370

Crusading may have manifested itself in the same variety of ways as in the thirteenth century, but there was growing in the East a threat more serious than any faced since the eighth century, a threat to Europe itself from the Ottoman Turks. Western Europe became really worried about them in 1369, when the Byzantine emperor John V journeyed to Rome to appeal for help against the Turks. So the history of crusading in the East between 1291 and 1523 falls into two periods. The first was one in which the aims were the reconquest of Palestine, but also the crushing of Mamluk Egypt, which was a necessary prerequisite, and the defence of the remaining Latin settlements, particularly against the piratical activities of the Turkish emirates of Menteshe and Aydin. This meant that crusading moved to the sea and became very largely naval. In the second period the advance of the Ottomans meant that the defence of Christian Europe itself came to have priority.

After 1291 the papal curia was concerned to organize the defence of Latin Greece, to send aid to Cilician Armenia which was still holding out against the Mamluks, and to enforce an economic blockade of Egypt, which most men agreed was a necessary prelude to a crusade. From Boniface VIII the popes promulgated decrees of increasing severity on the blockade. Clement V authorized the Hospitallers on Rhodes to capture the vessels of Christian merchants trading with the Mamluks and sequester their cargoes. Strict embargoes were imposed from the early 1320s, when it was laid down that merchants who infringed them were to be excommunicated. These measures were accompanied by direct approaches to western trading communities which were often persuaded to legislate in the way the popes wanted. The effectiveness of this blockade has been debated. There is no doubt that ports like Ayas which could act as intermediaries between Christians and Muslims grew in importance, but it is also clear that direct trading with Islamic centres continued, if on a reduced scale. And when the Mongol routes across Asia came to be temporarily disrupted in the 1340s with effects on the Black Sea traffic the Italians insisted that trade relations with the Mamluks be re-opened. From 1344 the Holy See, which was beginning to abandon hope for the recovery of the Holy Land, granted licences for such trade.

After the death of Pope Boniface VIII the growing French influence on the curia manifested itself in support for Charles of Valois, the King of France's brother, who in 1301 had married Catherine of Courtenay, the heiress to the Latin empire, and wanted to recover it. In 1306 the collection of crusade tenths in France, Sicily and Naples was authorized in favour of Charles and in 1307 crusade-preaching was ordered in Italy. Charles delayed so long that the coalition of powers against the Byzantine emperor on which he was relying collapsed, but meanwhile Pope Clement V had been considering the preaching of a general passage with the purpose of recovering Palestine. The attitude of the French and the trial of the Templars made this impossible, except as a long-term goal, so he turned to the organization of a *passagium particulare*, which was to consist of 5,000 troops, to remain in the East for five years under the command of the Hospitaller master to defend Cyprus and Cilicia and prevent Christian merchants engaging in illicit trading. The pope had to face the fact that King James of Aragon's crusade against Granada, planned at the same time, was siphoning off potential recruits, although it is indicative of the general enthusiasm for enterprises in the East that in the spring and summer of 1309 large numbers of rural and urban poor in England, Flanders, northern France and Germany were taking the cross and gathering in disorderly groups; in July, apparently, 30–40,000 of them arrived at Avignon demanding a general passage. In fact the expedition which sailed from Brindisi early in 1310 did little more than help consolidate the Hospitaller occupation of Rhodes.

In the years after 1310 the papacy still concerned itself with Latin Greece, granting Philip of Taranto crusade tenths and indulgences and authorizing crusades in favour of the Brienne pretenders to the dukedom of Athens against the Catalan Company: one was approved as late as 1330. But with the accession of Pope John XXII in 1316 crusading further to the east again came to the forefront of curial planning, in response to the enthusiasm that was showing itself in France, where in 1320 there was another outbreak at the popular level of the movement of the shepherd crusaders. At the Council of Vienne in 1312 Philip IV had agreed to prepare a crusade and a six-year tenth had been levied on the whole Church, of which the French contribution, increased for a seventh year, had been conceded directly to the king. At Whitsun 1313, at a great assembly held in Paris to witness the knighting of his sons, Philip himself, his sons and his son-in-law Edward II of England had all taken the cross. Philip IV had since died, but his son Philip V, who himself had taken the cross in 1313, was bound to carry out the project and to assist him John not only confirmed a new four-year tenth to be levied on the French Church, but also made a four-year grant of annates; this was followed in 1318 by another two-year tenth. Dr Housley has pointed out that the French crown had been given eleven years of tenths and four years of annates since 1312: the tenths alone would have raised 2,750,000 pounds *tournois*. But rebellion in Flanders held the king back and, with Cilicia again under threat, the various parties began to think of another *passagium particulare*, to be led by Louis I of Clermont. It was the naval vanguard of this which John directed in 1319 to the Italian wars, where it was lost. The French reaction was strong and the king took a very hard line, as we have seen. Philip, in fact, was a committed crusader who left 100,000 pounds in his will to a future *passagium* and might well have gone on crusade if he had not fallen mortally sick in 1321. Over the winter of 1319–20 he held a number of assemblies, to some of which he summoned many old war-horses from the provinces to advise him on the coming crusade: they probably included Odo of Grandson.

In January 1323 the new king of France, Charles IV, formulated another detailed proposal, this time for a three-part crusade: a *primum passagium*, to sail in the same year to the aid of Cilicia; a *passagium particulare* in the following year or soon afterwards; and, in the very long term, a general passage to reconquer the Holy Land. The planning ground to a halt over finance, since it was certain that the bulk of the costs would have to be borne by the French Church, which was in no state to take on such a commitment, and it was not until 1328 that King Philip VI, who was another enthusiast, revived the project. In 1331 the pope gave his consent to the preaching of an expedition to leave before March 1334. Philip's plan, which at first took the pope aback, was a very ambitious one: another three-stage crusade, for which the main French contribution would be to a general passage proposed for August 1336 under the command of the king himself as captain-general of the Church. On 1 October 1333, in another great ceremony in Paris, held in the meadows near St-Germain-des-Prés, Philip and many of his nobles took the cross.

The first of the two preliminary *passagia* was launched in 1334 and marked an important development in crusading. For what resulted was a naval league designed to deal with the Turkish pirates operating from the emirates of Menteshe and Aydin. The basis of it was an agreement drawn up between Venice, the Hospitallers and the Byzantine emperor Andronicus III on Rhodes in September 1332 to maintain a force of twenty galleys in the area for five years. In the autumn and winter of 1333–4 Philip VI and Pope John agreed to supply a further four galleys each. This fleet inflicted a heavy defeat on the Turks in the Gulf of Edremit. The league was also going to be involved in the second *passagium*, a force of 800 men-at-arms under Louis of Clermont, which was to invade Asia Minor: 400 were to be sent by France and the papacy, 200 by the Hospitallers and 100 each by Cyprus and the Byzantine empire, while Venice and Naples would contribute additional shipping. But this alliance came to nothing. Relations between France and England were being soured and Pope John died at the end of 1334. Under his successor, Benedict XII, the *passagium* planned for 1335 was shelved, but an attempt was made to revive the naval league, it seems unsuccessfully, although at one point the papacy, the Byzantine empire and France were preparing ships. In 1336 Benedict recognized that political conditions in western Europe were so unfavourable that the general passage would have to be cancelled as well, although he sent some limited aid to Cilicia. This led to bitter reproaches and disillusionment among contemporaries.

In May 1342 Benedict was succeeded by Clement VI, who had been a leader of the French delegation which had negotiated on behalf of Philip VI in the early 1330s. Clement made no plans for a general passage, which was now quite impossible, because of the war between France and England and the general economic depression in western Europe, but under him a new strategy, based on the successes of 1334, was developed. This involved the reconstruction of a naval league against the Turkish emirates, now at their most aggressive, and the interesting thing was that the recovery of the Holy Land was no part of the scheme; it is significant that Clement was the pope who abandoned the embargo on trade with Egypt. Responding to appeals from Venice, Cyprus and Rhodes, he sent a legate to Venice to plan the new league: the papacy and Cyprus would each provide four galleys, the Hospitallers and Venetians six each. He paid for his galleys by levying a three-year tenth, later supplemented by another two-year one, on certain provinces of the Church and by crusade-preaching to raise money through the sale of indulgences. In the spring of 1344 twenty-four galleys assembled off Euboea. This fleet defeated the Turks at sea and on 28 October took the port of Smyrna, the emirate of Aydin's principal harbour. Smyrna was to be held until it fell to the Mongol Timur in 1402. Its capture led to yet another outburst of crusading fever in the West and in response to a set-back early in 1345, when the leaders of the crusade were killed in an engagement with the Turks, the dauphin of Viennois, Humbert II, volunteered to defend the new beach-head and led an expedition which sailed from Venice in the middle of November. Humbert returned to the West in 1347 and the league broke up in 1351, by which time Venice and Genoa, which had been granted indulgences to defend its Black Sea station of Feodosiya against the Mongols in 1345, were at war. In a Europe coping with the results of the Black Death and against the background of the

Hundred Years War Pope Innocent VI spent most of his ten-year pontificate trying to revive it. Officially it was still in being in a joint responsibility for the defence of Smyrna, but it was not until 1359 that it was put on a more active footing. Crusade-preaching was authorized and a tenth was levied. Peter Thomas, the great Carmelite preacher and diplomatist, was appointed legate and that autumn with Venetian and Hospitaller ships he won a victory at Lâpseki in the Dardanelles.

For the next decade, however, the old idea of a general passage to Jerusalem was revived through the efforts of King Peter I of Cyprus, who succeeded to the throne in 1359. In the same year he used Cypriot ships abstracted from the league to occupy Corycus in Cilicia. In 1361 he captured Antalya. And on 15 June 1362 he addressed a circular letter to the West announcing his intention of leading a crusade to liberate Jerusalem. In October he set off to raise money in Europe and he met the new pope, Urban V, at the end of March 1363. A general passage was planned for March 1365. King John II of France was a fervent supporter and took the cross, together with several of his nobles. He was granted a six-year tenth and other revenues and was appointed captain-general of the enterprise. But he died on 8 April 1364, a prisoner of the English, to whom he had surrendered himself when one of the hostages for his ransom after his capture in the Battle of Poitiers had broken his parole. The dream of a general passage was, in fact, unrealistic, given the economic conditions in France. Peter, leading what was originally envisaged as a *passagium particulare* in advance of it, left Venice on 27 June 1365 with the crusaders he had recruited. His army was estimated as being c. 10,000 men and 1,400 horses. He adopted the thirteenth-century expedient of attacking Egypt, perhaps, as Dr Edbury has suggested, with the aim of at least strengthening the standing of the Cypriot ports by destroying a major rival, and on 10 October he took the city of Alexandria by surprise. But he could not hold it and his expedition, laden with plunder, withdrew to Cyprus six days later. In the following year Count Amadeus of Savoy left Venice with another fragment of the crusade, an army of 3–4,000 men. After retaking Gallipoli from the Turks in August he campaigned against the Bulgarians on the Black Sea coast, who had been holding up the return overland of the Byzantine emperor John V from Buda (Budapest): the towns of Nesebŭr and Sozopol were restored to the empire. Peter of Cyprus went on to lead a raid on Cilicia and Syria in 1367, but with his assassination in 1369 the old idea of the liberation of Jerusalem passed away, to be revived only in brief moments of euphoria in later centuries.

Concern about the Turks

In the following year there was a new pope, Gregory XI, and the rising power of the Ottoman Turks became for the first time a dominant factor in curial thinking. The Ottomans had emerged from the confusion in Asia Minor that followed the collapse of Selchük rule. After their defeat at the hands of the Mongols in 1243 the authority of the Selchüks had declined and there had been a fragmentation of the Turkish polity into principalities, of which the emirates of Menteshe and Aydin, although not the most powerful, were for a time the ones that worried westerners the most. Among the *ghazi* princes on the frontier was a man called Ertugrul who by the time of his death in 1280 seems to have founded a little state of his own. His son Osman came to prominence early in the fourteenth century; it was against him that the Catalan Company was employed by the Byzantines. He spread his rule over a significant area of north-western Asia Minor, as far as the Aegean, the Sea of Marmara and the Black Sea. He died shortly after taking Bursa in 1326 and under his son Orkhan the Ottoman state, well-governed and with a disciplined army, began to expand rapidly. In 1331 Nicaea was taken, in 1337 Izmit and in 1338 Usküdar, just across the Bosporus from Constantinople. Invited into Thrace as mercenaries, the Turks had established a beach-head in Europe by 1348 and they occupied Gallipoli, at the mouth of the Dardanelles, in 1354. By Orkhan's death in 1360 his rule stretched from western Thrace to Eskişehir and Ankara. Hordes of Turks were now pouring into Europe: Edirne was taken in 1361, Plovdiv in 1363 and in 1371 victory at Maritsa gave the sultan Murad I most of Bulgaria and Serbian Macedonia. The Turks achieved dominance of the Balkans after the Battle of Kosovo in 1389, on the morning of which Murad was assassinated. His elder son and successor, Bayazid I, took what was left of Bulgaria in 1393, invaded the Peloponnese in 1394, reducing the Christian lords to vassaldom, and defeated the crusade of 1396 at Nicopolis (Nikopol). Turkish expansion was halted by the Mongol Timur's victory at Ankara in 1402 and by succession disputes in the Ottoman family which lasted until 1413. But then, and particularly under Murad II (1421–51), the Turks resumed their advance, laying siege to Constantinople in 1422 and taking Thessaloniki in 1430. Eastern Anatolia was absorbed or cowed and in 1444 a crusade was routed at Varna. The Peloponnese was ravaged in 1446. Hungarian military power was decimated in a second battle at Kosovo in 1448. Under Mehmed II (1451–81) the Turks then prepared to turn on Constantinople. In spite of the efforts of the papacy and last-ditch attempts to unite the Catholic and Orthodox Churches, which split the Greeks themselves, the Western response was inadequate. Constantinople fell on 29 May 1453, after a siege of nearly two months, and the last Byzantine emperor, named, with a sad irony, Constantine, died in the fighting. In 1456 Athens was annexed and although Belgrade was held by the Hungarians until 1521, Serbia succumbed in 1459 as did most of the Peloponnese in 1459–60. Trebizond fell in 1461 and Lesbos in 1462. Euboea was taken in 1470 and under

Bayazid II (1481–1512) Lepanto (Návpaktos), Koróni and Methóni in 1499–1500. Under Selim I (1512–20) it was the Muslim Near and Middle East that felt the weight of Turkish assault, but with the accession of Suleiman I (1520–66) the Ottomans turned again on the West and, as has already been described, Rhodes was taken in 1522.

This inexorable advance provides the background to the efforts of the papacy from 1370 onwards. Pope Gregory XI, who came from a family with crusading traditions, had in mind the preaching of a general passage to the Balkans to defeat the Turks; here for the first time the defence of Europe against them came to the fore. But the Anglo-French war made this impossible and the pope therefore tried to unite those powers directly threatened and to encourage them to help themselves. This, of course, meant leagues. Plans for a new one had been hatched in 1369; they were revived in 1373 and 1374, but the proposals foundered on the refusal of the powers involved – Venice, Genoa, Naples, Hungary and Cyprus – to unite. Gregory's attempt to organize a Genoese expedition in 1376 came to nothing and another one forced on him by the Hospitallers in 1378 ended disastrously in Epirus as we have seen.

Crusades engendered by the Great Schism

Then came the Great Schism and from 1378 to 1417 there were two (later three) lines of popes in Rome and Avignon. Europe was split between those adhering to one line or the other – even the Hospitallers on Rhodes were riven with dissension – and a united response to any threat should have been an impossibility. There were, in fact, internal crusades generated by the Schism itself. In the early 1380s England, which backed Urban VI in Rome, was swept by crusading enthusiasm and two expeditions were planned, one under Henry Despenser, the Bishop of Norwich, against the 'Clementists', the supporters of Clement VII in Avignon, wherever they might be found, and the other under John of Gaunt, Duke of Lancaster, against Castile. The French, who were Clementists, controlled Flanders and the crusade of the Bishop of Norwich was a lost cause. It left with massive demonstrations of popular support on 16 May 1383 and, after taking several seaside channel towns, laid siege to Ypres. In early August the approach of a French army caused the siege to be abandoned and the English crusade withdrew. John of Gaunt's campaign, heralded by a ceremony in which his nephew King Richard II recognized him as king of Castile, began on 9 July 1386, when he sailed from England. A year later he had withdrawn to Gascony, having received a rich indemnity in return for his renunciation of the crown.

The crusades of Mahdia and Nicopolis

But more striking than these fiascos were two major ventures which demonstrated that the crusading movement was strong enough to transcend even the

Schism and unite the factions in Latin Christendom. In 1390 the continuing interest manifested itself in an extraordinary scheme, proposed to King Charles VI of France, who supported Pope Clement VII, by the Genoese, who supported Pope Boniface IX, for a crusade against the town of Mahdia in the Hafsid kingdom of Tunisia, which was a centre for what would later be called Barbary corsairs. These pirates had been raiding Genoese shipping; the Genoese, Sicilians and Pisans had already been involved in a major engagement and had occupied the island of Jerba in 1388. Pope Clement VII authorized the crusade, for which there was great enthusiasm in France, even though the king stipulated that knights must equip themselves at their own expense and that the number of *gentilshommes* in the army must not exceed 1,500. Genoa contributed 1,000 crossbowmen and 2,000 men-at-arms in addition to 4,000 sailors. Crusaders also came from England, Spain and the Low Countries. The fact that this venture was seen to transcend the Schism was demonstrated by an order from the high command that no one should refer to it but that in a spirit of fraternity all should unite to defend the Catholic faith. Louis II of Clermont, an experienced soldier, was appointed leader. In July 1390 the French and Genoese fleets made for the island of 'Consigliera', possibly Kuriate, where they halted for nine days. Late in the month they landed on the mainland, but the North Africans had had time to organize resistance and after nine or ten weeks besieging Mahdia both sides were exhausted. The Genoese secretly negotiated a renewal of an earlier treaty they had had with the Tunisians and Louis of Clermont returned to Europe in October with nothing achieved.

Perhaps because it had been a demonstration of Christian unity, perhaps because France and England were once again caught up in a bout of crusading fervour, this curious side-show actually fired more zeal and there now came into being the project of a general passage against the Turks in the Balkans which had been held up since 1370. The governments of France and England, already deeply concerned about the Schism, were actively discussing plans for a crusade to the East from 1392, and early in 1393 a small Anglo-French force was sent to Hungary. In the following year ambassadors from England, Burgundy and France travelled to Hungary and it was in response to them that King Sigismund of Hungary sent embassies to western Europe, the second of them led by the Archbishop of Esztergom to France, to appeal for help. The reaction in France, particularly in Burgundy, was strong and many leading nobles were recruited, including the Counts of Nevers, La Marche and Eu and Henry and Philip of Bar, all cousins of the king. King Charles himself wrote to King Richard of England, suggesting that they both enrol. Large numbers of men also took the cross in Germany. The pope in Rome, Boniface IX, proclaimed the crusade in 1394; he was joined by the pope in

Avignon, Benedict XIII, who granted indulgences to the French crusaders. An army of c. 10,000 men mustered around Sigismund at Buda in the late summer of 1396 before advancing to Orşova and crossing the Danube at the Iron Gate (Portile de Fier). In the second week of September they came before the city of Nicopolis (Nikopol), where they were joined by Venetian and Genoese ships and by a Hospitaller squadron under the master, Philibert of Naillac, which had sailed up the Danube. The Turkish sultan Bayazid was besieging Constantinople when the news of the crusaders' advance reached him. He at once marched to relieve Nicopolis, which he approached on 24 September. On the following day, in one of those futile acts of stupid bravery typical of feudal chivalry in the period of its decline, the French knights, in spite of their inexperience of the enemy or the conditions, insisted on being placed in the front line. They then charged up a hill straight for the Turkish position which was fortified by stakes and, slowed down by these obstacles, they were exhausted by the time they came face to face with the main Muslim body. In the confusion the crusaders began to recoil and this degenerated into a rout during which John of Nevers and many of the leaders were taken prisoner.

Crusading against the Turks, 1397–1413

The downfall of western chivalry at Nicopolis opened the rest of the Balkans to the Turks. In this moment of crisis the Hospitallers accepted the custody of Corinth from the Byzantine despot, Theodore of Mistra, who was even prepared to consider the sale of his entire despotate to them; he bought Corinth back from them in 1404 when the immediate danger had passed. Pope Boniface IX issued crusade encyclicals in favour of Byzantine Constantinople in 1398, 1399 and 1400, although the last of these was suddenly withdrawn, perhaps because the Roman curia had heard that the Byzantine emperor was appealing to his rival in Avignon. King Charles of France turned to John Boucicaut, who had been captured at Nicopolis and had been ransomed. He set sail in late June 1399 with 400 men-at-arms, 400 'varlets' and some archers. Joined by ships from Genoa, Venice, Rhodes and Lesbos he broke the Turkish blockade of Constantinople and with his substantial fleet of twenty-one galleys, three large transports and six other vessels pillaged the coasts in Turkish hands. After relieving Constantinople he brought the Byzantine emperor back to the West with him to appeal for help.

Eastern Europe was only saved by the Mongol Timur's invasion of Anatolia, which put back Turkish expansion for a while. In the wake of Timur's campaign and the temporary eclipse of Turkish power there was a revival of Christian activity. John Boucicaut, who had been appointed governor of Genoa, arrived at Rhodes with a Genoese fleet of ten galleys and six large transports in June 1403, with the intention of enforcing

Genoese claims in Cyprus but also raiding the Muslim coastline. He ravaged the port area of Alanya and then, unable to reach Alexandria because of contrary winds, he and the Hospitallers attacked Tripoli, pillaged Batroun and sacked Beirut: most of the loot appears to have been Venetian merchandise. After an unsuccessful descent on Sidon he returned to Genoa, fighting a sea-battle with the Venetians on the way. In 1407 he may have been planning a new attack on Egypt.

The Hussite crusades

The restoration of Turkish power after 1413 and the ending of the Great Schism in the West meant a revival of crusading plans. In 1420 Pope Martin V tried without much success to organize a crusade in aid of the Latins in the Peloponnese and in 1422, when Constantinople was being besieged by the Turks, he tried to arrange a league of Hospitallers, Venetians, Genoese and Milanese to go to its assistance. The problem at this time was that the western empire was caught up in the Hussite Crusades, the last great series of crusades against heretics. Although John Hus, who had criticized the granting of crusade indulgences by Pope John XXIII to those who waged war on King Ladislas of Naples, had been burned for heresy in 1415 on the judgement of the Council of Constance, Hussite strength in Bohemia was growing and the Hussite demands – communion in both kinds, bread and wine, the public suppression of sin, particularly among the clergy, with the threat of non-clerical jurisdiction in the field of morals, the freedom of preaching and a review of the Church's temporal possessions – were sharpened by their association with Czech nationalism at a time when the emperor-elect, Sigismund, was laying claim to the throne of Bohemia. In 1418 Pope Martin, who seems to have been particularly determined throughout, charged one of his cardinals with the preparation of a crusade. In March 1420 Sigismund held an imperial diet at Breslau (Wrocław) during which the papal legate publicly read the pope's proclamation of a crusade against Wyclifites, Hussites and their supporters. Early in May Sigismund led an army of c. 20,000 men into Bohemia, but many of them deserted and he suffered a series of defeats at the hands of the Hussites under their able leader Jan Žižka. But a feature of these crusades was the energy with which they were organized. By the time Sigismund was pulling out in March 1421 another crusade was being prepared. Two armies entered Bohemia, although they had withdrawn before Sigismund re-entered Hussite territory in the following October, only to be comprehensively defeated and forced out in January 1422. In the next autumn two more armies marched; they had withdrawn within months. A fourth crusade invaded Bohemia in July 1427, but it dissolved in panic after an engagement near Tachov and suffered huge losses, after which the Hussites themselves advanced into German territory. An extraordinary scheme to raise an English crusade in 1428–9 under Cardinal Henry Beaufort, who had been legate on the crusade of 1427, ended with Henry's army, financed with crusade taxes, being put at the disposal of the Duke of Bedford in France and being swallowed up in the French war. Against this background of failure a great imperial diet took place at Nuremberg in February and March 1431 and planned yet another crusade. In the summer three armies mobilized. One concentrated on re-taking those German territories which had been lost, the second, under Albert of Austria, raided Moravia, but the third, under Frederick of Brandenburg, was annihilated by the Hussites on 14 August. These five Hussite crusades, which included in their ranks participants from many parts of Europe, were almost the most futile of the whole movement; in the end the Hussites were brought under some measure of control by the Bohemian nobles themselves, although they were still worrying the papacy in the 1460s. But they point to the future. Sigismund had been the king of Hungary who had been the instigator of the Crusade of Nicopolis. If anyone had firsthand knowledge of the Turkish threat it was he. And yet he was prepared to divert energy and resources into an internal struggle within Christendom. This helps to explain why a century later, in spite of the Turkish menace, crusading would falter when the Latin Christian world was to be much more seriously divided by the Reformation and the ensuing wars of religion.

The crusade of Varna

By 1440 Turkish power was even more threatening. At the same time the union of the Catholic and Orthodox churches, for which the papacy had been working hard, looked promising. On 1 January 1443 Pope Eugenius IV issued a new encyclical, calling on all the faithful to defend the Christian East against the Turks. There was little response except in Poland, Wallachia, Burgundy and Hungary, where John Hunyadi, the ruler of Transylvania, had been engaged in heroic resistance. He and King Ladislas of Hungary planned a great expedition for the summer of 1443. They were joined by crusaders, routed the Turks at Niš and entered Sofia, after which they withdrew. The Balkans were now up in arms and although the king of Hungary may have been induced to pledge himself to a ten-year truce with the Turks in June 1444, he had already sworn to renew the war against them. A Hungarian and crusader army of c. 20,000 men advanced through Bulgaria and besieged the coastal town of Varna. At the same time a new naval league – twenty-four galleys provided by the pope, Duke Philip of Burgundy, Venice, Dubrovnik (Ragusa) and the Byzantine empire – sailed for the Dardanelles. The Turkish sultan Murad hurried to Varna's relief with a much larger army, some of it transported, it was rumoured, in Genoese ships, and on 10 November destroyed the Christians in a battle in which Ladislas of Hungary and the papal legate were killed.

Reactions to the loss of Constantinople

Varna paved the way for the final onslaught on the Byzantine empire. The news of the fall of Constantinople on 29 May 1453 was a sensation and the remaining Christian settlements in the Aegean were thrown into a state of terror: in November 1455 the pope was persuaded to grant plenary indulgences to the defenders of Genoese Chios. One result was seventy years of intense activity and propaganda on the part of the papal curia and Professor Setton has pointed out that the recovery of Constantinople became an ideal similar to the liberation of Jerusalem in earlier periods. The news reached Rome in early July 1453 and on 30 September Pope Nicholas V issued a new crusade encyclical and sent appeals to the courts of western Europe; for the first time printing-presses in Germany were used to advertise the crusade and print indulgences and propaganda. On 17 February 1454 Duke Philip the Good of Burgundy and his Knights of the Golden Fleece swore to take the cross at a magnificent feast in Lille during which a live pheasant, decked with jewelry, was brought to the table; among the side-shows an elephant was depicted carrying the Holy Church appealing for aid. A few weeks later there opened the first of a series of crusade assemblies in Germany, marked by intrigue and divisions of opinion, which in 1455 concluded by postponing the crusade for a year when the news of the pope's death in March reached the participants.

But the new pope, Calixtus III, was even more committed than his predecessor had been: he was reported to be 'always talking, always thinking about the expedition'. On 15 May 1455 he confirmed Nicholas's encyclical and he set 1 March 1456 as the date of the crusade's departure. Legates and preachers, especially recruited from among the Franciscans, were sent throughout Europe and a commission of cardinals under the Greek Bessarion oversaw planning. On 14 Feburary 1456 the great preacher St John of Capistrano took the cross at Buda and was empowered to preach the crusade: he was said to have recruited 27,000 men in Hungary alone. A major Turkish threat was developing against Belgrade. John himself led a force of 2,500 men to the town where he was joined by other Hungarian crusaders under John Hunyadi, who broke the Muslim blockade. In an extraordinary engagement a huge Turkish army was forced by inferior Christian forces to withdraw on 22 July. The Turks left their equipment in their disorderly flight and John of Capistrano went so far as to claim that the time had now come to recover Jerusalem and the Holy Land. In the following summer a papal fleet of sixteen galleys occupied Samothráki, Thásos and Limnos (Lemnos), for the defence of which Pope Pius II was later to found a new Military Order, of Our Lady of Bethlehem, and captured more than twenty-five Turkish ships at Mitilíni.

The stand at Belgrade and the razzia in the Aegean were not enough to stop the Turks, of course. And the European powers were not prepared to sink their differences and give full-hearted backing to a crusade, as the experiences of Calixtus's successor Pius II show. Pius was another enthusiast and had been a fervent supporter of the crusade from the start. Almost his first act as pope was to summon a crusade congress to Mantua. This dragged on for eight months, largely because the envoys of Germany and France, who were anyway inadequately empowered, arrived so late, but by Christmas 1459 a total of 80,000 men had been promised. On 14 January 1460 a three-year crusade against the Turks was proclaimed. But by March 1462 Pius was very nearly in despair:

> If we think of convening a council, Mantua teaches us that the idea is vain. If we send envoys to ask aid of sovereigns, they are laughed at. If we impose tithes on the clergy, they appeal to a future council. If we issue indulgences and encourage the contribution of money by spiritual gifts, we are accused of avarice. People think our sole object is to amass gold. No one believes what we say. Like insolvent tradesmen we are without credit (Pius II, *Commentaries* in *Memoirs of a Renaissance Pope*, tr. F. A. Gragg (abridged edn 1960), p. 237).

In fact, apart from a declaration of war on the Turks by Venice, the results of all the papal diplomatic activity were nugatory.

Pius, however, was determined that there should be a crusade and, like Gregory X two centuries before, he wanted to lead it himself, doing battle as a priest 'with the power of speech, not the sword'. He took the cross on 18 June 1464 in St Peter's and left Rome on the same day for Ancona, where he expected to be joined by a Venetian fleet. Some companies of Spanish, German and French crusaders arrived, but plague broke out and he died on 15 August, three days after the doge of Venice with twelve galleys had reached Ancona.

With the fall of the island of Euboea, Venice's chief naval station after Crete, the newly elected Pope Sixtus IV published a new crusade encyclical on 31 December 1471 and hurriedly went into league with Venice and Naples, spending more than 144,000 florins on a papal squadron under Cardinal Oliviero Carafa. The league's fleet, a really large one which comprised some eighty-seven galleys and fifteen transports, assembled off Rhodes in the late summer of 1472 and attacked Antalya and Smyrna, burning the latter town to the ground. Pieces of the chain from the entrance to Antalya's harbour were brought back in triumph and can be seen to this day in St. Peter's, over the door leading to the Archives of the Basilica to the right of the sacristy.

When it came, the Turkish response was startling and a remarkable display of the power now at the sultanate's disposal. In 1480 the Turks besieged Rhodes and at the same time their forces landed in Italy itself, near Otranto, which fell to them on 11 August. They had established a beach-head in western Europe and Sixtus, who even contemplated flight to Avignon, at once appealed for aid. He followed this by issuing a crusade encyclical on 8 April 1481, but on 3 May the great sultan Mehmed II died and on 10 September Otranto surrendered to Christian forces.

The conquest of Granada and the invasion of North Africa

In the midst of all this flurry of crusade propaganda the Reconquest in Spain, which had been dormant for over a century, was renewed. Since 1344 it had had a low priority in the minds of kings and frontier-fighting had been left to local nobles. In 1475 Pope Sixtus had gone as far as appropriating half of the *tercias reales*, which had long since ceased to be used for conquest, for the wars against the Turks. But with the union of Aragon and Castile in the persons of Ferdinand and Isabella in 1479 and the resurgence of crusading ideas that had followed the loss of Constantinople the Spanish court began to seethe with fervour. The paraphernalia of crusading – papal encyclicals and crusade privileges – were in evidence and the war was pursued with a remarkable single-mindedness at the expense of almost all Spain's other interests. The Christians were helped by the fact that Granada, which by seizing Zahara provided a *casus belli,* was torn by dissension set off by the rebellion of the king's son in 1482. Alhama fell to the Christians in that year and the western half of the kingdom, comprising Zahara, Alora, Setenil, Benameji and Ronda, was occupied between 1483 and 1486. Malaga was taken in 1487 and Baza, Alméria and Guadix in 1488–9. Ferdinand and Isabella laid siege to Granada itself in April 1490 and when their camp was destroyed they replaced it with a town, Santa Fe, the building of which demoralized the Muslim defenders. Granada surrendered on 2 January 1492 and the Spanish king and queen entered it on the 6th. On 4 February the Vatican and Castel St Angelo in Rome were illuminated with torches and bonfires and on the next day a solemn procession of thanksgiving was held and the first bullfights in Rome were organized by Cardinal Rodrigo Borgia. It was said somewhat grandiloquently that the taking of Granada offset the loss of Constantinople and it was assumed that this would be a prelude to the liberation of North Africa. In fact the invasion of Africa began in 1497 with the occupation of Melilla. This was followed by a remarkable series of conquests, authorized by the popes and even justified by the ancient idea of reaching the Holy Land by way of the African coast: Mers el-Kebir in 1505, Gomera (Canary Islands) in 1508, Oran in 1509 and the Rock of Algiers, Bejaïa (Bougie) and Tripoli in 1510. These Spanish beach-heads were to be the scenes of grim fighting, as we shall see.

Crusade plans, 1484–1522

But the Spanish advance in the far West was the only concrete result of all the papal efforts in spite of the curia's continuing commitment to the movement. The capitulations agreed by the cardinals before proceeding to the election of Pope Innocent VIII on 29 August 1484 included the pledge to summon a general council to reform the Church and initiate a new crusade, an old programme that was to be revived in the sixteenth century. As soon as Innocent had been elected the curia began to make plans, but it was not until 1490 that the political situation in western Europe began to look favourable; and that was deceptive. A congress to discuss a crusade was opened in Rome in March and was attended by representatives of all the major powers except Venice. It put forward very detailed proposals for two land armies, one comprising German, Hungarian, Bohemian and Polish crusaders, the other French, Spanish, Portuguese, Navarrese, Scottish and English, and a fleet, to be provided by the Holy See and the Italian states, the whole campaign being under the general command of the western Emperor Frederick III or his son Maximilian, the King of the Romans. One army was to attack the Turks on the Hungarian frontier while the other landed in Albania. The fleet would operate in the Aegean. The Turkish prince Jem, who was now being held by the papacy, was to accompany the crusade: everyone seems to have been convinced that his presence would be a major political bonus. No crusade resulted from these ambitious proposals – although plenary indulgences were given to those who went to the defence of Hungary in 1493 – and they were overtaken by the French invasion of Italy in 1494. But crusading was so much in the air that King Charles VIII of France, who was asserting his claims to the throne of Naples, seems to have been genuinely absorbed in the dream that his conquest of southern Italy would be a prelude to an invasion of Greece in the company of Jem, whom he collected in Rome. Jem soon died, the crusade plans faded away and although Charles entered Naples in triumph on 22 February 1495 and was crowned king on 12 May the hostility of Venice and Milan made it impossible for him to stay. He withdrew to France in November.

In 1499 news of extensive Turkish preparations reached Italy. It was feared that an attack on Rhodes was imminent, but in fact the assault fell on the Venetian possessions in Greece. Lepanto fell in August and Methóni, Pilos (Navarino) and Koróni a year later. Pope Alexander VI commissioned studies on the crusade and Europe seemed to be again aroused, with Henry VII of England expressing real concern. The pope tried to assemble another congress and on 1 June 1500 he issued a new crusade encyclical. Quite substantial sums were raised from a three-year crusade tenth and in the spring of 1502 a papal squadron of thirteen galleys sailed to supplement the Venetian fleet. But France and Spain were at each other's throats over the kingdom of Naples and the next few years were taken up with much talk and little action. Pope Julius II and Pope Leo X were indefatigable planners and propagandists, but the constant warring in Italy, the French invasions and the League of Cambrai against Venice nullified their efforts. Henry VII of England, Manuel of Portugal and James of Scotland pressed for a new crusade, while at one time or another Ferdinand of Spain and Louis XII of France were prepared to commit themselves to the enterprise. Crusading was discussed at the first, sixth, eighth, tenth and twelfth sessions of the Fifth Lateran Council between 1512 and 1517, with the stress on the old association of reform and crusade. Pope Leo X issued an encyclical for eastern Europeans in 1513 and a crusade army was certainly being raised in the following year. He pressed the political powers on the need to resolve their differences: in 1516 he even summoned the French to a crusade under their king, Francis I, whom he had persuaded to take personal leadership.

Then in 1516 and 1517 came the Ottoman conquests of Syria and Egypt. There is no doubt that public opinion was aroused and that people were terrified. The papal curia responded with a further burst of activity. On 11 November 1517 a special crusade indulgence was issued and the pope established a commission of eight cardinals which, after stressing the need for a general armistice in Europe, to be guaranteed by solemn oaths taken by all the princes in a sworn alliance entitled the *Fraternitas sanctae cruciatae*, proposed the raising of an army of 60,000 infantry, 4,000 knights and 12,000 light cavalry, together with a fleet. One force should land at Durazzo while the other advanced on Thrace from the north. The pope himself would accompany the crusade. Copies of this memorandum were sent to the western kings. The responses of King Francis of France and the Emperor Maximilian underlined their conviction that peace in western Europe was a prerequisite. On 6 march 1518 the pope declared a five-year truce in Europe and sent prominent cardinals as legates to secure the adherence of all the powers. So concerned were people at this time that it really looked as though the pope's appeal would be heeded. France, the Empire and Venice agreed to the five-year truce and in October France and England made the Treaty of London, establishing a defensive union which other powers could join. The pope ratified it on 31 December and King Charles of Spain a fortnight later: the Field of the Cloth of Gold in June 1520 was a demonstration of this new alliance. Plans for raising money and military forces went ahead. But with the news of Sultan Selim I's death in 1520 the preparations faltered and the crusade passed out of the limelight. The Christian princes were not to know that Selim's successor Suleiman was to be just as formidable a conqueror and they turned their minds to their political interests nearer home, the rival claims for the Empire and Naples of Charles of Spain and Francis of France; and the Lutheran revolt in Germany.

The inability of the popes and the Roman curia, in spite of continuing enthusiasm and tremendous efforts over seventy years, to unite the West behind a crusade reminds one of the periods 1150–87 and 1272–91. The nature of inter-state politics and the chaos into which Italy fell from 1494 onwards made it impossible to persuade the princes to sink their differences for long enough. They could always be convinced that a dispute with a neighbour or a righteous claim was more important than the Turkish threat to Europe. The question arises whether the crusading movement was now in serious decline. In so far as it was associated with the papacy and the papacy was no longer respected or really trusted it seems that in Germany and perhaps also in France papal appeals no longer met with a ready response. One can exaggerate this – there was still real enthusiasm in certain sections of society in both countries – but I discern an ebbing of the ideal in those regions distant from the Mediterranean region and eastern Europe, where the popes and the powers which had to face the Turks were still quite highly committed.

CHAPTER 10

The Old Age and Death of the Crusading Movement, 1523–1798

The Reformation

After the seventy years of intense effort in Rome following the fall of Constantinople, pressure for crusading seems to have relaxed in the third decade of the sixteenth century as the curia was distracted by the French and imperial invasions of Italy, and by anxiety about the activities of the reformers as the Lutheran revolt in Germany began to gain momentum. Pope Adrian VI's reaction to the news of the fall of Belgrade in 1521 and Rhodes in 1522 had been to declare a three-year truce in Europe to allow the mustering of forces to fight the Ottomans: King Francis of France was reminded by the Sacred College that the glory of his house rested not on wars with its neighbours but on the part it had played in crusades against the infidel. But the project collapsed in the face of yet another French assault on Italy. Adrian's successor, Clement VII, set out to organize a pan-European league against the Turks and it was no doubt with reference to this that Francis and Charles V expressed their desire for a 'general crusade' to be summoned by the pope in their treaty of Madrid in 1526. On 26 August of that year a Hungarian army under King Louis II was destroyed by the Ottomans in the Battle of Mohács and the king was killed. It is not surprising that the pope was still discussing the formation of a crusade league as an imperialist threat to Italy grew; and during the German occupation of Rome in 1527 Charles V's agents demanded of him the summoning of a general council to reform the Church and extirpate Lutheranism, and linked these aims with the preparation of 'the most desired expedition against the infidels'. This very conventional programme was proposed again in the abortive plans for a council at Mantua in 1537 and yet again in the summons to the Council of Trent (Trento) in 1544, which was convoked to resolve those matters

> which relate to the removal of religious discord, the reform of Christian behaviour and the launching of an expedition under the most sacred sign of the cross against the infidel (*Concilium Tridentinum*, ed. S. Ehses, for Görres-Gesellschaft, vol. 4 (1914), p. 387).

This agenda differed from those of the councils of the thirteenth century only in its reference to Protestantism.

The fact was that Catholics tended to believe that the Protestants were at least as dangerous as the Turks, if not more so. In February 1524 Pope Clement VII was expressing anxiety about both the Turkish threat to Hungary and the activities of Martin Luther, and two years later, as we have seen, a proposal for a 'general crusade' was incorporated into the treaty of Madrid between Charles V and Francis I with the aim of 'the repelling and ruin . . . of the infidels and the extirpation of the errors of the Lutheran sect'. In 1551 Pope Julius III threatened King Henry II of France with a crusade for aiding the Protestants as well as the Turks and in 1566 King Philip II of Spain's spokesman stated that the Turks were less of a menace than the 'internal evil' of heretics and rebels. This was typical: we have seen over and over again that internal threats, from heretics, schismatics or political opponents of the Church, were almost invariably treated more seriously by the popes, and indeed by the majority of Latin Christians, than external ones. If the Aragonese in Sicily had been able to cause the diversion of crusade resources on the eve of the fall of Latin Palestine, it is not surprising that the rise of the Protestants threatened to paralyze resistance to the Turks.

Protestant doctrines spread rapidly and by the end of the century a significant minority of western Christians were lost to Catholicism and therefore to the crusading movement. Many of the reformers, Luther in particular, were quite happy with the idea of righteous wars: the Lutheran princes and estates voted the emperor grants of supplies to fight the Turks; and in Protestant England a Form of Thanksgiving was said thrice weekly in the churches for six weeks after the successful defence of Malta in 1565. The Huguenot captain, Francis of La Noue, spent his time in prison in the early 1580s writing his *Discours politiques et militaires* which contained a project for a modified *passagium generale*, without an indulgence, to recover Constantinople. He hoped this would unite Christendom and end the religious wars. But the Protestants naturally rejected the notion of a holy war under the aegis of the pope and the appeal of crusading must have faded rapidly among them, although in the following centuries they were still occasionally to be found serving with the Hospitallers on Malta.

The Military Orders were, in fact, seriously weakened. The North German Hospitallers, who had already carved out for themselves a separate province in 1382, adopted Lutheranism and formed a Protestant bailiwick which eventually bought itself freedom from the grand magistry on Malta and remained in being as a Lutheran institution. In Denmark the Order also survived for a time as a Lutheran establishment, but then gradually ceased to function. In England, Norway and Sweden it was dissolved and its property was confiscated, although it was briefly revived in England under Queen Mary. In Scotland the last Hospitaller commander, James Sandilands, converted to Protestantism and was granted the Order's lands as a secular barony in 1564. A similar fate befell the Teutonic Knights. In 1525 the grand master, Albert of Brandenburg, adopted Lutheranism and was enfeoffed by the King of Poland as hereditary Duke of Prussia. In 1562 the last master of Livonia, Gotthard Kettler, also became a Lutheran duke. The Order survived only in southern Germany to play a part in the Hapsburg wars against the Turks and Protestants.

The Reformation obviously debilitated Christian resistance to the Turks, but, although the Ottomans were still a potent and terrifying force, their advance was becoming more spasmodic, at least on the eastern land frontier, where rapid moves were followed by intervals of relative peace. But by 1541 the Turkish frontier had been established in central Europe with its capital at Buda. Vienna was besieged in 1529 and again in 1683. In the Mediterranean the Turks were mopping up the islands and remaining mainland holdings of the Latin Christians. Naŭplion and Monemvasia were surrendered in 1540, Chios fell in 1566 and Cyprus in 1570–71, although Malta, an important link in the Christian defensive line from central Europe to North Africa, fought them off in 1565. Crete was to fall in 1669. And a grim battle raged in North Africa where the local Muslims recognized Ottoman overlordship and gained Turkish support in their struggle with the Spaniards. By 1578 the Christians had been pushed into the far west.

It was understandable for the Christian powers to try to limit the damage through diplomacy as well as meeting the Turks head on: Venice went as far as to congratulate Suleiman on his capture of Rhodes and his victory at Mohács, and she and the empire, which were bearing the heaviest losses, had to be prepared to make truces with Constantinople. France, on the other hand, allied herself with the Turks as part of a strategy to protect herself against the power of Charles V, although it is fair to say that the entente of 1536, reinforced by Selim II's capitulations of 1569, put her in the position to act as protector of Catholic merchants and pilgrims travelling in the Ottoman empire and her rôle in this respect was to prove beneficial. More surprising was the attitude of Pope Paul IV (1555–9), whose obsession with heresy left him with little time for crusades, although he threatened Charles V and Philip II, whom he feared and hated, with one. He even considered an alliance with the Turks against the Hapsburgs; this was among the charges for which his nephew Cardinal Carlo Carafa, who, incidentally, had been a Hospitaller, was later sentenced to death.

North Africa

Crusading was now confined to three zones. One of these was North Africa, where Spanish beach-heads had been established along the northern coast as centres of conversion and as bases for the mastering of the shoreline. The vast conquests in the Americas absorbed much of the energy of Castilian society – there is, in fact, evidence that crusading ideas were transferred across the Atlantic – but the efforts and resources put into the struggle for North Africa were striking. The Spanish crusading movement was a national enterprise under royal control, as we have seen, and it was self-reliant enough to be less affected by events elsewhere in Europe than was crusading to the East, but sooner or later it was bound to come up against the Turks, who had been casting their eyes westward since their occupation of Egypt.

An early leader of resistance to the Spaniards was a man called Aruj Barbarossa, a native of Lesbos and possibly originally a Greek, who took control of Miliana, Médéa, Ténès and Tlemcen. He was killed in 1518, but his younger brother Khair ad-Din Barbarossa took over, subjected the territories he ruled to the Turks and with their help took Collo, 'Annaba (Bône), Constantine, Cherchell and in 1529 the Rock of Algiers, which became his base. He soon built a reputation for himself as one of the most feared pirate captains in the western Mediterranean, leading large fleets of freebooters on raids as far as Italy. He was such a menace that in 1533 the imperial envoys treating with the Ottoman government on the exchange for Hungary of Koróni, which had been retaken by the Christians in 1532, wanted the Turks to include in the bargain the surrender of the Rock of Algiers to the Spaniards.

In August 1534 Khair ad-Din occupied Tunis, providing himself with a base of operations uncomfortably close to southern Italy. The Emperor Charles V's response was to organize an expedition to take it. A crusade was preached and indulgences were offered. The Emperor himself took command under 'the Crucified Saviour' and like many crusaders before him made a preliminary pilgrimage, in his case to Montserrat to invoke the aid of the Blessed Virgin Mary. Pope Paul III sent money and six galleys; the Hospitallers sent four; the Portuguese provided galleons and caravels. On 16 June 1535 a fleet of 74 galleys and 330 other ships disembarked an army under the Emperor's command not far from the spot where St Louis had landed in 1270. In a great crusading victory, which Charles claimed freed 20,000 Christian captives, the fortress of La Goulette was taken on 14 July, most of the Barbary fleet was captured, Khair ad-Din's troops were defeated and on the 21st Tunis was sacked. The lock and bolts of its gate were sent to St Peter's in Rome where Charles enjoyed an imperial triumph. Khair ad-Din withdrew, by way of Mahón on Minorca which he ravaged, to Algiers. He went on to become a Turkish admiral and the scourge of Christians throughout the Mediterranean region before his death in 1546.

In October 1541 Charles led the forces of his empire on an assault on

Algiers, which was unsuccessful because a gale scattered his fleet and convinced him that he could not properly supply the army he had landed: it is worth noting that among those with him who tried to persuade him to persist with the enterprise was Hernando Cortes, the conqueror of Mexico. Then in June 1550 Charles sent a fleet to besiege Mahdia which had been the goal of Louis of Clermont's crusade in 1390. It had recently become the base of Khair ad-Din's successor as the leading Barbary corsair, a native of Asia Minor called Turghud Ali (Dragut). The Christians took the town on 8 September, although Turghud Ali slipped away. The sultan appointed him governor of Tripoli, which had been given to the Hospitallers in 1530 but was surrendered by them to the Turks on 14 August 1551.

The Hospitallers, whose reputation had not been enhanced by their lacklustre defence of the place – 200 of them had surrendered – pressed King Philip II of Spain to re-occupy it. Pope Paul IV granted crusade indulgences which were renewed by Pope Pius IV and in February 1560 a fleet of at least forty-seven galleys, provided by Spain, Genoa, Florence, Naples, Sicily, the papacy and the Hospitallers, together with forty-three other ships, carried an army of 11–12,000 men – Italians, Spaniards, Germans, Frenchmen, Hospitallers and Maltese – to the island of Jerba at the southern entrance of the Gulf of Gabès and took possession of its fortress on 13 March as a first step towards the recapture of Tripoli to the east. The Christians knew that there would be a Turkish counter-stroke and they worked hard to improve the fortifications, although many of them were being struck down with typhus. In May the bulk of the army began to re-embark, planning to leave behind a garrison of 2,200 Spaniards, Italians and Germans, but there was no time to complete an orderly embarkation before a Turkish armada was upon it. On the 11th the Christian fleet was destroyed with the loss of twenty-seven galleys. The garrison of Jerba had very little water because the two cisterns in the castle were almost dry, but it managed to produce about thirty barrels a day through distillation. By 27 July it had run out of the wood needed to heat the stills and many men were dying of thirst and scurvy. The siege was over by the 31st. Many of the defenders, including the wounded, were massacred; 7,000 prisoners, of whom 5,000 had been captured in the destruction of the fleet, were taken to Constantinople.

In general Spain and Portugal were more concerned about North Africa than the eastern Mediterranean and the papacy understood this. By this time the Spanish Military Orders of Calatrava, Santiago and Alcántara had been converted into Orders of Chivalry, incorporated under the crown, with their knights permitted to marry – those of Santiago had always been allowed to wed – and their rôle, it has been written, was now 'one of social orientation and definition'. But Pope Pius V (1566–72) ordered the Portuguese Military Orders to take up position on the North African frontier and even decreed that no brother could be professed until he had served for three years there; he wanted to establish a seminary in Africa for the training of young brother knights. In the period leading up to the Battle of Lepanto in 1571 Spain was persuaded to subordinate its interests in favour of naval campaigns in the East, but this did not alter the fact that Tunis, which Charles V had restored to a dependent Muslim ruler in 1535, posed a constant threat to the Christian outpost at La Goulette. In 1569 Tunis was occupied by Uluj-Ali, another Algerian corsair and Ottoman admiral who, incidentally, was to be the loser at Lepanto, and this convinced the Spaniards that something must be done. With the collapse of the Holy League, which will be described below, Don John of Austria took Tunis with hardly a fight on 11 October 1573 and went on to capture Bizerte. The Turkish response was immediate. On 13 May 1574 an enormous fleet of 240 galleys left Constantinople for the Barbary coast. After a month's siege La Goulette was taken on 25 August and Tunis was recaptured on 13 September. The Turks now strengthened their grip on the North African coast and began to press on the Christian holdings in Morocco, assisting their own candidate for the sharifate to take Fez in 1576. The Spanish government began to look secretly for peace with them, but King Sebastian of Portugal, a romantic figure who was obsessed with the idea of crusading, launched himself into what may have been the last true crusade, fortified with indulgences and accompanied by papal legates. He landed at Asilah and led an army of 15,000 foot and 1,500 horse past Larache – Portuguese, Spaniards, Germans, Netherlanders and a papal force originally destined for Ireland under the command of the Englishman Sir Thomas Stukeley – together with several thousand non-combatants. By 3 August 1578 he had reached Ksar el-Kebir (Alcácer-Quivir), but he was now out of touch with his fleet and out of provisions. On the 4th he was faced by a greatly superior Moroccan army and in the ensuing battle 'of the Three Kings', Sebastian, the Ottoman puppet sharif and his predecessor, to whom Sebastian was allied, all succumbed. Stukeley and some 8,000 Christians were also killed; nearly 15,000 were taken prisoner.

The eastern theatre

The two other theatres of war, Hungary and the eastern Mediterranean, were linked strategically and so can be treated together. It is surprising how much activity there was in the Mediterranean in spite of the fact that the papacy and the western European powers were becoming increasingly hamstrung by the growth of Protestantism. In the autumn of 1529 the sultan Suleiman laid siege to Vienna for three weeks and anxiety about his advance impelled Pope Clement VII and the emperor Charles V into an alliance; Francis I of France, who had been at war with Charles, was forced to make peace. As far as the pope was concerned, therefore, a threat to the heart of Europe had brought into existence the general peace for which he had been striving. Now at last Christian arms could be turned against the Turks. On 2 February 1530, three weeks before the emperor was crowned by Clement in Bologna, the representatives of a dozen states, mostly Italian but also including the empire and Hungary, were asked by the pope to secure the necessary authority to commit their masters to a 'general expedition against the infidels'. Clement authorized crusade-preaching in the empire and for the next two years worked hard to get an expedition going, but his efforts were nullified by hostility between France and the empire and the Lutheran problem.

Charles V's triumph at Tunis revived the hopes for a crusade to the East. In January 1536 Pope Paul III assured King Sigismund I of Poland that he was working for the recovery of Constantinople and in the middle of September 1537 a Veneto-papal league was formed and a commission of cardinals was appointed to plan a campaign, although this coincided with an extraordinary alliance between France and the Turks to attack Italy, which in the event was a failure because their moves were not synchronized. In February 1538 Charles V joined the league. If it was successful he was to become emperor in Constantinople and the Hospitallers were to get back Rhodes. He was to pay half the expenses, the Venetians two-sixths and the papacy one-sixth. The pope, moreover, managed to persuade France and the empire to sign a ten-year truce. But in September the league's fleet was defeated by a Turkish navy under Khair ad-Din's command off Préveza at the entrance to the Gulf of Arta. The pope, who intended, he said, to go on crusade himself, encouraged Charles to take up arms again in the following spring, but the league faded away and in 1540 Venice made peace with the Turks, paying an indemnity of 300,000 ducats and ceding Navplion and Monemvasia, her last fortresses in the Peloponnese. She was not to recover any important holdings in continental Greece until 1685.

The disaster at Préveza put paid to crusading in the eastern Mediterranean for some time. There was activity in North Africa, as we have seen, but in the late 1550s Pope Paul IV was not interested and although Pius IV was more conventional – he said he would like to accompany the expedition of another league, for there was no more glorious way to die than on a crusade – the imperial government was anxious for peace on its eastern frontier: truces, interspersed, it is true, with war, were arranged with the Ottomans in 1545, 1547, 1554, 1562, 1565 and 1568. By the late 1560s, however, it was clear that the Turks were preparing to seize Venetian Cyprus. On 25 March 1570 their demands for its surrender reached Venice. The Republic, which had sought to avoid committing itself to an alliance with Spain which would involve it in the defence of the Spanish possessions in North Africa, now turned in desperation to King Philip II. A large fleet of papal, Genoese, Venetian, Sicilian and Neapolitan ships was hurriedly assembled, but after reaching Rhodes it withdrew to Crete on hearing of the fall of Nicosia. The Turks had landed on Cyprus on 1 July. Nicosia fell on 9 September 1570. Famagusta surrendered after a heroic defence on 5 August 1571.

On the previous 25 May a Holy League of the papacy, Spain and Venice had been formed after intense diplomatic efforts. As in 1538 Spain would pay half the costs, Venice two-sixths and Pope Pius V one-sixth. The Venetians would assist in the defence of Spanish North Africa. This was to be a perpetual alliance, committed to annual campaigns in the eastern Mediterranean and Don John of Austria, Charles V's bastard son and so Philip of Spain's half-brother, was to be its first commander-in-chief. John reached Naples on 9 August 1571 and was ceremonially presented with the standard which was to fly over his ship: an enormous embroidery of the crucifixion, embellished with the arms of the three allies. His command, the largest fleet assembled by the Christians in the sixteenth century, provided by the allies and also by Savoy, Genoa and the Hospitallers, consisted of 209 galleys, 6 galleases, 27 large ships and many smaller ones, carrying 30,000 men, 28,000 of whom were professional infantry. It set sail on 16 September from Messina with the aim of engaging a Turkish armada of 275 vessels which had been cruising destructively in the southern Aegean and the Adriatic. Battle was joined on 7 October at the point near Lepanto where the Gulfs of Corinth and Patras (Pátrai) meet. John had more heavy cannon, his gunners were better trained and the Turks were overwhelmed by the Christian gun-fire. Their losses were immense and were said to include 30,000 men killed or captured, 117 galleys taken and 80 vessels destroyed. Lepanto is not regarded nowadays as the watershed it once was, but the effect, however short-lived, on Christian morale can scarcely be exaggerated: in a sermon that was printed and widely circulated the French humanist, Mark-Anthony Muret, declared that the Christians must now push on to Judaea and liberate the Holy Sepulchre. In the Catholic Church the anniversary is still celebrated as the Feast of Our Lady of the Rosary.

The Holy League was reaffirmed on 10 February 1572. Pope Pius made great efforts to extend its membership and on 12 March he issued a long brief addressed to all the faithful, in which he renewed the crusade in terms that would have been familiar to Pope Innocent III nearly four centuries before:

> We admonish, require and exhort every individual to decide to aid this most holy war either in person or with material support. . . . To those who do not go personally but send suitable men at their expense according to their means and station in life . . . and to those similarly

who go personally but at another's expense and put up with the labours
and peril of war . . . we grant most full and complete pardon, remission
and absolution of all their sins, of which they have made oral confession
with contrite hearts, the same indulgence which the Roman pontiffs, our
predecessors, were accustomed to concede to crusaders going to the aid
of the Holy Land. We receive the goods of those going to war . . . under
the protection of St Peter and ourselves (Pius V, cited by K. M. Setton,
The Papacy and the Levant, vol. 4 (1984), p. 1076, note 126).

A large advance fleet engaged the Turks in early August; the encounters
were inconclusive, although they again demonstrated the superiority of
Christian gunnery. Joined by John of Austria and with the number of
vessels swelled to 195 galleys, 8 galleasses, 25 galleots and 25 other ships,
the Christians then tried to take Methóni and Pilos in the Peloponnese. But
they failed and in spite of the efforts of the papacy the Holy League
dissolved in 1573 with the Venetians making peace with the Ottomans and
the Spaniards turning their attention back to North Africa. Pope Gregory
XIII spent the rest of his pontificate trying to form another league, but he
was not successful.

It is clear that the crusading ideal was alive in the sixteenth century. It is
easy to find examples of the traditional language of holy war and grants of
indulgences and crusade tenths which, for instance, were being regularly
given to Venice, although some elements were now solidifying into forms
in which their original functions were obscured. Parts of the Spanish
cruzada, a tax which originated in the sale of crusade indulgences in return
for privileges, were diverted in the sixteenth century to defray the costs of
the rebuilding of St Peter's in Rome; the *cruzada* became so divorced from
its original purpose that its privileges were issued regularly until this
century and were only abrogated in the diocese of Pueblo, Colorado, in
1945. And since the indulgence was being granted to all who fought the
Turks, whether they had taken the cross or not, and the vast majority of
the men employed by the leagues were professional soldiers and sailors, it
is not entirely clear how many crusaders, that is to say volunteers who had
taken the vow, were to be found by the 1570s. But even if it was now
somewhat decayed, crusading was still too living a force to be ignored by
any Catholic ruler. There is no reason to suppose that kings were merely
paying lip-service to an ideal that no longer meant much to them, given the
general fear of the Turks: crusading fervour was in everybody's interest
anyway. And the treaties and peaces made with the Muslims by those
states like Venice and the empire which were in direct contact with the
Ottomans are not evidence of a failure to comprehend those ideals; in the
course of this book there have been many references to truces made with
the Muslims from the earliest times by rulers whose commitment was

incontrovertible. The Franco-Turkish entente belongs in a different category and the fact that a nation which had been the chief upholder of crusading for so long was now indulging in this kind of *Realpolitik* suggests that a change was in the air, as does the attitude of Pope Paul IV. But the use of Muslim power against fellow-Christians was also to be found in the thirteenth century. The scale of its use in the sixteenth century is a strong pointer to the decline of crusading, but against it must be weighed the overwhelming evidence for commitment to the old ideas.

That this can now be stated with conviction is due to the work of Professor Setton, who has uncovered enormous quantities of material to support the case. It is no longer possible for any historian to echo Karl Brandi's view that in the Treaty of Madrid the agreement of Charles V and Francis I to crusade was a 'strange reversion to the outworn beliefs of medieval France and Burgundy!' Historians only see what they are looking for. As more scholars begin to work on the ground cleared by Professor Setton more details will come to light and the state of the movement at the time will become clear. Once we pass 1571, however, we move from half-light into almost total darkness. A few examples suggest that crusading was still a force, even if it is impossible to make much of them in the present state of our knowledge.

In 1645 the Turks invaded Venetian Crete. In nearly twenty-four years of war, until Iráklion (Candia) surrendered on 26 September 1669, the Venetian fleet, supplemented by galleys and other ships provided by the popes and the Hospitallers, undertook a series of aggressive operations in the Aegean, with the aim of blocking the Dardanelles; in 1656 the islands of Bozcaada (Tenedos) and Limnos near the mouth of the Dardanelles were taken and were held for a year.

In March 1684, following the second unsuccessful Turkish siege of Vienna, a new Holy League with Poland, the empire and Venice was formed by Pope Innocent XI. It was supported by preaching, crusade tenths, enthusiastic recruitment and prayers of intercession at home, re-miniscent of crusading in earlier centuries. The League embarked on a war which lasted until 1699 and impoverished the papal curia. Buda was taken in 1686, Belgrade was held from 1688 to 1690 and there was a consolidation of Christian gains in Hungary and Transylvania. Between 1685 and 1687 the Venetians occupied almost the whole of the Peloponnese, and they held Athens from October 1687 to April 1688, blowing up the Parthenon in the process of taking it. They seized the island of Levkás in 1684 and they held Chios for five months in 1694–5.

The Turks went to war again in 1715, re-occupying the Peloponnese and taking the island of Tínos, which the Venetians had ruled for over five hundred years. In 1716 the Emperor Charles VI made an alliance with Venice and a Christian army under Prince Eugene of Savoy inflicted severe defeats on the Turks in the Balkans, taking Petrovaradin, Timişoara (Temesvár), the last Muslim fortress in what was then Hungary, and Belgrade in 1716–17.

Indulgences were issued for the defence of Crete and Vienna. The Holy League of 1684 was a good deal more successful than the leagues of the sixteenth century. Thousands of 'volunteers' fought in its armies. Were they crusaders? Ten years ago I appealed for researchers to examine these seventeenth-century conflicts in terms of crusading. No one has done so yet, but it seems that we are justified at least in supposing that the movement was still being expressed in them.

The Hospitallers of St John and Malta

It certainly still survived elsewhere, in the last order-state of a Military Order. It will be remembered that the Hospitallers of St John had lost Rhodes in 1522. By the end of the following year they were negotiating for a new base and on 23 March 1530 the Emperor Charles V granted them the islands of Malta and Gozo and the North African city of Tripoli, putting them in the front line of the defence of the Spanish African holdings in just the way his predecessors the kings of Castile had used the Spanish Military Orders. Eighteen months later they tried to demonstrate their worth to the general Christian cause by sacking Methóni in the Peloponnese. The pope was not particularly impressed and said that it would have been better for them to have occupied the place instead of looting it. But this raid probably led to the suggestion in 1533 that they be given charge of Koróni, which had recently been recaptured. Their surrender of Tripoli to the Turks in 1551 has already been mentioned, but any loss of prestige was more than compensated for by their heroic defence of Malta in 1565 against an enormous and well-equipped Turkish army, sent to clear Constantinople's line of communication with North Africa. On 19 May 1565 the Turkish invasion force of 25,000 men began to land. To resist them the grand master, John of la Valette, had 8–9,000, including c. 500 brother knights and some brother sergeants-at-arms, 4,000 arquebusiers and 3–4,000 Maltese irregulars. The assault lasted until 8 September when, having sustained very heavy losses, the Turks withdrew in the face of a relief force of c. 12,000 Spaniards and Italians. They left a scene of ruin and desolation on the shore of the Grand Harbour, in the midst of which stood only 600 of the original defenders still capable of bearing arms; of the 500 brother knights at the start of the siege, 300 were dead and most of the rest were wounded.

The Hospitallers had not been enthusiastic about Malta, a small and infertile island of ninety-five square miles with its fortifications in poor repair. Memories of the past were kept alive by the way the churches built by them – of St John, St Catherine, Our Lady of Victory – were given the same patrons as churches on Rhodes. Nor were they prepared to embark on an ambitious building programme at first: they satisfied themselves with a few simple conventual buildings and the construction of two forts. But after 1565, with their reputation enhanced and so much energy expended and blood spilt, their attitude changed. A new city, designed by Francesco Laparelli and named after John of la Valette, was built on the peninsula overlooking the Grand Harbour which had been the scene of some of the fiercest fighting. A feature of it was the incorporation of the Order's conventual buildings into the town rather than in a separate compound: the whole city became as it were a monastic enclosure. It was massively fortified and the Hospitallers continued to improve the fortifications around the Grand Harbour in the seventeenth and eighteenth centuries; in fact, although there was a large Turkish raid in 1614, no serious invasion came before 1798. Like Rhodes Malta became an important commercial centre, handling a growing volume of shipping and acting as the entrepôt for eastern goods on their way even to the Americas: the United States established a consulate there as early as 1783. Commercial relations with France were particularly close and half the shipping which called at Malta in the eighteenth century was French. It was from this that Napoleon's ambitions partly sprang.

The grand masters ruled their order-state as benevolent, if rather unimaginative, despots. They built hospitals, encouraged works of art, founded a famous school of anatomy in 1676 to supplement their hospital, and a university in 1768, and ran a kind of health service for the population, which rose from c. 20,000 in 1530 to over 90,000 in 1788. But Malta was not legally autonomous. It was a fief of the kingdom of Sicily and there was a political crisis as late as 1753 when King Charles VII of Naples claimed his rights as sovereign. In fact, stage by stage the grand masters had been assuming the attributes of sovereignty. They had begun to mint their own coinage as soon as they had conquered Rhodes, and from that island they had sent ambassadors to the courts of Europe. From perhaps as early as the fifteenth century they were creating honorary knighthoods for laymen closely associated with their work. Their claims to sovereignty were recognized in 1607 when, nearly four hundred years after the grand master of the Teutonic Knights, the grand master of the Hospitallers was made a prince of the Empire. The Order's ambassadors from Malta were officially received in Rome, France, Spain and Austria. Grand Master Manoel Pinto (1741–73) completed the process by adopting a royal crown.

The Hospitallers continued to fulfil their military rôle quite effectively. They played a part in nearly all the leagues and major campaigns against the Turks. To this day the keys of the fortresses of Passava, Lepanto and Patras in Greece and Hammamet in Tunisia, which were stormed between 1601 and 1603, hang in the chapel of Our Lady of Philermos in their conventual church in Valletta. In 1664 they attacked Algiers and in 1707 they helped the Spaniards hold Oran. Their ships were regularly at sea, cruising along the North African coast and throughout an area bordered by Sicily and Sardinia in the west and Crete and the Peloponnese in the east, with the aim of clearing the Mediterranean of Muslim pirates. As we have seen, they had a fleet of seven or eight war-galleys; after 1700 they gradually replaced these with a squadron of four or five ships of the line, mounting fifty or sixty guns each. Although the maintenance of this force was a very great expense – in the seventeenth century an average of 45 per cent of the headquarters' revenues was spent on it – they kept up an aggressive and quite damaging onslaught on Muslim shipping: the Turkish attack on Tripoli in 1551 was partly in retaliation for a series of assaults by them on neighbouring Muslim ports. As late as the period 1722–41 their line ships accounted for one Turkish and fifteen Barbary vessels and their galleys for a further five ships from Tripoli. The naval training the Hospitallers gave their knights was much admired. When the Empress Catherine the Great of Russia wanted a galley fleet in the Baltic she asked for the assistance of a knight of St John. Famous French sailors who were brother knights included the Chevaliers Tourville and d'Hocquincourt and the Marquis of Valbette in the seventeenth century and the great Bailiff de Suffren in the eighteenth.

By the middle of the eighteenth century, however, decline was setting in. This was partly because the war with the Ottomans was dying away and the Hospitallers' role was rapidly becoming out-of-date, partly because the Order had never had the benefit of internal reforms, in spite of the strictures of the Avignon popes and the efforts of a group of Hospitallers in the early seventeenth century who were proposing renewal in the wake of the Council of Trent. Signs of decadence are still visible on Malta today: the bare, simply designed lines of the conventual buildings were gradually softened internally with sumptuous decoration. The Order was devastated by the French Revolution and the revolutionary wars; it was, after all, one of the classic expressions of the *ancien régime*. In 1792 all its property in France was seized and by 1797 it had lost all its estates west of the Rhine, in Switzerland and in northern Italy. Its revenues fell by two-thirds. A new grand master, Ferdinand of Hompesch, made approaches to Austria and Russia which alarmed the French and in June 1798 Napoleon, who had his eye on Malta for commercial and strategic reasons, brought his fleet into Maltese waters on his way to Egypt and demanded admission to the Grand Harbour. When the knights tried to stand on their rights as neutrals he attacked and it is evidence of the extent to which the Order had decayed that it was in no state to resist him. Of 332 knights on the island 50 were too old or ill to fight. Command was in the hands of brothers chosen for seniority and not merit. The guns were ancient and had not been fired in anger for a century; the powder was found to be rotten and the shot defective. The urban militia, commanded by officers who had never bothered to learn the Maltese language, was undisciplined and frightened. Obsolete defensive plans were put into operation. In two days and with hardly any bloodshed the garrison, which was scattered throughout the island rather than concentrated in Valletta, had been overcome. Hompesch and his knights were ignominiously expelled.

The crusading movement ended with the fall of Malta on 13 June 1798, although the Order of the Hospital of St John survives today, still recognized as sovereign by many states, still an Order of the Church but, although technically still a Military Order, now devoting itself entirely to the care of the sick. There is real irony in the last act. Just over 700 years after Pope Urban II had called for the service of Christian knights, here these knights still were, still predominantly French and in fact obsessive about their status, as the armigerous mosaic memorials carpeting the floor of their conventual church in Valletta, the cenotaph of chivalry, testify. The order-state of these brothers, heirs of the men extolled by St Bernard, many of them descendants of twelfth-century crusaders, was a survival of the type of crusading state proposed by the theoreticians of the fourteenth century. It collapsed pathetically before the fleet of a French general bound for Egypt of all places. Napoleon, of course, was not a crusader, but he was more successful in Egypt than St Louis had been. And the story has a final twist to it. Napoleon confiscated the precious stones and metals that adorned the Hospitallers' relics, many of which they had carried with them from Palestine by way of Cyprus and Rhodes. Some of this treasure still lies at the bottom of Aboukir Bay, to which it was sent when Nelson attacked the French fleet, but Napoleon disposed of some of it in the markets of Alexandria and Cairo to pay for his troops. So precious metal acquired in the East by representatives of the crusading movement returned six centuries later.

Conclusion

The crusading movement had died a lingering death. By the late fourteenth century it may have been losing its grip on the masses. In the fifteenth century growing disinterest in Germany and perhaps in France witnessed to disillusionment with the papacy. In the sixteenth century the Reformation reduced the Catholic population of Europe and involved everyone in introspective and bitter conflict: in the circumstances it is remarkable how strongly the movement persisted. By the seventeenth century adherence to it was confined to the popes, those nations directly confronting the Turks and those families from which the Order of the Hospital of St John recruited its members. The last crusade may have been that of Sebastian of Portugal in 1578. The last crusading league was, the Holy League from 1684 to 1699. The last crusaders may well have been found in the late seventeenth or early eighteenth century. The last functioning brother knights of a Military Order running the last order-state were the Hospitallers on Malta until 1798.

In the light of the evidence presented in the last two chapters the old explanations of decline are no longer convincing. Failure in the East cannot have bred too much disillusionment and the rise of nation-states in the West cannot have created too alien a climate for the movement to survive if it continued for another five hundred years: even the Reformation and Counter-Reformation did not kill it off. It had, of course, changed by the sixteenth century but that only demonstrates its adaptability. It is surely the case that its decline and demise were the results of something more fundamental than sentiment or political environment. The moral theology on which crusading rested passed out of currency in the late sixteenth and seventeenth centuries as the idea of holy war was replaced by the concept of the just war. This meant that violence came to be regarded by most theologians no longer as morally neutral, but as something intrinsically evil and therefore an act which could be justified only as the lesser of evils. And at the same time the medieval view of a political Christ, committed to one particular political system, gave way to the conviction that Christ was politically neutral. By the eighteenth century holy war was becoming unfashionable and was being regarded as the product of a fanatical and quaintly superstituous age. Reasonable intellectuals looked on crusades with a mixture of sorrow and contempt. For Diderot, the *encyclopédiste*, the consequences for Europe of 'these horrible wars' were the depopulation of its nations, the enrichment of monasteries, the impoverishment of the nobility, the ruin of ecclesiastical discipline, contempt for agriculture, scarcity of cash and an infinity of vexations.

To David Hume they

have ever since engaged the curiosity of mankind, as the most signal and most durable monument of human folly that has yet appeared in any age or nation.

Edward Gibbon's judgement was that they

have checked rather than forwarded the maturity of Europe. The lives and labours of millions which were buried in the East would have been more profitably employed in the improvement of their native country: the accumulated stock of industry and wealth would have overflowed in navigation and trade; and the Latins would have been enriched and enlightened by a pure and friendly correspondence with the climates of the East.

Despised and disdained by fashionable opinion the last vestiges of crusading were too demoralized to survive.

'Malta [wrote Napoleon] . . . certainly possessed immense physical means of resistance, but no moral strength whatever.'

But the wheel is always turning and it is now the reasonable men of the eighteenth century who are looking distinctly unfashionable. It goes without saying that historians interpret the actions and judge the motives of the men and women they study in the light of their own preconceptions. In this respect history is a reconciliation of the past with the present; otherwise it would be incomprehensible to those for whom it is written. And since the present is always in a state of flux it follows that interpretations and judgements alter with time. For the last thirty years a section of Christian opinion has been advocating the use of force in the cause of liberation and has been using in justification of this a theology, including the concept of a political Christ, which is very similar to that which underlay the crusades. This theology has now been accepted in its essentials by the papacy, although the curia has rejected the use of violence except as a last resort. We do not have to agree with these contempories of ours to recognize that their existence among us makes the crusaders' ideals more comprehensible in our own time. A result, I think, is that we find it easier to accept the crusaders for what they were and, without endorsing what they did, can begin to understand why some of the greatest saints in Christian history – Bernard, Louis, Thomas Aquinas, Bridget, Catherine of Siena – were fervently on their side and why so many men and women were prepared to sacrifice wealth, health, life itself, in a cause which they believed to be just, even salvational. The actions of many crusaders were individual expressions of a piety that may be alien to us but was very real to them, as Humbert of Romans, an experienced crusade preacher, stressed in the early 1270s when he sought to answer the point that harm was actually done to Christendom by the deaths on crusade of so many decent men.

> The aim of Christianity is not to fill the earth, but to fill heaven. Why should one worry if the number of Christians is lessened in the world by deaths endured for God? By this kind of death people make their way to heaven who perhaps would never reach it by another road.*

---

* Humbert of Romans, 'Opus tripartitum', ed. E. Brown, *Fasciculus rerum expetendarum et fugiendarum* (1690), vol. 2, p. 193).

A select bibliography of secondary works

General

The best general bibliography is H. E. Mayer, *Bibliographie zur Geschichte der Kreuzzüge* (1960), supplemented, for works published 1958–67, by Professor Mayer's 'Literaturbericht über die Geschichte der Kreuzzüge', *Historische Zeitschrift* Sonderheft 3 (1969) and for works since 1967 by his reviews in *Deutsches Archiv für Erforschung des Mittelalters*. These bibliographies, however, concentrate on studies of crusades to the East. Professor Mayer is compiling the forthcoming bibliographical volume of K. M. Setton (editor-in-chief), *A History of the Crusades*. The best bibliographical guide to Islamic history is still J. Sauvaget, *Introduction to the History of the Muslim East*, recast by C. Cahen (1965).

Large-scale general works in English are:
S. Runciman, *A History of the Crusades*, 3 vols (1951–4), which is now over thirty years old, favours the Byzantine Greeks and concentrates on crusading to the East.
K. M. Setton (ed.-in-chief), *A History of the Crusades*, 2nd edn, 5 vols so far (1969 onwards). Again, rather dated. The contributions are variable in quality. The best are very useful; the worst are misleading. It does give some space to crusades in Europe.

The Church and crusading

Most of the surveys of crusading thought which have covered extensive periods of time have been of two types. First, there are those which approach the subject through canon law:
M. Villey, *La croisade: essai sur la formation d'une théorie juridique* (1942).
J. A. Brundage, *Medieval Canon Law and the Crusader* (1969)
F. H. Russell, *The Just War in the Middle Ages* (1975)
M. Purcell, *Papal Crusading Policy 1244–1291* (1975)
J. S. C. Riley-Smith, *What were the crusades?* (1977)
J. Muldoon, *Popes, Lawyers and Infidels* (1979).

Secondly, there are those in which crusading is viewed against a wider theological background:
C. Erdmann, *The Origin of the Idea of the Crusade* (1935; English trans. 1977). A work of seminal importance in its day, although Erdmann's opinions are now being challenged. See especially J. Gilchrist, 'The Erdmann Thesis and the Canon Law, 1083–1141', *Crusade and Settlement*, ed. P. W. Edbury (1985)

E. D. Hehl, *Kirche und Krieg im 12. Jahrhundert* (1980). An important work.

J. S. C. Riley-Smith, 'Crusading as an act of love', *History* 65 (1980)

B. Z. Kedar, *Crusade and Mission* (1984).

For the critics of crusading in the twelfth and thirteenth centuries, see

E. Siberry, *Criticism of Crusading 1095–1274* (1985).

For the theoreticians of the late thirteenth and fourteenth centuries, see

A. S. Atiya, *The Crusade in the Later Middle Ages*, 2nd edn (1965)

E. Stickel, *Der Fall von Akkon* (1975)

S. Schein, 'The future *regnum Hierusalem*: A chapter in medieval state planning', *Journal of Medieval History* 10 (1984)

J. N. Hillgarth, *Ramon Lull and Lullism in fourteenth-century France* (1971)

C. J. Tyerman, 'Marino Sanudo Torsello and the Lost Crusade: Lobbying in the Fourteenth Century', *Transactions of the Royal Historical Society* Ser. 5, 32 (1982)

N. Iorga, *Philippe de Mézières (1327–1405) et la croisade au XIVe siècle* (1896).

The most authoritative introduction to the ideas of militant Christian liberation is to be found in G. Gutiérrez, *A Theology of Liberation* (1973).

There are some good studies of the ideas and policies of popes:

H. E. J. Cowdrey, 'Pope Gregory VII's "Crusading" Plans of 1074', *Outremer*, ed. B. Z. Kedar, H. E. Mayer and R. C. Smail (1982)

A. Becker, *Papst Urban II (1088–1099)* 1 (1964)

R. C. Smail, 'Latin Syria and the West, 1149–1187', *Transactions of the Royal Historical Society* Ser. 5, 19 (1969)

H. Roscher, *Papst Innocenz III. und die Kreuzzüge* (1969)

C. R. Cheney, *Pope Innocent III and England* (1976)

J. A. Brundage, 'The Crusader's Wife: a Canonistic Quandary', *Studia gratiana* 12 (1967)

K. M. Setton, *The Papacy and the Levant (1204–1571)*, 4 vols (1976–84)

W. E. Lunt, *Papal Revenues in the Middle Ages*, 2 vols (1934)

——, *Financial Relations of the Papacy with England*, 2 vols (1939–62)

P. A. Throop, *Criticism of the Crusade* (1940). This is no longer acceptable for its conclusions on the critics, but it still contains the best treatment of the policies of Pope Gregory X.

N. J. Housley, 'Pope Clement V and the crusades of 1309–10', *Journal of Medieval History* 8 (1982)

——, *The Avignon Papacy and the Crusades, 1305–1378* (1986). The best book on crusading in the fourteenth century.

E. Ashtor, *Levant Trade in the Later Middle Ages* (1983), pp. 17–66 for the most detailed treatment of the papal embargoes of the early fourteenth century.

Crusades to the East

Contributions to the study of crusading in the period 1095–1291 include:

J. S. C. Riley-Smith, *The First Crusade and the idea of crusading* (1986)

R. Somerville, *The Councils of Urban II: 1. Decreta Claromontensia* (1972)

——, 'The Council of Clermont (1095) and Latin Christian Society', *Archivum historiae pontificiae* 12 (1974)

——, 'The Council of Clermont and the First Crusade', *Studia gratiana* 20 (1976)

E. O. Blake and C. Morris, 'A Hermit goes to War: Peter and the Origins of the First Crusade', *Studies in Church History* 21 (1984)

J. C. Andressohn, *The Ancestry and Life of Godefroy of Bouillon* (1947)

H. E. Mayer, 'Mélanges sur l'histoire du royaume de Jérusalem', *Mémoires de l'Académie des Inscriptions et Belles-Lettres* NS.5 (1984), which contains (pp. 10–91) interesting studies of Godfrey and Baldwin of Boulogne.

R. B. Yewdale, *Bohemond I, Prince of Antioch* (1924)

J. H. and L. L. Hill, *Raymond IV de Saint-Gilles* (1959)

C. W. David, *Robert Curthose, Duke of Normandy* (1920)

J. Prawer, 'The Jerusalem the Crusaders Captured: a Contribution to the Medieval Topography of the City', *Crusade and Settlement*, ed. P. W. Edbury

J. S. C. Riley-Smith, 'The Venetian Crusade of 1122–1124', *I communi italiani nel regno latino di Gerusalemme*, ed. B. Z. Kedar and G. Airaldi (1987)

G. Constable, 'The Second Crusade as seen by Contemporaries', *Traditio* 9 (1953). Still the best study of the Second Crusade.

P. Munz, *Frederick Barbarossa* (1969), pp. 370–96, for treatment of Frederick I's contribution to the Third Crusade.

J. B. Gillingham, 'Richard I and the Science of War in the Middle Ages', *War and Government in the Middle Ages*, ed. J. B. Gillingham and J. C. Holt (1984)

D. E. Queller, *The Fourth Crusade* (1978)

J. Longnon, *Les compagnons de Villehardouin* (1978)

R. H. Schmandt, 'The Fourth Crusade and the Just-War Theory', *Catholic Historical Review* 61 (1975)

A. Frolow, *Recherches sur la déviation de la quatrième croisade vers Constantinople* (1955)

J. Folda, 'The Fourth Crusade, 1201–1204: some reconsiderations', *Byzantinoslavica* 26 (1965)

J. P. Donovan, *Pelagius and the Fifth Crusade* (1950)

J. M. Powell, *Anatomy of a Crusade, 1213–1221* (1986). A study of the Fifth Crusade which has appeared too recently to be used by me here.

J. Richard, *Saint Louis* (1983)

W. C. Jordan, *Louis IX and the Challenge of the Crusade* (1979)

H.-F. Delaborde, *Jean de Joinville et les seigneurs de Joinville* (1894)

A. J. Forey, 'The Crusading Vows of the English King Henry III', *Durham University Journal* NS. 34 (1973)

S. Lloyd, 'The Lord Edward's Crusade, 1270–2: its setting and significance', *War and Government in the Middle Ages*, ed. J. B. Gillingham and J. C. Holt.

Our view of crusading after 1291 – 'The Later Crusades' – is being transformed, partly because of the interest of a group of younger historians, partly because Professor Setton in *The Papacy and the Levant* has revealed vast stores of material. These have still to be digested and analyzed and a start has been made by Dr Housley in *The Avignon Papacy*. Much of chapters 9 and 10 of this book is based on the work of these two historians. See also

S. Schein, 'Gesta Dei per Mongolos 1300', *English Historical Review* 94 (1979)

M. Keen, 'Chaucer's Knight, the English Aristocracy and the Crusade', *English Court Culture in the Middle Ages*, ed. V. J. Scattergood and J. W. Sherborne (1983)

C. J. Tyerman, 'Philip V of France, the Assemblies of 1319–20 and the Crusade', *Bulletin of the Institute of Historical Research* 57 (1984)

M. Barber, 'The pastoureaux of 1320', *Journal of Ecclesiastical History* 32 (1981)

N. J. Housley, 'King Louis the Great of Hungary and the Crusades, 1342–1382', *The Slavonic and East European Review* 62 (1984)

J. J. N. Palmer, *England, France and Christendom, 1377–99* (1972)

P. Rousset, 'Sainte Catherine de Sienne et le problème de la croisade', *Revue Suisse d'histoire* 25 (1975)

——, 'Un Huguenot propose une croisade: le projet de François de la Noue (1580–1585)', *Revue d'histoire écclesiastique suisse* 72 (1978)

A. C. Hess, 'The Battle of Lepanto and its place in Mediterranean History', *Past and Present* 57 (1972).

Crusading in Spain

This is, of course, referred to in many of the studies of crusading to the East. But in addition, consult

J. Goñi Gaztambide, *Historia de la Bula de la Cruzada en España* (1958)

E. Bernardet, 'Croisade (Bulle de la)', *Dictionnaire de droit canonique*, ed. R. Naz 4 (1949), pp. 773–99

D. W. Lomax, *The Reconquest of Spain* (1978)

R. A. Fletcher, *Saint James's Catapult: The Life and Times of Diego Gelmírez of Santiago de Compostela* (1984)

P. Linehan, 'The Synod of Segovia (1166)', *Bulletin of Medieval Canon Law* NS 10 (1980)

——, *The Spanish Church and the papacy in the thirteenth century* (1971)

R. I. Burns, *The Crusader Kingdom of Valencia*, 2 vols (1967)

——, *Islam under the Crusaders* (1973)

——, *Medieval Colonialism* (1975)

——, *Muslims, Christians and Jews in the Crusader Kingdom of Valencia* (1984).

The Reconquest in the fourteenth century is treated by N. J. Housley in *The Avignon Papacy*; its extension into North Africa in the sixteenth century is described by K. M. Setton in *The Papacy and the Levant* and A. C. Hess in 'The Battle of Lepanto'. Works on the Spanish Military Orders are included in the section on the Military Orders.

Baltic and north-eastern crusades

Central to this topic is the history of the Teutonic Knights. Works on them are included in the section on the Military Orders. See also

E. Christiansen, *The Northern Crusades* (1980)

F. Lotter, *Die Konzeption des Wendenkreuzzugs* (1977), although some of his conclusions have been challenged.

N. J. Housley, *The Avignon Papacy*, has interesting things to say about the fourteenth century, as has

M. Keen, *Chivalry* (1984).

Crusades against heretics and opponents of the Church

N. J. Housley, 'Crusades against Christians: their origins and early development, c. 1000–1216', *Crusade and Settlement* ed. P. W. Edbury

E. Kennan, 'Innocent III and the first Political Crusade: a comment on the limitations of papal power', *Traditio* 27 (1971)

S. Lloyd, '"Political Crusades" in England, c. 1215–17 and c. 1263–5', *Crusade and Settlement*, ed. P. W. Edbury.

M. Roquebert, *L'Épopée Cathare*, 3 vols (1970–86). The best study to date of the Albigensian Crusade; see also H. Roscher, *Papst Innocenz III.*

N. J. Housley, *The Italian Crusades* (1982). The standard work on the political crusades in Italy. Dr Housley continues the story in *The Avignon Papacy* (1986).

——, 'The Mercenary Companies, the Papacy and the Crusades, 1356–1378', *Traditio* 38 (1982).

The best treatment of the crusades against the Hussites is by

F. G. Heyman in K. M. Setton (ed.), *A History of the Crusades* 3, pp. 586–646. See also

G. A. Holmes, 'Cardinal Beaufort and the crusade against the Hussites', *English Historical Review* 88 (1973).

The Byzantine Greeks and the crusaders

A far more realistic attitude is now being taken towards their relationship.

R.-J. Lilie, *Byzanz und die Kreuzfahrerstaaten* (1981). This adds appreciably to our understanding of crusades as well as of the relations between the Byzantine empire and the Latin East.

C. M. Brand, *Byzantium Confronts the West 1180–1204* (1968)

For the centuries after 1204, see K. M. Setton, *The Papacy and the Levant* (1976–84). See also:

M. Angold, *A Byzantine Government in Exile* (1975)

D. J. Geanakoplos, *Emperor Michael Palaeologus and the West* (1959)

A. E. Laiou, *Constantinople and the Latins: The Foreign Policy of Andronicus II, 1282–1328* (1972)

J. W. Barker, *Manuel II Palaeologus (1391–1425)* (1969).

Muslims and Mongols, the crusades and the Latin East

P. M. Holt, *The Age of the Crusades: The Near East from the eleventh century to 1517* (1986). A first-class short introduction to the subject.

C. Cahen, *Pre-Ottoman Turkey* (1968)

E. Sivan, *L'Islam et la croisade* (1968)

M. G. S. Hodgson, *The Order of Assassins* (1955)

N. Elisséeff, *Nur ad-Din*, 3 vols (1967)

M. C. Lyons and D. E. P. Jackson, *Saladin* (1982). Much the best biography of him.

R. S. Humphreys, *From Saladin to the Mongols: The Ayyubids of Damascus 1193–1260* (1977)

H. L. Gottschalk, *Al-Malik al-Kamil von Egypten und seine Zeit* (1958)

R. Irwin, *The Middle East in the middle ages: The early Mamluk Sultanate 1250–1382* (1986)

D. O. Morgan, *The Mongols* (1986)

——, 'The Mongols in Syria, 1260–1300', *Crusade and Settlement*, ed. P. W. Edbury

P. Thorau, 'The Battle of 'Ayn Jālūt: a Re-examination', *Crusade and Settlement*, ed. P. W. Edbury

P. Jackson, 'The Crisis in the Holy Land in 1260', *English Historical Review* 95 (1980)

P. M. Holt, 'The treaties of the early Mamluk sultans with the Frankish states', *Bulletin of the School of Oriental and African Studies* 43 (1980)

——, 'Baybars's Treaty with the Lady of Beirut in 667/1269', *Crusade and Settlement*, ed. P. W. Edbury

J. Richard, 'Un partage de seigneurie entre Francs et Mamelouks: les "Casaux de Sur"', *Syria* 30 (1953)

R. Irwin, 'The Mamlūk Conquest of the County of Tripoli', *Crusade and Settlement*, ed. P. W. Edbury

H. Inalcik, *The Ottoman Empire* (1973)

S. J. Shaw, *History of the Ottoman Empire and Modern Turkey* 1 (1976)

Latin Palestine and Syria and Cilician Armenia

The history of the Latin East was revolutionized in the 1940s and 1950s. The first of the new histories was

C. Cahen, *La Syrie du Nord à l'époque des croisades et la principauté franque d'Antioche* (1940).

It was followed by

J. Richard, *Le comté de Tripoli sous la dynastie toulousaine (1102–1187)* (1945)

——, *The Latin Kingdom of Jerusalem*, 2 vols (1979; first published in French 1953). This is still the best introduction to the kingdom's history.

J. Prawer, *Histoire du royaume latin de Jérusalem*, 2 vols (1969–70)

——, *The Latin Kingdom of Jerusalem* (1972)

——, *Crusader Institutions* (1980). A most important collection of articles, of the writing of which Professor Prawer is a master.

J. S. C. Riley-Smith, *The Feudal Nobility and the Kingdom of Jerusalem, 1174–1277* (1973)

For the history of the Church in the Latin patriarchates of Jerusalem and Antioch see

B. Hamilton, *The Latin Church in the Crusader States: The Secular Church* (1980)

H. E. Mayer, *Bistümer, Klöster und Stifte im Königreich Jerusalem* (1977). A highly original collection of studies, containing by far the best treatment to date of the controversial career of Patriarch Daimbert. The author has made other important contributions to Church history.

——, 'Das Pontifikale von Tyrus und die Krönung der lateinischen Könige von Jerusalem', *Dumbarton Oaks Papers* 21 (1967), which is also important for political history.

——, 'Latins, Muslims and Greeks in the Latin Kingdom of Jerusalem', *History* 63 (1978)

——, 'The Concordat of Nablus', *Journal of Ecclesiastical History* 33 (1982)

Other recent studies of the Church which I have used are:

J. G. Rowe, 'The Papacy and the Ecclesiastical Province of Tyre (1100–1187)', *Bulletin of the John Rylands Library* 43 (1960–61)

P. W. Edbury and J. G. Rowe, 'William of Tyre and the Patriarchal Election of 1180', *English Historical Review* 93 (1978)

J. S. C. Riley-Smith, 'Latin Titular Bishops in Palestine and Syria, 1137–1291', *Catholic Historical Review* 64 (1978)

J. Richard, *La papauté et les missions d'Orient au moyen âge (XIIIe–XVe siècles)* (1977). The best book on the missions.

K. S. Salibi, *Maronite Historians of Medieval Lebanon* (1959)

On schools and learning, see

P. C. Boeren, *Rorgo Fretellus de Nazareth et sa description de la Terre Sainte* (1980)

B. Z. Kedar, 'Gerard of Nazareth: A neglected twelfth-century writer in the Latin East', *Dumbarton Oaks Papers* 37 (1983). This is also important for the origin of the Carmelites.

R. B. C. Huygens, 'Guillaume de Tyr étudiant', *Latomus* 21 (1962)

R. C. Schwinges, *Kreuzzugsidee und Toleranz: Studien zu Wilhelm von Tyrus* (1977).

For the culture of the nobility, see also

D. Jacoby, 'La littérature française dans les états latins de la Méditerranée orientale à l'époque des croisades: diffusion et création', *Actes du IXe Congrès International de la Société Rencesvals pour l'Étude des Épopées Romanes* (1982).

For art and architecture see K. M. Setton, *A History of the Crusades* 4, which is devoted to the subject; and also

C. Enlart, *Les monuments des croisés dans le royaume de Jérusalem. Architecture religieuse et civile*, 2 vols (1925–8)

Z. Jacoby, 'Le portail de l'église de l'annonciation de Nazareth au XIIe siècle', *Monuments et Mémoires de Fondation Eugène Piot* 64 (1981)

——, 'The Workshop of the Temple Area in Jerusalem in the Twelfth Century: its Origin, Evolution and Impact', *Zeitschrift für Kunstgeschichte* 45 (1982)

H. Buchthal, *Miniature Painting in the Latin Kingdom of Jerusalem* (1957)

J. Folda, *Crusader Manuscript Illumination at Saint-Jean d'Acre, 1275–1291* (1976).

Dr Denys Pringle is completing a survey of all the Latin churches in the kingdom of Jerusalem.

For political, legal and administrative history, see

J. S. C. Riley-Smith, 'The title of Godfrey of Bouillon', *Bulletin of the Institute of Historical Research* 52 (1979). For another view, see J. France, 'The Election and Title of Godfrey de Bouillon', *Canadian Journal of History* 18 (1983).

——, 'The motives of the earliest crusaders and the settlement of Latin Palestine, 1095–1100', *English Historical Review* 98 (1983)

——, 'The survival in Latin Palestine of Muslim administration', *The Eastern Mediterranean Lands in the Period of the Crusades*, ed. P. M. Holt (1977)

P. W. Edbury, 'Feudal Obligations in the Latin East', *Byzantion* 47 (1977). 'Service abroad' is also considered by H. E. Mayer in his 'Mélanges', pp. 93– 161 (see p. 261 above).

J. S. C. Riley-Smith, 'Further Thoughts on Baldwin II's *établissement* on the Confiscation of Fiefs', *Crusade and Settlement*, ed. P. W. Edbury

H. E. Mayer, 'Jérusalem et Antioche au temps de Baudouin II', *Comptes rendus de l'Académie des Inscriptions et Belles-Lettres* (1980)

——, 'The Succession to Baldwin II of Jerusalem: English impact on the East', *Dumbarton Oaks Papers* 39 (1985)

——, 'Studies in the History of Queen Melisende of Jerusalem', *Dumbarton Oaks Papers* 26 (1972)

——, 'Kaiserrecht und Heiliges Land', *Aus Reichsgeschichte und Nordischer Geschichte*, ed. H. Fuhrmann, H. E. Mayer and K. Wriedt (1972)

R. C. Smail, 'The international status of the Latin kingdom of Jerusalem, 1150– 1192', *The Eastern Mediterranean Lands*, ed. P. M. Holt

B. Hamilton, 'The elephant of Christ: Reynald of Châtillon', *Studies in Church History* 15 (1978)

P. Jackson, 'The End of Hoenstaufen Rule in Syria', *Bulletin of the Institute of Historical Research* 59 (1986)

H. E. Mayer, 'Ibelin versus Ibelin: the struggle for the Regency of Jerusalem 1253–1258', *Proceedings of the American Philosophical Society* 122 (1978)

——, 'The Double County of Jaffa and Ascalon: One Fief or Two?', *Crusade and Settlement*, ed. P. W. Edbury

——, 'John of Jaffa, His Opponents and His Fiefs', *Proceedings of the American Philosophical Society* 128 (1984)

P. W. Edbury, 'John of Ibelin's title to the County of Jaffa and Ascalon', *English Historical Review* 98 (1983)

J. Richard, 'Les comtes de Tripoli et leurs vassaux sous la dynastie antiochénienne', *Crusade and Settlement*, ed. P. W. Edbury

Recently Professor Mayer has been leading studies away from political and constitutional history and back to the detailed examination of individual lordships.

H. E. Mayer, 'Die Kreuzfahrerherrschaft 'Arrābe', *Zeitschrift des Deutschen Palästina-Vereins* 93 (1977)

——, 'Die Seigneurie de Joscelin und der Deutsche Orden', *Die geistlichen Ritterorden Europas*, ed. J. Fleckenstein and M. Hellmann (1980)

——, 'Die Herrschaftsbildung in Hebron', *Zeitschrift des Deutschen Palästina-Vereins* 101 (1985)

——, 'The Origins of the County of Jaffa', *Israel Exploration Journal* 35 (1985)
——, 'The Origins of the Lordship of Ramle and Lydda in the Latin Kingdom of Jerusalem', *Speculum* 60 (1985)
M–L. Favreau, 'Die Kreuzfahrerherrschaft Scandalion (Iskanderūne)', *Zeitschrift des Deutschen Palästina-Vereins* 93 (1977)
——, 'Landesausbau und Burg während der Kreuzfahrerzeit. *Safad* in Obergalilaea', *Zeitschrift des Deutschen Palästina-Vereins* 96 (1980)
P. Hilsch, 'Der Deutsche Ritterorden im südlichen Libanon', *Zeitschrift des Deutschen Palästina-Vereins* 96 (1980).

A University of London research student, Steven Tibble, has recently made some startling discoveries, which, when published, are likely to transform our view of royal policy towards the fiefs.

The best introduction to military history in the twelfth century is
R. C. Smail, *Crusading Warfare 1097–1193* (1956), which is also important for crusades. See also
——, 'The Predicaments of Guy of Lusignan, 1183–1187', *Outremer*, ed. B. Z. Kedar, H. E. Mayer and R. C. Smail
P. Herde, 'Die Kämpfe bei den Hörnern von Hittin und die Untergang des Kreuzritterheeres (3. und 4. Juli 1187)', *Römische Quartalschrift für christliche Altertumskunde und Kirchengeschichte* 61 (1966). This is the best analysis of the Battle of Hattin.

For castles, see
P. Deschamps, *Les châteaux des croisés en Terre Sainte*, 3 vols (1934–77)
M. Benvenisti, *The Crusaders in the Holy Land* (1970). This is a good survey of all surviving buildings in the area under Israeli control, including churches and agricultural structures.
D. Pringle, *The Red Tower* (1986). A revolutionary work, not only for the thoroughness of the archaeological investigation of a small castle, but also for the way it places it and neighbouring castles in their social and economic context.

Recent works on social and economic history, including trade, are:
D. Pringle, 'Two Medieval Villages North of Jerusalem: Archaeological Investigations in al-Jib and ar-Ram', *Levant* 15 (1983).
——, 'Magna Mahumeria (al-Bīra): the Archaeology of a Frankish New Town in Palestine', *Crusade and Settlement*, ed. P. W. Edbury
D. M. Metcalf, *Coinage of the Crusades and the Latin East* (1983)
P. W. Edbury, 'The baronial coinage of the Latin kingdom of Jerusalem', *Coinage in the Latin East*, ed. P. W. Edbury and D. M. Metcalf (1980)
J. H. Pryor, 'The Naval Architecture of Crusader Transport ships', *The Mariner's Mirror* 70 (1984). Dr Pryor is engaged in a full-scale study of shipping in the period.
J. S. C. Riley-Smith, 'Government in Latin Syria and the Commercial Privileges of Foreign Merchants', *Relations between East and West in the Middle Ages*, ed. D. Baker (1973)
H. E. Meyer and M.–L. Favreau, 'Das Diplom Balduins I. für Genua und

Genuas Goldene Inschrift in der Grabeskirche', *Quellen und Forschungen aus italienischen Archiven und Bibliotheken* 55–6 (1976)

M.–L. Favreau, 'Graf Heinrich von Champagne und die Pisaner im Königreich Jerusalem', *Bolletino storico Pisano* 47 (1978)

——, 'Die italienische Levante-Piraterie und die Sicherheit der See-wege nach Syrien im 12. und 13. Jahrhundert', *Vierteljahrschrift für Sozial- und Wirtschaftsgeschichte* 65 (1978). Dr Favreau's study of the Pisans in the Levant is forthcoming.

D. Jacoby, 'L'expansion occidentale dans le Levant: les Vénitiens à Acre dans la seconde moitié du treizième siècle', *Journal of Medieval History* 3 (1977)

——, 'Crusader Acre in the Thirteenth Century: Urban Layout and Topography', *Studi Medievali* ser. 3, 20 (1979).

Outside the general works there is little to recommend on Cilician Armenia.

T. S. R. Boase (ed.), *The Cilician Kingdom of Armenia* (1978).

Latin Cyprus

An up-to-date history of Latin Cyprus in the thirteenth and fourteenth centuries is being written by Dr P. W. Edbury. In the meantime one still has to rely on

G. F. Hill, *A History of Cyprus* 2–3 (1948).

But a modern approach is to be found in the following:

J. Richard, 'Le casal de Psimolofo et la vie rurale en Chypre au XIVe siècle', *Mélanges d'archéologie et d'histoire de l'école française de Rome* 59 (1947)

——, *Chypre sous les Lusignans: Documents chypriotes des archives du Vatican (XIVe et XVe siècles)* (1962)

D. Jacoby, 'The Rise of a new Emporium in the eastern Mediterranean: Famagusta in the late thirteenth century', *Meletai kai Upomnemata* 1 (1984)

P.W. Edbury, 'Latin dioceses and Peristerona: a contribution to the topography of Lusignan Cyprus', *Epeteridos* 8 (1975–7)

——, 'The Crusading Policy of King Peter I of Cyprus, 1359–1369', *The Eastern Mediterranean Lands*, ed. P. M. Holt

——, 'The Murder of King Peter I of Cyprus (1359–1369)', *Journal of Medieval History* 6 (1980).

For art and architecture, see

C. Enlart, *L'art gothique et de la Renaissance en Chypre*, 2 vols (1899).

Latin Greece

The history of Latin Greece has had detailed, if rather unanalytical treatment, in K. M. Setton (ed.), *A History of the Crusades* 2–3 and K. M. Setton, *The Papacy and the Levant*. See also

J. Longnon, *L'empire latin de Constantinople et la principauté de Morée* (1949)

N. Cheetham, *Mediaeval Greece* (1981)

D. Jacoby, *La féodalité en Grèce Médiévale: Les "Assises de Romanie": sources, application et diffusion* (1971)

——, 'The Encounter of Two Societies: Western Conquerors and Byzantines in the Peloponnesus after the Fourth Crusade', *American Historical Review* 78 (1973)

——, 'Catalans, Turcs et Vénitiens en Romanie (1305–1332): un nouveau témoignage de Marino Sanudo Torsello', *Studi Medievali* ser. 3, 15 (1974)

G. Fedalto, *La chiesa latina in Oriente*, 3 vols (1973–8)

J. M. Buckley, 'The Problematical Octogenarianism of John of Brienne', *Speculum* 32 (1957)

A. Bon, *La Morée Franque: Recherches historiques, topographiques et archéologiques sur la principauté d'Achaïe (1205–1430)* (1969)

F. Thiriet, *La Romanie vénitienne au moyen âge* (1959)

P. Argenti, *The Occupation of Chios by the Genoese and their Administration of the Island, 1346–1566*, 3 vols (1958).

The Military Orders

There is no good book in English on the general history of the Templars.

M. L. Bulst-Thiele, *Sacrae Domus Militiae Templi Hierosolymitani Magistri* (1974)

R. Hiestand, *Papsturkunden für Templer und Johanniter*, 2nd edn (1984), for their ecclesiastical privileges and those of the Hospitallers.

J. S. C. Riley-Smith, 'The Templars and the Teutonic Knights in Cilician Armenia', *The Cilician Kingdom of Armenia*, ed. T. S. R. Boase (1978), for their march in the Amanus.

R. B. C. Huygens, *De constructione castri Saphet* (1981) and the review of this by D. Pringle, 'Reconstructing the Castle of Safad', *Palestine Exploration Quarterly* 117 (1985), for the rebuilding of Safad.

A. J. Forey, *The Templars in the Corona de Aragon* (1973). The best book on their provincial structure.

——, 'Recruitment to the Military Orders', *Viator* 17 (1986).

——, 'Novitiate and Instruction in the Military Orders during the Twelfth and Thirteenth Centuries', *Speculum* 61 (1986)

M. Barber, *The Trial of the Templars* (1978). A good description of their fall.

For the Hospitallers of St John before the fourteenth century, see

J. S. C. Riley-Smith, *The Knights of St John in Jerusalem and Cyprus, c. 1050–1310* (1967)

T. S. Miller, 'The Knights of St John and the Hospitals of the Latin West', *Speculum* 53 (1978)

A. J. Forey, 'Constitutional Conflict and Change in the Hospital of St John during the Twelfth and Thirteenth Centuries', *Journal of Ecclesiastical History* 33 (1982).

Good work is now being done on the management of the Hospitallers' European estates. See especially:

M. Gervers, *The Hospitaller Cartulary in the British Library (Cotton MS Nero E VI)* (1981)

——, *The Cartulary of the Knights of St John of Jerusalem in England. Secunda Camera Essex* (1982)

A.–M. Legras, *Les Commanderies des Templiers et des Hospitaliers de Saint-Jean de Jérusalem en Saintonge et en Aunis* (1983).

A history of the Order's occupation of Rhodes is very badly needed. It is sincerely to be hoped that Dr A. T. Luttrell, the world's leading authority on the subject, will publish one. Meanwhile his many articles should be consulted. Some of these have been collected in two volumes:

A. T. Luttrell, *The Hospitallers in Cyprus, Rhodes, Greece and the West (1291–1440)* (1978)

——, *Latin Greece, the Hospitallers and the Crusades, 1291–1400* (1982).

See also the comments in N. J. Housley, *The Avignon Papacy* and
A. Gabriel, *La cité de Rhodes (1310–1522)*, 2 vols (1921–3).

For the Order's occupation of Malta, see
R. Cavaliero, *The Last of the Crusaders* (1960)
J. Q. Hughes, *The Building of Malta during the Period of the Knights of St John of Jerusalem, 1530–1795* (1956)
A. Hoppen, *The fortification of Malta by the Order of St John, 1530–1798* (1979)
——, 'The Finances of the Order of St John of Jerusalem in the sixteenth and seventeenth centuries', *European Studies Review* 3 (1973)
A. T. Luttrell, 'Eighteenth-Century Malta: Prosperity and Problems', *Hyphen* 3 (1982).

Besides the general works, especially E. Christiansen, *The Northern Crusades* and N. J. Housley, *The Avignon Papacy*, one should consult for the Teutonic Knights and other German Orders
M.–L. Favreau, *Studien zur Frühgeschichte des Deutschen Ordens* (1974)
M. Tumler, *Der Deutsche Orden im Werden, Wachsen und Wirken bis 1400* (1955)
M. Burleigh, *Prussian Society and the German Order* (1984)
F. Benninghoven, *Der Orden der Schwertbrüder* (1965).

For the Spanish Military Orders, see
A. J. Forey, 'The Military Orders and the Spanish Reconquest in the Twelfth and Thirteenth Centuries', *Traditio* 40 (1984)
D. W. Lomax, *La Orden de Santiago, 1170–1275* (1965)
J. F. O'Callaghan, *The Spanish Military order of Calatrava and its Affiliates* (1975)
L. P. Wright, 'The Military Orders in Sixteenth- and Seventeenth-century Spanish Society', *Past and Present* 43 (1969).

For the English Order of St Thomas of Acre, see
A. J. Forey, 'The military order of St Thomas of Acre', *English Historical Review* 92 (1977).

A note on sources in translation

I have always had doubts about the utility of advising students to read individual sources, because historical research is built on the comparison of related pieces of evidence, rather than on a line-by-line interpretation of a single text. But the fact is that the study of sources now plays a large part in history teaching in British schools, which serve the interests, after all, of all pupils, not simply those of future academic historians. A selection of crusade texts is to be found in

L. and J. Riley-Smith, *The Crusades, Idea and Reality, 1095–1274* (1981).

Five eyewitness accounts of the First Crusade are:
Gesta Francorum et aliorum Hierosolimitanorum, ed. and tr. R. Hill (1962)
Peter Tudebode, *Historia de Hierosolymitano itinere*, tr. J. H. and L. L. Hill (1974)
Raymond of Aguilers, *Historia*, tr. J. H. and L. L. Hill (1968)
Fulcher of Chartres, *Historia Hierosolymitana*, tr. F. R. Ryan, ed. H. S. Fink (1969)
Anna Comnena, *The Alexiad*, tr. E. A. S. Dawes (1928).

See also
A. C. Krey, *The First Crusade: The Accounts of Eye Witnesses and Participants* (1921)
S. Eidelberg, *The Jews and the Crusaders* (1977), for the Hebrew sources on the pogroms that marred the First and Second Crusades.

Two of the main sources for the Second Crusade, one covering the fighting in Asia Minor, the other the engagements in Portugal, are:
Odo of Deuil, *De profectione Ludovici VII in orientem*, ed. and tr. V. G. Berry (1948)
De expugnatione Lyxbonensi, ed. and tr. C. W. David (1936).

Two narrative accounts of the Third Crusade are:
Ambroise, *L'Estoire de la guerre sainte*, tr. (as *The Crusade of Richard Lion-Heart*) M. J. Hubert and J. L. La Monte (1941)
Baha' ad-Din, *Kitab an-nawadir as-sultaniya*, tr. (as *The Life of Saladin*) C. W. Wilson (1897).

The two chief eyewitness accounts of the Fourth Crusade are:
Geoffrey of Villehardouin, *La conquête de Constantinople*, tr. M. R. B. Shaw (Penguin Classics, 1963)
Robert of Cléry (Clari), *La conquête de Constantinople*, tr. E. H. McNeal (1936).

For an eyewitness narrative of the Fifth Crusade, see
Oliver of Paderborn, *Historia Damiatina*, tr, J. J. Gavigan (1948).

A marvellous eyewitness account of St Louis's first crusade is John of Joinville, *La Vie de Saint Louis*, tr. M. R. B. Shaw (Penguin Classics, 1963).

For the German crusades of the thirteenth century, see
Henry of Livonia, *Chronicon Livoniae*, tr. J. A. Brundage (1961).

For Latin Jerusalem, Tripoli, Antioch, Cyprus and Greece, see
Fulcher of Chartres, *Historia*, tr. F. R. Ryan, already mentioned
William of Tyre, *Historia*, tr. E. A. Babcock and A. C. Krey, 2 vols (1943), although this translation of the most famous of all the histories of the Latin East was made on the basis of an obsolete edition of the work.
Philip of Novara, 'Memoirs' from the *Gestes des Chiprois*, tr. (as *The Wars of Frederick II against the Ibelins in Syria and Cyprus*) J. L. La Monte and M. J. Hubert (1936).
Crusaders as Conquerors: The Chronicle of Morea, tr. H. E. Lurier (1964)
Leontios Machairas, *Recital concerning the Sweet Land of Cyprus*, ed. and tr. R. M. Dawkins, 2 vols (1932).

Various itineraries and pilgrimage descriptions of the Holy Land were translated by the *Palestine Pilgrims Text Society*, 14 vols (1896–1907). A new collection of the twelfth-century accounts is being prepared by Dr J. Wilkinson for the Hakluyt Society.

For the internal legislation of the Hospitallers of St. John while their headquarters were in Palestine and Cyprus, see
The Rule, Statutes and Customs of the Hospitallers, 1099–1310, tr. E. J. King (1934).

For Muslim accounts of relations with the settlers, see
F. Gabrieli, *Arab Historians of the Crusades* (1969)
Ibn al-Qalanisi, *Dhail tarikh Dimashq*, extr. tr. (as *Chronicle of Damascus*) H. A. R. Gibb (1932)
Usamah ibn Munqidh, *Kitab al-i 'tibar*, tr. (as *An Arab-Syrian Gentleman and Warrior in the Period of the Crusades*) P. K. Hitti (1929)
Ibn Jubair, *Rihla*, tr. R. J. C. Broadhurst (1952)
Baha' ad-Din, *The Life of Saladin*, tr. C. W. Wilson, already mentioned.
Ibn al-Furat, *Tarikh al-Duwal wa'l Muluk*, part ed. and tr. U. and M. C. Lyons, 2 vols (1971)
Ibn 'Abd al-Zahir, *Sirat al-Malik al-Zahir*, part ed. and tr. S. F. Sadeque (1956)
Abu'l-Fida', *al-Mukhtasar fi akhbar al-bashar*, extr. tr. (as *The Memoirs of a Syrian Prince*) P. M. Holt (1983).

An account of the siege of Rhodes in 1480 was translated within two years.
William Caoursin, *Obsidionis Rhodiae urbis descriptio*, tr. (as *The dylectable newesse and tythinges of the glorious victorye of the Rhodyans agaynst the Turks*) J. Kaye (1482). See the edition by H. W. Fincham (Order of St John of Jerusalem, Historical Pamphlets no. 2, 1926).

For the siege of Malta, see

Francisco Balbi de Corregio, *La Verdadera relaçion de todo lo que el año de MDLXV ha succedido en la Isla de Malta*, tr. (as *The Siege of Malta, 1565*) E. Bradford (1965).

Index